Communication and Society
Editor: Jeremy Tunstall

Big sounds from small peoples

This book is also No.7 (1984) in the series of reports
from The Gothenburg University Department of Musicology

ROGER WALLIS and KRISTER MALM

Big sounds from small peoples

The music industry
in small countries

Constable · London

First published in Great Britain 1984
by Constable and Company Limited
10 Orange Street London WC2H 7EG
hardback ISBN 0 09 465300 3
paperbacks ISBN 0 09 465360 7
Copyright © 1984 by Roger Wallis and Krister Malm
Set in Linotron Times 10pt by
Rowland Phototypesetting Ltd
Bury St Edmunds, Suffolk
Printed in Great Britain by
St Edmundsbury Press
Bury St Edmunds, Suffolk

Contents

Illustrations

(Unless otherwise mentioned, photos are by Roger Wallis)

Diagrams

Tables

To those who made this possible . . .

Thanks to

The Bank of Sweden Tercentenary Foundation for their
financial support towards the costs of research and printing;

The Gothenburg University Department of Musicology for help
with administration and practical advice;

MEDIACULT, the international institute for audio-visual
communication and cultural development in Vienna, for
rewarding co-operation;

Rikskonserter (The Institute for National Concerts), Sweden,
for financial and material support;

and to all those government representatives, phonogram
company staff, musicians, broadcasters and others in our sample
countries who have devoted so much time and effort to
providing the information we have requested.

Special thanks to our wives and families who have had to put up
with a lot (including our absence) during the past four years.

And to Suzie Feingold in Stockholm, who devoted many late
nights putting the manuscript together. To Monica Menges for
translations and other assistance. Also to Elfreda Powell of
Constable Publishers, who helped us with the final editing of the
manuscript.

Roger Wallis
Krister Malm
Stockholm 1983

Introduction

'Not for the first time, we got screwed . . .' A boss at one of the world's largest record companies mused sardonically over their embarrassing bankruptcy in a small African state. Five years later, another giant company moved into the same territory and was soon claiming 30% of the market. The point here is not that one or other of these companies is more or less gifted in the art of transnational operations, but that they should involve themselves in such a tricky market.

The reason is twofold. Small countries fulfil a dual role for the music industry. They provide marginal markets for international products. They also, by virtue of their unique cultures, can provide the sort of talent that comprises invaluable raw material for international exploitation. Jamaica has given us reggae. Trinidad the calypso. The small countries of South America, with a little help from Simon and Garfunkel, gave us the music of the Andes. We know about these. Others are waiting to emerge. Kenyan and Tanzanian Swahili pop is well on its way through the transnational phonogram pipeline to Europe. Sweden has given the world ABBA (though their music has nothing to do with their country of origin). But Sweden, a rich country, still has problems keeping its own recording industry alive. Investments in Swedish records and cassettes merely for a local market are too much of a financial gamble for the local phonogram industry (or at least the large percentage which is controlled by a small number of transnational companies). This is not a reflection on the cultural intentions of their local employees; it is a fact of the business.

The music industry, like so many others, has gone through a period of amalgamations and collapses. Through integration and diversification the larger companies in the music industry have become bigger in size and fewer in number. Many of them are owned by, or themselves own, other portions of the media and electronic industries. This too has affected the music life of small nations. Decca used to have the most comprehensive catalogue of Welsh music. Shortly after Decca was bought up by Polygram in 1979, their Welsh catalogue was discontinued as part of a rationalization drive. At the same time in Wales, however, there was an expanding number of small producers documenting and spreading more Welsh culture via sound recordings than ever before.

The reason for this encouraging development, once again, is twofold. Every country, every culture has its enthusiasts who lead the way when they feel their identity is threatened. The other reason is found in the accessibility of technology. Throughout the Seventies, music industry technology has found its way into every corner of the world. The most isolated village can get its first cassette recorder before it has running water or mains electricity. Even the absence of power lines has not always hindered the spread of electric instruments – portable generators are just as good. The last ten years have encompassed the final break-through of stereo HiFi, the global introduction of the sound cassette and the spread to most countries of video cassettes.

The Eighties poise us on the brink of laser, digital, satellite and cable technology, all of which can radically change and increase the spread of music via different media. The Seventies have taught us that music industry technology penetrates faster than any other technological development in the history of mankind. No-one really knows what effect the new technologies of the Eighties will have on small countries and their attempts to retain and develop their cultural heritage. All one can say, for sure, is that there will be an effect.

Big sounds from small peoples represents an attempt to penetrate this exciting (and sometimes frightening) scenario. The results are not all so bleak as one might expect from a cursory glance. Human beings have incredible qualities of resilience which can be called upon when things dear to their hearts are threatened. The threat of being flooded by a nationless transnational music culture leads to counter-actions in the form of local sub-cultures. But will this always be so, with the advent of a music media saturation on a scale never witnessed before? Or will other processes, triggered off by economic factors, regulate the effects of the new music industry technologies? Will we have one global music featuring a limited number of superstars on compact laser disc, or will we have many types of music supporting and cementing the cultural identity of different groups?

Studying these questions in a sample of small countries is a practical approach to a complex problem area. Concentrating on the experiences and possible developments concerning small countries is of relevance, not only for those nations themselves, but also for music as a whole. Small countries, by virtue of their vulnerability, are more likely to provide evidence of patterns of change at an early stage than larger nations.

THE MISC PROJECT

This book suggests some possible future developments in the field of international and national music. It also summarizes the information collected within the framework of a three-year research project known as 'the Music Industry in Small Countries'. (This is why the four-letter word MISC will be seen frequently to adorn the pages of this volume.) MISC gathered its information in fact-finding missions to 12 countries on 4 continents; Jamaica and Trinidad in the Caribbean, Tunisia in the Arab world, Tanzania and Kenya in Africa, Sri Lanka in Asia, the Nordic nations (Sweden, Finland, Denmark, Norway), Chile in South America and Wales. These visits were complemented by trips to world centres of the music industry, such as London and New York. Absent from the sample are small countries belonging to the socialist block. The indirect links between the state-run music industry in these countries and the transnational music industry pose very special problems of analysis. Some pilot interviews made with informants in Czechoslovakia indicated that the situation in many ways is similar to that in Western Europe, but that there also were substantial differences which could not be explored within the limited resources available.

In the 12 sample countries our sources of information include interviews with people ranging from doormen at less respectable night clubs and musicians to top level industrialists and politicians. Most countries have received two visits, the second time with a film crew in conjunction with a television series based on this research. By producing audio-visual material it is hoped that the results of MISC will not merely suffer the fate of collecting dust on the shelves of some university cellar, but will be accessible to as many people in as many countries as possible. Without music, life would lose much of its value. This concerns our future.

1

The MISC project

In every society throughout history there has been a cultural phenomenon labelled 'music'. Musicologists' studies have tended to centre on the history of western music and most of them deal with its development during the last 100 years. Only very few studies have been concerned with the most profound change ever in the field of music: its industrialization.

Its evolution during the last 100 years has been multifarious, the only factor common to all its branches being that music in any civilization exists as a social and cultural necessity. The music industry has developed in two particular categories: the production of hardware, the 'music machines', and the production of software, i.e., the music sounds to be mass-produced, including the vehicle on which the music is recorded and its packaging. (The term 'phonogram' has been used throughout the book to denote the latter, and refers generally to records and tapes.)

The first industrialization of hardware began during the 1830s and 1840s when brass instruments and accordions were gradually developed and adapted to industrial mass production. Such mechanical and semi-mechanical instruments as were *invented* during the nineteenth century were never more than curios, with the possible exception of the pianola. However, during the final decades of the century several inventions were created which led to the industrial production of phonographs and gramophones by around 1900. By 1920 the industrial production of radio transmitters and receivers was gaining momentum. Already electronics were beginning to revolutionize music machines, a process which has been going on ever since with increased momentum. The loudspeaker, valve amplifiers and optic sound registration of the Thirties, the open reel tape-recorder and television of the Forties, the long-playing disc and stereo technique of the Fifties, the transistorized amplifier, the compact cassette and electronic instruments of the Sixties, are some of the milestones in the development of more and more sophisticated music machines.

It is hard to pinpoint exactly the first industrial production of software in the field of music. Mass-produced broadsheets were mostly just printed texts of well-known melodies, but a few carried musical notation, and can thus be termed mass reproduced music. The second half of the nineteenth century saw the full development of mass-produced music albums and sheet music. At the turn of the century, the 78 r.p.m. record supplemented sheet music. The trend towards production of pieces of music which could be printed on two pages was fortified and standardized by the three-minute format of the 25cm 78 r.p.m. record. The acoustic recording techniques used at the time favoured the loud noises made by industrially produced instruments like the brass and the accordions.

Conditions within urbanized, industrial society combined with new instruments and new media forged new kinds of music and a new structure of music life. Gradually, a wide range of music businesses emerged: publishing houses, managers, record companies, broadcasting companies, and different kinds of hardware-producing manufacturers. More and more kinds of music were brought into the market place. International copyright conventions were amended to cover music and the new media. Performing rights societies and musicians' unions were formed.

The industrial and business aspects of the production and selling of hardware are relatively easy to analyze. However, the processes involved in the mass production and selling of music are more complex and harder to grasp. Here social, cultural, technological, economic and organizational factors interact in a complicated pattern.

Even so, surprisingly few studies have been made of this 100-year-long industrial processing of music. No general descriptive model has been established. Researchers have dealt with the industrial production and distribution of music within several frameworks, all of which focus on the links of decisions and actions that make up the process of collaborate production.[1]

The oldest of these frameworks is that of the *assembly line*, where the music is said to pass through a number of distinct stages of fabrication before it is released on the market. Metaphors such as 'tune factory' and 'song mill' have been used.[2] In the assembly-line process the know-how is built into the machinery combined with procedural rules for the operators. The pure assembly line produces a number of identical products. This, of course, is not strictly applicable to the music industry where the products have to be at least marginally different. However, some types of industrial processing of music come close to the assembly-line process, e.g. the production of background music (muzak).

Another framework is that of *craft and entrepreneurship*. Most persons involved in the collaborative production of music could be called artisans (hit song writers, sound engineers, producers, studio musicians etc). They have the requisite skills and experience to perform a technical task, but are told by their employers when, where and in what style.[3] Sometimes one single person makes all crucial decisions in the production process. This is often the case in small phonogram companies run by enthusiasts[4]. It can also be the case of the powerful rock music producer in a big company. This has been referred to as entrepreneurship.[5]

A third framework is that of a *formula consensus*. The co-ordination of the efforts of many skilled specialists in collaborative production, according to this framework, is based on a set of shared standards of evaluation. People working in a particular branch of the music industry have a common basis for forming a judgement of what constitutes a good performance or work, and what the ulti-mate result should be like. The concept 'art world' has been used to denote this area of consensus.[6]

A more comprehensive framework is that built around the con-cept of *product image and the decision makers' visions of the use and function of the phonogram*. In the music industry, music is regularly referred to as 'product'. There are also numerous other terms used at different stages in the processing such as 'a copyright', 'a property', 'a demo', 'a tape', 'a dub', 'a transcription', 'a cut', 'a master', 'a side', 'a release', 'an A side', 'a pick', 'a plug', 'a selec-tion', 'a hit' or 'a dud', etc.[7] A similar vocabulary is used in France.[8] All these expressions show that the attention of creative and other people involved in the process is focused on the commercial values of the music – 'the product'. The aim is to make money. The music company tries to direct production towards a final result corresponding to the directors' and owners' image of what is a saleable product.

The industrial processing of music involves creating a number of links between the music makers and the recipients of the music. The most important link in this system is the phonogram, that is to say primarily gramophone records and cassettes. The phonogram stores the results of the efforts of the production team, and distri-butes it to the recipients either as sales via the wholesale and retail trade or via some other medium such as radio, television or film. Most broadcasting companies use phonograms as their main source of programme material. Since the second World War the phono-gram has come to be the focal point of the music industry.

A number of technical innovations have changed phonogram technology profoundly during the last forty years or so. Around 1950 the tape-recorder and the long-playing record introduced new possibilites for editing music recordings, ousting the previous 3–6 minute limit on continuous listening. During the 1960s multi-track recording technique was gradually developed together with a num-ber of electronic sound processors, enabling a wide range of effects

The music industry is everywhere. A mobile 'Record Shack' in Kingston, Jamaica

in recorded music. Stereo technique together with corresponding hardware brought a far more intricate world of sound right into the living-room. These developments in recording and phonogram technology were closely associated with the emergence of rock and pop music with its emphasis on 'sound'. Simon Frith has called his comprehensive sociological study of rock music *Sound effects*.[9]

Throughout the 1950s and most of the Sixties the gramophone record was the only widespread phonogram, the use of the open reel tape-recorder in the home being fairly limited. LP record technology requires quite elaborate production facilities: engraving ('cutting'), electroplating, pressing etc. In the early years, both the production process as well as the playback units required mains electricity. This was a decisive factor in restricting the phonogram industry and with it the other branches of the music industry to the USA, Europe and a few urban centres in other parts of the world.

The old 78 r.p.m. records could be played back on gramophones with clockwork mechanisms and were more wide-spread than LP and EP records, especially in Africa and Asia.[10]

At the end of the Sixties two major technological advances began to influence the music industry; silicon chips/integrated circuit technology and the compact cassette. The combination of these two made it possible to play recorded music anywhere, any time. Playback units became cheaper and smaller. This, together with the expansion of the broadcasting sector, meant that the products of the music industry could be consumed in any part of the world. The music industry had its boom. From 1970 onwards, phonogram sales expanded by more than 20 per cent annually (excluding sales of blank cassettes!). In the USA the retail value of phonograms sold in 1970 was just over 1 billion dollars. By 1978 the corresponding figure was over 4 billion dollars. Sales had increased by 400 per cent in eight years! Sales of hardware also rocketed with stereo gramophones, cassette players and of course blank tapes finding their way into virtually every corner of the world, in both industrialized and developing countries.

The gramophone record is a one-way medium. You can only play back. The cassette is a two-way medium or a read-on/read-off medium. You can both record and play back on most cassette players. Cassette equipment is easy to handle – no advanced technological knowledge is required as long as they function and don't have to be repaired or serviced. Even servicing has been made fairly simple. When something goes wrong whole units or sub-units are simply replaced. With the combination of radio and cassette player

TABLE 1

SALES OF BLANK AND PRE-RECORDED CASSETTES (MILLIONS) 1971/81

Country/year	1971	1973	1975	1977	1979	1981
United Kingdom	6	21	40	60	75·4	100
Sweden	1·0	3·9	11·3	14·0	16·0	16·0
Sri Lanka	—	—	very few	0·1	1·1	2·4
Tunisia	—	—	very few	0·3	1·2	app. 3

Sources: *UK* 1971–77, British Phonographic Industry (pre-recorded) and Government Green Paper on Copyright (blanks). 1979–81 based on estimates from Mechanical Copyright Society. Tape manufacturers' statistics are far lower. *Sweden*, State Price and Cartel Committee investigation. *Sri Lanka*, Customs import statistics. *Tunisia*, statistics from local manufacturers.

Cassettes finding their way into every corner of the world. A market in the isolated town of Doez, in the Sahara desert, Tunisia

into the radiocassette anyone could record music from the radio. To connect a gramophone to a cassette player or to join two or more cassette players together for dubbing recordings is a fairly simple operation. Cassette technology brought the possibility of recording through microphones or the duplication of recordings within the reach of everybody. In the 1970s home-taping grew rapidly with far-reaching effects, not only on the spread of music but also for the artists and the industry that produced it. In 1983, the Japanese hardware manufacturer AIWA even introduced into the open market a cheap 'tape to tape' cassette recorder that could duplicate from one cassette to another at high speed.

The compact cassette and home taping have been blamed for many of the financial problems that beset the phonogram industry in the late Seventies. It is interesting to note in retrospect that when Philips, who pioneered the sound cassette, introduced it ten years earlier, the patent was given away free to anyone who wanted to manufacture. This was partly to get it accepted by the market, and partly to oust its main competitor which at that time was much stronger, the stereo 8 cartridge. Philips won that battle at a time when few could foresee the long-term consequences. With the improvement of its sound quality in recent years, the cassette also started to compete with the vinyl disc as a medium for mass-reproduced music. Record technology requires a bigger initial investment. It also involves sophisticated industrial processes which demand highly skilled labour. In tropical climates the operations of heating and cooling the vinyl plastic pose many problems. Gramophone records also easily get ruined in hot climates if they're not stored in a cool place, or when left inadvertently in the sun. In all these respects, cassette technology is easier to handle and thus more accessible. (We will delve deeper into the repercussions of cassette technology on the music industry later).

The technological changes following the Second World War have coincided with structural changes in the music industry, the most important being the growth of the transnational or multinational corporations in the media and culture sectors. This growth and some of its general effects have been described by researchers such as Herbert Schiller[11], Armand Mattelart[12] and Jeremy Tunstall[13]. These large electronics and media corporations have incorporated substantial parts of the music industry through mergers and integration of operations (cf Chapter 3). Most of the transnational concerns are dominated by interests in the USA. In the music industry sector the USA also dominates by sheer virtue of the size of the American market. The US phonogram market has a turnover as big as the whole of Western Europe. A phonogram that is even a moderate success in the USA is sure to generate quite substantial profits. Thus a major part of production planning in phonogram companies even outside the USA is geared towards attaining successes in the US market.

There are clear historical and economic reasons for the US domination of the music industry. Politicians interested in matters of culture in many countries have noted the world-wide implications of this fact. There is even some evidence that the US uses this dominant position strategically. A report produced in 1974 by a group of strategic researchers at the Pentagon National School of War states that:

On this ever-smaller globe of ours, all societies, all cultures are engaged in an inevitable competition for predominance and survival. Those who will fashion tomorrow's world are those who are able to project their image (to exercise the predominant influence and a long range influence) . . . If we want our values and our life style to be triumphant we are forced to enter a competition with other cultures and other centers of power. For this purpose the multinational company offers considerable leverage. Its growing business arsenal with its foreign bases works for us 24 hours a day. It is a fact of osmosis which does not only transmit and implant entrepreneurial methods, banking techniques and North American commercial relations, but also our judicial systems and concepts, our political philosophy, our mode of communication, our ideas of mobility, and a way of contemplating literature and art appropriate to our civilisation.[14]

This statement can be juxtaposed with the policy slogan originally coined by the Ford Motor Company and sometimes cited as a code of conduct: 'To be a multinational group, it is necessary to be national everywhere.'

To what extent do the transnational music corporations live up to these principles? What are their strategies? It's clear that, even in the early Seventies, the transnationals were well aware of their worldwide influence. The EMI company, one of the three biggest transnational music corporations, presented this picture of itself in 1971:

It (EMI) operates in every continent, through group companies in 33 overseas countries. Using hundreds of promotion men and over a thousand salesmen it has the power to stimulate demand both in quantity and quality and to meet the demand when sales accelerate.[15]

During the following decade this marketing power of the transnationals was used to create immense sales of hit records, especially with disco music. A new term, mega-sellers, was coined for phonograms that sold billions of copies.

A great deal of writing has been devoted to the output of the music industry, the artists and music they record. On the other hand, only a handful of comprehensive studies have been made of how the post-war music industry actually functions. Hirch[16] concentrated on the financial and organizational structure, though much of the data has been superseded by the dramatic developments of the Seventies. Denisoff[17] has reported on business and contractual relationships within the industry and Blaukopf[18] covers historical aspects. A much quoted study of the transnational phonogram companies and their global market was produced by two Finnish researchers[19] who have attempted to describe the structure of the industry, providing market statistics gleaned from company reports and trade publications.

Another small group of studies deals with specific areas of the industry. Gillet[20] covers phonogram company activities concerning the development of blues and rock. Hennion and Vignolle[21] analyze the economic structure of the industry in France. Three years later, Hennion[22] published a sociological study of different roles played by those involved in the production of phonograms (looking at who decides what gets recorded, how and why). In Britain, Peacock and Weir[23] have analyzed the role of the composer in the market-place through a study of the activities of copyright protection organizations and legislation.

The music industry has seen many rapid changes during the past 10–15 years, but we still know very little about the nature of these developments and their effects on music and life and music activities. The MISC research forms the basis of this book. MISC's aim has been to contribute towards an understanding of the different phases in the growth of the music industry during the Seventies. MISC pays particular attention to the interests of small countries, to their ability to use technological know-how in the development of their own cultural heritage, without being swallowed up by the global expansion of the cultural industries.

PROBLEMS SPECIFIC TO SMALL COUNTRIES

Rapid changes in the music industry prompted the Swedish National Council for Cultural Affairs in 1976 to set up a committee to investigate the field of sound recordings in Sweden. Some of the questions posed were: Which phonograms are produced in Sweden and by whom? How are phonograms distributed and how are they used? The committee's extensive report[24] was published in 1979 and gave this summary of the tendencies observed in the field of sound recordings.

There has been rapid concentration and integration on the international level. Production and sales at the beginning of the 1970s were in the hands of a large number of companies. By 1978, they were largely controlled by five multinational concerns responsible for a joint total exceeding 60 per cent of world record sales. The pace of this concentration process has increased during the 1970s. At present these concerns are planning to expand extensively in the Third World during the 1980s.

The number of records sold in Sweden doubled between 1970 and 1976. However, this powerful expansion has not entailed a larger or broader repertoire. The repertoires of the large companies have increasingly been concentrated to a few types of music, in particular 'super hits' in pop music, Western art music, and disco music. Marketing resources have also been increasingly concentrated on these products, with the result that a few products are responsible for a large proportion of sales.

Large-scale production, large editions, and the fact that record production does not require a large commitment of capital have resulted in a high level of profitability for the large companies. In 1976 the profits of the larger companies in Sweden ranged from between 21 and 125 per cent with an average of 55 per cent profit on invested capital.

In the beginning of the 1970s, the speedy repertoire concentration led to reactions from groups of musicians who were playing music which the large companies were not interested in releasing on record. The founding of a number of relatively small Swedish record companies was one of the ways in which these reactions were manifested. A sharp increase in sales has contributed to the ability of these companies to survive economically in spite of limited resources. However, during 1977 and 1978 sales increases have tapered off.

Most Swedish-owned record companies have remained small, nevertheless playing an important part in the world of Swedish music, since their activities forge an important link between large groups of Swedish artists and their public.

The number of sales outlets for records in Sweden has greatly increased during the 1970s. At the same time the average breadth of repertoire for sale has decreased, partly because fewer records are kept in stock and partly because service and information to customers are structured in such a way as to make it difficult to get information about records and order those not in stock at the sales outlet. More and more sales outlets have relinquished their power to choose which records to buy and sell, leaving this instead to rack firms and central buying departments. Thus the personnel at the points of sale know less about the trade today than their counterparts did at the beginning of the 1970s.

The amount of time spent listening to records has greatly increased, in particular among lower age groups.

Typical of the 1970s are the definite breakthrough of stereo and rapid developments in the field of recording techniques. Many of today's studio-recorded products consist of music which is impossible to reproduce live.

The gramophone record is basically the same technical construction it was when it was invented. The cassette has also arrived during the 1970s. Both of these media use analogue storage of sound. The possibilities of transferring and storing sound digitally, however, have increased rapidly during the 1970s. One of the advantages of the digital technique is the elimination of loss in quality due to tape noise and poor frequency range in the processes of transference and storage.

Due to the swift development of microprocessor technology and minicomputers it is now possible to store large amounts of sound in a digital state in a very small space.

Digital technology is used for example in video records, prototypes of which have been available since 1978. These records are read by laser beams. If they are used only to register sound, then up to sixteen hours of stereo sound can be accommodated on a video record the same size as a conventional LP.

Minicomputers with extensive memories will soon be on the market at reasonable prices. These computers will most definitely radically change the whole situation in the field of sound recordings.

In terms of cultural policy, it is important that the state is continually aware of technical advances and is able to take action to direct the results of those developments into channels consistent with the aims of state cultural policy.

The committee found that both the current situation and future perspectives called for intervention by the government to ensure the continued release of a wide range of phonograms with Swedish music and Swedish musicians in the future. The main conclusion was that the Swedish market is not big enough to support financially both the output of 'international' music and a diversified output of Swedish music on phonogram.

Similar problems concerning sustaining phonogram production with a high content of local music have been reported from Austria, Denmark, Norway and Finland. The pattern that emerges seems to be the same everywhere. Small countries, small culture and language areas mean small markets with difficulties in making phonogram production commerically viable. The result is a dominance of imported 'international' (in fact mainly US) repertoire on phonograms, difficulties in maintaining or setting up local phonogram production facilities within the country and less local music on the radio in small countries. With investigations of listening habits indicating the increased importance of recorded music in media as opposed to live performance, the process outlined above would seem to lead to the marginalization of local music traditions, posing a threat to musical heritage.

An Austrian researcher, Kurt Blaukopf, states the problem in these terms:

The difficulty of developing creative talent and of giving them access to communication via the phonogram is especially apparent in small countries that have no national phonographic industries. Austria is a good example of this phenomenon.

The Austrian market is dominated by the products of foreign companies. Their distributing organizations are linked in a cartel.[25]

During the late Fifties and Sixties, many countries in Africa and Asia gained political independence. At that time most of them had a very limited music industry sector, but towards the end of the 1960s this started to grow. Wolfgang Laade noted a startling change in music life linked to the operations of the music industry in his 1969 survey of music life in African and Asian countries[26]. He also noted that phonograms with local types of music were issued in more and more of the developing countries and compiled a discography of these phonograms.[27] In the 1970s the trend that Laade noted developed into a veritable media explosion in many Third World countries.

Are problems and effects the same or different?

Most developing countries are not small in terms of population or area, but many of them are small in terms of material resources. Would this mean that these countries are experiencing the same difficulties regarding the music industry sector as the small countries in Europe? Does the fact that a country is small mean that it has specific problems regarding the impact of the music industry on music life in common with other small countries? Do the technological, economic and organizational developments in the music industry during the 1970s have the same effects on musical activities in all small countries? Or are the general conditions in a small industrialized country in Europe so different from the conditions in a small country in Latin America, Africa or Asia that all comparisons are meaningless?

It may seem surprising but the developments we are charting here seem to cut right across national barriers, geographical areas and political systems. Even a study of developments from around 1900 to the early 1970s in countries as different as Sweden, Tanzania, Tunisia and Trinidad[28] shows interesting similarities in the patterns of change within their music cultures. As we shall see from a summary of this study, the notion of comparing small countries with very different general backgrounds is not so far-fetched as it might seem. There now follows a short digression for those who might have any intellectual doubts about the validity of this study.

On the face of it the music cultures of Tanzania, Tunisia, Sweden
and Trinidad might seem to be very dissimilar; traditional music
styles from these countries sound completely different. But the
processes of change in all four have a number of common elements,
particularly in these areas: mode of performance, music style and
structure, organization on a national and local level, as well as use
(or reception) and function.

Mode of performance
The folk music cultures of all four countries have experienced a
development towards 'stage shows' (organized performances by
music and dance groups for an audience). This would appear to be a
significant change with other developments following in its wake.
Organized performances require a selection of artists. In all four
countries this often occurs via competitions with adjudicators. The
'best' musicians join together to form 'super groups' and their music
is adapted to meet the demands of a stage performance. The
emphasis is on technical prowess and spectacular, almost acrobatic
qualities of performance. The same is true of stage performers
amongst Swedish folk fiddlers where high tempo is a criterion,
amongst Tanzanian traditional musicians who try to play as many
drums as possible simultaneously, or steelpan beaters in Trinidad where virtuosity is a prime virtue.

More recently, orchestras with elements of Western instruments
have been formed in all four countries for the purpose of playing
different types of popular music. These orchestras (or bands)
normally perform in various dance halls, but their role has more of a
background nature than the more spectacular folklore ensembles.
Instead they provide a background to other activities (in a res-
taurant or accompanying an artist in a radio/TV studio). Examples
are the Tunisian radio orchestras, 'dance bands' in Sweden, the
house bands in a calypso tent in Trinidad, and the Tanzanian jazz
bands.

Music style and structure
The development towards performance in concert form also involves a departure from some of folk music's spontaneity. Concert
performances require a greater degree of organization and disci-
pline. Pieces of music are linked together to form a programme,
where every item has a defined length. In each piece, the music
tends to be arranged in a particular fashion (according to series of
norms that develop based on, for instance, the acoustics of the halls,
the demands of the audience, the organizers and sometimes the

sponsors, the technical abilities of the musicians etc.).

In the area of traditional music, there is a clear tendency towards a decrease in the number of stylistic variations. Particular styles are regarded as being of higher quality and, although they might be affected by elements from other music forms (art music, religious songs etc.), they become the norm for the traditional music of a particular country. Examples are calypso in Trinidad, the music of the Gogo tribe in Tanzania, music from the provinces of Dalarna and Hälsingland in Sweden and 'Malouf' music in Tunisia.[29]

The organizational changes that can be observed are also similar. All four countries have built up a national apparatus for music administration, with the state getting involved in various decision-making processes. National folklore ensembles are established as well as various national education institutions. On the local level, there is a variety of new venues where music is performed: community centres, people's houses, and *maisons de culture* replace the traditional venues for ceremonies and rites.

The music life of the four countries has noticeably become more and more integrated into the economic system. Specialization increases. A group of professionals emerge who live entirely off music, as do different types of enterprises such as phonogram companies and concert agencies.

Use and function
These changes are all accompanied by changes in the use and function of music. Music is used more and more as a symbol of identity for a nation or different groups within a nation. Art music had been performing this function for some time, but from 1900 onwards, folk music became a symbol for country and people. It was used to strengthen feelings of national unity and seems to have had a unifying function between different ethnic groups and social classes in society. Many forms of popular music also serve to strengthen group identity for sub-groups within a larger community. Thus soul music had this function for students in Dar es Salaam around 1970 – at the same time as progressive pop played a similar role in Sweden. Steelband music had the same function for the poorest groups in Trinidad around 1950.

In another common development, music is used to a greater extent as a medium for different propaganda activities, for political or commercial information (advertising). Its use as entertainment as a 'time-filler', also increases as a professional corps of entertainers emerge, often performing to a large audience via mass media. Music gradually assumes a new function, different from that in traditional music cultures where it had a primarily communicative or ritual role.

Removing music from its traditional context also results in society changing its attitude to music. Traditionally, music is not an isolated phenomenon but one which is intimately related to different contexts where it is used. Thus many traditional societies did not even have a separate word for music – the word *musiki* in Swahili is a modern addition to the language. With specialization, professionalism and 'mediaization' (adaptation to modern media), music becomes an independent phenomenon, a sound structure which can be performed outside its original context. At the same time, other art forms (drama, dance, sculpture etc.) also attain independent status, and together with music become known as 'art' or 'culture'.

A streamlining of music's form and content can also be observed in each of the four countries covered in this summary. Not only have Western art music and popular music forms been adopted, but a rich flora of traditional music forms has been rationalized to a limited number of standard forms. This process is particularly noticeable in song lyrics. In the more modern versions of folklore music, nationalistic idioms dominate, whereas songs about love and individual problems are most common in popular music.

So why all the similarities?

All the observations above indicate that there are many similarities in the patterns of musical change noted in Tanzania, Tunisia, Trinidad and Sweden since the early years of this century. There seem to be two main directions of change, which interact with each other. The first involves developments following attempts to create national music styles and forms. The other is the development of popular music.

The types of change we've described occur in all four countries, but at different times; earliest in Sweden, but in Tunisia from around the Twenties with the most spectacular changes in the Fifties. In Trinidad, the development of popular music can be noted from the Thirties onwards, but attempts to develop a national style of music come later, around 1950. In Tanzania, these developments did not start until 1950, with the most radical changes occurring in the mid-Sixties.

The sort of developments we are noting here (music as an independent phenomenon, devoid of links with a traditional way of life etc.) first occurred in Central Europe before the turn of the century. A partial explanation of our observations is that all four countries have gone through similar developments in their economic and production systems, but at different times. This, however, cannot be the whole explanation. Tanzania in 1970, for instance, still had an economic system similar to that of Sweden around 1900. If economic changes were the only relevant factors, then one would still hardly expect to observe the sort of changes that can be noted in the music life of Tanzania. Another important factor must be taken into consideration, namely the education of the elite. This has its origin in a system resulting from the global domination of the states of Central and Western Europe during the first half of this century. Not only Sweden was affected, with an educated elite holding certain views about music, but a local elite with a European education established itself in Tanzania, Tunisia and Trinidad. These groups adhered to the same value system that had stimulated the growth of the independent European states, that had also led to the development of national music styles. The leaders of the groups that fought for independence in the colonies shared the European educated middle class' admiration for the independent national state. These groups often applied the same value systems to their own traditional forms of music, organizing folk music competitions, folk dance troupes etc. in Tanzania, Trinidad and Tunisia. They were moved by the same motivations that had inspired Sweden's national romantics previously. This postulate is supported by the observation that members of the educated middle class dominate the groups who organize music institutions, associations, and run companies in the music sector (including popular music) in Tanzania, Tunisia and Trinidad. The situation is largely the same in Sweden.

To sum up: value systems and knowledge spread through the European education system, together with changes in the economic and production systems are the main reasons for the similarities noted in the observed patterns of change. These similarities are so marked that any comparison of a number of small countries (industrialized or developing with a colonial heritage) is far from being a meaningless exercise.

Diagram 1 summarizes the process of change up to 1970. The middle column represents the music culture, the left column basic factors such as production and economy. The column to the right represents general cultural factors. The arrows indicate the channels and directions of influence. The vertical axis represents time. The developments take place at different times and at different rates in the four countries. The process in Sweden stretches over almost a century while in the case of Tanzania most of the changes have taken place after 1955. Thus, in certain areas, developments in Tanzania towards the end of the 1960s were catching up with the developments in Sweden. As time passes, one can observe more and more similarities in the types of change affecting the music cultures of these small countries. The influence of basic economic and production factors seems to decrease throughout this process,

DIAGRAM 1: PATTERNS OF CHANGE IN MUSIC CULTURE

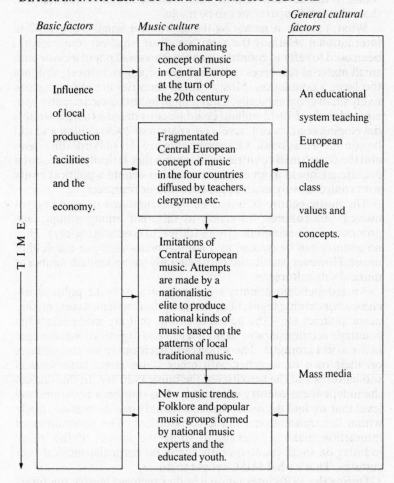

Basic factors

Influence of local production facilities and the economy.

Music culture

The dominating concept of music in Central Europe at the turn of the 20th century

Fragmented Central European concept of music in the four countries diffused by teachers, clergymen etc.

Imitations of Central European music. Attempts are made by a nationalistic elite to produce national kinds of music based on the patterns of local traditional music.

New music trends. Folklore and popular music groups formed by national music experts and the educated youth.

General cultural factors

An educational system teaching European middle class values and concepts.

Mass media

TIME

whilst the influence of mass media has increased, radically affecting life styles and value systems. The transistorized cassette recorder replaces pearls and trinkets as a status indicator – unlike jewellery it also disperses ideologies.

ASSUMPTIONS AND QUESTIONS

Our summary of four music cultures indicates that perhaps the most important reason for the similarities noted is the fact that the countries are small and thus subject to cultural domination. The assumptions can therefore be made that common patterns can be found in the development of music culture in small countries and that relevant comparisons can be made.

What, exactly, is meant by the expression 'small countries'? In international relations the term 'small' or 'smaller' countries has been used to refer to countries either with a small population or with small material resources (so-called developing countries), with not too large a population. Most of these countries are also comparatively small geographically. Thus a small industrialized country with a population of 10-12 million could be considered as small, while a developing country can have a population of 20-30 million and still be considered as small. Of course there are lots of borderline cases and the term 'small countries' will remain theoretically vague, but it is quite adequate in an empirical study to denote a political entity with comparatively small population and/or resources.

The music culture of any country is composed of a number of musical sub-cultures belonging to different ethnic groups, age groups or socio-economic groups (different classes in society). Thus no country can be treated as a homogeneous entity in the field of music. However, small countries generally have a limited number of musical sub-cultures.

An independent country's government can make political decisions concerning legislation, the education system, taxes, media, music policies etc – the actual decisions that are made affect the country's relationships to technological and organizational changes in the world around it. The actions and decisions of sovereign states on their own or together with other states affect both musical sub-cultures and the activities of the music industry. In this respect the independent country is an entity. It is only on a governmental level that we find decisions that can possibly match decisions made within the transnational music corporations. The possibilities of interaction make it relevant to study the impact of the music industry on small countries rather than on particular musical sub-cultures. That's what MISC set out to do.

During the 1970s international bodies such as Unesco, the International Music Council (IMC) and the International Society for Music Education (ISME) as well as a number of national institutions for cultural policy began to focus their attention on the role of the music industry and particularly the phonogram. The 1977 Unesco conference in Nairobi and the cultural symposium held later the same year in conjunction with the Festival of Black and African Culture in Lagos discussed the role of the phonogram in contemporary society. Politicians expressed their concern that economic processes might force the music industry to concentrate on a limited number of artists whose products can be produced in long series, rather than maintain a wide repertoire that includes phonograms with a limited relevance in, say, one single small country. These worries were based on the well-established and accepted thesis that cultural activities related to one's own heritage, history and immediate environment play a vital role in enriching the quality of life for individuals, groups or nations as a whole. This is also a basic thesis behind the MISC study.

Representatives of the music industry have expressed concern about fiscal levies on phonograms (value added taxes, import duties etc.), as well as lack of copyright protection in many countries. How do these matters apply to small countries? Is the industry's interest in attaining a flow of cultural products free from fiscal constraints compatible with the national cultural interests of small countries? What about the international agreements covering the rights of composers, performers and producers of phonograms that have developed over a number of decades? Their growth has been closely geared to the changing conditions in the music cultures and business climate of the larger industrialized countries. Such agreements, however, do not always lend themselves to rapid universal enforcement. What effects does legislation based on these international conventions have in a small country with a large heritage of folklore, where the concept of ownership has different connotations, where music traditionally has a close relationship to the activities of daily life, and where an administrative infrastructure does not exist?

Other important questions posed are:

– What kind of policies have governments in small countries applied or tried to enforce in the field of music?
– Which grassroots activities are taking place? What opinions have been expressed publicly on changes in music culture? Who lobbies who, and with what aims in mind?
– What is the nature and role of 'national' types of music in different small countries?
– Does the influx of Western music produce reactions in the form of strict musical traditionalism or popular types of 'counter-music'?
– How accessible are the technologies developed by the electronic media and music industries, and how are they used in different small countries? Have inventions such as the cassette provided new ways and means of documenting and expanding local kinds of music?
– Does the spread of music industry technology produce a shift from an emphasis in musical activity on function and communication to a 'product-orientated' view of music where mechanical reproduction and consumption dominate?
– How active is the music industry in different countries? Which business enterprises operate? Do the large transnational corpora-

tions working with music have identical strategies in small markets, or are they heterogeneous in this respect?

There are many more questions like this that could be asked and at least one very basic assumption behind the MISC study that should be stated: Small countries both in the industrialized and developing world have a lot to learn from each other regarding their relations to the music industry and the methods that can be applied to protect and develop their own cultural traditions in the field of music. An exchange of experiences can help them make the appropriate choices out of the flood of technological innovations and organizational models offered by the music industry and the big nations of the world.

AN INTERACTION MODEL

The interaction model in Diagram 2 represents the area investigated in the MISC study. The model should be valid for most small countries from the 1960s and onwards. There are three main levels of action:

- the *international* level includes international organizations, the transnational music industry and related media and electronic industries,

- on a *national level* we find the local music industry, related industries, mass media, music institutions and organizations (this includes phonogram companies, radio and television, the press, music colleges etc),

- the third level refers to the aggregate of *music activity* in a country, including the actual music played by musicians and listened to by members of different musical sub-cultures, the organization of musical sub-cultures, musical preferences etc. This is the level of the 'public at large'.

All the bodies in this system interact directly or indirectly. They are also influenced by factors which have their origin in processes outside the area covered by the model. By mapping out the processes that have been going on in the interaction model during the past 10–15 years, many of the questions posed in the previous section can be fully or partially answered.

DIAGRAM 2: MISC INTERACTION MODEL

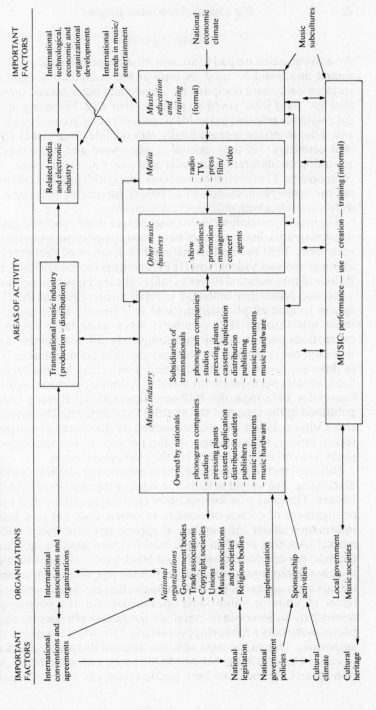

RESEARCH METHODS

An early question we had to ask was what methodological approach should and could be used. A look at the available international statistics on culture compiled by Unesco and other bodies showed that few 'hard facts' could be gathered that way. Not many up-to-date statistics relevant to the MISC area of research could be found and those available seemed hardly very reliable. Statistics in different countries – if they existed at all – were and are compiled according to different standards and are thus hard to use for comparisons. One even comes across contradictory figures concerning the same phenomenon in a country (invariably presented by different parties with different vested interests).

The most commonly available statistics are those concerning sales of phonograms. Such statistics have been compiled on a worldwide scale since 1970 by the International Federation of Producers of Phonograms and Videograms (IFPI) and from the mid-1970s by the Billboard International Buyer's Guide. The IFPI gives the figures in wholesale prices and Billboard in retail prices. Some of the IFPI figures include all phonograms sold in a country and some only those sold through IFPI members. When using these figures in calculations one can end up with completely different results. Kurt Blaukopf has computed the sales per capita of phonograms in 1977 in different countries and found that Switzerland has the highest figure of sales per capita in the world.[30] A similar computation using figures for 1976 from the Billboard International Buyer's Guide published in the report of the Swedish Committee on Phonograms and Cultural Policy proclaims Sweden as the world phonogram record holder, with the highest sales per capita. The same report ranks Switzerland as number 9 in the phonogram league.

Different methods of measurement are often used in international statistics. The weight in kilos, the value or the number of items all feature. The same goes for imports of electronic equipment. A total consignment of x kilos of cassette recorders does not give much information about the number of apparatuses introduced into a market. Another problem in the hunt for quantitative data is that records, pre-recorded cassettes and blank tapes are often lumped together. Even sprocketed film, perforated tape and 2-inch computer tapes can appear in the same statistics making measurements in terms of units or value fairly meaningless for the phonogram researcher. In some small countries the largest phonogram companies make only a modest appearance in official lists from customs authorities. One of the most vivid examples of this was Sri Lanka's so-called Cassette King, Mr Atu Moolchand, who according to his own advertising and other local businessmen, was involved in most

Sri Lanka's cassette king, Atu Moolchand

deals concerning imported cassettes. The Cassette King only features officially in the customs files as the importer of less than
100,000 or so cassettes per annum (in a market of over 2 million
cassettes).

Some statistical results do emerge from market research and
different kinds of polls. All sociologists are aware of the hazards

attached to such results. For instance, many contradictory research results have been presented regarding the nature and effects of 'home-taping', i.e. private taping from radio or discs on to cassettes. The Nordic members of the IFPI commissioned an investigation that showed that the majority of home-tapers use their cassette recorders to copy records to tapes. However, in a similar investigation, the audience research unit of the Swedish Broadcasting Corporation came to a completely different result, namely that the majority of home-taping took place off the radio[31]. In October 1982 a front-page headline in *Music Week* read: 'Home-taping isn't killing sales claims US survey.' The text continued:

A new market research survey of consumer home-taping habits – commissioned by an association of US hardware manufacturers and retailers – has, perhaps not surprisingly, reached the conclusion that, 'most audio home-taping is for reasons that have nothing to do with pre-recorded music.'

Backing this claim, which directly contradicts music industry surveys on taping, are figures from the survey of 1,000 home-tapers which apparently reveal that '52 per cent of the home audio cassette recordings made during the three month period prior to the survey were made of something other than pre-recorded music'.[32]

One can assume that the phonogram sector of the music industry would not agree that such findings were valid.

Difficulties regarding reliable statistics have been encountered in every country in the MISC sample. The lack of comparable statistics in the field of sound recordings has also been dealt with in detail by Pekka Gronow in a paper prepared for the Unesco office of statistics.[33] One can assume that it will be a long time before his recommendations are implemented. Of course, during three years of MISC studies we have encountered some statistical data that are reliable. Statistics from the Swedish Price and Cartel Board probably give an exact picture of the number of phonograms sold in Sweden in 1977, as do figures concerning records pressed in Kenya after 1976 from the only pressing plant in the country. Approximations and estimates given by experts can often be shown to be more correct than official figures. To be of any use, all the available scattered statistics relevant to MISC have to be supplemented with other data. MISC is primarily a qualitative study. Most of our data were collected through interviews, by consulting the memory of individuals representing different areas of activity in the interaction model (Diagram 2). A conventional way to do this would have been to distribute a questionnaire to a sample of informants in small countries. Anyone who has tried this method in studies involving developing countries knows that it just does not work. In 1980 Mediacult in Vienna distributed a questionnaire with questions regarding phonogram production to government offices and music corporations in all the member states of the Arab league. Only two questionnaires with very brief answers were ever returned. The only sure way to collect this type of data is to make personal interviews with the informants. This method has been used here.

The informants interviewed include representatives of transnational music corporations and of international organizations. In the small countries we have interviewed politicians (e.g. those with responsibility for culture), civil servants dealing with music, educationalists, representatives of music organizations, mass media (radio–TV people, music journalists), the music business (both bosses and employees right down to doormen at night clubs) and of course music-makers. In short, the sample of informants in each country has been made as wide as was practically possible.

The interviews were geared at getting the informants to identify *significant incidents* in the field of music during the period from around 1970 through to the early Eighties. The interviews were not conducted according to a fixed questionnaire but adapted to the specific competence of the different informants. Thus it was possible to filter out incidents considered significant by people in different positions and to throw light on these incidents from several angles.

For instance the Voice of Kenya radio monopoly decided in 1980 to change radically the music policy on one of its channels, by replacing international hit songs with local music. The experiment turned out to be very traumatic for the VoK and was discontinued after a fortnight. Virtually all our informants had a different picture of the background to this event, but their variety of opinions taken together gave us a clear insight into the tensions and structure of the local phonogram industry. The answers we received were certainly biased according to various vested interests, but the sum total provided excellent qualitative data on the popular music arena in Kenya.[34]

For obvious reasons the method was first tested in Sweden, our home base, where the results could be compared with a wealth of data on the music field collected by several researchers using other methods. It was found that a fairly limited sample of 15 informants were able to pinpoint significant incidents and facts leading to a picture of developments in Sweden that tallied with what was already known.

The information gathered was sorted into the following categories:

1. The formation of new music institutions significant changes affecting existing music institutions.

    Examples of music institutions: educational establishments, national concert organizations or orchestras, cultural or research institutes.

2. The formation of new music organizations or changes in existing music organizations.

    Examples of music organizations: musicians' unions, composers' organizations, concertgoers' associations, other groupings of active musicians or people actively supporting music.

3. Changes in legislation. The introduction of new national or international agreements.

    Examples: legislation intended to stimulate or control music activity, legislation or agreements affecting copyright, introduction of duties or taxes affecting music productions, legislation or regulations controlling the role of music in the education system.

4. Changes regarding business activities in the music sector.

    Examples: changes in the structure of the music industry – record companies, publishers, music periodicals, concert promoters and associated operations. Significant campaigns promoting national or other music. The investment climate for domestic as opposed to imported music.

5. Changes in the music policies and activities of radio/TV/press organizations.

    Examples: changes in the emphasis on coverage of national as opposed to global music phenomena. The relative roles of live and recorded music. The extent of mass media's commitment to informing about and reviewing music activities such as concerts, workshops, festivals etc.

6. Other changes or significant events not covered in the above categories.

    Examples: major festivals. Cultural debates. Acts of individuals. Changes in the economic climate. Introduction of new music cultures by immigrants/tourists or other processes.

Once the significant incidents are identified and categorized the oral data can be supplemented by relevant documents such as laws, agreements, annual reports from organizations, articles in the press etc. When all these data are referred to the interaction model a description of change can be made.

The significant incident method is a method of data reduction that produces a description of developments that is not too detailed and which can be handled with limited resources. The resulting patterns of change in the MISC countries are presented as a series of profiles in the Appendix. By consulting these profiles it is possible to relate the specific developments in special areas that are dealt with in this book to the total pattern of change in a country.

With very few exceptions all the hundreds of informants interviewed in this project agreed to having their statements taped. Two respondents who refused to be recorded, however, were lawyers at a copyright organization. Another was a director of a small Jamaican phonogram company. We also experienced people asking us to turn off our tape recorders when they wished to say something particularly controversial or offensive. In these cases we made notes instead. In principle, all interview quotes in this book have been transcribed from the tapes in the MISC files unless stated otherwise.

Clearly with the resources at our disposal, a limited sample of small countries had to be chosen for the study. Ideally countries in such a sample should represent not only different historical, political and economical backgrounds, but also some of them should have similar general conditions or backgrounds. Such a mix should make it possible to evaluate what is unique in a single country or in a certain kind of country as well as what is common to small countries in general. Another criterion was that some general research results should be available concerning the traditional kinds of music of each sample country.

FROM JOIKS TO REGGAE: MUSIC OF THE SAMPLE COUNTRIES

The following short descriptions of the music cultures of our sample countries do not claim in any way to be comprehensive. They are intended to give the reader a general idea of the music traditions and historical development of music life up to the start of the MISC study period.

When referring to different kinds of music a common-sense terminology will be used in this book. The term 'traditional music' refers to established musical traditions especially in fairly egalitarian rural societies. 'Art music' and 'folk music' refer to the music traditions of the higher and lower stratas of a stratified society. 'Popular music' refers to types of music which have emerged mainly as forms of entertainment in industrialized societies.

The Nordic countries, (*Denmark, Finland, Norway and Sweden*) comprise a similar group of small industrialized nations in northern Europe. Their cultures are closely related, the languages of Denmark, Norway and Sweden being very similar. Finland also has a sizable Swedish-speaking minority. They are all modelled on the welfare state concept, with considerable state and municipal involvement in culture. Their music cultures are very similar.

Prior to the Sixties, there were three main kinds of music; traditional folk music, Western art music and popular music. More recently there has been a considerable amount of overlap between these genres, producing forms such as folk-rock (electrified versions of old Scandinavian tunes) as well as experimental developments in the areas of jazz and electronic music.

Traditional Nordic folk music had its roots in the agrarian society that was dominant until the start of this century. It was often related to work on the farms, especially herding the cattle in their summer pastures. When the snow melted in the spring, the cows were often taken up into the hills to graze. Calls were sung in a piercing high falsetto to round them up at sunset. Horns were used for signalling and wooden flutes for leisure-time music. Herding music was mostly performed solo; neutral and diminished thirds were common features. It probably represents the oldest type of music in the Nordic countries, apart from the even older solo songs called *joiks*, sung by the Lapps, a minority group who live a nomadic life in the far north. All other styles contain features common to music over the whole of northern Europe, e.g. diatonic scales (made up of 5 whole tones and 2 semi-tones), strict rhythm, simple metre and relaxed, unvaried voice timbre.

A division can be made between secular and religious songs in Swedish folk music. Songs were used at work and play, normally without instrumental accompaniment. Over the past 100 years, instruments such as the zither and the guitar have been gradually introduced as accompaniments. In the religious sector, Lutheran chorales and from the mid-nineteenth century, non-conformist hymns have dominated. Traditional dance music was and still is played by folk fiddlers and other instrumentalists playing the keyed fiddle (*nyckelharpa*) and the clarinet. The accordion was introduced in the late nineteenth century. Percussion instruments have not been used in traditional Nordic dance music. The most popular dance used to be the *polska* in intricate triple metre. During the nineteenth century other dances such as the waltz, mazurka and polka were transformed into local Nordic versions.

Towards the end of the nineteenth century a choreographed 'folk dance' emerged, performed in peasant costume by university students. This later developed into the folklore shows that have become so popular amongst the nationalistic middle class, the music for these dances being composed music in folk-fiddling style. From 1910 onwards these activities grew more organized. Folk fiddlers started to congregate at large annual get-togethers (*spelmansstämmor* or fiddlers' conventions) open-air meetings in the summer which still attract several thousand participants, who will spend a weekend playing in small improvised groups. Concurrently, a system of folk musician contests developed in Norway. Some fiddlers also started to tour the country playing virtuoso tunes. The performance of folk music became generally more structured. Folk music orchestras were formed with 5–20 or more musicians.

There has been a marked interest in folk music throughout the Nordic area during the Seventies. This has been particularly noticeable amongst certain youth groups who have developed a concern for their own cultural roots.

The art music of the Nordic countries has always been dependent on developments in Central Europe. This music has been performed within the church, at the courts and amongst the upper class population of the towns. Over the past 100 years, institutions for art music such as opera houses and concert hall societies have been established in the major Nordic cities. The music performed in these institutions is the standard repertoire of Western art music sprinkled with works by Nordic composers writing within the same stylistic framework.

Popular music emerged during the nineteenth century as a result of the industrialization process, and made for sale as entertainment to a mass audience. Until then, the ordinary worker hardly had any spare time for popular music. Such 'popular' music at this time had its stylistic roots in art music, practised by the middle class.

From the turn of the century working hours were gradually reduced and wages increased. A popular music for workers emerged with many features borrowed from the folk music idiom. Orchestras with accordions, guitar, double bass, and (in Finland) the harmonium played versions of modern dances like the tango, the one-step, the foxtrot etc. adapted to Nordic folk music styles. Nordic variants of variety shows and music hall developed. From the Twenties musicians tried to copy Afro-American music and German *schlager* music. Later jazz music (particularly 'trad jazz' in the New Orleans style) became popular and in the Fifties rock 'n' roll. Throughout the Sixties thousands of youngsters started electric bands based on the styles of British pop with lyrics often in phonetic English. All these types of music were partly transformed into Nordic variants, thus preparing the way for the unique forms, often with local language lyrics, that were to emerge in the Seventies.

The Nordic countries were supplemented in the MISC study by *Wales*, also an industrialized area in western Europe. Wales was chosen in order to find out what parallels there are between developments in a minority culture area in a big country and those in a small country. Wales, together with Scotland, Ireland, Cornwall and Brittany (France), traditionally belongs to the Celtic culture complex, though throughout the past three centuries, however, Wales has been constantly influenced by the dominant English culture. The Welsh have a long tradition of song. Welsh folk music originally consisted mainly of the epic songs of the bards and other kinds of vocal music. A five note scale without semitones was used. Through the Anglo-Saxon influence hybrid styles have developed including mixtures of church modes and major/minor scales.

Mainly through its religious function during the eighteenth century, Welsh vocal tradition was gradually transformed into chorale singing. In 1819 an important competition in music and poetry was held. This was to become a yearly event under the name Eisteddfod and represents a revival of the meetings of bards at yearly feasts in earlier times. The Eisteddfodau have become the main forum for Welsh music. (As one Welsh musician put it: 'For one week a year, at the National Eisteddfod, you can feel really Welsh'). The choral singing that was developed in the churches and chapels was taken up by the coal miners, who developed the concept of the Welsh choir. Large choirs of miners developed a very distinctly Welsh style with a timbre coloured by the Welsh language. After the second World War the Eisteddfodau, particularly the national gathering in the first week of August, have become very large events attracting tens of thousands of participants and visitors. The competitions are usually divided into categories: adult choirs, solo singing for males and females, children and youth choirs and solo singing, folk singing and folk dance, and poetry recitation.

The music performed at the Eisteddfodau is both conventional Western art music and mixtures of art music and various revival forms of Welsh folk music. Before the Sixties Welsh popular music was totally dominated by the Anglo-American styles but during the Sixties and Seventies Welsh-language popular music developed from a Country and Western style to harmonically more advanced and sometimes more recognizably Welsh forms.[36]

For decades prior to 1970, both the Nordic countries and Wales had had a firmly established music industry which issued records of mainly Anglo-American popular music and art music. In the Nordic countries German popular music and local popular music started emerging on records even before the first World War. By the end of the Twenties this sporadic output had developed to a regular flow. During the Thirties a few small locally owned phonogram companies in Sweden released Swedish-language popular songs on 78 r.p.m. discs. During the Sixties and Seventies, the high purchasing power of the Swedes attracted the transnational phonogram companies, who consolidated their control over the established local music industry. Manufacturing resources in Scandinavia were also concentrated to the richest nation, Sweden.

Kenya, *Tanzania*, *Jamaica*, Trinidad and Sri Lanka are five countries in our sample that have a common historic background. They have all been under British colonial rule. All five are classified as developing countries. Four of them (Kenya, Tanzania, Trinidad and Jamaica) comprise two pairs with similar cultural backgrounds but different political situations during the post-colonial period, that is since the early Sixties.

Kenya and Tanzania represent the East African section of the sub-Saharan culture area. In both countries a multitude of ethnic groups exist, each with their own language. More than 140 languages are spoken in the two countries. Swahili and English serve as languages for general communication with Swahili being the national language of both Kenya and Tanzania. In Kenya two tribal groups dominate: the Kikuyu and the Luo. In Tanzania no special ethnic group dominates. In the post-colonial period Kenya has politically and economically belonged to the capitalistic market economy system while Tanzania has developed a political and economic system built on the principles of socialism. Tanzania has less natural resources than Kenya and according to UN statistics, is one of the ten poorest countries in the world. The traditional music of the area consists of a multitude of styles practised by different ethnic groups but with some common features. They are traditionally integrated into a social context. There is no sharp dividing line between music, dance, drama, dress, masques etc. In most of the indigenous languages there is no word merely for music. A common word in many East African languages is *ngoma* which denotes a combination of music, dance and drama. *Ngoma* often also means 'drum', the main music instrument for many, but not all, of the ethnic groups. In the non-literate traditional cultures *ngomas* were used to retain usable knowledge. Laws, history, cosmology and medical care were taught through the medium of song, dance and drama. In most ethnic groups this teaching by *ngoma* was and still is an important part of religious practices. As in most other cultures, one also finds music used for facilitating work, in different types of therapy and for celebrating important events in the community or the life cycle of individuals (harvests, weddings, funerals etc.).

Since the music of East Africa is almost always connected with movements of the body, rhythm is the most important element. This is emphasized by the division of the words of texts into strongly rhythmical groupings. A very basic feature is that a steady tempo is maintained over long periods, sometimes hours. Each participant in the music-making process refers all the other elements of the musical structure to a steady basic beat or pulse. On top of this pulse, a texture of rhythmical patterns is laid out (ployrhythms). An important means of creating accents and stresses is the shifting of the timbre, especially in drumming. The melodies are often built on five-note scales. The melodic phrases in polyrhythmic music are very short and are repeated continuously in *ostinato* patterns.

Multi-part music is common. In *ngoma* there is a great variation of dancing styles. Usually each participant dances without physical contact with other dancers. The movements of different parts of the body can follow different patterns in the musical texture. Most of the dancing is performed 'within the body'. The dancer moves in a very limited space.

Rattles, drums and other kinds of rhythmical instruments are the most widely used, and in coastal region simple xylophones. The *mbira* or hand piano (metal or bamboo reeds of different lengths mounted on a wooden box giving different notes when plucked) is common in the coastal region and in the central region of Tanzania. Bowl lyres and tube fiddles are played in northern Tanzania and Kenya.

Christian missionaries have exerted a marked influence on the music scene around the missions, trying to stamp out traditional 'heathen' music and introducing Christian hymn-singing instead. The Christian schools fostered an African elite with European values, thinking and habits. Their official ceremonial music was European. During the 1950s the urban areas expanded rapidly. They were filled with single men who had come to look for work, often far away from their relatives and villages. A new culture dominated by men emerged in the pubs and ballrooms. Western popular music influenced the music of these new lifestyles. This trend continued into the Sixties when, for instance, Chubby Checker's 'Twist' became very popular in Kenya and was copied in a number of local variants. After independence other new forms of popular music developed alongside Western music, these East African variants being often sung in local languages.

In the late Sixties, Congolese music came to be the dominating form of pop throughout East Africa. This kind of music was based on Latin-American rumba-type rhythms (though made more poly-rythmic by the introduction of more African influences) with short melody sequences sung in Linguala or Zaïrean patois. It developed in the urban areas of the former Belgian Congo (e.g. Kinshasa, Katanga) and spread to Kenya, initially via phonogram companies importing 78 r.p.m. discs. This diffusion was then backed up by live groups of Congolese musicians, many of whom had left Zaïre during the turmoil of the Congolese war and had settled in Kenya. By 1970, Zaïrean bands had virtually taken over the local pop scene in Kenya and neighbouring Tanzania. Local musicians singing in Swahili or the major Kenyan tribal languages had a hard time being accepted. This situation changed gradually through the next decade. Luo musicians in Kenya developed their own *Benga* beat. Tanzanian musicians borrowed some ideas from their 'Zaïrean colleagues, extended the melodic lines and, by singing in

Swahili, produced what has now become the popular Tanzanian jazz band style. Some Zaïrean groups who had been very popular in Tanzania in the early Seventies adapted to this new style and stayed on. More recently international phonogram companies such as CBS, Island and Virgin, have been making efforts to record these groups in order to test their potential in the Western world. Most of these operations have been organized through the Kenyan capital, Nairobi, since Tanzania lacks sophisticated recording and manufacturing facilities.

Jamaica and Trinidad are West Indian islands. Both have a history of plantations worked by slaves brought from Africa. Quite a few indentured workers imported from India were also brought to the islands, especially to Trinidad. Others came from China and the Middle East.

The music culture of these islands comprises many different styles ranging from pure African and East Indian music to locally developed Caribbean music. One distinct group consists of the African and Afro-European music played within the many religious cults and sects. Music played in African cults such as the *Shango* is slightly modified West African music with an ensemble of three or four drums of different sizes, rattles and call-and-response singing with a leader and a group of dancers alternating. In the revivalist Christian churches, however, rhythmical choral singing dominates, sometimes together with percussion instruments. The songs of these churches, especially those of the so-called Spiritual Baptists, can be termed Caribbean Spirituals.

The Afro-European types of music have resulted from the combined effects of European cultural domination, the disintegration of African culture brought about by slavery and the direct banning of certain types of African music and instruments. Dance melodies of Northern Europe have also had a considerable influence. Their melodic phrases were shortened and adapted to call-and-response style of singing and more complex rhythms were added. When dances like the waltz, the polka etc. were adopted together with their music by the black slaves and their descendants, the period structure, metre and rhythm were kept more or less unchanged. However, the sound of the voices and the instrument used were varied according to African tradition. Another very important feature of the musical results of this process was improvisation. Often binary and ternary metres were superimposed on each other, a modification of the African polyrhythms common also in Spanish and Latin-American music.

Afro-Caribbean music is a further development of this Afro-European style. It is mainly dance music played during community festivals such as the Trinidad Carnival and the Jonkunno mas-

querades and village dances of Jamaica. Well-known forms of
Afro-Caribbean music are the Jamaican *mento*, with its strong
accent on the fourth beat of the four-beat metre, and the Trinidadian calypso with its many forms.

Older calypsos are in two styles. One is more African, based on
the Kalinda music with call-and-response singing, quick tempo and
many percussion instruments. The other one is more European with
long stanzas and short refrains or no refrain. The melodic style is
dominated by minor modes. The basic rhythm is the paseo rhythm
borrowed from Afro-Spanish music from neighbouring Venezuela
(Venezuela is very near Trinidad). The singing of witty stanzas was
accompanied by guitar and maracas. During the Twenties and
Thirties the *merengue* rhythm and wind instruments were introduced into the calypso together with major modes. From the Sixties
to this day, calypso singers have been accompanied by big bands
with brass, wind and rhythm sections. The present trend includes
the use of larger PA systems and electronic instruments to facilitate
more exact reproduction of the sounds produced in the recording
studios (in other words a departure from the traditional importance
of improvisation).

Calypsos are sung mainly in the pre-Lenten carnival season. The
texts carry serious social commentary, but often mixed with jokes
and what white listeners would refer to as 'smut'. Calypso melodies
also serve as music for the carnival masqueraders dancing in the
streets of the towns in Trinidad.

For the past forty years during carnival season, calypso melodies
have also been played by steelbands – orchestras with instruments
made out of oil drums, so-called steel pans. The different notes are
produced by beating differently shaped bosses in the metal surface
of the top of the oil drum. In a modern steelband there are six or
more kinds of steel pans ranging from the tenor pans covering the
high register to the bass pans for the very low notes. Much research
has been carried out into the tonal qualities of a steel pan. 140
metals and alloys have been tested from which the 16 best have been
chosen. Over the years a great number of steelbands have been
formed in Trinidad. In 1971 the number of bands was estimated at
over 400 with 20–100 musicians in each one. Because of the costs
involved – a chromium-plated tenor pan of high quality costs over
£200 – most steelbands rely on private sponsors, often manufacturers of beverages, cigarettes and other healthy products or insurance companies.

Trinidad has a large East Indian community, so that East Indian
and African music have been infused into the *tassa* drumming of
Trinidad. Some calypsos also have melodies with East Indian
features.

Reggae music started developing in Jamaica in the late Sixties as a mixture of the chants of the rastafari cult, the mento and popular music styles from the USA. The Trinidadian calypso has been marketed worldwide on records since the Forties and Jamaican reggae music since 1975 – a fact that contributed to the choice of these two countries in the sample. Jamaica and Trinidad had only a rudimentary music industry before 1970. Jamaican reggae is now very much a studio product. Live concerts with reggae groups are rare occurrences. Calypso is still performed live, though even this form of live music on Trinidad is feeling competition from discothèques.

Sri Lanka is one of the few countries in Asia that could qualify as being 'small'. The bulk of the population of the country consists of the Sinhala people. A considerable minority of Tamils from southern India live in the northern part of the island. Another group of Tamils live in the centre area but many of these are stateless, having been 'imported' during the colonial days to work on the tea plantations. The culture of the Tamils is the same as that of the inhabitants of south-eastern India from whence they hail.

An important category of Sinhala music is that connected to Buddhist rituals. The chanting of the scriptures is done in two different styles, *gatha* and *pirith*. The *gatha* rendering preserves the metrical order of the scriptures while the *pirith* is in free rhythm with prolonged syllables. Both styles are recitative. Another type of music connected with Buddhist worship is the *hēwisi* music. This music is played by two drums, the *daula* which plays the basic rhythm and the *tammätta* playing elaborations, together with a double reed shawm called *horanewa*.

Other forms of traditional Sinhala music are found in the drum music used to accompany dancing. There is the 'up-country' dancing with roots in the Sinhala court of Kandy up in the hills, where kings ruled until they were finally conquered by European colonizers, and the 'low-country' dancing from low-lying lands in the south. A special form of low-country ceremony with dancing to drum music is the *tovil*, a healing ritual in which the famous Sri Lankan medicine masks are used (different headgear in conjunction with music and dance is used for healing different ailments). There is also a wide repertoire of songs sung at work ('carting songs' or 'paddy-field songs') or in traditional folk dramas like the masked drama known as *kōlam* in the coastal region or the *sokari* of the Kandyan region. In the latter the hourglass-shaped *udekki* drum is used.

The first European people to land in Sri Lanka were the Portuguese, in 1505. They tried to conquer the country but never really managed. However, they left a strong musical influence in the coastal areas. This has survived as *kaffrinna* and *baila* music which

resembles Afro-Portuguese music forms in Brazil. The explanation
for this is probably that the Portuguese army consisted mainly of
Africans from what is now Mozambique. The word *kaffrinna* can be
derived from a Portuguese word for negro: 'kaffir'. The word *baila*
means 'dance' in Portuguese. *Baila* music has developed into the
main popular music of Sri Lanka today, supporting a thriving local
cassette industry.

Strangely enough, the Dutch who ruled Sri Lanka from 1658 to
1796 and the British who ruled from 1802 to 1948, seem to have left
few musical traces in Sri Lanka apart from an amateur symphony
orchestra.

During the first decades of the twentieth century theatrical troups
from Bombay brought the popular Indian *nurti* songs with instruments like the harmonium, violin and tabla to Sri Lanka. These
tunes were based on North Indian *ragas* and *talas* (melodic and
rhythmic systems). Thus began a period of dominance of North
Indian music which has lasted more or less until today. In the
Thirties, the *nurti* music drama had a centre in the Tower Hall
Theatre in Colombo – in 1981 the President took this institution
under his wing and personally sponsored its rejuvenation as a centre
of North Indian music.

Sri Lanka had no locally established music industry before 1970.
EMI (India) did visit the island once a year for the purpose of
making local recordings. These were manufactured in India and
re-exported to Sri Lanka, and there is now an active local cassette
industry spreading music which is rarely played on the official
broadcasting station.

Sri Lankan media have had an important role in music dissemination throughout Asia. The commercial and external service of the
SLBC has had the same role in the Indian sub-continent as Radio
Luxembourg in Europe. For many years it was the sole broadcaster
of Indian film music which was not featured in broadcasts on
mainland India.

Tunisia represents the Arabic-Islamic culture in the MISC–
sample. Due to the geographical position of the country between
two fairways, the Mediterranean and the Sahara, its music culture
has been influenced from several directions. Originally Tunisia was
inhabited by the Berbers whose music was built on pentatonic
scales. Their influence can still be traced in much Tunisian folk
music. Later the Phoenicians and the Romans left their mark on the
culture. The most important single influence came with Islam
around the year 700 A.D. From the sixteenth century, Tunisia
belonged to the Turkish Ottoman Empire until the country became
a French colony in 1881. Tunisia gained political independence in
1956.

There are two main traditions within Tunisian music. The music of the towns, which can be called art music, and the music of the countryside, the folk music. Over the centuries the confrontation of these two traditions has resulted in a number of music types with a mixed style.

Since Tunisian culture is a variant of Islamic culture, many phenomena in the field of music have emerged from the tensions between the rules of Islam and pre-Islamic traditions. Music has been and still is a subject of contention among followers of Islam. In the Koran certain poets and singers are condemned. This has led some orthodox Islamic leaders to condemn all types of music except the prayer calls (*azan*) and recitations from the Koran. In spite of this negative attitude from some leaders, Islam in Tunisia has been fairly tolerant towards music.

The traditional music of Tunisia bears features common to many types of music in the Arabic–Islamic area. This is particularly the case with the music of the towns, the art music. Many of these features have Asian roots.

Music is often performed by a solo singer or instrumentalist. Small orchestras are also common, while larger orchestras with 20 or more members are a fairly new phenomenon. The timbre of the voice is tense, but not so tense and nasal as in more Eastern Arab countries.

The music of Tunisia is monodic. If several musicians play a piece of music they all perform the same melody line, each one with a personal touch, thus creating heterophony. The shape of the melody line is regulated by a system of rules called *nagam-at*. This word also denotes the pitches of the notes included in the melody line. The system of nagam-at corresponds to the *maqam-at* of Eastern Arab countries.

There are two main rhythmical variations; music in free rhythm and music in strict rhythm. Music in free rhythm is usually performed by a soloist but is sometimes played by a small ensemble. This music is very often improvised. Music in strict rhythm is the most common type of music in Tunisia. The rhythmical patterns used are called *iqa-at*. Each *iqa* is made up of a certain pattern of heavy and light beats and rests. Every iqa as well as every nagam has its own name.

In folk music, different types of antiphonal singing are common. In music for dancing short melodic formulas are varied and repeated. Separate instruments are used in folk music and art music respectively.

Folk music instruments are *gasba* (end-blown flute), *zoukra* (an instrument of the shawm type), *mezued* (bagpipe), the drum types *tabal, gasaa, darbukka* and *bendir,* and *qarqaba* (metal castanets).

A traditional Tunisian group performing at the Cultural House in Kairouan

Art music instruments are *nai* (end-blown flute), *el oud* (lute), *kanoun* (a psaltery), *rebab* (a bowed two-stringed fiddle), *naghrat* (a pair of small kettle drums) and *tar* (tambourine). The European violin is also used.

The traditional art music of Tunisia is called *malouf,* a rather general term used in the same way as the term 'classical music' in Europe. The music types called *malouf* are of different origins. Some types have roots in Andalusia, others in Turkey, Syria or Egypt. *Malouf* is performed today by small orchestras of three to eight musicians who both sing and play, or by larger orchestras where a division between singers and instrumentalists is made.

Within the folk music sector there are numerous types of music belonging to different ethnic groups. The music of the nomadic desert Bedouin is distinguished by narrow melodic formulas and very few instruments. Bedouin in agricultural areas have more varied melodies and more instruments. A great deal of the folk music is combined with dancing, usually different types of chain dances. Music for dancing is strongly rhythmical with short melodic phrases. Songs used in different ceremonies have a more complicated rhythmical structure and longer melodic phrases.

Folk music is often played at local religious centres called *marabouts*, which also serve as a kind of music school. Folk music plays an important role in all kinds of festivities, especially weddings and circumcision ceremonies. While art music is played by professional musicians folk music is played by semi-professionals. The latter have to have other sources of income since festivities only give them employment during two or three months a year. An indication of their importance in folk ritual is that a normal circumcision ceremony for a young boy might take about a whole week, including performances by two or three folk groups and a brass band. In the Seventies some folk musicians and dancers were introduced into the tourist entertainment sector. This gave them the opportunity to enjoy employment almost twelve months a year by providing a selection of more spectacular and virtuoso samples of their own culture.

The period of French colonial administration has left its mark on Tunisia. Tunisia still has radio channels in Arabic and French. Many of its television programmes are taken from a French satellite. Even if the music conservatoire in Tunis has formally relinquished its emphasis on European art music in favour of Arabic music, both European and Arabic music traditions are still represented.

Themes from Egyptian films and songs by popular artists from other Arab countries account for most of the imported music distributed on phonograms. In the Seventies, students returning from Europe started singing songs in Arabic with political texts, either to French-style popular melodies or in the style of traditional Tunisian folk music (*musique engagée*).

Tunisia had no established music industry prior to 1970. Phonograms had been imported for a number of years from Egypt and Europe. Some pre-recorded cassettes and discs are still imported – this trade goes mainly via Athens or Cairo. There is also a local cassette production, with three factories making blank tapes. The music sold on these tapes is mainly popular folk music which is rarely played on the official radio station.

Chile is a Latin American country which has experienced vast political and economic changes during the Seventies. One interesting feature is that the economic monetaristic theories of the Chicago School has been applied more thoroughly in Chile than anywhere else.

The music of the Catholic church and other kinds of Western art music have been an integral part of Chilean music life since the

seventeenth century. During the nineteenth century philharmonic
societies and opera houses were established in most cities. In 1929 a
faculty of fine arts was established at the Universidad de Chile in
Santiago, offering free higher education in Western art music. The
promotion of Western art music in Chile culminated in the creation
by a Bill of Congress of the Instituto de Extensión Musical in 1941.
Its vast programme began with the establishment of the Symphony
Orchestra of Chile and the National Ballet, the University Choir,
the periodical *Revista musical chilena*, the biennial Chilean music
festivals and the sponsoring of various chamber and choral ensembles. These all date from the Forties. By the beginning of the
Seventies, Western art music had achieved a very strong position in
Chilean music life thanks to long-term sponsoring by government
authorities.

There are two main kinds of folk music in Chile: the Amerindian
and the Hispano-American. Many hybrid forms exist, however, and
most of the music of the Amerindian peoples of Southern Chile has
been submerged into the mainstream of Hispano-American music.
Only the Aymara people of the Andean highlands and the Mapuche
people of the Atacama desert still maintain their traditional types of
music.

Andean music in Chile shares many features with Bolivian and
Peruvian Amerindian music. Five-note scales without semitones
dominate. The melodies have strophic form with frequent repeti-
tions of whole sections. Simple binary, ternary or mixed metrical
patterns are generally used. The music can consist of vocals to
instrumental accompaniment or pure instrumental dance music. It
is played on different types of flutes and string instruments such as
guitar, *bandola* and *charango*. Andean music was popularized in
Europe and the USA in the late Sixties through versions played by
folklore groups who visited Paris and other European cities. This
popularity was augmented by the duo Simon and Garfunkel who
picked up an Andean song, *El condor pasa,* and made it a worldwide hit.

The music of the Mapuche has some features in common with the
Andean music, but has a distinct style of its own. This music has not
influenced other Chilean music to any great extent.

The Hispano-American folk music consists of dances and songs.
Typical stylistic features are parallel motions in thirds or sixths,
simple three- or four-chord harmony, mostly·major mode, predominance of fixed tempo with alternations between slow and fast
sections and compound metrical structures. Solo or duo vocal
performances with slightly tense and nasal sound and frequent use
of *glissandi* and other ornaments predominate. The music is played
mainly on plucked string instruments like the five- and six-string

guitar, rattles, scrapers and occasional accordion and harp.

The most common dance is the *cueca* or *zamacueca*, characterized by dance movements imitating the courtship of hen and rooster, performed by couples with handkerchiefs in their right hand. The melodies are sung and accompanied by guitar and handclapping. The metre alternates between 6/8, 3/4 and 2/4 time within a set number of rhythmic formulas.

Narrative song types like *tonada*, romance, *corrido* etc. are common in Chile, as in neighbouring countries. During the Fifties and Sixties, a modern popular song style grew out of this song tradition called *El nueva canción* (the new song). These were created by singer-songwriters (*cantautores*) and were mostly sung solo with guitar accompaniment. Prominent exponents of this style were Violeta Parra and Victor Jara. The new songs very often had leftist political texts and were part of the movement leading to the election victory of Salvador Allende. (Victor Jara was also assassinated in the 1973 military coup.) These new songs started to re-emerge after a few years' absence in the mid-Seventies. They are usually sung at small music cafés called *penas*.

During the past decades the music scene in Chile has also been profoundly influenced by Spanish and Latin American popular music and from the Fifties onwards more by music from the USA.

Throughout the Seventies in Chile, traditional folk instruments have become more expensive. Liberal import policies have also led to an influx of electric instruments and domestic electronic equipment. The number of groups playing imitations of Western rock music has increased and access to the cassette has also enabled people to listen to types of music not officially approved by the government of General Pinochet. The Cuban singer, Sylvio Rodriguez, for instance, has retained the popularity he enjoyed in the early Seventies (prior to the coup), in part thanks to underground distribution via cassettes.

2

Who's on the scene?

The interaction model (Diagram 2, p.21) included three main levels or aggregates of action: the international, the national and the local. Originally, of course, all activity occurred on the local level; types of music have traditionally been created and used in local communities. Still this is normally the case, even if some kinds of music are spread far afield outside their original context through the megaphone of modern mass madia. Every style of music is 'understood' and kept alive by a group or groups of people at a local level.

A system of kinds of music which are usually stylistically related exists within any limited geographical area. These are normally 'dialects' of music found in a larger area and comprise the musical traditions of an ethnic group. Different kinds of music in such a music system each have their own use and function in society: in rituals and ceremonies like weddings and burials, in feasts with dancing and 'boy-meets-girl' situations, as means of communicating education, political or other messages. Some kinds of music are known and can even be performed by the majority of a community or society. Other kinds are restricted to special groupings.

A common restriction is music that is reserved for specific age groups. In many traditional societies there are various maturity rites where members are introduced into a new age group via a new music, maybe with song texts that reveal the secrets that are to be kept from the younger ones. In urban societies music preferences are related to generations, who tend to stick to the kind of music they heard during their youth. Music sociologists and psychologists have noted that people hardly change their musical preferences after the age of 25. This is particularly noticeable in Europe where different generations tend to retain the 'loyalty' they developed to the styles that moulded their musical value system during their formative years. The generation that grew up with the Beatles still like the Beatles. Those who played and listened to jazz or rock-'n'roll in the Fifties often return to these music forms later in life (thus the re-emergence of 'big bands' and the market for Fifties rock'n'roll nostalgia). This process can also lead to musical conflicts. A generation of urban youth who have never been exposed to anything else but Western or local pop music would find it hard to appreciate the traditional music of their parents, music which might have other types of relevance in society. 'Some young people buy Kenyan traditional music purely to have something to joke about.' (Local phonogram producer of tribal music in Nairobi).

Both in traditional and urban societies the music of a certain group of people is only part of a collection of attributes. Particular clothing and hairstyles are others. This is just as true of the Masai warrior in Kenya or Tanzania as it is of the 'punks' of Western Europe. The musical focus of these informal groupings is on the music specialists, those musicians who are considered skilled or 'the best'. In many groupings these musicians also are amongst the leaders of the group. In their music they speak both to the group and on behalf of the group and thus enjoy a position of power.

Awareness of the dangers associated with this position leads many musical leaders (in consumer societies at least) to avoid as far as possible making any statements with political implications. Their power is directed towards persuading their fans to buy as many of their products as possible. The fact that the 'punks' of the late Seventies seemed to do just the opposite was a reflection of their reaction against the outward affluence of a society which couldn't satisfy many of their basic needs, above all, meaningful employment.

Many formal groupings associated with music on the local level can be found in most countries. In traditional societies there are often special associations for the upkeep of certain musical traditions. Two examples are the Nindo music groups of the Wagogo people in Central Tanzania or the local fiddlers' associations in Sweden formed to play the traditional fiddle music of a certain county. In urban areas there are the concert hall societies and other local bodies supporting the performance of art music like the local symphony orchestra associations in Swedish towns, the Dar es Salaam Music Society in Tanzania or the Society for North Indian Art Music in Colombo, Sri Lanka. One also comes across societies for different kinds of dances and their corresponding music. Some of these local associations and societies have joint organizations on a national level and sometimes even on an international level.

The informal and formal local groupings in the music sector comprise the backbone of any music culture. The activities of these groupings are interwoven with other activities in the local community. Together with language, music seems to play a decisive role in the formation of the identity of individuals and their feelings of belonging to a group. Such a group can have historical dimensions, carrying on the traditions handed down from its ancestors, or it can be a revolting 'here and now' group. All these groupings are very important actors on the music scene.

On the local level there also are different kinds of music businesses, institutions for formal music education, mass media and government institutions. In almost all cases these are extensions or variants of phenomena that exist all over a country. Thus they can be summed up in the description of the national level. However, today these businesses, media and institutions are very important interaction channels in the music life of most countries. The way in which local government authorities and media support or put constraints on different local music groupings moulds the shape of music life on a local level. Local music businesses can concentrate on local music activities and musicians or they can act mainly as agents for other kinds of music. Via these channels local kinds of music can also be spread. An example of this is jazz music, which started as a local music in southern USA and via music business activities and media spread all over the world.

A type of informal business activity on the local level which has grown in significance with increased access to technology is piracy in its different forms. Piracy, essentially, refers to some form of unauthorized duplication where the business relies on making an economic gain at the expense of other copyright holders (composers, performers or phonogram companies). Entrepreneurs in this field are involved in a number of activities; piracy in general, counterfeiting and bootlegging.

Piracy in general refers to the unauthorized duplication of an original phonogram producing a product where the sound is similar, but not usually as good as on the original, and where the packaging (record sleeve or cassette inlay) is similar but not usually identical. The operator does not try to hide the fact that the phonogram is 'unofficial'. Typical tools for this sort of operation are a gramophone player, one or more cassette recorders and a photostat machine. Such activities can be found virtually everywhere.

Counterfeiting involves producing an exact replica which is hard to distinguish from the original phonogram. This requires more sophisticated equipment and more capital investment.

Bootlegging includes the unauthorized recording of an artist's performance prior to duplication. A cassette recorder at a live concert or connected to a radio as well as a co-operative duplicator or record manufacturer are the technical prerequisites.

Pirates are usually local operators. Organized piracy can also occur, however, on a national and international level. The production of pirated cassettes in Singapore has been such an important export earner that one must regard it as a national activity in the country.

A photostat machine comes in handy when pirating music. A picture from Dar es Salaam, Tanzania

THE INTERNATIONAL SCENE

A number of international organizations deal directly or indirectly with music. Most of these have a membership consisting of nationally based organizations. They function therefore as international federations of national organizations with a common interest. On the international scene there are music corporations with varying degrees of international activity.

Non-commercial international organizations, apart from those dealing with copyright, are mostly members of an umbrella organization, the International Music Council (IMC). The IMC has its headquarters in Paris and has consultative status with Unesco. The IMC also has national committees in countries. When the IMC was formed in 1949 it represented only a few national groupings in Western countries; the music it dealt with was almost exclusively

Western Art music. Now there are committees in all parts of the world, organized in very different ways in different countries. There are IMC committees in all the MISC sample countries except Tanzania and Trinidad. The IMC's main forum for international discussion is its biannual world congress held every alternate October. Some of the subjects discussed at the 1983 General Assembly give a good indication of the expansion of the IMC's frame of reference since its conception over thirty years ago: Music and modern media, cross-cultural processes in Africa, the IMC and musicology.

Many international organizations representing different aspects of the world music are also members of the IMC. Amongst the more important and active of these are:

– The International Federation of Musicians, representing national unions for musicians.
– The International Society for Music Education (ISME) which promotes music education as part of general education as well as music as a profession.
– The International Council for Traditional Music (ICTM), which coordinates activities, especially research activities, within traditional, folk and popular music. ICTM like IMC has a number of national committees.
– The International Publishers' Association, made up of music publishers.

Other IMC members are the International Society for Contemporary Music, the European Association of Concert Managers, the European Association of Music Festivals, the International Association of Music Libraries, the International Jazz Federation, the International Federation of Festival Organizations etc. Most of these organizations are based in Europe. They all function as more or less organized international lobbies, trying to further their own special interests in the field of music. Most of them arrange international conferences and seminars.

Music provides a major part of the output of most broadcasting organizations. On the international scene there are a number of broadcasting associations such as the European Broadcasting Union, the African Broadcasting Union and the Asian Broadcasting Union. A certain exchange of music programmes takes place between radio and TV stations in these regional unions, especially in the field of art music. Joint music programme production occurs in connection with so-called 'rostrums for young performers and composers', arranged in collaboration with IMC. In Europe there is also some co-operation in the field of popular music. This includes joint compilation of a European hit list as well as the infamous Eurovision Song Contest ('A song for Europe').

The oldest form of organized international co-operation in the field of music concerns copyrights of different kinds. It dates back to the last century and the Berne Copyright Convention of 1886. That convention has been amended several times, but the basic principle remains the same: the creator of a work of music or a text is entitled to some kind of remuneration when the work is performed in any country that has ratified the convention. The same principle provides the foundation of the Universal Copyright Convention of 1952, which differs in some details from the Berne Convention. Over the years, more and more countries have agreed to adhere to these conventions. Signatories have also gradually introduced more or less similar legislation concerning copyright.

Of the MISC sample countries, Chile, Denmark, Finland, Kenya, Norway, Sri Lanka, Sweden, Tunisia and Wales (via the United Kingdom) have ratified one or both copyright conventions. Jamaica, Tanzania and Trinidad all have national copyright legislation. Jamaica, Trinidad and Kenya are linked into the international copyright system through the British Performing Right Society (a heritage from colonial times). Tanzania was not a colony but a protectorate and has very loose links with the international system which means, in effect, that Tanzanian composers enjoy little or no protection internationally.

With the growth of phonogram technology the international copyright agreements have been supplemented by two other conventions: the Rome Convention of 1961 and the Phonograms Convention of 1971 (otherwise known as the Geneva Convention). These aim at international protection of the rights of performers, phonogram companies, broadcasting and TV organizations. The conventions give the performers the right to stop mass reproduction without their consent of recordings of their performances. The same right is given to phonogram companies concerning their recordings. According to 'Rome' the performers and phonogram companies are also given the rights to remuneration when a phonogram is used for broadcasting or telecasting. These rights are sometimes referred to as 'neighbouring rights', i.e. 'neighbours to the copyright'. (The rights of composers to receive remuneration when a work is mass reproduced on phonograms are known as the 'Mechanical Rights'). As few as 25 countries have signed the Rome and Geneva conventions. Of our sample countries only Chile, Denmark, Norway, Sweden, Finland and Wales (via the UK) have signed both conventions, and then not always in their entirety. Kenya has signed the Phonograms Convention which deals only with the protection against unauthorized duplication of phonograms. Many smaller countries that are not net exporters of music have been dubious about the Rome convention since it would be a drain on their foreign currency reserves. They would have to pay out far more than they got back.

A copyright owner such as a composer, lyricist or musical arranger, can make a deal with a publisher or a performing right society to look after the interests of part or of the whole of the copyright. In most countries that have signed a copyright convention there are national performing right societies which are mostly members of CISAC (Confédération Internationale des Sociétés d'Auteurs et Compositeurs), an international body formed in 1926. There are also collecting societies for payments of neighbouring and mechanical rights. According to the principles of the conventions, all the rights of all members in collecting societies should be protected in all other convention countries. The money collected should be transferred to the owner of the right through the collecting societies' international exchange system. In practice, however, numerous difficulties are encountered and departures from this principle frequently occur. Thus neighbouring rights payments accruing to Swedish performers in West Germany never actually get transferred to Sweden. West German musicians retain this money and Sweden retains monies arising there from performances of West German phonograms. Other countries have similar arrangements which do not tally with the principles of international conventions.

Other copyright problems stem from the fact that these conventions are based on a view of the creation of music and a concept of ownership of 'intellectual property' which grew out of traditions and conditions in late nineteenth century Europe. (We will return to these difficulties in a later chapter.) An organization which tries to develop the different aspects of copyright is a Unesco body, the World Intellectual Property Organization (WIPO).

The International Federation of Producers of Phonograms and Videograms (IFPI) is an international organization for phonogram companies. The IFPI has members in some 60 countries. In most of these countries the IFPI members have formed a national IFPI group. Such national groups exist in Chile, Denmark, Finland, Jamaica, Kenya, Norway and Sweden. IFPI also have one or two members in Sri Lanka and Trinidad. During the Seventies, the IFPI has been very active trying to persuade governments to sign the Rome and Phonograms conventions. The IFPI has also helped performers (via musicians' unions) set up collecting bodies in order to prepare an infrastructure to facilitate the signing of the Rome convention. IFPI has also been active in encouraging governments of countries that have signed the conventions to enforce and implement the articles of the conventions, for instance by introducing legislation criminalizing illegal copying and distribution of phonograms (the activities of phonogram 'pirates'). The IFPI, as its full name suggests, is also keen to act as spokesman for the fast-growing video industry.

In some small countries like the Nordic ones and Kenya many small local phonogram companies hold the view that IFPI is mainly furthering the interests of the transnational corporations. Thus in the Nordic countries a regional organization separate from IFPI was formed in 1975, the *Nordiska Icke-Kommersiella Fonogram-producenters Förening* – NIFF (the Federation of Nordic Non-Commercial Phonogram Producers). The Kenyan Record Produc-ers Association was started in 1971 by small phonogram companies owned by Kenyans who did not want to become members of their local IFPI branch. The IFPI deny that they favour the large com-panies, and declare that they wish to represent all phonogram companies, big and small.

The big, internationally active music corporations are very im-portant actors on the international scene. Through subsidiaries, licensees and agents they have established a worldwide network for marketing their products, both hardware and software. At the centre of these musical activities are the transnational phonogram companies, also called 'the majors', and in particular the Big Five: CBS (USA), EMI (UK), Polygram (German Federal Republic – Holland), WEA (USA) and RCA (USA). The country of origin given in brackets is merely an indication of an historical past, since today these corporations are true transnationals – active all over the world. All the majors are part of bigger media and hardware production concerns. EMI is owned by Thorn Electrics Ltd., WEA by the Kinney group of companies, Polygram by Philips and Sie-mens. Each of the majors issues records on tens and hundreds of different record labels.

The internationally active makers of musical instruments have become more and more important during the 1970s. One of the most active is the music instrument branch of the Yamaha copora-tion, which has ventured into music education in many countries to promote sales of electronic and other industrially produced instru-ments. Representatives of the 'Yamaha Cultural Foundation' fre-quently put in an appearance at various international cultural gatherings.

The transnational music industry is a jungle of relationships which is very hard, not to say impossible to untangle. Through a network of holding companies and licence deals, different parts of the big corporations are linked together. However, to describe the impact of these big concerns and their operations it is not necessary to know all the details of ownership and financial relationships within. We will return to the structure and role of the transnationals in the following chapters.

The meeting place for many actors on the local and international scenes is the national scene with all its government bodies, the mass media and various organizations with different vested interests. As an agent of change on the national scene, the music industry plays a crucial role. Much of the activity of the music industry on a national level is related to different phases in the process of recording and marketing phonograms. Diagram 3 presents an outline of this process. In small countries the activities of each company usually only cover some of the phases in the process. A large subsidiary of a transnational phonogram company or a larger company owned by nationals however can be involved in most or all of the phases in the production and distribution process.

DIAGRAM 3: THE DIFFERENT PHASES IN PHONOGRAM OPERATIONS

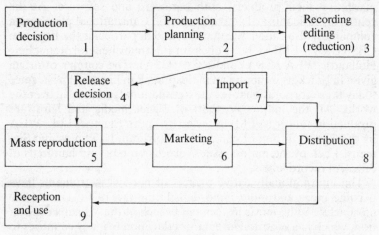

The decision to produce a phonogram, the production planning and the actual recording normally occur within the same phonogram company. Sometimes, however, recordings are supplied by independent companies who 'lease tapes' to a phonogram company with larger distribution resources. The producer of the recording would normally receive a royalty based on sales of the phonogram. A '10/90 deal' would indicate that the producer should receive 10 per cent of the retail selling price less tax on 90 per cent of sales. (The 10 per cent deduction from 100 per cent is a strange relic of the days of 78 r.p.m. bakelite records when one in every ten used to get broken in transit.)

Some phonogram companies have their own resources for mass reproduction of phonograms (record pressing plants or cassette duplication). The majority, however, purchase these services from larger companies that offer 'custom pressing' or cassette duplication facilities.

Marketing is normally planned jointly by the phonogram company (the producer) and the distribution organization that wholesales phonograms to retail outlets.

The *Production decision* (1) covers the type of material on the phonogram and the artists involved. It can apply to a single phonogram or a whole series.

Production planning (2) covers the exact choice of a number of variables: repertoire, performers, extra musical assistance from arrangers, studio and required studio technique, design of printed matter (the sleeve or cover and the inner bag in the case of discs, the 'inlay' in the case of cassettes). Production planning can also cover such aspects as the forms of marketing or the number of phonograms to be manufactured.

The date when the final product is put on the market, the *Release date* (4), is often decided after the *Recording Phase* (3) has been completed and the management can deem how attractive the product will be for the market. The exact nature of the marketing resources that are to be employed are often decided at this stage. The exact details of these decisions vary from company to company and from artist to artist. The management of a large phonogram company would rarely wait to hear the results of a recording with a super-star before deciding on a marketing campaign or a release date. Nor would stringent restrictions be placed on how much studio time a top artist used. Lesser known artists, on the other hand, might be lucky to get more than a few hours in a studio to record a couple of short pieces of music.

Sometimes all the production planning functions are in the hands of one person. Larger companies have a division of labour with A & R (Artists and Repertoire) men, producers, marketing and PR specialists.

A & R men (they usually are men!) seek out artists, sign contracts with them and help in the choice of repertoire. The A & R men are expected to be constantly aware not only of trends in the market so that current demand can be met, but also of new things coming on the scene that could be the trends of the future. A & R men spend much time listening to demonstration recordings (demo-tapes) from would-be artists, composers or publishers.

Producers have many different tasks. The main one is functioning

as a link between artist and recording technology. Sometimes the
producer also functions as recording engineer, thus playing a vital
role in developing the acoustic picture or 'sound' of the artist(s).
The producer endeavours to make sure that the artist and the A & R
man's intentions are satisfied by the sound produced. Particularly in
popular music, the producer will often introduce many of his own
musical ideas, small 'gimmicks' such as handclaps or other sound
effects which can make the final recording more attractive or
unique. The result, however, can sometimes be quite the opposite
with the producer having the streamlining effect of making the
recording sound just the same as everything else in a similar genre.
The producer's role is described in detail in Stuart Grundy's and
John Tobbler's collection of interviews with a number of influential
producers.[1]

Note that the term producer as used here should not be confused
with the term 'phonogram producers' used in copyright discussions
and descriptions of business structure to denote companies that
make (produce) phonograms. The International Federation of
Phonogram and Videogram Producers (IFPI) is the organization
representing phonogram companies, not only the people who spend
hours in studios trying to get the right 'sound'.

Marketing and PR Officers plan through which channels and in
which way information about the artist should be fed to the mass
media, to the retail trade and to the public at large.

Returning to the different stages in the production process,
Recording (3) usually takes place in a permanent studio with a
sound engineer in charge of technical equipment in a control room,
and the performers in an adjacent soundproofed room. Recordings
can also be made outside the studio, for instance by using mobile
equipment at concerts. Such recordings are generally referred to as
'live'. Multi-channel technique is frequently used in phonogram
recordings. The sound from different artists or instruments is
recorded on separate channels running in parallel on a magnetic
tape (8, 16, 24 or even 32 channels are common). At many recording
sessions where popular Western music is being put on tape, only a
few instruments are recorded at a time. Often the vocals are
recorded last of all. The same technique is also applied in Sri Lanka,
though with less sophisticated equipment. Artists in East Africa are
more accustomed to performing live and tend not to use multi-
channel technique, even if it is available, for fear of losing their
spontaneity, and/or to save studio costs.

After the recording session, multi-channel tapes are reduced to
2-track stereo; electronic effects such as echo are added with the
producer making particular use of his expertise. Different pieces of
music are then edited together in the right order for the phonogram.

The phonogram company decides when to release and how much to make available to the market and the *mass-reproduction* (5) phase gets underway.

Reproduction on to gramophone discs which can be played back on analogue reproducers (with a needle that follows a groove so that mechanical vibrations transmit signals) involves many separate stages:

1. The sound on the tape from the final sound mix (the 'master tape') is transferred via a lathe with a sharp needle on to a disc covered with soft material (an 'acetate' or 'lacquer'). This process of engraving is often known as 'cutting'.
2. The acetate is sprayed with a thin layer of silver and an electroplating process is then used to produce metal matrices. The ones used for pressing discs are known as 'stampers'.
3. Stampers which are mirror images of the surface of the original acetate are inserted in a press. Soft vinyl plastic (PVC) is placed between the stampers and is moulded into a disc when pressure is applied. Each set of stampers can normally produce up to 1,000 discs before they have to be replaced.

In recent years some of the know-how required in the pressing process has been eliminated by the introduction of automatic presses. The acetate-matrix transfer can also be eliminated by using a process known as Direct Metal Mastering (DMM). With DMM cutting occurs directly on to a copper disc from which stampers can be produced through electrolysis. This technological innovation has the advantage of improving sound quality (less echo, rumble and crackle) and dramatically decreasing the incidence of costly rejects in the process.

Record labels are fixed to the disc at the same time as the plastic mass is pressed. They are printed in normal off-set presses, but the type of paper used, particularly its humidity, is a critical factor. Sleeves are also printed in normal presses. The lamination and gluing processes require special machines.

The techniques used for reproducing discs with digital as opposed to analogue information are similar in part to those described above. Similar electroplating and pressing equipment is used. The engraving procedure for the Philips Compact Disc uses lasers. A laser beam also replaces the needle in traditional playback equipment, reading the digital pulses optically. RCA's Selectavision system, however, reads programme information by measuring capacitance.

Duplication of cassettes normally involves a master tape running at high speed connected to a number of 'slave' recorders, running at

Europa Film equipment for the production of copper-plated cutting masters for use in the new Teldec DMM system

the same speed. High speed duplication cuts down the time required but also leads to a loss in quality. This is one reason why some people prefer to copy material on to tapes on their own equipment at normal speed rather than purchase commercially available musi-cassettes. The electronic industry is continuously developing new magnetic materials in order to improve the sound quality in high speed duplication.

Import of phonograms (7) occurs in different ways. Complete products (discs in sleeves or cassettes) can be imported from a foreign phonogram company either by a local subsidiary or the local agent who has been given a distribution contract for that particular geographical area ('territory'). Sometimes shops or private indi-viduals import directly from wholesalers in other countries spe-cializing in phonogram exports. Large shops often do this in an attempt to procure attractive phonograms before the local agent has

An automatic disc press made by Alpha-Toolex of Sweden

managed to supply the market. Another method of import is licensed production. A copy of the master tape is imported by a company that has been granted a licence to manufacture (a lease-tape deal). When phonograms can be expected to sell more than a thousand copies as discs this is normally a more economic solution than direct import (discs are bulky and transport costs high).

A particular case of import is that involving semi-finished products. A company in one country might produce a lavish recording of the accompaniment to a song (a 'backing track') which can be distributed to different countries, whereupon vocals in different languages can be added in different markets. This practice is not normally approved of by musicians' organizations since it decreases work opportunities for local musicians who earn part of their living providing their services in recording studios ('session musicians').

The *marketing* stage (6) covers all forms of information to sales outlets and presumptive purchasers. A marketing strategy normally concentrates on helping the artist create as much attention as possible in the press and on radio/TV, thus providing a suitable platform from which to spread information about the phonogram. For instance when an artist performs on television, it is not unusual for the phonogram company to present the latest phonogram in an advertisement that refers to the television programme. It is also becoming more common for phonogram companies to provide promotion films on video tapes of their major artists (often produced for large sums of money) for a nominal fee or entirely free of charge.

Information to the retail trade is normally transmitted via travelling salesmen, printed matter (including catalogues), display material and articles in trade papers.

Distribution (8) covers different ways of physically bringing the phonograms to the recipients. The most common pattern is that phonograms are transported from the wholesaler's warehouse to retail shops which sell to the general public. There are more direct methods. One involves the wholesale company, or an associated company putting phonograms on display in various outlets (shops, supermarkets, petrol stations etc.). This is known as 'rack-jobbing'. The 'rack' companies supply a limited number of attractive phonograms and service the racks. This cuts the costs of distribution but decreases the range of music available to the public on phonograms. It also makes it harder for specialist music shops offering a wider range of music to survive.

Yet another more direct method of distribution involves mail order supplies either from shops that specialize in this type of activity or from 'record clubs'. Record clubs are usually controlled by large phonogram companies or book and periodical publishers (e.g. *Readers' Digest*).

Another form of distribution which has become more and more common is so-called 'home-taping'. Individuals copy directly from a disc on to a cassette or from the radio/TV. This individual activity is not illegal in most countries and should not be confused with illegal commercial activities that come under the category of piracy.

A sophisticated form of individual taping verging on piracy is provided by some retail shops, notably the 8,000 'record bars' in Sri Lanka. A customer gives the shop a list of favourite songs in the morning and collects a cassette with his or her personal compilation in the afternoon.

Reception and use (9) of phonograms is the last stage in the process. The phonogram is listened to via play-back equipment or via the radio or television. The degree of attention involved in listening can vary, ranging from active concentration to passive reception. The term 'wallpaper music' has been used to denote the function of music in the latter.

In a small country there might be one or more record pressing plants (e.g. Jamaica, Sweden) or none at all (Tanzania, Denmark). There will probably be large and small phonogram companies, some of which are subsidiaries or are closely linked to the trans-nationals, and some of which are owned by nationals. These companies may have very different policies, or they may be divided into groups with similar policies.

Musical instruments

In small countries the manufacture of musical instruments occurs, with a few exceptions, in small production units as handicraft or semi-handicraft. Such production units can be vitally important for the survival of national types of music played on traditional instruments. Both Western orchestra and electric and electronic instruments, however, are usually imported into small countries by sales agents for big manufactuers. Hardware like gramophones and cassette players are either imported or are assembled from imported parts in local plants.

Work opportunities

Artist managers and concert agents are active in almost all countries. Their business can exist in many forms ranging from the godfather type of operation where a boss 'controls' several bands and star musicians, to the musicians' co-operative kind of self-help booking and management agency. There are bigger and smaller enterprises involved in various kinds of promotional activities in the field of music. Business companies or organizations and associations can play an important role in the music life of some countries by sponsoring musical activities for reasons of goodwill.

Music pubs, dance halls, night clubs, hotels providing folklore shows for tourists etc. are all part of show business and the music scene. In some places the show business sector is the main employer of musicians. The demands of organizations within the entertainment sector are important factors in steering the process of change in music.

Radio and TV organizations contribute to the music scene in different ways, depending on their policies. Special publications catering for different musical sub-cultures as well as the music columnists of the dailies and the weeklies also have an influence. So too, do importers and producers of films and videotapes with music.

Government policies

In many countries the government plays an increasingly active role on the music scene. Through legislation, subsidies, different bodies such as ministries of culture, cultural councils, music councils and committees for music policy-making, governments support and suppress different kinds of music. Government-supported institutions of different kinds are generally responsible for formal music education, both general and at advanced level.

Government music policies are often influenced by what could be termed the 'cultural climate' of a country. This climate is partly a product of the music industry and the media, but is also affected by the views of the music establishment, organized in different national groupings. Here one finds different associations for amateur music-making, symphony orchestras, brass bands, rock groups, choirs etc, etc. For instance there are no less than 45 different Swedish music organizations affiliated to the Swedish national committee of the IMC. They range from the relatively small Swedish association for teachers of stringed instruments to a powerful choral association that can claim no less than 250,000 members.

Associations for European art music exist in almost all the small countries in the sample, from the chamber music societies in Sweden to the Dar es Salaam Music Society or the Colombo Symphony Orchestra in Sri Lanka. There are also audience and concert-goers' associations in some countries; sometimes they appear in the form of fan clubs for different popular musicians. Religious organizations too play an important role in the promotion of their special kind of music as part of their rituals. Religious organizations can also be very active in condemning and restricting those kinds of music considered sinful and harmful. Religious pronouncements condemning music vary in the extent of prohibition. The Bilal Muslim mission in a book entitled *Music and its effects*[2] advocates a total rejection of all music. Other religious spokesmen reject some forms of music and dance because they claim they encourage moral depravity. Religious organizations can be quite active in the phonogram industry selling large quantities which rarely appear in any official statistics. Some popular artists have been quick to note how a pronouncement that their souls have been 'saved' gives them access to what is a lucrative and fairly stable market (the subjects of evangelical popular songs being fairly predictable).

Trade unions for musicians, composers, music teachers and others working professionally with music have been formed in many countries to negotiate fees and working conditions. Related to these unions are the different collecting societies set up to collect money accruing from users of music as a result of copyright legislation. Counterparts to the unions are the associations formed by different kinds of music businesses (the national groups of the IFPI, hotel associations, retailers' associations etc.).

All these organizations act as pressure groups on the national music scene. The exact pattern and power structure differs from country to country, but most of these actors are to be found in most small countries. Details of who's on the scene and when they came on the scene in the MISC sample of small countries can be found in the charts of the Appendix which present a profile of change for each country.

3

The plight of small countries

We live in a changing world where no individual, organization or community is unaffected by their environment. Small countries wishing to retain some semblance of national sovereignty and independence are particularly vulnerable to events above and beyond. Fluctuations in the value of the dollar probably have a greater effect on the wellbeing of a rich country like Sweden than any policies its government might try to implement. Countries that have to spend a large portion of their foreign exchange on the oil bill (Tanzania 50 per cent, Kenya 40 per cent) have very little economic freedom; particularly as regards generosity towards aesthetic pursuits in the area under scrutiny in this study.

Even having your own oil is not always a guarantee for a rosy economic climate, a point which was made very strongly by one of Trinidad's singing poets. Calypsonian Ortniel Bacchus (Tobago Crusoe) was crowned 1983 Calypso Monarch after singing 'Trinidad ain't no right to be crying now' at the Carnival celebrations. This is part of his lyrics.

A worldwide recession worse than in the thirties
is causing concern internationally.
This worldwide recession and world economy is
the reason for alarm by the authorities.
Poorer countries catching their tail to keep head over water.
Richer countries don't want to fail, but they can't make it no
  better.
Now here at last, things begin to get hard.
What is the position in Trinidad?

We have oil in abundance, plenty, plenty money
We even have a high standard of living also
Man, the way things were really going well, I was always saying
This is the land where milk and honey flow.
Citizens exposed to millions, Government playing with billions
More cash in the place than the law allow
Now that rainy day is here, I don't see why Trinidad
  didn't prepare
Trinidad have no right to be crying now.

The whole place in a quandary, we get rich so suddenly,
Nobody don't want to work hard again
We send for some workers from dem foreign countries
When they rip we off everybody start to compalin.
Farmers turn their backs on the land, no agriculture,
    no farming.
They've getting money from special works who pay them
    for doing nothing.

The whole place became a pigwell, more pay, no production
We didn't know that the oil money would have done
We spend millions on food when we could have grown we own
We have chance to spend when what we all can buy
was jet planes to Miami, spending sprees in New York City
and the import bill just rocket to the sky.

Economic games and video, morality went down so low
A bit out of reach for Trinidad somehow
Well now that the tables are turned and it seems as
though the money gone down
Trinidad have no right to be crying now.

Different types of factors impinge on small countries, affecting
what they can or cannot do internally. Economic, cultural, technological and legislatory factors, separately or in combination,
provide constraints. The results of such dominance in any country
also depend on its own particular traditions and historical accidents
(wars, colonialization, occupations by foreign powers, religious
upheavals and the like). It could be argued that the influence of
larger cultures, technological advances or international legislation
on small countries is all basically a question of economic power.
Possibly so in a historical context, but for our purposes the division
is a useful starting point for a description of the Big and the
Small.

FOREIGN INVESTMENT IN SMALL COUNTRIES

To pay their bills, small countries have often had to take loans from
other nations (usually oil suppliers), from banks or international
finance organizations such as the IMF. Strings are normally
attached to the latter. When Jamaica signed an IMF agreement in
1981, one of the conditions was that the management of the
state-run tourist hotels would be handed over to 'reputable international operators'. In other words, the Hiltons and Intercontinentals
of this world would decide what went on inside the hotels, i.e.

ultimately, which Jamaican entertainment (culture) would be allowed in.

If tourism is chosen to be a major currency earner, then it would appear to be impossible wholly to avoid its detrimental effects on local culture. Even Tunisia, a country more aware of these dangers than many, has not escaped the negative effects of tourism. It becomes more important for a folk musician performing at a hotel to show that he can balance five beers and three Cokes on his head whilst blowing his *zoukra* (shawn), than demonstrate how the music functions. And this is understandable. How could one recreate the right atmosphere for, say, a traditional wedding tune in a 25-minute show at the grill bar of a ****hotel?

Small countries often go out of their way to attract foreign investment. Indians build hotels in Sri Lanka. Saudi Arabians do the same in Tunisia, providing havens where both they and the tourists can do things they would never do at home. Since hotels offer entertainment, this provides a major source of employment for musicians. Its nature also places restrictions on the music they are expected to play. In their search for a steady job, many of Kenya's best musicians find their way to the hotels on the Mombasa coast where they are expected to perform their ABBA/Boney M/Frank Sinatra repertoire for affluent German tourists. By and by, hybrid forms emerge with snippets of Swahili song on a West European disco beat ('Afro Disco' as performed by Neville and the Savannahs can be heard on Polydor POL 7–388).

Free-trade zones are also attractive industrial perks. A Saudi Arabian company has opened a video complex in such a zone in Sousse, Tunisia. The Zinifilm organization uses its hyper-modern German television equipment to record television series for the Middle East. Different versions are made for different countries, according to respective censorship requirements. The operation enjoys full tax exemption in Tunisia as long as none of the products are sold within the country. Zinifilm use a lot of music on their sound tracks. Most of it, according to the staff, is taken from existing phonograms – 'not compositions by top composers and artists because they make a fuss. Lesser known composers are only too happy to have their works exposed.'

The nature of economic effects also depends on which Nobel prize winner governments put their faith in. Milton Friedman's policies have been applied more totally in Chile than in any other countries where this Chicago economist has been accorded guru status. An authoritarian government has helped, of course. The policy of maintaining high bank rates (35 per cent in 1981) with a free exchange system attracted much foreign capital in the late Seventies – this provided the basis for a gigantic hire-purchase

It becomes more important to balance 5 beers and 3 cokes whilst playing the *zoukra* than demonstrate how the music is played

market. 'It's easier to buy a car than a kilo of meat' was a much heard comment. The free import policies led to a veritable flood of electronic goods, including many electric instruments. Anyone who could afford a down payment could get an electric guitar. To acquire a traditional folk instrument such as a *charango* (a stringed instrument made from an armadillo shell) was an entirely different matter. Folk music being identified with the Allende period and still having a tarnished reputation with the military, traditional instruments would not be the sort of article shopping centres put on display. Excluded from the hire-purchase system, one would have to pay an instrument maker cash for the labour involved. Thus a *charango* became far more expensive in reality than an electric guitar. Ten years earlier the situation had been very different. During the Allende period, traditional and folk music was the rule. Instruments were in demand. Many were made, and they were cheap. Once again we see how economic policies can cut right across traditional patterns of culture.

EXTERNAL CULTURAL FORCES

External cultural forces – albeit in combination with economic factors – often decide the availability of culture within small nations. When the global products of the cultural industries, particularly films, TV shows and strip cartoons, have made their money 'first time round' in the richer nations, they are offered cheap to those who are less well off. Thus the Tanzanian Film Company's choice of Anglo-American films on release in Tanzania might give the average film critic a heart attack, but it's that or nothing. Foreign currency restrictions require the TFC to wait up to two years before remitting distribution fees. The only film distributors willing to wait as long as that are those who really scrape the bottom of the bucket.

The same process affects television. All small countries that have television would probably like to augment the local content of their TV programmes. But this becomes a financial impossibility. It's so much easier to pick up material from the barrage of cheap culture waiting outside. Thus all over the world one finds the same mixture of old episodes of *Dallas*, *Muppet Shows*, *Bonanza* etc.

On a more local level, a suprising number of small cultures are overshadowed by more powerful neighbouring cultures. Reactions to the Big Brother syndrome vary from sad inferiority complexes to remarkable resilience. *Welsh* culture, for instance, seems to have survived despite the dominance of Anglo-Saxon language and media – possibly this is due to the support Welsh cultural traditions have received from the local intellectual elite. The intellectual establishment in *Tanzania* certainly supports the development of modern popular music trends in the country. Ten years ago Tanzanian jazz bands were very much in the background, with visiting rumba-style groups from Zaïre commanding all the attention. Now, thanks partly to widespread media support, the Tanzanian musicians have emerged with a buoyant popular music culture. Even the Zaïrean groups still in the country have mostly given up singing in Linguala (their language from Zaïre) and now perform in Tanzania's national language Swahili. *Kenyan* musicians, on the other hand, never seem to have recovered from the deluge of Zaïrean music in the late Sixties. In 1982, however, the government of Kenya did give the impression of being keen to tackle the problem; a Presidential National Music Commission was appointed with a brief to find ways of increasing the status and quality of local music culture, which is not easy. Kenya, in common with many other former colonies suffers from a post-colonial cultural burden, manifesting itself frequently as a confusing mixture of Shakespeare, Gilbert and Sullivan, missionaries and cocktail parties. After the first whisky, the language becomes English and the pitch becomes augmented by half an octave. ABBA, The Bee Gees or James Last provide the background. Any artistic expression of local cultural roots would be an anachronism in such an environment.

We mentioned missionaries. The religious revivalists were well on their way in nineteenth century *Sweden* towards exterminating traditional music in that puritan, Lutheran country. The fiddle was the invention of the devil. The art of making the *nyckelharpa* (keyed fiddle), the instrument used for accompanying many Swedish traditional dances, would have probably died out altogether, had it not been for a national folk music revival in the last decade or so.

Quite a few Swedes, in common with the inhabitants of so many small nations, still feel an inferiority complex towards their own culture. The elite favour Central European art music as the only aesthetically acceptable form of musical culture. On the other hand, large sectors of youth, with no small measure of encouragement from the media, assume that anything from the other side of the sea (in a westerly direction) must be better than locally grown music. Somewhere in between these two extremities you find groups of enthusiasts trying to define their own local, cultural frame of reference. In the Fifties and Sixties the balance was not in their favour. There were said to be anywhere up to 5,000 electric groups in Sweden, singing rock or pop, often in phonetic English. Some of the rock'n'roll artists with the largest Anglo-Saxon repertoire couldn't speak a word of English. Vietnam, independence movements and student revolts brought about a change in the late Sixties. Groups of enthusiasts emerged from their cellars, cottages and garages, doing things that would have been unthinkable ten years before, singing rock in Swedish, playing traditional tunes with electric guitars. A new type of music movement gathered momentum. This is but one illustration of a pattern of resilience that has emerged in many small countries during the Seventies, a resistance to being culturally sat upon.

Jamaican reggae is another example. It is not the music of the middle or upper class elite. It is the music of the ghetto, expressing

the wrath, aspirations and hopelessness of people who feel down-
trodden. The USA has had a traditional cultural 'big brother' role
vis à vis the Caribbean, despite the British colonial influence.
Calypso singers from Trinidad always used to go to New York to
record their records. Jamaicans used to listen to American blues
records. Reggae was a fusion of Jamaican rhythms and American
rock and blues – typically, it didn't make a world impact by
converting the Americans first. Little Jamaica made its impact
through London and the immigrant market in the UK. Roots never
die, small cultures are resilient. Upper class intellectuals in Jamaica,
however, still look down on reggae as something artistically in-
ferior.

Sri Lanka presents a similar, yet more complicated picture. Over
the years various external cultures have descended on the peoples of
the island, who themselves are divided into two main cultural
groups. The Tamil minority have a strong, natural cultural affiliation to Southern India from whence they hail. The Sinhalese
majority, on the other hand, have not found it so easy to define their
own culture. They live with a mixture of legacies, from their own
dynasties of the past who ruled from Kandy up in the mountains,
and from various colonizers, first Portuguese, then Dutch and
finally British. As regards music, many intellectual Sinhalese have
looked to Northern India for inspiration, claiming that ragas should
provide the basis for an aesthetically high quality Sinhalese musical
tradition. The argument is similar to that put forward by groups in
the West who regard Central European art music as the only
acceptable art form, rejecting jazz, rock and folk music as something of lesser quality. More recently in Sri Lanka some music
researchers have mooted the view that there is a more geniune and
national Sinhalese form of music, which can be found in the
drumming and vocal singing traditions that are still practised on
ceremonial occasions[1]. Such counter-claims have sparked off a
debate – quite violent in tone at times – with most of the more
dramatic passages being staged at the Sri Lanka Broadcasting
corporation. Should the radio devote more time to Sinhalese traditional drumming and singing or should it concentrate on North
Indian art music? Whilst the intellectuals have been exerting no
small measure of emotional energy tackling this apparently insoluble problem, the masses have been listening to totally different
sounds thanks to the cassette. Any number of cheap cassettes with
Western music are available. But the Sinhalese have also created a
thriving local cassette industry based on their own popular music
forms, in particular the *baila* rhythm, a jerky 6/8 tempo, halfway
between a calypso and a samba – originally introduced 400 years ago
by the Portuguese. Most *baila* cassettes are not deemed suitable for

Sinhalese drumming traditions, not appreciated by all sections of the Sri Lankan elite, and only occasionally played on radio

radio performance. They cost twice as much as foreign music cassettes, but do well in the market even without a large media back-up. Clearly they represent something close to the hearts of many Sinhalese.

It has been claimed that the North Indian art music lobby in Sri Lanka has its origins in political aspirations during the move towards independence when India presented an ideal for many nationalists.

> Indian intellectual leaders had called for a return to their own cultural – and musical – heritage. The Sinhalese took Indian music as the symbol of these and their own cultural aspirations and totally forgot their own musical tradition.[2]

The same might have happened in *Tunisia*, which had long been under the cultural yoke of both France and Egypt. The situation

prompted a group of local musicians in the Thirties to get together
and put a lot of effort into saving a particularly Tunisian form of
music culture, *malouf*. Malouf has its roots in Andalousian culture
and thus differs from other Arabic music. In 1934, at the beginning
of the movement for national independence, the Rachidia association was formed for the preservation of *malouf* – not only as an
antidote to the influence of French colonial culture but also in
response to the strength of Egyptian music. The Rachidia still
exists, *malouf* is still enjoyed and practised, but mainly by upper-
class Tunisians – in fact it is their national 'classical' music. The
Egyptian culture is still present too, through the film industry. But
with the introduction of the cassette, Tunisians have been able to
get access to a popular Tunisian form of folk culture which has been
adapted to the cassette media. These are the songs of the artists who
perform at weddings and other festivities. Just as with Sri Lankan
baila music, these cassettes are rarely deemed to be suitable for
performance on the national radio network. Whatever one thinks of
the quality, at least this new local music industry provides an
alternative which probably has more relevance to the lives of those
who enjoy it than the mass-produced songs of make believe from
the Egyptian film industry.

TECHNOLOGY FROM OUTSIDE

It stands to reason that small countries can only engage in limited
participation in the development of high-cost technology. Consequently, they can enjoy limited control over the spoils of such
research. Even rich Sweden finds it hard to participate in the race to
bung communication satellites into orbit. But Sweden will be on the
receiving end of the mass of fuzzy footprints which will shortly cover
Europe, providing individual homes with access to umpteen TV
channels, depriving governments the traditional means of control
over the media. Even without the satellites, music can be picked up
over boundaries, television waves can travel over frontiers. The
rooftops of Tunis consist of a jumbled maze of aluminium bars and
poles – all vying to pick up Italian TV signals from across the
Mediterranean. Even in the far south of Tunisia, in the isolated
troglodyte village of Matmata, where 800 families still live in caves
under the ground, there's no shortage of television antennae growing out of the rocks. Some families even have videos. The local hotel
proprietor – the hotel is itself a system of caves – has even installed a
rotating aerial with a remote controlled motor on the top of a nearby
mountain. He claims to be able to pick up TV signals from as far
afield as Tel Aviv via this arrangement.

In another developing country, Sri Lanka, a local television

At Matmata where 800 families still live in caves, there's no shortage of TV aerials growing out of the rocks

entrepreneur succeeded in picking up signals from a Soviet satellite in the summer of 1980. Direct reports from the Moscow Olympics were relayed over Colombo via the tiny little ITN station. A year and a bit later, Sri Lanka started a national television channel, Rupavahini. The service was made possible by a foreign-aid gift from the Japanese government. They supplied a transmitting station complete with studio facilities. Cynical voices were heard to mutter that the Japanese just wanted to sell television sets. The Japanese ambassador reacted indignantly to such accusations. The Sri Lankan government said they had accepted the gift because of the role they believed television could play in education. The Japanese electronic industry must have deemed it a good affair – for months prior to the opening, the radio commercials on the SLBC were full of ads for Hitachi and National receivers. Once again observers pointed out that with sales fast approaching 100,000 sets on the island, suppliers had done business worth around 15 million dollars – the value of the Japanese 'gift'. What exactly did the Sri Lankans get? An international adviser described the equipment as "obsolescent but not obsolete". A local television enthusiast described the government instructions to Rupavahini to maintain a 60 per cent level of local material as an "illusion". It remains to be seen whether Sri Lanka ends up with the same mix of international cultural product, with the same assortment of sports, blood, violence, cartoons and glitter that adorns the screens of many other poorer countries.

The only country in the sample of small nations that can boast of being on the forefront of at least one aspect of music industry technology is Sweden. Sweden has a unique position as regards access to the techniques of manufacturing gramophone records simply because two wholly Swedish-owned companies have specialised in the areas of electroplating and pressing. Important to note is that they haven't been absorbed by the international phonogram industry with whom they partially compete. There are different reasons for this. Toolex, the makers of Alpha automatic record presses, are already a lucrative division within a Swedish multinational, Atlas Copco. The other firm, Europa Film, design and manufacture the electroplating equipment that turns acetates with grooves into stampers. They are a successful family enterprise that is rapidly expanding with the video boom in Sweden. The presence of these two companies has been very important for the development of independent manufacturing facilities for gramophone records, not only in Sweden, but in many other countries. Both Alpha-Toolex and Europa Film have supplied much of the equipment for the new video disc plants.

Technology is everywhere, be it a cassette factory in Tunisia churning out two million blank tapes per annum, a satellite in the sky or a transistorized cassette-radio. They all bring us the output of the transnational cultural industries. Whether we like it or not, we're all exposed to an etherial mixture of mass culture and propaganda of various complexions. Small countries cannot stop it coming in. All they can do is decide which local alternatives to offer with the limited resources at their disposal.

INTERNATIONAL LEGISLATION

Few, if any, small nations have legislatory systems that have developed in total isolation from other larger systems. Most colonies have taken over the legal legacy of their former masters. British copyright law, for instance, reappeared almost verbatim in the new law books of the former British colonies when independence was granted.

Small nations are under pressure to abide by numerous international conventions and agreements, many of which have been developed to suit the interests of the larger, richer nations. The diplomatic hiccups hampering cooperation between the industrialised nations and the third world, the call for a new 'world information order' or discussions within UN organisations such as GATT regarding Third World economies illustrate how hard it is to change the established order of things. A music copyright system based on the concept of an individual being solely responsible for the creation of a work might not be suitable for a society where composition is a collective activity and where the creative results are traditionally regarded as general property in the 'public domain'. For many small nations, strict adherence to international agreements such as the Berne or the Rome convention might merely lead them to pay out a lot of money to the Boney Ms and ABBAs of this world, and not get very much in return. International bodies, such as the World Intellectual Property Organisation (WIPO) encourage adherence. But for small countries with foreign currency problems, any net outflow of cash is not welcome, whatever the morals involved.

Even the small nations' ability to affect international decisions is limited, They might enjoy safety in numbers in the international family at the UN, in Unesco etc, but the big powers have engineered the system, and often have the right of veto. Sometimes even international commercial organisations are better at effecting change. International bodies provide at times the forum where transnational cultural industries try to get results that cannot be achieved through normal business practices or individual lobbying of governments. The international phonogram industry's own organisation, the IFPI, has waged a campaign directed at Unesco to get phonograms classed as cultural products on a par with books, which should enjoy duty-free importation. This campaign was organized by the deputy director-general of the IFPI, Gillian Davies, herself recruited by the industry from the World Intellectual Property

Organisation. The campaign got under way in 1972 when Unesco held a regional conference in Helsinki, Finland.

The IFPI onslaught 'involved bombarding the various ambassadors with literature stating the industry's case . . . So well had the IFPI's lobbying been carried out that there was a unanimous recommendation that European states should recognize the cultural rights of records. All was set for a successful assault on the Unesco general conference in Paris later the same year. This time, thanks to the support of the Record Industry Association of America (RIAA), the United States undertook to sponsor the resolution.' Finally the Unesco general conference in Nairobi (1976) did formally accept a resolution confirming that phonograms are culture. The report quoted above from *Music Week*[3] concluded that 'by the end of 1977, some signs of commercial implementation should be evident.' In fact countries didn't adapt to club rules as fast as the IFPI had hoped. Four years later, a senior planner from Polygram wrote in a paper for the Council of Europe:

> The industry still looks forward to the day when complete justice will be done and recordings will be universally acknowledged as the cultural medium they *truly* are – as was accepted in the General Conference of the Unesco in Nairobi in 1976 – and are added in a new Protocol to the Florence Agreement, treating the record as the book by according it the status of cultural material. We are still waiting for the ratification of this agreement in various parliaments.
>
> It is unacceptable that pornographic books are treated as 'culture' in many countries just because they are printed, and are consequently tax exempted or low-rate taxed, while a Beethoven symphony on records is taxed at luxury rates. It is even more ridiculous that in some countries the *live* performance and the *printed* music of Beethoven symphony is 'culture' taxed and the production on records 'luxury'.[4]

From a democratic point of view, this argument is convincing. Why indeed should a pornographic record – there are such things – be taxed when the book isn't? Phonograms undoubtedly are culture, a means of communication. But they communicate different ideas. Should the cultural value of Beethoven be cited as a valid argument for the removal of taxation from the majority of the industry's international mass products? It's just possible that certain governments and societies might regard a lot of international pop as being of dubious cultural value. It would be very undemocratic, and rather foolhardy to forbid it. But when young people can afford to devote *x* hours a night to disco records, one should not be surprised

if governments are tempted to tax them for the luxury, irrespective
of any Unesco resolutions about the cultural value of phonograms.

The point we are making is that international legislation and
recommendations impinging on small countries are rather like the
Ten Commandments. They enjoy high status, but are not always
applied or applicable. Their form is also the result of historical
power structures and current lobbying, in which the Big have a
greater say than the Small. A contributory factor is that there is very
little independent consultation between small nations in different
parts of the world regarding international legislation – Kenya
doesn't get in touch with Jamaica when it wants to get advice about
copyright. Lobbying can be met by lobbying, but only if you've had
time to decide where your common interests lie. ˙

The music industry is everywhere – there's no corner of the earth
where its effects cannot be felt. Through radio, television, phonograms and videograms the same sounds can be enjoyed by listeners
anywhere on the globe. But do people just listen to the same sounds
when the products of the electronic industry become available? The
answer, of course, is yes and no, for two reasons. One is the relative
availability of low-cost phonogram technology. The other is the
complex relationship between the big and the small in the phonogram industry. The big get bigger by swallowing up the small. But
the small keep on cropping up. Fortunately, size does not guarantee
total control.

4
The strategy of large
and small phonogram companies

Today, social scientists as well as all those concerned with cultural activities at different levels are faced with a central problem: the growing internationalization of the cultural industry with its qualitative and quantitative aspects. It may well be that no other sector of this industry has reached a degree of international concentration comparable to that of the record industry . . .

. . . The cultural industry, once a light industry dominated by individual know-how, has developed into a heavy industry whose survival depends on its success in international markets on account of the enormous investments involved.[1]

The major transnational phonogram companies are not only gigantic, they're also integrated into even bigger organizations operating in the communications and entertainment field. The growth picture, with the large phonogram companies becoming bigger in size and fewer in number has been encouraged by the belief in the large-scale economies of size.[2] The result is that the Big Five (CBS, EMI, Polygram, WEA and RCA) control a high percentage of the market in many countries. This applies to large nations such as the USA, France and the United Kingdom and to smaller countries. These 5 companies controlled 97 per cent of the phonogram market in Denmark in 1977[3] and only 6 per cent of phonograms sold in Canada – also a small country in relation to its neighbour – were of Canadian origin.[4] The Big Five's world percentage, based on retail sales, varies somewhat according to the state of the American market and fluctuations in the dollar, but an average of 60 per cent in the free market economies is generally accepted. If furious negotiations between WEA and Polygram are not hindered by anti-trust laws or other legal and financial considerations, then the Big Five will become the Big One and Three Others.

Concentration, integration and diversification

Growth has been achieved by various means other than merely selling more phonograms within the same company. *Concentration* has been a normal strategy, i.e. buying up another organization engaged in the same activities as oneself. The most spectacular example is the growth of Polygram. Polygram was formed in the late Seventies by the amalgamation of two established names in the recording business, Phonogram (formally Philips) and Polydor. Over the years the Polygram group have also acquired:[5]

Mercury	(US)	1962
MGM	(US)	1972
RSO	(US)	1976
Barclay	(France)	1978
Decca	(UK)	1980

Polygram now control around 15 per cent of the world market.

Another method of expansion has involved integration, in contrast to the early seventies when different stages in phonogram production were spread over many companies. Integration can be *horizontal*, involving mergers between similar activity groups such as those involved in TV, radio, film production, manufacture of electric instruments etc. Thus EMI used the profits from the Beatles to get involved in television companies, cinema chains – which gave access to a network of concert venues – and guitar amplifiers. *Vertical* integration involves the merging of distinct stages in the path of a record from idea to record buyer such as production, marketing, distribution and retailing. Thus a phonogram company might establish or buy recording studios, record pressing and cassette-copying plants, printing works, distribution companies and retail outlets.

Phonogram companies also expand their turnover through diversification into totally new areas. When Warner Bros became WEA with a little help from the Kinney group, the phonogram company found itself related to a car hire firm and a variety of parking lots. The Swedish group ABBA have preferred diversification rather than concentration when disposing of the profits from their phonogram company, Polar. They have built up a network of interlocking companies that indulge in anything from art and real estate speculation to bicycle and car-tyre manufacture. The rapid growth-rate of successful phonogram companies and the variety of methods of expansion applied make it extremely hard for the researcher to know who owns who or what, and thus understand the complicated relationships within the industry. However, one can derive a small measure of comfort from the fact that people within the industry do not always know who their relations are, or how the networks are linked together. ABBA's legal advisers, in the course of some financial gymnastics, even managed to hold an Annual General

Meeting of the 'wrong' company on one occasion. A financial report in the press described the consternation amongst the participants when the error was detected, *after* the chairman had closed the meeting.[6]

The processes of integration take place at all levels, internationally and nationally, in large or small countries. And they rarely leave the environment unaffected.

When CBS decided to establish a proper footing in the affluent Swedish market, it purchased a local distributor, Cupol (1969). At the time Cupol was one of the few outlets through which small local phonogram producers could distribute their records. Looking after them was not a very profitable occupation and the new owners, CBS, decided to clear out the shelves, ousting some of the lesser customers. One positive effect of this was to stimulate local small independents to engage in vertical integration. Some of them already had their own studios. One year later they decided to start a joint distribution company, SAM-distribution. Five years later, the same group of 16 independents went one stage further, building their own record pressing plant, mainly as an insurance against the Big Five oligopoly.

The expansion process whereby the big companies increase their influence includes not only the purchase of competitors, but even extends to financial actions aimed at making sure competitors do not enter the scene.

Polygram Kenya's only manufacturing competitor in East Africa, Sapra, went bankrupt in 1976. Polygram International moved in and bought up most of the machines, freighting the majority out of the country. Local independent producers claimed this was a conscious move to foil their attempts to start a collectively owned pressing plant. Polygram described the move in terms of logical business strategy – the machines were going cheap through the local receiver.

As the CBS Sweden example showed, concentration and integration are the methods preferred when transnationals wish to establish or extend their influence in small countries. The examples are legion. When Decca, now itself part of Polygram, wished to establish a Welsh catalogue in the late 60s, this was done not so much through Decca's own recording activities, but mainly through absorbing local catalogues and companies. Thus Qualiton, a local company based in Wales with its own manufacturing facilities, was bought up. Decca took the pressing plant away from Wales to London and subsequently closed it. Local phonogram producers lost another local resource.

Money doesn't always buy happiness. When the big move in and buy up the small, the process can be quite painful for those involved.

WEA sold a lot of phonograms in Sweden, thanks partly to the efforts of its Swedish licensee, a respected local independent, Metronome. Metronome's business complexion was 50/50 local/ foreign repertoire. The desire of the owners, themselves musicians, to keep the company Swedish attracted many local artists, and a lot of progressive sounds emerged. In 1979 Metronome suddenly announced they had sold out to WEA. The owners explained that the alternative would have been to lose the WEA catalogue, and half the jobs in the firm, since Warners otherwise would have started their own company. The contract had been signed 'under certain pressure'. In the short term, the Metronome take-over was natural and financially correct from WEA's point of view. In the long term, however, the benefits are not so clear for Metronome's domestic image, its operations with domestic artists or for Swedish music culture as a whole. It will probably become primarily a distribution outlet for WEA's sound and video recordings (indeed in 1983 WEA's Swedish company announced the sale of its record-ing studio which had been a prerequisite for the Metronome company's contribution to domestic music).

HOME-TAPING

The growth of the major phonogram companies has provided a close relationship to other hard- and software sectors of the enter-tainment and electronics industry. Philips, for instance, are at the forefront of the development of radios, sound and video cassette recorders. BASF (part of Siemens who own half of Polygram) make a lot of blank tape that is sold for domestic consumption. Such relationships can be both advantageous and problematic. Thus the managing director of Polygram Kenya in his office in Nairobi bemoans the fact that home-taping is undermining his attempts to sell records and pre-recorded cassettes. But in another wing of the same building a conveyor-belt is churning out Philips radio cassette recorders, i.e. the very hardware that makes home-taping possible. And one of the biggest neon signs in the centre of Nairobi reminds passers by that BASF is the best tape to use.

The cassette is a fact of life. In the early Seventies the compact cassette – pioneered by Philips – won the battle in the marketplace by pushing aside RCA's stereo 8 system. Since then cassette sales have expanded the world over, penetrating almost every commun-ity. In some territories, e.g. Sri Lanka and Tunisia, cassettes have virtually replaced disc recordings. But the phonogram industry continues to believe it loses money. Chief executives and their organizations continue to moan. Clearly the main losers are the artists and composers.

Recent shock waves went through the European phonogram industry when certain top groups such as the Rolling Stones agreed to partake in tours sponsored by tape manufacturers. The official voice of the British phonogram companies, the BPI, published a booklet claiming that with actual sales of phonograms in the UK valued at £424m, home-taping was losing the industry another £304m. The BPI also expressed disappointment that artists should 'have a commercial link-up with an organization whose products jeopardize (their) future in the recording industry'. A rather embittered representative for one of the targets of this attack retorted that the phonogram industry was guilty of hypocrisy. 'The majority of major record companies are hypocrites. Name one that isn't involved with a blank tape company in one way or another.'[7]

The problems associated with the integration of hard- and software manufacture within the transnationals would appear to be something the industry cannot solve internally. Presumably this is because the Big Five do not control all manufacture of magnetic tape. Companies outside the phonogram industry such as Maxell (Japan) and the fast growing Agra group, with roots in Iran, pursue an independent course. Even if the parent companies of the transnational phonogram companies did control most blank tape manufacture it would be risky to compensate for home-taping by putting too big a surcharge on tapes – they would soon find themselves transgressing monopoly and anti-trust laws. The entertainment industry has preferred to pass the buck on to governments, with extensive lobbying for a levy or tax on tape sales, the proceeds of which could be phased back into the industry to compensate for the losses their own products cause to phonogram sales. Sweden is one of the few countries to have introduced such a levy on blank tape sales, but the construction chosen by the Swedish government, as we will note in a later chapter, was hardly what the major phonogram companies wanted or expected.

The phonogram industry has invested large sums in developing gadgets or techniques for hindering home-taping (spoiler signals on phonograms etc.). So far these attempts have not been successful, mainly because of the ease of producing devices which neutralize their effects.

MUSIC PUBLISHING: MONEY FOR NOTHING?

If hardware-software integration has caused problems for the phonogram industry, another area of expansion would appear to have provided almost unlimited advantages. In recent years, phonogram companies have virtually taken over the lucrative activities of the music publishers.

If a composer assigns to a publisher the right to look after the copyright of a work, then the publisher can expect to earn anything up to 50 per cent of all the performing fees as well as cash from phonogram sales (mechanical royalties) generated by the same piece of music. Relatively little effort is required of the publisher, apart from access to good lawyers and certain minimum 'watchdog' functions – indeed most of the latter are performed, not by publishers but by the composers' own copyright societies where these are functioning well (PRS in the UK, STIM in Sweden, SACEM in France etc.). Thus publishing can boost the income of a phonogram company, particularly when recording contracts are closely coupled to publishing agreements. This is why many artists/composers on Polygram labels are published by Chappell (acquired by the same organization in 1968). Even though there is no functioning publishing system for local artists in Kenya, despite the presence of the PRS for numerous years, local composers who record for Polygram are expected to assign their rights to Chappell, who will look after their songs should they become popular, say, in Europe. Such rights can be picked up quite cheaply in the developing world. In Europe such rights are more expensive, but the potential for profitability is clearly present.

An example of the relation between a major record company and its associated music publishing company is that of CBS Germany and their acquisition of the recording services of a Swiss musician/composer, whose first independently-produced LP was selling very well in Switzerland and parts of Germany. When the artist was signed to CBS, sales of that LP were taken over by CBS for all territories. The primary effect was to multiply turnover by a factor of 5 for the year 1982, thereby creating CBS Germany's best-selling artist in the German-speaking countries.

During the course of 1982, the artist's management was approached by the English and French managers of April Music, CBS Records' publishing arm, to acquire the artist's publishing rights. Records' sales in the first six months of 1982 in Germany, Austria and Switzerland were so high that April Music obviously felt that the artist's potential was as great outside the German-speaking territory as inside, so much so that they decided to offer the artist a substantial advance payment against future publishing income in other European territories. April's awareness of the artist's potential would surely have been affected by their sister record company's experience in the German-speaking territory, and the nature of the deal proposed was a significant indication of the corporate attitude to an obvious profit-centre. When the contract was finalized, April had agreed to advance the artist £20,000 against copyright income from mechanical and performance royalites from all territories except Germany, Austria, Switzerland and North America. Though this might sound like an enormous sum, it would only require sales of approximately 90,000 units to recoup it from mechanical royalties alone. To underline the economics of this decision, April's involvement was reinforced by the continuing growth of sales in Germany and, at the end of 1982, by the first substantial sales in 'their' territory, when the artist's first album sold 10,000 copies in Holland in three months.

Yet another example of the investment attraction of publishing for phonogram companies is provided by the Swedish group ABBA. One of their first priorities when the money from international record successes came pouring into Sweden – before they got into bicycles and sauna baths – was publishing. They bought a number of Swedish publishers and now control a fair percentage of the heritage of Swedish popular song. Should ABBA ever grow tired of the business and sell out to a big transnational, Sweden would lose control of a tidy chunk of the country's culture.

The scramble to buy publishing organizations has continued with undiminished intensity during the Seventies. EMI, for instance, doubled its publishing revenue after buying Screen Gems. The Beatles lost the financial battle for control of Northern Songs, the owner of many of their own creative achievements. By 1982 there was only one large independent publishing company left in the UK (Campbell Connelly) and that too was put on the market. 'Publishing was indeed a very safe investment. There were virtually no production costs and songs had a much longer life than records – the money kept coming in.'[8] In 1979, a London firm of business analysts in a report on the music industry concluded that 'publishing cannot help making money, whether on the domestic or export market.'[9]

Bearing in mind that these easy profits are made by retaining a portion of the income generated by the creative efforts of composers, what should the attitude be of the composer to these 'new' publishers? Should the composers seek or shun their services? Such questions are particularly pertinent in small countries where most publishers are merely subsidiaries of large phonogram companies with their activities mainly directed at exploiting large catalogues of international material acquired elsewhere. As we'll note in a later chapter on copyright, composers in many small countries often find themselves in a Scylla and Charybdis situation; if they do use the services of a publisher, they'll have to accept that up to 50 per cent of their earnings go to someone else. If they don't, they probably won't get anything at all.

The military connection

Publishing is only one of the business areas into which the phonogram companies have expanded or been absorbed. Links can be found in almost every corner of the leisure industry, the electronics industry and even military research and production.[10] Knowledge of the connection with the war machine must have come as a surprise to many of the international artists who have used the phonogram to spread the message of peace and love. Even the Rolling Stones expressed concern:

> We found out, and it wasn't for years that we did, that all the bread we made for Decca was going into making little black boxes that go into American Air Force bombers to bomb fucking North Vietnam. They took the bread we made for them and put it into the radar section of their business. When we found that out, it blew our minds.[11]

Joan Baez, Pete Seeger, Paul Simon, Bob Dylan and many others must have had similar thoughts.

The transnationals in our sample, a summary

The picture of developments that emerges during the last decade is of a handful of major phonogram companies getting involved in larger and more diversified conglomerates. They have subsidiaries or affiliates in many countries – with sometimes more than one operation in the same country. Thus EMI have 32 subsidiaries in 29 countries and 28 licensees in as many countries. Polygram have 48 different operations in 30 countries and a total of 182 other phonogram companies working for them as licensees all over the world.[12]

Polygram have a 100 per cent control of domestic manufacture of gramophone records in East Africa; EMI enjoy the same position along a good portion of the west coast of South America, namely in Chile. But power is not always a blessing. Too much power can be an embarrassment, involving local subsidiaries in complex tightrope walking. EMI in Chile have to humour a military government that dislikes critical songs. Polygram in Kenya and the local producers are frequently at odds over manufacturing prices, and the locals have a lot of support from the government. Some countries are regarded as so troublesome that the transnationals have never moved in or have got out in a hurry. We have come across all these different situations in our study.

Jamaica, for instance, one of the sources of much international music over the past decade, until recently had no multinationals at all. In this small country of little more than 2 million people and at

No shortage of technology in Jamaica. The console in Aquarius studio, Kingston

least 7 record factories, manufacture and distribution have long been in the hands of a number of local companies. These locals also account for the distribution of the major record companies' products in Jamaica and the other Caribbean territories via licensing agreements. However, in 1981 CBS decided to break the trend. Overtures were made regarding a move into Jamaica, offering a partnership deal to the owner of the largest local company, Byron Lee of Dynamic Sounds.

The Jamaican move was the same type of agreement CBS had tried a year earlier in Kenya. Anxious to have access to growing attraction of East African popular music, CBS offered the owner of a local studio in Nairobi a 30 per cent stake in a joint venture. This, it was felt, gave CBS the opportunity of being in the forefront of what could be a new world trend – as well as having the added advantage of being able to use the London office as a clearing-house for material from East Africa on its way to the lucrative market in South Africa.

The fear that material might end up in South Africa was probably one reason why Kenya's neighbour, Tanzania, broke off a tentative joint production agreement with CBS after a handful of singles had been produced in 1980. Polygram used to have good contacts with Tanzania. Philips still have an assembly plant for radios and cassettes, and the Polygram company has contracts,on paper at least, with some of the major Tanzanian jazzbands. But nowadays Tanzania is a closed country for most transnationals. Most of the major phonogram producers would be dubious about opening in Tanzania for fear of not getting their money out of the country, despite the lure of the buoyant Tanzanian music scene. However, Tanzanian music finds its way out of the coutry by a variety of means, usually via the flow of tape dubs from Radio Tanzania, many of which appear on discs in Kenya (e.g. Dar International Band on AIT Records Moto Moto label and Safari Sound on CBS Kentanza). The legality of these records is debatable. Radio Tanzania claims the tapes have been stolen, the artists say they don't know how they get to Nairobi, and the Kenyan record companies claim they have bought the tapes in good faith. From Kenya these phonograms can turn up virtually anywhere in Africa or even in Europe. Needless to say, it is hard for the artist to get a fair deal under such circumstances.

Two other countries where the majors are conspicuous through their absence – but for different reasons – are Sri Lanka, and Tunisia. Sri Lanka is situated near one of the centres of world cassette piracy, Singapore. Since import restrictions were liberalized in 1977, a thriving cassette market has developed which sells about 1 million cassettes of pirated international repertoire (ABBA, Boney M, Jim Reeves etc.) and about as many of local artists per annum. Thanks to the extent of piracy and lack of enforcement of copyright laws, the transnationals have been content for Sri Lanka to remain a blank spot on the world phonogram map. The local market is not deemed to be big enough to warrant local operation, nor is the 'artist talent' regarded as being internationally exploitable. EMI used to service the needs of the local Sinhala music sector producing 78s in Sinhala via India, but no longer. 'It's a damn boring place where nothing ever happens' according to one senior executive. Boring or not boring, local Sinhalese repertoire is in high demand in the Middle East amongst the many Sri Lankan migrant workers – something which the Singapore cassette industry was quick to discover. Even without help from the transnationals, local music in Sri Lanka finds its way across the world to where the demand is. Someone is always around to do the job in the music business – legally or illegally.

Tunisia applies strict controls on the operations of foreign companies. Since two local firms started manufacturing blank and pre-recorded cassettes (Oasis and Mellouliphone) the import of tapes has been virtually prohibited. But many of Tunisia's citizens who are migrant workers in French-speaking Europe also want Tunisian music. This has allowed EMI to get involved via its Greek subsidiary; a convenient exchange agreement between Athens and Tunis involves licensing foreign material (often from other Arab countries) for manufacture in Tunisia in return for the right to manufacture Tunisian material in Europe. Unfortunately, however, these activities seem to have had little or no effect on the amount of copyright money returning to the Tunisian copyright society SODACT. Another reason why the transnationals have expressed little interest in the current Tunisian phonogram market is the high incidence of piracy (up to 80 or 90 per cent according to one local record producer). Exact copies of any new pre-recorded cassette, printed matter and all, are available in the bazaar areas within three hours of its release on the market! The only legal local operators who can survive are those who combine blank tape manufacture or studio services with phonogram company activities.

Trinidad is another country with a lot of live music but no transnational phonogram companies. RCA did have a subsidiary and a pressing plant, but they sold out in 1975, apparently because the market was too troublesome. One reason mooted for the absence of the traditional names of the phonogram world is that, as late as the early Seventies, most calypso recordings by Trinidadians were made in New York.

Throughout the Seventies, some resources were established on Trinidad. In 1981 the island had three studios and two pressing plants. But then these operations ran into financial and practical problems – part of the blame was put on exorbitant taxes on spare parts. By 1983 most of the calypsonians were manufacturing their phonograms in Barbados or the USA. As usual when social comment is needed in Trinidad, one of the calypsonians wrote a song about it. Here are a couple of verses from William Harris's (Lord Relator) 'Fading Industry'.

> We throw away the franchise
> We no longer monopolize
> We're treating calypso like some prostitute or whore,
> So now she pack up she grip and gone
> She's disenchanted with this place where she was born.
> Since the local recording industry in a total mess
> I must let you know, Madame Calypso
> Just changed she home address.

For Calypsonians to make a record
They now have to go abroad
It's a fact of life but it is sad.
No records are made here in Trinidad.
The music that they jump to and play mas today
Is now mass-produced in the USA
It is a bad blow
For Trinidad and Tobago.

In case you don't know
We're now importing we own calypso.
Calypsonians in trouble, no studios available
Mankind making horrors, Barbados and New York making
   stampers.
Tax and import duty cannot be denied
Because the records are manufactured outside.
Recently, you know, we closed down a pressing plant
It's a real pity our record industry is non-existent.

Another problem facing the calypsonians (who mainly have their own small phonogram companies) is that piracy has extended from small activities in certain shops to a large-scale operation on the streets. Venders sell pirated cassettes for 20 Trinidad/Tobago dollars a time (app. 8 US$), thus making a profit somewhere in the region of 14 TT$ per sale. A very lucrative operation indeed.

The personal aspect of legal phonogram activity in Trinidad is illustrated by the fact that even the most established artists can be seen selling their own discs from the boot of their car.

THE INDEPENDENTS

Despite the growth of the Big Five, there seems to be no decrease in the number of small independent phonogram companies, or 'indies', that are often responsible for much of the creative activity in the music industry. The term 'independent', though generally accepted, is really a misnomer. The smaller companies might be free to make creative decisions regarding repertoire, but they're invariably dependent on larger companies for various services such as manufacturing and distribution. Despite difficulties of nomenclature, it is fruitful to analyse the difference between big and small phonogram companies, especially in small countries with limited local markets.

It is generally true that a large organization makes more money selling 1 million copies of 1 product than 10,000 copies of each of 100 products. Longer series of fewer products offset the high adminis-

Cassettes and oranges. Threats to the calypsonians. (Pirates in the streets of Port of Spain, Trinidad.)

trative and running-in costs as well as some of the inflexibility of giant organizations. Especially when the company in question might have invested anything up to £250,000 in TV advertising alone for a new phonogram. And the profits on a grand slam, a world-wide 'hit', are enormous. Thus it often becomes safer for subsidiaries of

Even the most established artists can be seen selling their own discs from the boot of their car. Here the Mighty Sparrow

the transnationals in smaller territories to import cultural products that are paying their way internationally, rather than to gamble in local production for a limited geographical and/or language market. Pressing up a Boney M LP is a safer bet than investing in a new production of local folk songs.

There seems to be a clear relationship between size, creativity and break-even points. In order to break even, a major company might have to sell up to half a million copies of an album which has been granted the honour of a television advertising campaign in one of the major world markets. This might even require the global spin-off effects in smaller markets that follow in the wake of a success in, say, the USA or Britain. The macro effects on the industry of television advertising also have negative cultural effects through decreasing the available range of phonograms. In the last four months of 1978 British phonogram companies spent no less than £6.4m on TV spots for 66 albums – about £100,000 per album.

It's not surprising that sales resources were concentrated on a small number of products, thus decreasing the ability to stock older records. A senior Polygram manager admitted that 'TV advertising has now replaced the healthy back catalogue market. Economic circumstances dictate that we now must all advertise on TV. That means a lot of competition in the medium and unfortunately smaller companies without money to spend on good advertisements will suffer'.[13]. The fact that this concentration on a few products affects the international activities of the transnationals becomes clear in this report in the trade press of an EMI international meeting

Emphasizing the importance of international considerations in A & R, Brian Shepherd (General Manager, A & R) said: 'It's just about impossible to make a major deal profitable in the UK alone, so we sign acts we can develop worldwide.' International Division General Manager, Paul Watts, reiterated the need not only to break acts, but develop techniques to maximize sales by reach new markets. Ideas from Canada, Denmark, Sweden, France, Italy and Germany were discussed.[14]

The situation for small phonogram companies is very different. Despite the pressures from above, there are still any number of small producers round the world who are quite content to invest in a phonogram which is likely to sell only 5,000 copies. The same small independent might even willingly produce a phonogram that only sells 500 copies, as long as sales of the other products in the catalogue cover the loss. This is because small independents normally are not guided solely by economic constraints; cultural goals, belief in what constitutes good music that should be spread around, provide an equally powerful motive force.

Decca in Wales

The effects of size are amply illustrated by the case of Decca in Wales. Decca was one of the few international record companies that devoted its efforts to developing a fully fledged Welsh catalogue. As we have noted, this was mainly achieved by absorbing small local producers in the late Sixties and early Seventies. By the late Seventies, Decca could offer phonogram buyers about 60 LPs of Welsh music featuring a variety of vocal soloists, choirs, folk artists etc. In 1980 Decca ran into financial trouble and was bought up by Polygram. Shortly afterwards the new Decca management decided to delete the Welsh catalogue. Raymond Ware, a senior producer at Decca, motivated the deletion, somewhat regretfully, in this way:

It's a great pity, artistically, to lose the catalogue. But in the end it's purely a question of economics . . . some companies, the size of this one, feel that if a record isn't selling 1,500 copies a year, then it costs too much to keep it on the shelves in the factory.[15]

Decca's retreat from Wales has not left the Principality's 500,000 Welsh speakers without any phonogram producers. The main independent, Recordiau Sain (Sound Records) has continued to supply the market with about 30 new albums and cassettes a year. Many of these releases make a resounding loss. Some do relatively well. And Sain operations as a whole are typical of many independents in small language areas – financially, they just about break even. Their constant liquidity crises are solved through a combination of voluntary labour, loans from artists, cultural grants, bank manager generosity or gifts from philanthropists. The same Decca producer quoted above had this to say about Sain.

Sain deals in ethnic material. That's something we can't get involved in. They are talking in terms of one, two, or three thousand. We're talking in terms of 30 to 40 thousand per item . . . Polygram is a company with wide international interests. I doubt whether we would make a particular record just for one particular market. It's too expensive.

A French view of large and small

The Decca statement would indicate that financial constraints in large companies tend to restrict the freedom for creative activity. It costs so much and requires so much bureaucratic energy to get the wheels moving in large organizations that many projects with uncertain financial possibilities never get off the ground. It's safer to leave smaller companies to act as risk-takers and market testers of new musical trends. This somewhat stereotyped view has inspired the French phonogram researcher, Antoine Hennion, to offer a caricature (see over page) of what he believes is an often accepted picture of the big and the small in the cultural industries . . .

Hennion hastens to add that he rejects such a simplification of reality, but claims that it is attractive to certain cultural elitists since a simple analysis of this kind 'combines in a mixture pleasing to the cultivated palate, a portion of cultural snobbery, a dose of sharp distrust for the actions of tradespeople in the sacred domain of culture, and a snatch of patronizing contempt for popular taste.' In fact he believes the big and the small need each other, and are mutually dependent in a 'complex system characterized not by out-and-out opposition between two watertight networks but by a

DIAGRAM 4: CULTURE INDUSTRIES

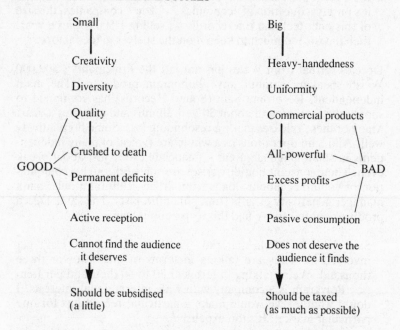

rich fabric of judiciously negotiated relations of reciprocity, inter-change and complementarity'.

Hennion, who has carried out numerous studies of the phonogram industry in France, rejects the notion that creation is dominated by distribution or that the international Anglo-Saxon oligopoly, by virtue of its size, can dictate which cultural products are sold in national markets. Despite the Big Five's 70 per cent of the French market, 50 per cent of production is French in the cultural sense. And 'none of the three French subsidiaries of American firms achieved any business success until they adopted French methods and recruited French teams'.[16]

This enthusiastic national cultural report, however is not mir-rored everywhere. In Canada, despite its strong cultural affiliation to France, only 6 per cent of all phonograms sold are of Canadian origin.[17] This illustrates an important point regarding big and small nations. Big nations, such as France, with a strong national culture are resilient enough to ward off much of the Anglo-Saxon aspects of the transnational music industry. Smaller countries are in a much weaker position. Canada might be geographically large, but it is still overshadowed, culturally and economically, by its neighbour, the USA.

The views of the independents

Hennion's enthusiastic picture of the dynamic relationship between small private companies and large transnationals would not be shared by Tony Stratton-Smith, the owner of one of Britain's most well-known independents, Charisma. After terminating an 11-year distribution agreement with Polygram, Stratton-Smith concluded:

> I have come to believe what I always thought emotionally, which is that big groupings are dangerous, and a partnership with them is dangerous . . . . the industry [has become] like an artificial stock exchange where companies trade in second, third and fourth contracts of established artists and try to do their competitors in the eye, rather than giving real backing to the people who know about talent . . . . I feel very strongly that since lawyers and accountants started to take control of this industry from record people, it has run into more marketing problems and vast philosophical problems . . . . I feel it's important to justify the need for independents, as I like the entertainment industry too much to see it slaughtered by the profit motive – which is a quite separate thing from proper financial control.
>
> I want to see another 100 independent companies, for I feel that the aims of the independents and majors are ultimately incompatible.[18]

A point to remember here is that the majors are not homogeneous colossi made up of totally programmed human nuts and bolts. The transnational phonogram companies are staffed by individuals representing a wide range of norms and values. Strict limits to their 'freedom' are imposed by the system, but the limits vary from organization to organization, from country to country. The Charisma boss might have received some comfort from this statement made by a WEA executive vice-president (Stan Cornyn) in a speech to American retailers (March 1979): 'The record industry has a responsiblity to culture. The industry should foster artists and products whose only justification is their own merit. If the accounts department queries the economic viability of a culturally worthwhile recording project, just hang up on them.'

Certainly many independents would pay lip-service to this view of an unpredictable phonogram world – as indeed most small phonogram producers would accept an inevitable relationship in one form or another with the major companies. Alternatives have been noted in the MISC-sample, notably in Scandinavia, and of course in the countries where the transnationals are absent but these are exceptions rather than the rule.

THE DEPENDENCY OF LARGE AND SMALL

EMI's international manager, Richard Lyttleton, who learnt his
trade running the company's subsidiary in Finland, believes the
dependency of large and small stems from the impossibility of
attaining total efficiency in the phonogram business. 'I think it's
very difficult to rationalize an industry which basically is irrational.
If it could be rationalized, we'd all be millionaires . . . but it can't.'
The independent's specific competence, Lyttleton too admits, is in
the area of creativity. But they still need to work closely with the
larger companies, particularly if they aspire to distribute internationally.

> What the independents can do, often better than us, is produce
> extremely sound marketable material. I think there's room in the
> world for both of us. But, as has happened over the past five
> years, they won't be able to attain total independence. We'll see
> creative satellite companies being born, retaining their artistic
> integrity, but using the larger companies for distribution. I don't
> think anybody can distribute records from scratch, on a world-
> wide basis, more efficiently than the large multinationals can.
> We've been doing it for a long, long time, and we've built up
> heavy networks.

Another EMI executive, Mike Wells, who runs the company's
African operations is even more outspoken about the attraction of
the multinationals in many small territories. International companies can be trusted to give royalty statements. 'That's why
Africans go to the European companies rather than their brothers.
One would think that if the big producer was a member of their tribe
then they would flock to him. But they don't, 'cause they know
they'll get screwed. That's really why the CBSs, EMIs and Poly-
grams survive. At least they're honest.' EMI, however, did not
survive when it ventured into the Kenyan market in the mid-
Seventies. The tale provides an illuminating picture of what happens when the relationship between a transnational and a local
producer in a small country goes wrong.

THE KENYAN EXPERIENCE: EMI and CBS

EMI's decision to establish a subsidiary in Kenya in 1977 was a
natural one. Nairobi was the commercial nerve of East Africa with

manufacturing resources and some rudimentary studios. Music by Congolese bands accounted for about 80 per cent of the phonogram market but this was nothing new for EMI, thanks to EMI-Pathé in France which had built up a strong African catalogue comprising a great number of Zaïrean recordings. The other big companies already operating out of Nairobi were Polygram (Phonogram at that time) and AIT, a subsidiary of Tiny Rowlands' Lonrho organization. AIT had also had some success with a new Kenyan sound, the *benga* beat sung in the language of the Luo tribe.

EMI decided to establish the East African operation in partnership with Mr Kanindo – partly for reasons of politics, partly to get access to local know-how. Things didn't work out as EMI expected. Their own expatriates in Nairobi lost control of the operation. They left sadly bitten and twice shy – with a loss of several hundred thousand pounds. Mike Wells, responsible back in London for clearing up the mess, gave us this version of the story.

Kenya is a relatively small territory. Kanindo is a very shrewd, very clever man. We had a partnership agreement whereby he did the distribution, and we produced the repertoire, both international and his own. We provided the records, as it were, and he would go out and sell them.

This was set up in 77/78. We put in inexperienced management, to say the least. The people at the time said: Kenya's a small country, send in a small boy. I got involved in this when I came back from New Zealand in January 1978. It was quite clear to me, the only way was bankruptcy.

Q: How much did EMI lose?
A: We shipped out about £100,000 to pay for liabilities. We owed Phonogram a bit, via debts to EAR [East African Records, Polygram's pressing plant].

Shortly after the demise of EMI Kenya in 1978, CBS decided to have a go. The reason, according to CBS headquarters in New York, was not so much to find a new market for CBS international products, but rather to sap local talent for the African market, 'to provide a base for future African expansion . . . Kenyan's relatively advanced music industry was also a factor. Finally, since the domestic market in Kenya is miniscule, our hopes are more toward developing local talent for sales in the East African region than for selling international product in Kenya.'[19]

Peter Bond, who had previously worked for Polygram for thirteen years, was given overall responsibility for CBS African

operations. Bond certainly knew Africa well, having done spells in
Kenya, Zaïre and Nigeria – he is Kenyan by birth and has the added
advantage of speaking Swahili. Maybe this is why CBS Kenya at first
sight appears to be very un-European. CBS chose a partnership
arrangement with a local studio owner, Simeon Ndesandjo, who
was given 30 per cent of the shares. Within three years of starting
up, the staff were claiming one-third of the Kenyan market. CBS
Kenya give the impression of being a local company deeply involved
in the cause of Kenyan nationalism and culture. An editorial in the
first issue of CBS Kenya's own magazine, *Music Scene*, praises the
government for deciding to establish a school for music, drama and
dance.

> Such a school would fill a gap in the cultural activities of this
> country. It could utilize the magnificent talents of Kenyan youth.
> It should polish and intensify the talents of African people in all
> fields of culture in order to enable us to compete on the interna-
> tional market. We don't have to borrow anything from the
> Western world to show that we, as Kenyans, have our own
> cultural indentity. We are strong and we know it. Let's strive for
> perfection in our own ways. Our roots shall guide us more than
> anything else.[20]

Strong stuff to come from a giant transnational phonogram company! But probably a true reflection of the feelings of the local
employees, particularly the chief A & R man, Livingstone
Amaumo. CBS Kenya have also demonstrated an extraordinary
feat of tightrope walking. Local African phonogram producers have
their own organization, the Kenyan Record Producers Association
(KRPA), which is very much in opposition to the local branch of the
International Federation of Phonogram Industries (IFPI). The
KRPA have been constantly at loggerheads with the IFPI, particularly with Polygram over prices for manufacturing services. The
local IFPI branch mainly represents the interests of the large 'white'
phonogram companies, AIT and Polygram. CBS is a member of
both organizations. A & R boss Livingstone Amaumo is even
secretary of the KRPA!
Peter Bond back in London sees this as a pragmatic solution to a
current situation.

> We're in both. We're a member of the Producers' Association
> since one of their functions is to make sure prices ex-factory are
> fair. As a customer, we're no different from them.
>   But I think it's ridiculous that in a market the size of Kenya
> there should be this division between the so-called multinationals

and the local companies. We want no part in such a division and we want to take no part on either side.

The apparent freedom allowed to the Kenyan operation would appear to be typical of CBS's approach to local operations in small countries. This policy even allows activities in the short term that could undermine the global interests of the transnationals, activities in support of nationalism, anti-establishment movements etc. – as long as the operation is profitable. CBS have learnt the rock lesson: that money can be made even out of revolutionaries, as long as you're willing to push in where other transnational angels fear to tread. This is a sound but daring policy. Good music is all about feelings and communication. People with an emotional involvement often produce the best sounds, which can make most money as phonograms. But things can get out of hand. The waters haven't been too calm even for CBS in Nairobi. Their local shareholder's other studio interests ran into financial trouble in 1982 and instead of being a sleeping partner he began to devote much more time to executive chairman activities within CBS. Despite success in chewing its way deep into the market, CBS Kenya was not making a lot of money. In 1982 the international firm of accountants, Price Waterhouse, were called in to overhaul the administration and advise where the brakes should be applied.

Despite temporary setbacks there's no doubt that CBS are among the top seeds, should East African popular music attain global popularity. CBS Kenya has the most advanced recording studio in East Africa which has already been used by other phonogram companies (e.g. Virgin) wishing to sample sounds for the European market. CBS staff have probably the best network of contacts in the region, including the vibrating scene in neighbouring Tanzania. CBS knows and plays the local rules of the recording game. A typical feat of bravado was getting the best musicians in a leading Tanzanian band (Mlimani Park Orchestra), which has a five-year exclusive contract with Polygram, to come to Nairobi and record two albums under another name. Thus a studio product – The Black Warriors – (CBS Ken-Tanza KTLP 002/4) was born. Polygram were not amused but regarded the incident as yet another case of contracts not being worth the paper they're written on.

Back over the border, the TFC (Tanzanian Film Company) with the government monopoly on records, was furious. Not only had the TFC just concluded a short flirtation in the form of a licensing deal with CBS London – TFC suspected that CBS were shipping Tanzanian music to South Africa – but also the 'Beauty and the Beast' design chosen by CBS Kenya for the Black Warriors sleeve was hardly compatible with official Tanzanian cultural values.

CBS Kenya bravado: the Mlimani Park Orchestra from Tanzania (contract with Polygram) become the Black Warriors with a gorilla and a brown lady. . . .

A TRANSNATIONAL IN DENMARK: CBS

Kenya is far from being the only case of CBS 'daring' or 'tolerance' – depending on which way you look at it. This transnational had a very successful run in Denmark in the mid- and late Seventies. CBS Denmark even attracted many radical rock musicians, who certainly would have had doubts about some of the giant's global communications activities. The formula for success was similar to that applied later in Kenya. A local A & R man (Paul Bruun), well versed in the Danish rock scene, was given almost total freedom, so long as the records sold. His task was made easier by the fact that most of the alternative, more ideologically motivated local phonogram companies were in political or financial disarray. CBS Denmark had a good run and even produced a benefit record, the royalties from which went unabridged to Copenhagen's largest squat, the Christiania barracks. CBS probably made more than a penny on distribution and helped give pecuniary support to one of the most blatant threats to the Danish establishment in recent times. Paul Bruun is no longer with CBS Denmark – like many other successful A & R men, he left to start his own 'independent' company, Medley.

CONFLICT IN JAMAICA: CBS

CBS have made two serious attempts to establish themselves locally in Jamaica. Their first unsuccessful overture was made in 1976, when the reggae market was fast expanding. Neville Lee, owner of a local company, Sonic Sounds, takes up the story.

> The CBS move was blocked, by myself – I was working for a local company, Dynamic Sounds, at the time – and another company, Record Specialists. We went to the Ministry of Trade and said: no way could we allow the multinationals to come into the country. At that time the whole attitude was very nationalistic. Michael Manley had injected this strong feel against multinationals. So it was null and void.[21]

With Manley ousted in 1980 and replaced by the more liberal government of Edward Seaga, CBS made a second attempt to get a Jamaican foothold. A bid was made for a large stake in Dynamic Sounds, which was then owned completely by Neville Lee's brother, the artist, band leader and entrepreneur, Byron Lee.

Neville Lee, who had built up his own company, Sonic Sounds, based 80 per cent on local music, was concerned.

> CBS policy world-wide is not to give licences but partnership; it's a 49/51 per cent deal. I don't know what effect this will have here. Personally, I'm concerned. I can't vie against CBS to get distribution for Peter Tosh, the Third World, Jimmy Cliff etc. There's no way I can win. So although there's a lot of exuberance and excitement at my brother's place, for me it might be a bad day. CBS are extremely aggressive. They do go for the local artists where they invest. I've spoken to my brother and said: Sure it might be good now, but what happens when CBS decide to dig in and get rid of you? You can't separate and say: You have that artist and I'll have this one. They want the best! That's the record industry . . . This is going to affect our industry. The question is, can we withstand the tremendous giant that is now being formulated?

This last question was probably a reference to the fact that Dynamic Sounds already had the licence to distribute Polygram and WEA material before the CBS deal. Buying its way into Dynamic Sounds would give CBS three clear business advantages.

1. Most successful Jamaican artists have come out of the ghettos, places into which few transnational directors would venture with chequebook and contract forms. The Dynamic Sound tie-up would provide clearer access and channels of information to local artists with international potential.
2. CBS could also monitor and control the fate in the Caribbean of two of its major competitors in the Big Five, and 3. Above all, with the CBS catalogue augmenting the percentage of foreign repertoire in Dynamic's operations to 85 per cent, and 70 per cent of their sales going as exports mainly to the other West Indian islands covered by the Caricom trade agreement, CBS would be part-owner of an ideal 'mini transnational' or 'trans-island' set-up serving the Caribbean area out of Jamaica. This is something CBS would never have been able to organize on their own from scratch.

Back at Dynamic Sounds, Byron Lee clearly did not share his brother Neville's anxiety.

CBS terminated their deal with Federal Records (another local company) – for what reason I do not know – and apparently they were thinking of giving the contract to Barbados. But the Prime Minister insisted that we should try to keep the label here.*
Apparently CBS looked us over and decided that we could act as caretaker for their repertoire until they were ready to start up their own company, CBS Caribbean, which is good, because we keep the foreign dollars here and we can boost our exports.
I think when CBS start up here, they'll have a partnership, allowing us to do their manufacturing. They don't want to get involved in that, they just want to market and promote.
Here in Jamaica, CBS would be allowed to own up to 70 or 80 per cent of the shares in a local company, if they were not taking out too much, but really want to help the local industry. They want to get involved in reggae – they've just signed a long term contract with the 'Third World', and they are looking at reggae, very peculiarly, for the Latin market, down in South America, and for the African market.
Maybe they'll come in and acquire us entirely sometime, and

---

* The Jamaican PM, Edward Seaga used to work as a record producer. In fact he produced Byron Lee's first recording.

that wouldn't be such a bad thing. Then we would be entirely a CBS company. I don't want that at present, because I'm heavily committed to WEA and Polygram. We control the three heaviest labels and that's quite hard at times.

The reference here, recorded in 1981, to selling reggae in Africa is interesting. Only a year later, CBS Kenya's marketing of the parent company's international product was leaning heavily on recent reggae acquisitions (Third World, Jimmy Cliff etc.) – a shrewd policy considering the current awakening in Black Africa of a desire to re-establish cultural links that were once so harshly severed by the slave trade.

CBS' actual move into Dynamic Sounds did not, however, go as smoothly or as quickly as either Byron or Neville Lee anticipated. In early 1983, CBS Records President Dick Asher explained that politics were still a hindrance.

> We had tried for a long time. At one point and I don't know if it was politics or what, but we just weren't given permission. We tried to form a company there with a local partner. We had agreements and everything which were contingent upon making submissions to the government, you know, where the government then was to give you your charter, and we didn't receive permission.
> Question: But it is better now?
> Answer: Sometimes you never quite get an explanation to these things. In a small country like that they don't necessarily explain their decision, they are not required to. So we really never got an explanation. Just knew we were turned down.
> Question: But now that you are moving in there, isn't it a bit late? Isn't it the end of the reggae bandwagon?
> Answer: We've always had contact with the musicians there, even though we didn't have a company there. For one thing the musicians travel. For another thing, although we weren't permitted to start up a company there, there was never a restriction on travelling to Jamaica. In fact, I encourage travel to Jamaica, it's a lovely place to spend a few days' holiday and it is interesting musically. So there's been contact there right along and we've been in touch. Peter Tosh has been on the label and has left us and come back several times.[22]

But political problems had not affected CBS increasing its catalogue of reggae artists to a point where in 1982 Neville Lee wondered if he was going to survive in the business. Things did go better for Neville Lee's Sonic Sounds in 1983 mainly thanks to a policy of developing new local artists and cooperating with local producers such as Jungo Lawes (producer of Yellowman, Little John, Don Carlos etc.). Neville Lee survived by working with a new generation of artists when CBS took the cream of the established names.

CHILE BEFORE AND AFTER THE COUP: EMI

EMI has acquired a manufacturing monopoly in Chile – strangely enough partly thanks to its successes during the Salvadore Allende period. Under the Unidad Popular government, imports of foreign phonograms were heavily restricted. On the other hand local music was lively, cheap and plentiful. Gramophone records, particularly those with folk music and political songs, assumed the same role as they have in Jamaica. A way of life, encouraged and supported by the government.

There were two pressing plants at the time (the early Seventies). One was owned by RCA but was nationalized by the Allende government. EMI's plant, on the other hand, was not taken over, probably because the local employees adapted well to the Unidad Popular situation. 'The former A & R director made sure EMI Chile was the first capitalist company to release anti-capitalist music.'[23] Their pressing plant could produce half a million singles and as many LP discs per annum on one shift-working – it was running at full capacity up to 1973, up to the cultural black-out caused by the military coup. No exact figures, however, are available. The Allende period, officially, is a blank space in time. All records, officially, have been obliterated. Thus a request to EMI for production statistics during these remarkable years evoked a quick response: 'Gentlemen, please don't ask the impossible of us!'

The only problem for EMI during the golden record days of Allende was that it could not get the millions of pesos it was making out of the country (partly thanks to the various activities of North American origin which were slowly throttling the Chilean economy). The staff still admit that the years of Unidad Popular were their best ones for music – and money-making:

Many products had fixed prices at that time. Records were regarded as basic necessities and the price was fixed at a low rate. Despite small profit margins we sold so much that business was fine. When Allende came to power the factory was working at 50 per cent of its capacity. One way of decreasing unemployment at the time was to give factories the impulse to produce more. This policy gave quite an impetus to the record industry. 1970–72 were the best years ever in the history of this plant – we were running at full blast. Our success was the result of volume, not high profit margins.[24]

Then came the coup. Price control was removed, imports of foreign products were encouraged. Record companies were forced to totally restructure their activities at a much lower level of local activity. EMI have still access to material recorded with artists such as Quilapayun and Violetta Parra, but regard most of it as too controversial even if it would make a lot of money. EMI leave this sector to small independents who continually test the system to see what can be released without getting into trouble.

Some years into the Pinochet period of military rule and Milton-Friedman-type economy, RCA was re-offered its confiscated pressing plant. RCA declined, the plant was closed and EMI was left with a tricky monopoly situation.

South American folk music, the main medium of musical expression prior to the coup, was taboo. The government associated the sounds of the Andes with nasty revolutionary tendencies. And EMI found itself with a dual problem. Not only did it have the same type of monopoly difficulties experienced by Polygram in Kenya (the only domestic factory independents can turn to), but the company also had to play a censorship role, making sure that nothing slipped through the factory that might offend the military.

> We can produce folk music, but only the sort that's completely 'pure' – a lot of it's too controversial. We'd get political problems. The government does support some cultural activities; things like handicraft. A wooden horse is always a wooden horse and it can't get mixed up in politics. But folk music is basically a music of protest, so most of it's impossible.[25]

This type of control is not something which is normally relished by A & R staff, whose hearts are with the music, but it is a situation many have to live with under military dictatorships.

In 1982, EMI-Chile had new problems. CBS decided, in line with their expansive policy, to open up in Chile. This meant that EMI, who had previously distributed CBS product, now lost an attractive part of their local catalogue.

ENTRY AND WITHDRAWAL FROM SWEDEN: EMI

EMI is a company that based its expansion in the late Sixties and early Seventies on one Golden Goose. As late as 1973, well after the heyday of those four lads from Liverpool, it was assumed that two Beatles anthologies would account for almost 30 per cent of the phonogram company's pre-tax profits.[26] This is probably the explanation for many of its problems in recent years. The conglomerate that referred to itself as the world's largest record company seemed unable to adjust to new situations. The late Seventies were characterized by decreased operations in various parts of the world. A typical EMI story was that of their giant manufacturing facility in Scandinavia.

Prior to 1975, EMI manufactured gramophone records in all the Nordic countries. The company had its own factories in Denmark, Norway and Sweden and ordered custom pressing facilities in Finland. EMI approached the Swedish government and offered to create 120 jobs in a regional development area if state funds for a record factory were forthcoming. Sweden provided a loan worth about 1½ million pounds at the time and a grant of approximately 500,000 pounds. The Åmål factory was built in Western Sweden. 120 jobs were created. EMI's factories in Norway and Denmark were closed, with a loss of jobs for Sweden's Scandinavian brothers, and the machines in the old Swedish factory were sold to a new operator for a small nominal fee. The new plant has a single shift capacity of 5 million LPs/annum, i.e. a 3-shift capacity of 15 million units, virtually the total size of the Swedish market. Fortunately most of the Swedish independants did not put all their pressing eggs in the EMI basket, because six years later, after some major upheavals at the top of the EMI ladder, their Swedish plant was abandoned. The machine park once again was sold this time to three local employees, for another nominal fee. And EMI asked the Swedish government to waive the outstanding debt on their loan, for the sake of the workers keeping their jobs. Part of the loan was waived. The local municipality took over the factory building. By 1983 fewer than 40 jobs were left.

EMI is still suffering from the turmoils of being bought up by the very electronics company to which it once sold off its radio and gramophone manufacturing interests. It is doubtful whether the company would engage in expansion of the same degree or as daringly as CBS within the immediate future.

POLYGRAM, WEA AND RCA

CBS Records, as we have noted, seem to prefer to keep creative managerial talent close to the organization, within the various CBS subsidiaries. Their large Dutch/German competitor, Polygram, has been content to allow satellite production companies to provide the creative impetus whilst retaining financial control through loans or shareholdings. Their production companies might give the impression of being independent and enjoy a large measure of freedom in their operations, but Polygram can disband them at will should they cease to provide the goods the market appears to want.

Wolfgang Arming, head of Polygram Austria, told the 1979 Vienna conference on the role of the phonogram in contemporary society how this policy has been implemented in an Asian country where he had previously been stationed.

Polygram Japan was not making enough money and the diagnosis was that there were too many A & R people on the staff. Most of them were asked to leave but were given the opportunity to start up their own production companies with loans from Polygram. The result, according to Arming, was excellent. The A & R men worked much harder in 'their own' business, and Polygram did much better out of them. An incentive system had been introduced, but Polygram retained ultimate control.

The most spectacular examples of this Polygram policy came from the USA.

The most successful 'independent' operator in the 1970's, for example, was Robert Stigwood, manager of the Bee Gees and boss of RSO Records, the man behind the film *Saturday Night Fever*. In fact, though, a 50 per cent controlling share of RSO is held by the world's largest recording conglomerate, Polygram, who advanced Stigwood the capital necessary for his film activities, Polygram have a deliberate policy, in other words, of using Stigwood as their 'creative' consultant. His job is to come up with ideas which they're prepared to bankroll, taking their cuts of the profits but quick to discard if there aren't any. Polygram had a similar relationship with Casablanca records which pioneered the huge sales of disco in the USA. When Casablanca began to lose control of this market (as the competition from other companies intensified) Polygram closed the company down and sacked Neil Bogart, its head.[27]

These cases also illustrate the difficulty of referring to the concept of 'independence' too carelessly (more on this later).

In the majority of our sample countries, with the exception of high piracy countries such as Tunisia/Sri Lanka, Polygram seems to be just ticking over without doing anything extraordinary. There are probably four reasons for this. Polygram is already established in most free market economies, either with subsidiaries or through local licensees. Profits from *Grease* kept Polygram financially happy for a few years. And thirdly, the organization has been kept busy internally absorbing new acquisitions (e.g. Decca) and amalgamating the two established names in recording, Philips or Phonogram and Polydor. This amalgamation process has been quite painful at times with more than one faithful servant finding there was no room in the new, combined, Polygram organization.

Fourthly, the Philips-Siemens-Polygram conglomerate is one of the contestants in the video disc race, hoping to win international recognition for its standard, rather in the same way that the Philips compact cassette once ousted RCA's stereo-8 cartridge. Such activities devour a gigantic amount of capital and curtail investments in other areas. Philips had invested 400 million US$ in its optical disc system by the end of 1981. At the same time, another contender on the videodisc marathon is RCA, who had invested 250 million US$ in their own system.

Unlike CBS, RCA have not been so keen to open up subsidiaries in small countries. RCA still have not bought up their local distributor in Sweden, a move that has been expected for some time. They did not move back into Chile when the government gave them an invite. RCA do not seem to be particularly interested in what is going on in the West Indies – they pulled out of Trinidad in the mid-Seventies – or East Africa.

WEA, Warner Electra Atlantic, have expanded rapidly over the last decade. The initial impetus came when Warner Bros. was absorbed by the Kinney Group and received a boost of liquid capital. Warner are big in video soft-ware and are also in the fast growing computer games sector. Atari was bought by Warner in 1976, and was expected to have a turnover of around 2 billion dollars in 1982.[28] (Representatives of the phonogram industry have complained bitterly that video games present one of their most serious threats.) If WEA and Polygram amalgamate, then this situation could change radically

As regards phonogram production and sales WEA have developed from being mainly an American operation to being Euro-American. The story of their take-over of a Swedish distributor in 1979 has already been related. As regards other continents, they seem more content to concentrate on selling their international products rather than discovering new talent in strange, far-away places.

SOME CONCLUSIONS

Bearing in mind that about 70 per cent of the legal world phonogram market is concentrated to five territories (USA, UK, Japan, Germany and France), why do the transnationals bother about retaining a presence in so many small countries? As the examples quoted above indicate, there is no cut and dried, black-and-white answer. Various shades of grey emerge in an analysis, with certain relevant factors predominating.

DIAGRAM 5: FACTORS AFFECTING THE ACTIVITIES OF
TRANSNATIONAL PHONOGRAM COMPANIES IN SMALL COUNTRIES

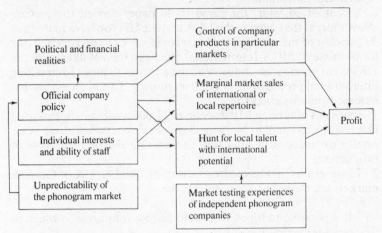

The final goal, of course, is *profit*. The *unpredictability of the
market,* however, means that the major companies never really
know when and where the next big trend is going to emerge. Even if
star artists often mould their careers in the big markets, they can
emerge originally from small countries – e.g. Bob Marley, Peter
Tosh (Jamaica), Osibisa (Ghana) and ABBA (Sweden). The *individual interests and talent spotting qualities* of the staff affect the
ability to discover new sounds from unlikely places, even if independent companies often pave the way. Thus Island Records'
Chris Blackwell – himself a Jamaican – pioneered the exploitation
of reggae in Europe during the Seventies. In 1982, another fast-
growing British phonogram company, Virgin, invested in a Kenyan
recording of an East African group based in Tanzania, the Orchestre Makassy. CBS were eagerly waiting on the sideline, ready to go
with their own East African groups if the British market accepted
what Virgin had to offer.

The transnationals' interest in picking up *extra sales of international product* in small countries varies from time to time, in
accordance with the realities of finance and politics. Policy decisions
can include instructions to subsidiaries to exert less effort on
providing distribution and manufacturing services for local companies ('third party product') and to do more for selling the parent
company's goods. This is a natural strategy to adopt in times of
global economic recession, or internal financial troubles. Thus in
1979, some of EMI's international label managers were told of the
need to 'redress the balance between group and non-group repertoire', in other words to increase the EMI-originated share of

phonograms, as opposed to third party product being sold through subsidiaries and affiliates.[29]

A year or so later, the same trade paper carried the caption 'Never forget that outside the USA and the UK you have more than 50 per cent of the world record market in which to make a hell of a lot of money!' MCA International manager John Wilkes gave the UK-based phonogram industry a lesson in how to profit from selling international productions in small territories. Two main points that emerge from this article are

1. that sales of foreign LIP discs up to 12,000 copies are not unusual in a country as small as Norway. Similar sales in two or three more small territories go a long way to covering the original costs of production.

2. Phonograms that have already 'broken' the US, UK or German markets are the ones to concentrate on.

> It is possible to break the world up into four areas in which to aim for maximum sales.
> – The US. If an act breaks in the US, there is a good chance that the act will break in most markets.
> – The UK. The UK's influence is still second to the US, and the majority of acts which break big here will break in most countries outside the US and Japan.
> – Germany. The only other country to influence other markets. If handled correctly an international record big in Germany should break in most European markets outside the UK.
> – Rest of the world. Outside of the three territories above, it is a matter of working individual countries. Spain can influence South America outside of Brazil, and a hit in Holland can sometimes be picked up by Germany and then onwards. Also East Europe is a vast, generally untapped market, but one which needs a specialist approach, and cannot be worked like other territories.

> Apart from those four areas, it is important to remember that all countries should be worked. To write that a few thousand sales in Argentina, El Salvador and Finland all add up and can make the difference between a profitable deal or not, may seem obvious, but we are so intent on going for the big ones all the time and making a 1000 per cent profit that we forget that 100 per cent profit should still be a target.[30]

Such a policy often receives enthusiastic support from local managers of transnationals, partly for reasons of personal satisfaction, partly because their progress within the company is geared to achievements such as selling 50,000 LPs of a British group in a country with less than four million inhabitants. 'Selling 50,000 records with the Shadows in Finland gives me personally more satisfaction than selling 700,000 copies in Germany. Actually, it's a greater achievement. Selling 25,000 copies in Singapore is equivalent to selling 1½ million in Germany or America.'[31]

Lyttleton's views on operations in small countries support our observations that the transnationals can balance on different legs when formulating local policy.

> EMI has local companies in 32 countries. Obviously if you do no local recordings, you're not going to pick up the major talent from each country. If they do too much local recording, they might go bust because the local market can't take it. My own view is that if each territory could break even on its local output, then you'd get sufficient spread for one of them to pick up the ABBA, the Baccara or the Boney M. I would never criticize the manager of a local company for breaking even or better. I think if you go into a loss it becomes arguable about the advisability. And you might argue that you need 28 companies in loss to get two big hits. I think CBS have some of that philosophy – I'm not quite sure if I subscribe to it. I think you need the commercial discipline.

Once again we have CBS propensity to gamble as opposed to the more careful, British approach of EMI.

Financial constraints within the parent company and local successes are not the only factors that limit the activities of phonogram company subsidiaries. As small countries have become more concerned about controlling their national destiny, political and financial restrictions have been applied to the workings of foreign companies. The downward global trend in the last decade that followed in the wake of the 1973 oil crisis has created foreign currency problems in small nations. Problems of getting money out combined with political constraints have had a negative effect on profit and a dampening effect on some companies' desire to invest. EMI have found the situation in Africa particularly disheartening.

> There are not many countries where you can go in, set up an EMI or a CBS and own all the shares. You have to have local interests, and you can only control 49 per cent of the shares. Theoretically this means that the IFPI man must be a local man . . . we all learnt during the last ten years that being associated with a major politician is a decidedly two-edged sword. But taking it all together – the corruption, the politics – all read up to the fact that we really don't want to know.
> (About money)

Madagascar hasn't paid since the revolution in 1972. Tanzania doesn't pay. Zambia does pay, but about two or three years late. In fact, Kenya, at the moment, is the only country in Black Africa remitting royalties on time, in that whole goddam continent.

What's going to stop people like us is that, basically, it's a one way stream. They want it all, and absolutely nothing comes out. Basically, they either play the rules of the international business game, or they forget about it.[32]

One can understand the frustration felt by EMI's African manager. The countries at the receiving end of his wrath would probably defend their actions by pointing out that in a situation where anything up to 50 per cent of one's foreign currency is devoured by the oil bill, then paying royalties on sales of Beatles records does not rank highly in the treasury's foreign payment priorities. Food and survival come first.

CBS, not surprisingly, have their own partial solution to the problem. The company invests, say, in Kenya, hoping that CBS Kenya recordings will find a market in the whole of East and Southern Africa. But incomes from successful sales in say, Zimbabwe, or Zambia, are not paid back directly to Kenya. If the money can be got out, it is transferred to CRI, the international headquarters in New York. There it appears only as a credit in favour of CBS Kenya. This presumably is an attempt to ensure that the proceeds from a successful operation in East Africa do not get blocked in Nairobi, should the Kenyan economy collapse.

There is one other reason (which we have not yet referred to) why transnationals can establish themselves in a particular territory. That is the desire to exert greater control over what happens to their repertoire. Transnationals often suffer losses because of the phenomenon known as 'parallel imports'. If phonograms in one country (e.g. Portugal) are cheaper than in neighbouring nations, then importers in other countries (say the UK) will try to purchase attractive phonograms in Portugal rather than from local companies. It is hard to control this if the phonograms are manufactured by a licensee in the low-price country. This is probably why CBS has opened a subsidiary in Portugal, to be able to exert more control over local financial dealings in its own products and the flow of parallel imports.

The potential for this is always very real and very difficult to stop, so almost in self-protection we have opened up five or six companies in recent years in places where in the past we wouldn't necessarily have considered opening up.[33]

Despite their power and size, transnational phonogram companies still have to do things they do not actually want to do.

THE ELUSIVE CONCEPT OF 'INDEPENDENCE'

Most phonogram companies – transnational or local, big or small – either claim or admit that the 'independents' are responsible for much of the creativity in the music industry. If a maximum of creative activity in a society is a reasonable goal of cultural policy, then it becomes important to understand the workings of the independents. To do this, the elusive nature of the term has to be unravelled.

Throughout the whole of our description of the operations of big and small phonogram companies, the word 'independent' has been used very loosely. The only common denominator immediately emerging is that *independents* are normally *dependent* on someone else. Some authors use the term solely to refer to a company which has the resources to bring a phonogram to the point of release, but which does not have the facilities to manufacture, fully promote and rapidly distribute records to the users.[34]

Such a description would hardly fit the small 'independent' companies in Sweden who have their own, collectively run distribution and manufacturing organizations.

Another definition links the concept of independence to the introduction of simpler technology, cutting the cost of entry into the market. Thus the advent of cheaper tape recorders and retail sales of reel-to-reel tape in the Fifties led to the 'creation of numerous small independent companies'.[35] A similar upsurge could be observed twenty years later with the widespread introduction of cassette technology. This link with cheaper technology tells us little about the activities or the raison d'être of the independents. Other factors have to be introduced to understand their cultural role.

David and Goliath?

Different sets of opposites are frequently applied when describing different types of phonogram operations. Some observers, noting the ups and downs of the smaller producers, conclude that the scenario is one of constant conflict between competing David and Goliaths. This is too simplistic. There are the large and the small, but except in extreme cases, size doesn't tell us much about the exact relationship involved. Indeed the detective work involved in finding out who really pulls the economic strings in some small 'independents' is immense. A philanthropic millionaire, a mafia tycoon, the local builder or a group of frustrated musicians might have provided the finance. They would give different explanations for their involvement, and their reasons for devoting cash and/or time would undoubtedly affect the creative direction of the resulting company.

National-transnational

Another common assumption is that independents often operate within one country and specialize in certain kinds of repertoire, trying to cover small segments of the market which are not considered worth exploiting by the transnationals. Thus 'national' and 'transnational' become two frequently quoted opposites, often with a positive loading for the small, local operator.

'The assumption is . . . that the products of small, independent, local musicians and labels are better aesthetically and ideologically than the products of multinational companies.'[36] Once again, as Simon Frith points out, this is too simplistic a view of independence. But it does help explain some of the phenomena we have witnessed.

Frustration with and suspicion about the role of transnationals was clearly a prime motivation for the growth of small local companies in Scandinavia during the Seventies. The enthusiasts involved shared a political view of the world that had been moulded by the horrors of the first televised war, Vietnam. They put much of the blame on the imperialist activities of big business. The transnationals were seen to be part of a global conspiracy in which no self-respecting, politically aware artist should get involved. The Do-it-yourself or DIY type of company was seen as a way of making sure that one's artistic endeavours and the profits they generated were not controlled by the servants of the evil transnationals.

Small, local phonogram companies, however, can be started for many other than ideological considerations. National ownership tells us little about the cultural nature of activities and thus is unsatisfactory as a criterion for 'independence'. It can have limited relevance. For instance, in Canada, the CIRPA (Canadian Independent Record Producers Association) accept membership of companies where more than 50 per cent of the shares are owned by Canadian nationals. This definition functions since such companies constitute a group with identifiable common problems stemming from a low local percentage of market penetration (only 6 per cent). The local producers' association in Kenya (KRPA) clearly wishes to further the business interests of African-owned phonogram companies. CBS Kenya is accepted because there is not a white face in the office. The KRPA gets on far better with CBS Kenya than it does with another large local company, AIT's owners are white Kenyans.

Small is not always beautiful. Some local companies can be more evil to local musicians than the transnationals. Many lesser-known Jamaican musicians would testify that tapes of their work have slipped away on the British Airways Jumbo to London (the 'tape shuttle') and not a penny came back. The blame isn't always on the producers, of course. Musicians also learn to play the game, selling the same tape with a different title or artist name to different phonogram producers. The lack of trust that develops between small producers and musicians is particularly noticeable in Trinidad. There most calypsonians record their own records, pay the bill at the pressing plant, put them in the boot of their car and do all the selling themselves. 'National' as a characteristic of independence is not a guarantee for honest dealings, or indeed for wide tolerance in freedom of expression.

Another complicating factor in any national/transnational analysis is that large locally based companies often indulge themselves in international activities. Thus ABBA's Polar company licenses the quartet's tapes to different distributors in different countries – CBS in the United Kingdom, Polygram in East Africa etc. Sonet, another wholly Swedish-owned company, have an operation in London which has released quite a few hit singles, not of Swedish artists but of British and American – they have the European rights for Bill Haley and the Comets.

Sonet would probably be regarded in Sweden as more of a musically laudable independent than ABBA's company, Polar. Sonet produce a greater range of local artists and appear to feed back a large percentage of their earnings into music production. ABBA's earnings have been mainly fed into a network of investment companies. ABBA have succeeded in doing what many multinationals would like to do; they have achieved a large percentage of successes from a small number of products. In 1976 Polar enjoyed 16 per cent of the sales of Swedish phonograms in Sweden, but accounted for only 3 per cent of the releases.

Even a commercial operation like Polar does invest in products that are likely to make a loss – albeit for cultural, good-will or fiscal reasons. It is a pragmatic business operation. ABBA's manager is violently and outspokenly anti-socialist, anti-state cultural policy, but he does some of his most successful business in Eastern Europe. Whatever their feelings about the business strategies and ideologies of the ABBA gang of five, few musicians would say no to a recording contract with Polar. ABBA's independence has a magic aura both in musical and financial circles. They found the right formula for the international phonogram market.

TABLE 2

THE BIG AND THE SMALL: THE PHONOGRAM INDUSTRY IN MISC SAMPLE
COUNTRIES

Situation 1981–82 in the phonogram industry	Sweden	Jamaica	Trinidad	Wales
Dominant phonogram (records/cassettes)	Records. Many blank tapes sold	Records. Cassettes on the increase	Records. 8-track cartridges still in taxis	⅔ LP records, ⅓ cassettes
Best/latest estimate of market size	15 million records (mainly LPs) 4 million cassettes	2·5 million singles 800,000 LPs	800,000 LPs 600,000 singles	3·3 million units based on % of total sales in UK
Relative dominance local/foreign music	App. 40/60	App. 40/60	App. 50% Caribbean (20% Trinidadian) 50% non-Caribbean	Mainly English language pop
Exports of local music	ABBA dominate by far (mainly via licence deals)	Much reggae exported, often via tapes to London	Some calypso exported in small quantities	Some to expatriates in Canada, Australia etc.
Phonogram companies – foreign owned	EMI, CBS, WEA, Polygram have subsidiaries	Dynamic Sounds planned partnership with CBS not finalized (1983)	None	No local offices of international phonogram companies. Some produce occasional records (EMI, Decca, RM)

Tanzania	Kenya	Sri Lanka	Tunisia	Chile
No phonograms manufactured or imported officially	Single records. LPs. Cassettes increasing	Cassettes, very few discs	Cassettes, very few discs	Records. Cassettes increasing
40,000 records in 1978. Many cassettes circulate	1·8 million singles. 200,000 LPs 100,000 pre-recorded cassettes	2 million cassettes per annum	150,000 discs 500,000 pre-recorded tapes (legally). App. 3 million blank tapes	1·3 million singles 500,000 LPs, 500,000 pre-recorded + 4 million blank cassettes
Local music on the radio. Some foreign phonograms played at discos	East African music dominates (mainly Zairean and Tanzanian)	50/50 (Foreign music Western or Indian)	60/40 (foreign music mainly Egyptian and French)	30/70 (70% mainly other Latin American music)
Unofficially via Kenya	Some to West Africa. More to central and southern Africa	Cassettes to migratory workers in Middle East	Via Athens to Tunisians working in Europe (mainly in France)	Some Chilean artists released in Latin America. Many in exile
None	Polygram, CBS, AIT (used to be owned by Lonrho)	None	None	EMI-Odeon, Philips (Polygram) and, as of 1982, CBS

TABLE 2 – *cont.*

Situation 1981–82 in the phonogram industry	Sweden	Jamaica	Trinidad	Wales
– locally owned	1 state owned (Caprice) 2 large locally owned (Sonet, Polar). Numerous others. 16 have own organisation (NIFF)	4 larger local companies in IFPI. Numerous other producers	5 larger companies + several labels owned by calypsonians	1 large (Sain) and a handful of small independents
Studio resources	At least 20 professional studios (8, 16, 24 track). Many advanced studios at Broadcasting Corp.	At least 7 professional studios (many with 16 track)	Sporadic activity in 3 multitrack studios + a few mono. Studios used mainly by local groups	At least 4 multitrack, some only for visiting English groups
Manufacturing resources – record factories	4 pressing plants, many with automatic machines. 1 manufacturer of pressing machines (Alpha) and electroplating equipment (Europa Film)	7 pressing plants, mainly fairly small operations	2 pressing plants but 1 closed since 1981 and other only just functioning (Discs pressed mainly in USA or Barbados)	1 plant
– cassette manufacture	1 locally owned	None	None	2 plants for sound and video tapes

Tanzania	Kenya	Sri Lanka	Tunisia	Chile
Tanzania Film Company has monopoly on phonogram production	AIT (now officially owned by Kenyan nationals). Numerous local producers, 30 organised in KRPA	8 larger cassette producers, numerous small producers and importers	2 larger private producers, 1 state controlled company, and numerous small, mainly pirates	5 local account for 15%. One of these (Quatro) has 11%
1 studio (2 track) run by TFC	1 16- and 1 8-track in Nairobi. Various other small studios for commercial purposes	11 commercial (4 with 4-track) Mono studios at Broadcasting Corporation	1 commercial studio outside state radio and film corporations	4 multitrack studios
1 plant has been under construction for 3 years hampered by currency problems	1 plant (Polygram) – only one in East Africa	1 small plant produces mainly samples for radio use	1 state controlled plant producing very few records	1 plant (EMI)
None. (Some cassettes have been assembled in the past)	2 plants	None	3 plants producing	None

TABLE 2 – *cont.*

Situation 1981–82 in the phonogram industry	Sweden	Jamaica	Trinidad	Wales
– cassette duplication	7 larger plus numerous small operators	Small operators	Small operators. Often done in shops. Street pirates supplied by a bigger operator	Small operators
Distribution and retail sales	Super-markets, specialist shops, petrol stations and clubs. 26% through racking companies. 4 large distribution companies cover 80% of the market	Larger companies distribute themselves to record stores	Distribution by each label owner. Imports done by a few bigger record shops. Retail through small shops in urban centres. Substantial tourist sales	Specialist shops, 'High Street' stores, racks. 'Welsh' shops, tourism

A commercial/non-commercial scale

The previous minor digression into Swedish idiosyncrasies brings us to one more set of opposites which crop up in connection with the 'indie' debate, namely commercial and non-commercial. Almost all phonogram companies are commercial entities in that they wish to sell the sounds they record. Possibly the only exception we've come across was in the early days of Tunisia's state-run company, En-nagham. Its original brief was solely to produce records with the speeches of President Bourghiba – as such its costs were presumably underwritten by the state.

Even if all companies, big and small, have to sell to survive, they can have very different attitudes to factors such as the range of music available, the length of life in the market etc. Large organiza-tions prefer a quick turn-around of product, rather than a slow

Tanzania	Kenya	Sri Lanka	Tunisia	Chile
Small operators, mainly in shops	Mainly small operators	2 main operators. Many small. 6,000 record stores provide services	3 main duplicating plants. Numerous small operators mainly pirates	5 high speed duplicators (largest 25,000/month). Many small operators
Unofficial distribution	Record stores. Large companies distribute themselves. Small producers often have own shops	Mainly through the 6,000 'Record Bars' all over the island	Some music shops – mainly via small time pirates who sell from small stores or stands	Music stores. Large unofficial distribution of home-copied cassettes

trickle over a long period. They tend to concentrate on attaining global hits with safe bets. Thus, in a sense they are more commercial than small companies that often have to respond to specific markets or subcultures, focusing on aesthetic values and/or expressed needs regarding the use and function of music.

The concept of a commercial/non-commercial scale would seem to be a better tool in the analysis of phonogram company operations than many of the other opposites discussed so far. Admittedly there are no phonogram companies that are 100 per cent non-commercial. Total isolation from commercial goals is as impossible for organizations as it is for individual musicians. The only case of the latter on record is that of the avant-garde jazz musician who disbanded his group every time more than fifty people came to a concert – he thought he was getting too commercial. With phonogram producers such extreme cases exist only in theory. However, certain characteristic trends can be isolated and related (see Table 2 and Diagram 6).

In any given phonogram company, the more activity that occurs in the lower part of the flowchart, the more commercial the company is. The mainly commercial company tries to direct its activities towards a final result which corresponds to the directors' and owners' image of what is solely a saleable product. But to reach maximum profitability, and to survive socially or politically in the market, a commercial company often has to take into consideration goodwill factors such as keeping a powerful cultural establishment satisfied by producing phonograms with non-profitable art music. When the international record industry wishes to persuade governments to ease taxation on phonograms, it refers to the plight of Beethoven, not to the success of Kiss. Another example of non-commercial trends in highly commercial companies would be the production of less profitable phonograms with minority types of music in order to open up the market to reach a new stratum of buyers.[37]

DIAGRAM 6: CHARACTERISTICS OF COMMERCIAL AND NON-COMMERCIAL PHONOGRAM ENTERPRISES

Characteristics of commercial phonogram enterprises
Decisions are made by shareholders and management. Writers and artists are aligned in a strict hierarchy. Tasks are highly specialized in the production process. Planning is governed mainly by the lust for profits. Profits go to shareholders.

The aim of marketing is to create a demand by manipulating recipients. Mass distribution of each individual product to as many people as possible.

Characteristics of non-commercial phonogram enterprises
Representatives for the recipients and collectives of authors and/or performers make the decisions (sometimes singly). Planning is governed mainly by expressed needs and artistic innovation. Profits, if any, are used to promote new products or for other nonprofit purposes.

Marketing is focused on consumer information. An effort is made to distribute to specific consumer groups who often share the same interests and values as the employees of the company.

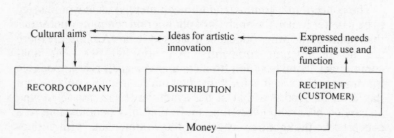

What we are saying here is that both paths of circulation in the flowchart are present in the activities of most phonogram companies. Even if there are no 100 per cent pure extreme cases, it should be possible to evaluate the general activities and overall strategy of any particular company and place it on a scale ranging from non-commercial to commercial. In this way it should be possible, and valuable, to distinguish between those who wish to make a lot of music and break even, and those whose prime consideration is that Number One Hit. Or put another way: those who want to minimize their losses and those who want to maximize their profits.

Having clarified the non-commercial aspect and its contribution to cultural activity let us return to using the term 'independent'. Independent companies in big countries seem to act as risk-takers and testers of new types of music on the market. Some of them also cater specifically for the needs of various subcultures. These functions are important, but seldom crucial for the upkeep of mainstream musical traditions of national importance in a large country. The situation in smaller countries with differing language areas is somewhat different.

In a small country or small language area small phonogram companies are of great importance for the retention and development of national music. The local independent company, as a rule, is far more deeply rooted in the music culture of the small country. With cultural life becoming more and more orientated towards mass media, the possibility of issuing and distributing phonograms with national music becomes increasingly important for the cultural identity of small countries.

5

The enthusiasts

Plenty of money does not necessarily result in plenty of cultural creativity – passive consumption might dominate. Governments can pump billions into the cultural sector and only give a certain amount of pleasure to a very limited number of people. On the other hand living off bread and water is not a prerequisite for attaining the pinnacles of creativity either. Culture cannot survive in urbanized societies without some money and some bureaucracy. The crucial link is human enthusiasm and action. Without this the finest goals of any cultural policy become worthless.

Because of its intangible nature culture needs a constant flow of new visions and ideas. Culture needs enthusiasts, people who feel motivated to work hard, often for unimpressive salaries, for the sake of creative activity they feel is important to themselves and to those with whom they associate. Culture needs not only the people who retain and develop traditions through their own artistic activity but also the enthusiasts who provide a necessary infrastructure. In the world of music the enthusiasts are the sort of people who start phonogram companies, music clubs, who organize concerts, tours and so on. Their motivations vary; they can be political, nationalistic, anti-establishment revolutionary, or just a vague 'love of music'. Their primary interest is rarely financial speculation. Neither their motivations nor their engagement, however, are permanent. They can change. The enthusiast who starts a music café might change priorities from minimum loss to maximum profit after a series of financial successes. And others may come on the scene with other ideas about what constitutes good music which should be supported.

This chapter describes some of the enthusiasts we have met in our travels, their motivations, goals and achievements. Particular attention will be paid to the process whereby small phonogram companies keep on emerging, and to what happens to them afterwards. We start in Scandinavia.

THE MUSIC MOVEMENT: SWEDEN

The musical happening of the Seventies which gave rise to more sounds, inches of newspaper column, praise and anger than any other series of events in Sweden was the development of the so-called Swedish Music Movement. This was the conglomerate term used to describe the network of music clubs, phonogram companies and bands that emerged, covering the whole country in the early years of the decade. Most of the participants were between 15 and 35 years of age. Swedish language songs as opposed to the English of the Sixties predominated, and Swedish folk music, became important. And the 'Do-It-Yourself' spirit prevailed as a result of widespread suspicion regarding the musical values of the established gatekeepers in Swedish society.

The visual presentation on page 122 is taken from a pamphlet on the music movement's activities published in 1976 by Rikskonserter (the Swedish national concert agency – a state organization).

The roots of the music movement were to be found not so much in the music establishment (art or commercial) but in the alternative and political youth movements of the times. As Sweden entered the Seventies, a group of enthusiasts in Stockholm succeeded in arranging mammoth free festivals on a public heath in the city. Groups no one had ever heard of emerged from their cellar dens and performed. The music featured not only rock groups singing in Swedish and jazz bands, but even Swedish folk music put in an appearance. The same organizers produced this for three years in a row. The next year, 1973, there was no music festival on the big heath – the organizers thought the whole thing had become too institutionalized, losing its spontaneity. But they had started a ball rolling.

The reaction of the established record companies was interesting. Both local and transnational, thinking the whole exercise was just a passing fad, showed little interest, thus demonstrating their preference for established trends and their difficulties in adapting to new directions. So the new Swedish musicians and their friends had to do it themselves or leave it, if they wanted to release phonograms of their artistic efforts. One group of musicians took over a near-bankrupt studio (the cash was put up by a rich philanthropist/ musician). They were soon producing between ten and fifteen LPs per annum, solely with artists/composers living and working in Sweden. Some of their releases were remarkably successful, selling up to 75,000 copies in Sweden alone. The company, MNW, was still ticking over ten years and over 100 LPs later.

Another group who gave their phonogram company the very coy name 'Silence Records' recorded the organist Bo Hansson, after he had been turned down by most of the other, established companies. His records, released through the British independent Charisma, were worldwide successes (distributed, of course, by the transnationals). Silence's share of the proceeds were ploughed back into the company's studio project. MNW and Silence were the first of a whole group of such independents, all of which labelled themselves

The spread of the Swedish Music Movement

The record pressing plant
LJUDPRESS AB
Montörsvägen 26
S-831 00 ÖSTERSUND
Tel 063/11 62 85
(Founded in 1976)

The music magazine
MUSIKENS MAKT
Språngkullsgatan 19 A
S-411 23 GÖTEBORG
Tel 031/11 62 15
(1973. 10 issues yearly)

The National Organisation for a
Non-Commercial Culture
KONTAKTNÄTET
Fack
S-402 30 GÖTEBORG
Tel 031/13 38 09
(1974)

＊

Record companies distributing
through Plattlangarna:
Amalthea, Malmö
(1977) 3 LP
Avanti, Göteborg
(1974) 4 LP
Barrikaden, Stockholm
(1974) 1 LP
Kofia, Göteborg
(1977) 1 LP
Levande Improviserade Musik
(LIM), Göteborg
(1975) 4 LP
Mora Träsk Musik, (MTM), Gävle
(1974) 5 LP
Musiklaget, Stockholm
(1974) 8 LP
Nacksving, Göteborg
(1975) 14 LP
Proletärkultur, Göteborg
(1970) 7 LP

Address:
PLATTLANGARNA (PL)
Norra Hamngatan 4
S-411 14 GÖTEBORG
Tel 031/13 31 33
(1975)

＊

Record companies distributing
through ENGELBREKT distribution:
Oktober, Stockholm
(1973) 21 LP
Folksång, Stockholm
(1971) 2 LP
Opponer, Stockholm
(1973) 1 LP
Befria Södern, Stockholm
(1968) 2 LP

Address:
ENGELBREKT distribution
Box 19009
S-104 32 STOCKHOLM
Tel 08/34 80 39
(1977)

Record companies distributing
through SAM-distribution:
A-disc, Stockholm
(1971) 1 LP
Alternativ, Sollentuna
(1973) 8 LP
Bruksteatern, Löderup
(1976) 1 LP
Cockroach Records, Vaxholm
(1975) 1 LP
Dragon Records, Saltsjö-Boo
(1975) 17 LP
Ett Minne för Livet, Stockholm
(1977) 3 LP
Forsa Ljud, Forsa
(1975) 7 LP
Giga, Falun
(1976) 1 LP
Hurv, Malung
(1974) 4 LP
Jatari, Stockholm
(1977) 1 LP
Kampen Går Vidare, Stockholm
(1974) 4 LP
Kung Karls Spira, Umeå
(1977) 1 LP
Lautaro, Norsborg
(1976) 1 LP
Lekstulaget, Östersund
(1977) 1 LP
Manifest, Luleå
(1974) 12 LP
Maskros, Värmdö
(1977) 1 LP
MNW, Vaxholm
(1971) 88 LP
Musiklaget, Stockholm
(1975) 1 LP
Narren, Stockholm
(1975) 4 LP
RKOB, Stockholm
(1974) 1 LP
Silence, Koppom
(1970) 50 LP
SJR, Stockholm
(1967) 3 LP
SUB, Uppsala
(1974) 3 LP
TALL, Stockholm
(1971) 2 LP

Address:
SAM-distribution Musik AB
Fack
S-185 00 VAXHOLM
Tel 0764/315 90
(1971)

Luleå

Östersund

Stockholm
(Vaxholm)

Göteborg

Malmö
Lund

Key to the signs:
○ = record companies
□ = distributors
● = Music Forums
◉ = record pressing plant
■ = Kontaktnätet
(Contact Network)
＊ = Musikens Makt (The Power
of Music), local offices

Wernqvist & Co. Stockholm 1979
Printed in Sweden

The spread of the Swedish Music movement

as 'non-commercial', indicating that speculation in music and maximum profit were not their main motives. Unlike many other
phonogram companies which continually concern themselves about
the nine out of ten releases that do not make a profit, these Swedish
companies supported the ideology that phonograms were not culturally less valuable or relevant because they made a loss. The
critical factor was that the operation as a whole broke even. An
extension of this ideology was a clear desire to extend the life of
phonograms. Phonograms were not regarded as products that the
recipient purchased, consumed and discarded after a short period.
The principle applied was that phonograms should be available as
long as there was the slightest demand. Whether it was a result of
this policy or merely an indication of quality, the fact is that MNW's
first releases from the early Seventies were still selling over a decade
later. The figures in Table 3 are quite extraordinary considering that
the phonogram industry normally refers to life spans of phonograms
in terms of months rather than years.

TABLE 3

LONG-LIFE PHONOGRAMS FROM A SWEDISH NON-COMMERCIAL COMPANY

Catalogue No.	Year of issue	SALES/year				TOTAL SALES UP TO 1981
		1972	1975	1978	1981	
MNW 1P	1969	351	369	145	110	4,525
MNW 17P	1971	3,823	2,155	884	251	24,941
MNW 20P	1971	4,809	3,845	1,793	242	28,903
MNW 35P	1972	6,772	8,763	4,870	1,549	75,586

The only way of realizing a goal of maintaining availability of as
much 'back-catalogue' material as possible was to control wholesale
distribution. The Swedish non-commercials started three different
distribution companies, of which the most important was Sam
distribution (1971). Sam expanded, with an acceleration towards
the end of the decade, co-operating with similarly minded companies in Norway, Finland and Denmark. Sam has also undertaken
the import of some phonograms from independents in other countries (notably the Scandinavian distribution of Rough Trade, UK).
However, increased size, even for a relatively small organization
like Sam, does not necessarily lead to large-scale economies. Sam's
distribution fee (including marketing costs) increased from 18 per
cent to 30 per cent of the wholesale price during the Seventies.

TABLE 4

THE GROWTH OF AN INDEPENDENT DISTRIBUTION COMPANY IN SWEDEN

Year	Turnover (millions of Kronor)	App. number of phonograms
1973/74	3·0	150,000
1976/77	3·9	156,000
1978/79	3·2	130,000
1979/80	6·0	222,000
1980/81	8·8	325,000
1981/82	12·5	426,000

The Swedish non-commercial producers expanded in numbers and regionalized during the Seventies. The latter was an interesting development, since phonogram production and resources had previously been concentrated in Stockholm. New phonogram producers appeared in Luleå in the far North (over 700 kilometres from Stockholm), in Malmö in the south, and in Gothenburg on the West Coast. The new phonogram producers were very different from their colleagues in the established companies. Company cars, wall-to-wall carpeting and cocktail parties were not the sort of perks they wanted or would enjoy. They maintained a grass-roots profile, close to the people who made the music and consumed it.

New Swedish organizations-builders

The vinyl products of the Swedish music movement did not merely reflect activities going on within a number of recording studios. There was a close relationship to the live music scene. All over the country numerous groups of enthusiasts started music clubs, so-called music forums, where musicians could practise and perform. Most music groups had one member who devoted much of his or her time to arranging appearances at different clubs and venues, thus eliminating the cost of a traditional middleman, the 'manager'. The music forums soon organized their own national organization, *Kontaktnätet* or 'Contact Network', which provided the means of lobbying official institutions and organizations for support. In this context, the music forums often came into conflict with more established popular movements, particularly those associated with the labour movement. The Social Democrats had governed Sweden for over 30 years and some of them liked to think they had a monopoly on the distribution of culture to the people.

The small Swedish phonogram companies also formed their own organization, NIFF (Nordic Non-Commercial Phonogram Producers Association), which soon became a pressure group in Swedish culture, begging to differ on virtually every matter with the local IFPI branch.

NIFF was particularly dissatisfied with the treatment (exposure) its phonograms received on the Swedish radio monopoly. NIFF companies had recorded many ironic songs about the activities of the USA in Vietnam. The Swedish Broadcasting Corporation used to put a skull and crossbones mark on such phonograms when they were catalogued in the record library. This indicated that producers should 'exercise care' when programming such records. Consequently they were rarely played. On the other hand, the library had numerous American Country and Western imports with songs in praise of the Vietnam heroes, but no such restrictions were placed on these. The Swedish Government-appointed phonogram committee reported in 1978 that the small producers in NIFF accounted for 7 per cent of all phonogram releases, had a 4 per cent market share but were only represented in 1.5 per cent of all the phonograms played on the Swedish radio monopoly. One of the highest hurdles enthusiasts working in new cultural directions have to contend with is resistance from the establishment, in this case the senior producers or 'gatekeepers' in the light music departments of the Swedish radio. Similar experiences have been noted in other small countries. Musicians in Jamaica and Trinidad have complained about the difficulties in getting local music on their radio stations (strike action in Jamaica in 1972 led to a marked improvement). Musicians and small producers in Kenya are still fighting what they regard as unfair treatment on the Voice of Kenya. Producers of Welsh-language phonograms have the same complaints – their music virtually never gets played on national UK radio. It seems to be a universal phenomenon that cultural visionaries are rare animals in the establishment – careful bureaucrats tend to dominate.

Getting at the hated Eurovision Song Contest . . .

One of the highlights of the Swedish Music Movement was the so-called Alternative Festival in 1975. A year earlier, the Eurovision Song Contest, organized by the ostensibly 'non-commercial' television companies of Europe, had provided the launching pad that boosted ABBA into worldwide orbit. Because ABBA hail from Sweden, Sweden was expected to pay for the finals a year later. Playing host to Eurovision Song Contests is something any small nation in Europe dreads. It digs such a deep hole in the budget that some countries decline, even after a win and despite any advantages for the tourist industry. In 1975 Swedish Television had budget problems and the money available for local musicians and free-lancers was being cut back. It seemed natural to many observers to say no to Eurovision, but the management decided otherwise; Swedish television had to honour its obligations to its European partners. This decision sparked off a remarkable reaction in the form of the biggest music manifestation Sweden had seen for years. The music movement was at the forefront and its motives were easy to understand. Not only was the country's television monopoly not spending as much on local music, but the money was going to an event which was the epitome of commercialism, giving profits to international phonogram companies (who sell the hits afterwards), and being paid for by licence fees. This was the way not only the music movement felt but also some thirty other music organizations who got involved in an alternative festival. The message was that happenings such as Eurovision Song Contests do more to dig holes in the cultural identity of participating nations than to achieve a valuable exchange of culture (anyone who is fool enough to sing a song in their own folk idiom comes last in the contest). The 1975 alternative festival did try to put on an alternative, one that involved hundreds of performers, from some twenty different countries, playing and singing different types of music; jazz, choral, classical, rock and folk. The aim was to demonstrate that genuine cultural exchange, across territorial and musical boundaries can take place without eroding cultural identity; all songs do not have to sound the same just to try to get a hit on the world market. The results of the 1975 Alternative Festival were documented on a phonogram (MNW–58;59P), in a feature film ('We have our own song') and in a number of radio and television programmes (Swedish Television's Channel 2, which was not involved in Eurovision at the time allowed some coverage). The finale was a grand carnival demonstration in Stockholm attended by no less than 5,000 people. Visiting gossip-columnists who follow things like Eurovision Song Contests shrugged their shoulders in amazement, wondering what on earth those crazy Swedes were up to.

The long term effects of such a musical manifestation are difficult to gauge. It probably helped (albeit slowly) to convince the estab-lishment (particularly the broadcasting monopoly) that a wider range of local musical activities should have a place in the media.

The reaction of the established phonogram companies to the progress of the Music Movement and activities such as the Alterna-tive Festival was that it was all a subversive plot designed to lead the youth of the country astray. ABBA's manager, Stig 'Stikkan' Andersson, publicly accused the organizers of the anti-Eurovision

The 1975 Alternative Festival in Sweden. 5,000 took to the streets of
Stockholm to protest about the commercialisation of music

manifestation of being members of a small revolutionary Marxist sect. Little did Stig Andersson know that the hard-line extremists on the left had already dismissed the Alternative Festival as something politically and culturally worthless. They proclaimed that the only correct line of action was to blow up the television transmitters on the night of the Eurovision Song Contest. Needless to say, nothing like that ever happened.

Internal squabbles and ideological battles

The second half of the Seventies was not an easy time for the Swedish music movement. There were differences of opinion between different phonogram producers regarding strategy. Should one try to remain alternative; should one try to retain the grass roots qualities of the early years by emphasizing content rather than technological quality (alternativism)? Or, should the whole exercise be seen as competition with the established music industry, trying to do the same thing but better (professionalism)?

The 'professionalists' insisted that the music movement must invest in studio resources that could produce the same sound effects as those from the transnational companies' hyper modern complexes. The relatively simple equipment that had produced big-selling phonograms five years earlier was dismissed as inadequate.

The 'alternativists', on the other hand, were more interested in the acoustic solutions to recording problems, applying mathematics, hammers and nails rather than investing in expensive technological gadgets. It's interesting to note that the main 'alternative' company, Silence, survived the Seventies far better than those who advocated a policy of trying to produce music that sounded like products from the transnationals, but with more meaningful songs. The noisiest debater amongst the 'professionalists', a company called Nacksving in Gotherburg, went bankrupt in 1981.

The Swedish music movement was to be beset by more ideological trouble in the late Seventies. Not only was some of the original enthusiasm waning, but a puritan, almost conservative streak developed. Sweeping judgements on the sincerity of various musicians were passed in its own newspaper (*Musikens Makt,* 'The Power of Music'). A certain intolerance frightened many musicians away. This was particularly true of younger Swedish musicians who had been inspired by the Do-it-yourself spirit of the British punk movement. Generation gaps are always hard to bridge in culture – this was no exception. Fortunately, when these words are being written (1983), things are looking brighter. The 'Power of Music' paper died a quiet death, but people from the movement have established a new, less intolerant (and more commercial) publication, *Schlager*. The distribution company (SAM) that was started in 1971 as a result of CBS' purchase of the only other Swedish independent distributor, is still expanding whilst sales for the transnationals are going down (SAM is owned collectively by the employees and the non-commercial phonogram companies' own organization, NIFF). NIFF's pressing plant (started in 1976 and owned collectively) is also expanding – two other Swedish plants have closed down. Co-operation has been extended to similarly-minded organizations in other countries: Danish SAM-distribution and Rough Trade in Britain to name but two.

Positive aspects
+ The Swedish language has been accepted in rock and pop lyrics. This has not only helped to balance the Anglo-Saxon dominance, it has also increased the quality and relevance of lyrical content in music.
+ Locally owned resources for production and distribution have been established which have survived crises both in the oil industry (the plastics shortage) and in the transnational phonogram industry. Whilst the transnationals have decreased their investment in local recordings in recent years, the music movement phonogram companies have increased their number of new releases.
+ Musicians have realized that they are not totally incapable of understanding and controlling the business aspects of their music. The old axiom that 'I don't care who exploits me as long as I can do my music' has been discarded.
+ A slight change of policy can be discerned at the Swedish Radio monopoly – more attention is paid to local phonograms by a wider range of producers. Local phonogram companies no longer have to rely merely on the support of isolated visionaries amongst the producers at Swedish Radio. This process was facilitated by a change of staff in the late Seventies when new blood replaced a number of conservative clots in top management.
+ The music establishment and the state cultural authorities have overcome most of their initial fears regarding what they preceived as anti-establishment tendencies within the music movement. Political action in the wake of the music movement has included the decision to instigate a study of the problems of the Swedish phonogram industry. This in its turn led to the introduction of a tax on blank cassettes, with part of the fiscal income being returned to producers of phonograms and music associations in Sweden.

Negative aspects
- The Swedish music movement suffered a period of isolation in the late Seventies when its music was little more than the 'left-overs' from student activities at the beginning of the decade. An excess of lyrics about Revolution, Oppression and other subjects approved by various ideological gurus alienated many musicians who did not feel qualified or motivated to adopt their creative activities to such lyrical constraints. Some artists left the 'non-commercial' phonogram companies and returned to the older established companies. 'Music movement artists sing about the workers. We sing for the workers'.[1]
- A concentration on professionalism coupled with a dissociation from alternativism led to ever-increasing demands on investments in studio equipment. Internal competition developed between the different non-commercial companies where the emphasis was on form rather than content (a recording from a 24-channel studio must be better than 8-track etc.). Much of the energy that was needed for dealing with the environment was wasted internally on ideological disputes and power struggles.
- The music movement did not succeed in communicating with either the older audience ('just a lot of music for student rebels') or the younger generation who felt a greater affinity for the punk 'anti-everything' ideology than for the relatively respectable remnants of the early Seventies fight against imperialism.
- The principle that a phonogram should not be a goal in itself, i.e. that it should be a reflection of live music, partly lost its significance. When the first groups of enthusiasts working with concerts, music forums and music cafés had expended their energy, substitutes were not waiting to come in and take over. The number of clubs where music movement artists could communicate live with their audience became less and less. This was not all the fault of the people in the movement. A tremendous amount of energy was wasted on fighting conservative elements in local authorities who frequently did all in their power to thwart the efforts of enthusiasts who wanted to arrange concerts. It was often a matter of prestige; local authorities in Sweden are responsible for providing places where young people can congregate, which they are hopelessly bad at doing. At the same time they could not accept the loss of control that would ensue if someone else (the musicians or their friends themselves) took the initiative. Another negative factor for live music was the disco trend of the mid- to late-Seventies. Spinning records provided such a cheap alternative that live music, despite its communicative attraction, suffered.

Despite the difficulties enumerated above, the Swedish music movement has achieved what will hopefully be many positive, irreversible changes in the Swedish music scene. The early visions of a mass-movement sporting enough creativity to replace much imported culture did not materialize. But the enthusiasts have kept active, without being swallowed up by the establishment or the transnational music industry.

NUESTRO CANTO: CHILE

During the Allende period (1969–73) music was regarded as a basic need. The music, recorded and live, that was heard everywhere was influenced by folk music traditions. Imports of foreign phonograms were heavily taxed and phonograms of local music were cheap.

Prior to 1973 folk traditions had a natural influence on popular music. We had *La nueva cancion chilena* where composers tried to combine elements of anything from the Beatles to classical with folk music. Chilean composers working with classical music stopped looking to Europe for inspiration. It was a development that concerned both the content of music and the ways of spreading it.[2]

This development was not entirely new. It was the culmination of a music policy which had been introduced way back in the Thirties, one of giving official support to folk traditions. Money was provided for the study of folk music at the universities. The development accelerated in the Sixties. The Frei government stipulated that at least 25 per cent of music on radio should be Chilean in origin. Folk music was present in school curricula as well as in the everyday life of a wide range of people.

In 1973 the military coup brought this to an abrupt halt. Victor Jara was murdered. Many musicians, composers and enthusiasts left the country in a hurry, taking as many master tapes and instruments with them as was possible. They took up residence in North America, France, Italy, Scandinavia and many other places.

Some enthusiasts stayed on, but it took about three or four years before they could emerge publicly. Shortly after the coup in 1973, a military spokesman had informed local musicians that their traditional instruments such as the *charango* were *instrumenta non grata*. 'You hardly dared be seen carrying a *gena* (flute) on the street.' Gradually the music returned, mainly as an underground activity centred in the universities and in the slum areas and shanty towns round the cities. The latter half of the Seventies saw this activity surfacing in various ways, through radio programmes, concert activities, phonogram production and music research.

In 1976, the Catholic church provided the forum for a new music programme, *Nuestro Canto*, on its station Radio Chilena. This was during a period when the church was particularly concerned about human rights in General Pinochet's Chile, and Radio Chilena was still living up to its old slogan 'The Voice for those who haven't got a voice'. *Nuestro Canto* presented a mixture of live recordings with amateurs and gramophone records. It was a resounding success, particularly when those responsible gradually introduced records by artists that had not been heard for some years (Victor Jara, Violetta Para and some artists who had left the country after the coup). Despite its popularity, however, *Nuestro Canto* was gradually throttled; not by direct involvement of the military which was still wary of its relations with the church, but by financial pressure. The advertisers, on whose revenue Radio Chilena depended, recognizing what they thought were left-wing tendencies in the music, removed their support for the station (they had plenty of others to turn to, there being 250 stations in all in Chile). This turn of events was not appreciated by the upper echelons of the Catholic church and *Nuestro Canto* was removed to an insignificant radio slot late on Sunday nights. The programme director responsible for building up the programme lost his job.

But *Nuestro Canto* had started a chain of events. It provided a forum where the enthusiasts behind a new record company, Alerce, could test the tolerance limits of the Chilean authorities. *Nuestro Canto* also provided local subsidiaries of the transnational phonogram companies with important information. EMI in particular had access to rich archives of Chilean folk music with untold commercial potential which the company would dearly like to release. *Nuestro Canto* and Alerce provided a testing ground.

Various 'supporters clubs' had grown up in the wake of *Nuestro Canto* and these gradually started arranging small concerts with artists 'from the universities and the slums'. Small music cafés or *penas* opened up in the cities. They were very popular but experienced numerous problems ranging from official harassment to direct violence, including the occasional bomb. Despite this, people could once again hear instruments that had been banned since the coup.

In 1978, Nuestro Canto became a concert agency. The authorities, of course, were not idle. With Radio Chilena not giving *Nuestro Canto* any more prime time slots, the police authorities applied rules and regulations to harass their concerts. Details of

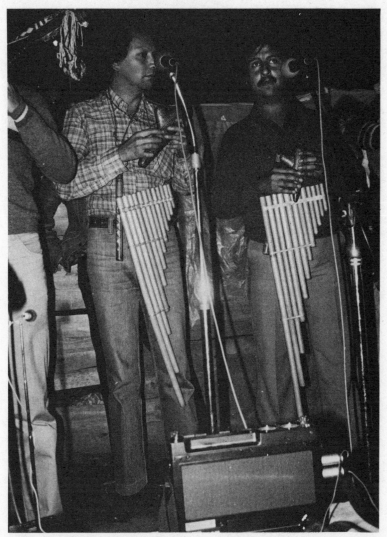

Gradually traditional instruments have started to reappear in Chile. A Saturday evening concert in a slum area outside Santiago

artists, songs including full lyrics had to be supplied to the police before a concert permit was granted.

Nuestro Canto's next move was to transform itself into a private company, which as such can enjoy a well-defined legal status. Business and private enterprise, according to the military's Friedman-influenced economic doctrine, must be encouraged at all costs.

This legal manipulation gave Nuestro Canto a breathing space and allowed them to put on 24 concerts a year in 1978-79.

> How easy it is depends on the opportunities available. In the beginning the authorities' reactions were quite illogical. One day they'd say one thing; the next day something else. Now we all know more about the rules of the game. We are a company and we have a legal defence.[3]

The legal antics involved in organizing activities as private companies are common to many enthusiasts in Chile. Music teachers who lose their jobs at the university start private teaching establishments. Musicologists and sociologists keen to engage in 'forbidden' areas of research do likewise. Those who wish to spread music on phonograms either rely on the unofficial distribution of music via cassettes, or they do it within the framework of company law. The Alerce company, started by well-known TV and radio personality Ricardo Garcia, is the most startling example. He started Alerce in 1976 in an attempt to provide a media alternative to the ever-increasing dominance of Anglo-American music on Chilean radio. It has not been plain sailing, as one might expect. There have been problems with the police, problems with the customs confiscating consignments of Alerce cassettes (on one occasion the claim was that Victor Jara singing folk songs was pornography) . . . But Ricardo Garcia, like Nuestro Canto, has used the system to fight the system for the sake of what he believes to be worthy cultural goals.

> We've learnt. We've developed a certain intuition. Of course there's always self-censorship, but also a margin of risk. We must continually try to find new openings.[4]

Alerce, like many independents, are dependent on the transnationals for services. Philips distribute their products. EMI press the records. But they are out at the front, in a difficult market, taking all the bashing. One can only admire their stamina.

BOB MARLEY'S SOUL GOES MARCHING ON: JAMAICA

It has been said that there are three alternatives to unemployment and poverty for young male Jamaicans in the poorer suburbs of Kingston. You either become a revolver man (police or gangster), marry a foreign lady and leave, or become a reggae musician. There is a lot of enthusiasm and a lot of tragedy amongst the reggae community – one driving force is the possibility of getting 'the big hit', the money-maker that can lift the artists out of ghetto poverty. Many have succeeded, even in the white world, but not all the proceeds have found their way back to Jamaica. Some artists did not bring it back for fiscal or currency reasons (Bob Marley transferred his membership of PRS to the American composers' organization ASCAP in 1972 so that his composer's income went to America). Others did not get anything back in Kingston because they were cheated. You have to be enthusiastic to continue making music commercially when you have no idea whom you can trust.

In the last few years of his life, Bob Marley decided he wanted to do something practical for the people and especially the musicians of Jamaica. After his death, the onus was on his wife Rita to continue the crusade through the record company they had founded, Tuff Gong. The principle at Tuff Gong was that all stages in the production process should be incorporated in the organization thus providing flexibility, and an insurance against the activities of other manufacturers and distributors (a similar ideology to that of the Swedish 'non-commercial' phonogram companies). Thus Tuff Gong owns a studio (in an old colonial mansion on Hope Road, Kingston), a pressing plant and printing press, a shop and a distribution outfit with three salesmen on the road covering the island.

Tuff Gong, as a record label, was started in the late Sixties. The record and distribution company was registered in 1973 but operations only got under way properly in 1978, the year before the pressing plant was purchased.

Since Bob Marley's death there have been many changes at Tuff Gong. In 1981, the employees clearly had an ideological motivation that extended beyond the purpose of keeping Bob Marley's memory alive, even if his wife Rita referred and still frequently does refer to Bob's spirit as the thing that keeps them going.

Interviews with the staff in 1981 indicated the following priorities.

- Tuff Gong should use their control over the production process to exert downward pressure on market prices (Tuff Gong should maintain lower charges for studio rental and custom pressing).
- Tuff Gong should concentrate on local music. 'We're not interested in foreign music. Our objectives are geared towards developing our local talent.'
- Political activity. Once again, following the paths trodden by Bob Marley, Tuff Gong should find it natural to propagate ideas about what the Jamaican government should do to help musicians, e.g. the government should provide assistance to help new, young artists get studio resources cheaply, the government should investigate producers and see contracts, because reggae is getting exploited and the artists are getting 'ripped off like murder'.

Rita Marley – rowing the Tuff Gong Boat ashore?

Few of the employees of Tuff Gong had much faith in the honesty of the international phonogram industry, or the workings of the international copyright system.

Copyright money, too, was an unknown quantity according to Tuff Gong.

This is part of the suffering of small countries. It doesn't help to join a copyright society. The only thing that might help is to change the wording round the labels from 'all rights reserved' to 'anyone who copies this record will get shot'.[5]

Tuff Gong's ideology at this stage could best be described as a pragmatic mixture of spiritual and earthly aims; 'It's something Bob wanted. Not just a money-making thing but a message of love and peace being spread through the whole world, a message of unity. Behind that spiritual message, of course, you have other things attached just for making money.'

Would Tuff Gong make enough to survive? Some of the more established Jamaican companies expressed their doubts (as one might expect, since odd men out who do not follow the rules are never appreciated in any business sector). 'There's not a lot of artists who have the business ability to go beyond producing music. Bob Marley's experience is new. Your creativity you can arrange and control, but beyond that . . . I wonder.'[6]

So much for the Tuff Gong scenario in 1981. Two years later, in 1983, the situation was very different. As one observer put it: 'There's been quite a turnover of staff at that place over the past two years'. The name had been changed to Tuff Gong International. What had been an oasis of love and music in a quiet residential area of Kingston had become a veritable fortress swarming with guards behind big iron gates. One of Bob Marley's former lovers (the mother of one of his children) complained that even she was not allowed through the outer gates. Rita Marley still seems to be in control of the operation but outside people with international experience of the record industry have been brought in, apparently to streamline the operation. Questions about the current ideology of Tuff Gong were answered with confused references to God and Love.

Maybe this was the only way for Rita Marley (who is generally acknowledged to be a shrewd businesswoman) to keep the ship afloat. Tuff Gong is certainly adapting itself to standard practices of international showbusiness, departing from being merely a group of idealistic enthusiasts.

Tuff Gong also have a major asset in the form of Bob Marley's estate, which should keep them in healthy finances for some time. In view of the interest the phonogram industry shows for releasing the works of famous artists after their death (e.g. Jimi Hendrix, Bob Marley), there should be a steady flow of copyright and royalty income from the flood of posthumously released Marley recordings – *if* Tuff Gong can get the right people to chase up the spoils.

Whether or not they live up to Bob Marley's ideals or become like just another record company remains to be seen.

A PHONOGRAM COMPANY AND 90 PER CENT PIRACY: TUNISIA

How on earth can anyone be fool enough to start a small phonogram company in a country where nine out of every ten cassettes sold are pirated products on which the producer earns nothing? This is exactly what our ultimate enthusiast, Mounir Ghattas, did when he started Studio 18 in Tunisia in 1981. Prior to this he had spent a number of years in Sweden gaining inspiration from the Scandinavian 'music movement'. He had seen what musicians and enthusiasts had achieved in Sweden. He had saved up enough to buy some TEAC 8-track equipment and a mixing console, and knowing that there was no commercial sound studio in his own country, he returned to start something embryonic. With the aid of a few thousand egg cartons, ten kilos of nails and a hammer, he turned a rented house outside the tourist resort of Sousse into a small studio. His first commercial cassette production featured a local popular folk singer from Tunis, Zoubaier (an extraordinary artist who prepares himself for performing by consuming a number of raw eggs and a litre of olive oil).

Mounir's method of selling the Zoubaier cassette was to prepare a sampler cassette with short excepts from the songs. This was played to 'official' music shops who could order copes, knowing that they at least would have it in stock before the pirates took over. In fact Mounir Ghattas' first venture into the tricky Tunisian cassette business only sold about 800 copies legally. But it became a great hit amongst the pirates. In one back street of Tunis where there are about thirty operators, each with about ten cassette recorders coupled together, the pirates were reporting sales of about twenty-five copies each daily of Zoubaier's cassette. If, at a conservative estimate, they sold about 50,000 copies then this would be equivalent to a loss for Zoubaier of copyright money in the region of £10,000 (he'd composed all the songs and artist royalties had been paid as a lump sum), and an even greater loss for our enthusiast.

Mounir and Zoubaier's attitude to the success of their product amongst the pirates was philosophic. Zoubaier saw it as a means for poor people who could not afford the prices in the big stores to get access to his music (his cassettes are rarely played on radio). It also benefited him indirectly as an artist since more people heard him, and he could get more work singing at weddings and other festivities. Mounir Ghattas accepted the loss as a fact of life. No tears were shed because he was more interested in developing the studio operations than phonogram production. Prior to the arrival of his

A Tunisian enthusiast in his little studio (Mounir Ghattas)

studio, the only recording facilities which could be rented were at the State Broadcasting Corporation (RTT) or at the State Film Institute.

Mounir Ghattas is one of those optimistic, idealistic enthusiasts for whom access to relatively low-cost technology has provided enormous opportunities. He has ambitious plans for discovering and encouraging the unknown sides of Tunisian music. Whether he survives within the peculiar business and legal constraints of Tunisian society remains to be seen – it will depend much on the business acumen and honesty of those with whom he co-operates, at least until Tunisia finds a solution to the piracy problem.

CELTIC ROCK: WALES

Sweden, Chile, Jamaica and Tunisia are certainly not the only places where we have found groups of enthusiasts surviving and thriving under difficult conditions. Take *Wales* or *'Cymru'*, as the 500,000 Welsh speakers (out of a total of 2.3 million) prefer to call it. The language issue and nationalism were the main motives for the enthusiasts who worked throughout the Seventies with phonogram projects, music clubs, festivals and publications.

Few people outside Britain today know that there is a living Welsh language. Indeed it had been predicted by many people in Wales after the Second World War that Welsh would soon die out altogether, with the language only surviving for a few decades in remote areas of the North. Remarkably, the tide seems to have turned now with pro-Welsh activities covering every media form. Once again this was mainly thanks to the efforts of enthusiasts, people who felt they were losing part of their cultural indentity with the demise of the language their parents spoke.

The late Seventies saw the main enthusiasts' phonogram company, Recordiau Sain (Sound Records) celebrating a decade of ups and downs, but still surviving. Most of its thirty or so annual releases made a loss but were balanced by one or two commercial successes. Sain was located in the rural North and the need for local resources in the South was slowly being satisfied by new small companies, many working mainly with small issues of cassettes. Most of these independents concentrated on Celtic folk music or rock/pop sung in Welsh, as well as with traditional Welsh forms of music such as choral singing.

Seen from the outside, the task many of these activists set themselves would appear to be gigantic if not impossible. Here they were with London only two hours away by train from the Welsh capital Cardiff, in a country where the media were almost totally dominated by Anglo-Saxon culture (no daily newspaper in Welsh, most radio consisting of non-stop English pop). They set themselves the task of trying to save something that was fast disappearing. Why? It's difficult for those involved to articulate their reasons. The nearest one gets to an explanation is an answer like this from a record store owner and concert organizer:

Towards the end of the Sixties, young people who had been through the Beatles started to look to their own culture . . . . Young people were thinking a lot more then than they do now. I'm 33. I for one went through a period in the early Sixties when I was very anti-Welsh. I looked upon the Welsh language as something useless, part of an old culture, part of a chapel-going, hymn-singing culture. Possibly a pang of conscience came over me – and possibly over others,

'Cultural identity' and 'national culture' might be controversial concepts which are hard to define, but they are clearly very real to people like this.

As usual with grass roots enthusiasts, the established order of things was one of the main targets for Welsh cultural activities. Primarily the English establishment came under attack, but even their own Welsh establishment received some criticism. The Welsh Arts Council, for instance, has never given any support to rock or folk music sung in Welsh despite the council's official dedication to the language and culture of the country. The annual cultural highlight of the Welsh year, the Eisteddfod Welsh-language music and poetry festival, however, has changed its attitude to contemporary culture, allowing rock and folk musicians to perform alongside the bards and choirs on the official site. This was after the enthusiasts had organized their own 'fringe' concerts for three years in a tent five miles further down the road.

The sounds that the Welsh music movement have preserved on phonograms cover a wide spectrum. It covers sophisticated pop productions such as Endaf Emlyn's *Dawnsionara* ('Slow dancing' Sain 1206M) to the provocative songs of Hywel Ffiaidd and Dafydd Iwan. The group Hywel Ffiaidd record for a small company in South Wales (123 Recordiau); their songs include *Croeso Diana* ('Welcome Diana', a none too complimentary song about Princess Diana, wife of Prince Charles and thus, officially Princess of Wales) and 'Bobby Sands' (a song about the Irish Republican Army member who died in prison whilst on hunger strike). These two songs are only distributed on cassette and then mainly by mail order.

Dafydd Iwan was one of the original enthusiasts who started the Sain company in 1969. This was when Decca were moving into the market and the other local producers offered no attractive alternative. Dafydd Iwan, a former chairman of *Cymdeithas Yr Iaith Gymraeg*, (the Welsh language society), has used the phonogram to communicate with fellow Welsh-speakers and tease the establishment. A typical example is his ode to the Prime Minister of Britain, Margaret Thatcher. This single was banned on BBC and commercial radio, and possibly for this reason sold well. Here, for the benefit of those who do not read Welsh, is an English translation of the lyrics.

(by Dafydd Iwan)

Come to the fire, listen to my song
I'll sing to Maggie Thatcher,
the iron lady, queen of the earth
No less than Maggie Thatcher.

The lightning flashes when thatched-roof Maggie
comes to lay the law down.
Chorus:
It's all up with Wales, let's go back to the Llymru'*
Hail! Oh Maggie Thatcher!

Simple people think that their fate
is in the hands of Destiny and so forth.
And she Madame Sarah† says in the morning
that it's the moon and stars which have the power.
But that's a lie, the one who decides
is Maggie, the thatched-roof woman.
Chorus: . . . .

The Russians pale when they hear
the name of old Maggie Thatcher.
And the Ayatollah Khomeini, he also trembles
when he sees a picture of Maggie Thatcher.
The Common Market is weak like a fly
when Maggie shouts from afar.
Chorus: . . . .

She's like a rock, let's praise the Dragon.
There's no moving or turning Thatcher
But the lady turned on the TV channel,
a U-turn by Maggie Thatcher!
The land of my fathers is a rash of cuts.
The axe-woman is coming.
Chorus: . . . .

If your husband hasn't got a job,
the answer's clear – move! says Maggie Thatcher.
Uproot your tent, and move to Kent,
like your fathers, says Maggie Thatcher.
But the Welsh intend to stand
without moving their tents (pavilions).
They'll challenge old Maggie and her crew.
For language and work, boys, let's fight now, boys.
We'll get rid of Maggie Thatcher.

As with their Swedish counterparts, the Welsh popular music
scene has not been without its conflicts. Musicians working with

---

* Traditional peasant dish similar to 'curds'.
† Fortune-teller on Welsh radio.

Welsh-language material may be increasing in numbers but they are still a minority in Wales. On the other hand they have certain advantages – Welsh-language radio and television have expanded and they have a monopoly on that. This causes some annoyance to English-speaking musicians living in Wales who find it hard to get access to a medium that is controlled from the big cities of England.

There is also friction between different generations of Welsh-speaking musicians. Sain, in recent years, have become more commerical in the interests of survival, releasing songs that ABBA and Elvis Presley have made popular, sung in Welsh, of course. Sales successes with a popular tenor (Trebor Edwards) have underwritten some of the losses made on rock productions, but even so Sain has been criticized for not putting more money into lesser-known Welsh rock groups. Part of the reason for this criticism was the virtual monopoly position Sain achieved with regard to Welsh phonograms in the late Seventies, a situation which became more monopolistic when Decca pulled out. (cf page 000). As a monopoly, an organization can expect to be the target of much scrutiny, especially when the issue involves such emotional aspects as cultural identity and nationalism. Sain was certainly scrutinized, particularly by Welsh language publications such as *Sgrech*, the organ for many younger Welsh-language rock fans. Fortunately for Sain, the early Eighties saw a number of small recording facilities appearing in different parts of the country. Other people got involved, relieving Sain of some of its cultural responsibility in the phonogram field, allowing some of those working at Sain to become active in the next significant media development, the introduction of a new Welsh-language television channel (S4C, opened in November 1982). The decision to start S4C, which involved a complete political turn-around for the conservative British government, was the result of heavy cultural lobbying and political actions including a well-known and respected intellectual threatening to hunger strike in Wales. The fact that the new channel would need between about twenty-five hours a week of Welsh material stimulated a whole range of activities, with production companies cropping up here and there, many of them producing video programmes featuring Welsh music and artists. The establishment had succumbed to yet another cultural demand from Welsh enthusiasts.

AN ORGANIZATIONS TREATY: KENYA

Sain in Wales had problems with its monopoly position in the Welsh phonogram industry. Monopoly problems in Kenya had the effect of bringing local musicians and phonogram producers closer together. Some of their common problems arose from the fact that

Local music magazines keep local phonogram companies on their toes.
Sgrech from Wales

Polygram had the only manufacturing facilities in East Africa, and
could thus dictate prices, delivery times and conditions. Local
phonogram companies needed a strong organization to negotiate
with Polygram – the Kenya Record Producers Association (KRPA)
tried to fulfil this function. Some enthusiasts at the KRPA also took

the next logical step, investigating the possibility of building their own manufacturing facility. In 1979, a musicians' cooperative association was formed in which local producers and performers could buy shares. The intention was to get a government loan and start a local pressing plant.

Polygram were not impressed by these plans. A spokesman referred to 'another pressure group that wants their own factory . . . they've no resources of their own. I've spoken to them and I gather that they think they can get records more or less free of charge if they have their own factory.'[7]

The plans to build a factory never materialized. This was not because of a marked improvement in relations between the KRPA and Polygram Kenya. The driving force behind the project the KRPA's enthusiastic secretary, found there were too many hurdles to clear and retired to other activities. This person was Adam Kutahi, a remarkable man who started Kenya's first African-owned phonogram company, Mwangaza Music, shortly after independence in 1965.

One of Adam Kutahi's major achievements in his organization-building activities was the signing of a treaty spelling out rights and obligations concerning different local organizations involved in the music industry. Kenyan musicians and music organizations have not had an easy time during the last decade. They have had to compete both with Anglo-Saxon pop which is highly favoured at the Voice of Kenya radio monopoly, and the influx of talented Zaïrean and Tanzanian musicians. Some Kenyans have survived by providing music for a limited market such as their own tribe, and various organizations have been formed to protect their interests and promote local music. Those involved are a very heterogeneous bunch. Some do not trust each other, others are not to be trusted. Some have a genuine concern about the music culture of the country, others see music as a purely commercial operation where subject matter for songs is chosen solely with reference to what is deemed politically opportune at the time. Adam Kutahi managed to find a common denominator everyone could at least pay lip-service to, namely the desire to 'make the greatest possible contribution to the success and prosperity of Kenya'. This was a preamble to a charter which regulated the dealings of phonogram producers, composers (through the local performing right society, the MPRSK), and musicians (through the musicians' union).

The treaty recognized some of the specific conditions that apply in the Kenyan music industry. For instance that performers invariably are considered to be the composers of the songs they sing. One royalty (12.5 per cent of retail price) is agreed upon, payable as an advance of 1,000 Kenyan shillings per single recording. The treaty specified how the organizations should attempt to get remuneration when Kenyan records are used commercially, and how the proceeds should be divided up between the members of the different organizations. The treaty also provided a basis for coming to terms with some of the common malpractices of the local industry, general distrust, poaching of artists, stealing of tapes etc.

All in all the Kenyan National Music Organizations Treaty is a remarkable document – particularly if one considers that the major phonogram companies would almost certainly dismiss those involved as a bunch of small-time crooks with one aim, 'to get rid of the white companies'. It is probably true that most African phonogram producers tend to put the blame for all their troubles on the activities of transnationals, but the treaty shows that some in their midst are willing to make their own attempt at tackling the organizational problems brought about by the growth of the music industry.

GYPSY RECORDS: SRI LANKA

Sri Lanka has one of the youngest music industries in our sample. Local cassette production exploded after the liberalization of import restrictions in 1977. Since all cassettes are imported, the people who control the music industry are mainly businessmen with interests in textiles, films, electronics etc rather than music. There are indications that musicians are becoming aware of how much money is being made out of their music and that the do-it-yourself enthusiasts are likely to emerge here as everywhere else.

One unusual group of Sri Lankan producers are the Perera brothers, who run a company called Gypsy Records in Colombo. They started off as a family band when their father lent them the money to buy electric instruments in the early Seventies. The brothers then built their own studio and it was a natural step to start a phonogram company, first with their own recordings and then with releases from other artists. This development was facilitated by the fact that their family business provided a ready-made distribution system. Their father had built up a confectionery business, and they had vans that traversed the island delivering sweets to small kiosks. Kiosks were the ideal place to sell cassettes. Gypsy Records were in business.

Some more Sri Lankan experiences will be quoted in the next section where an attempt is made to analyse why enthusiasts start phonogram companies, and what happens when they do.

ENTHUSIASTS' COMPANIES: A CHOICE OF STRATEGY

Model 1. The prerequisites (figures in brackets refer to boxes in the diagram on page 148).

At any point in time, record companies in a small country with a relatively free market economy have a choice of strategy. They can concentrate on producing phonograms with local repertoire and artists (5). The can choose to import foreign repertoire (4). Or they can operate on a combination of the two.

The subsidiaries of transnational record companies (3) are obviously under pressure to market products produced within their own concern in other territories, since the longer the series, the greater the overall profit. And even local entrepreneurs (2) can find dealing in international recorded material attractive. ABBA sells virtually everywhere, whether it's been obtained legally through agreement with ABBA's record company, or 'unofficially' in the form of pirated records and cassettes. A variety of factors decide on the actual strategy pursued.

- *The perceived profitability* (9, 10) from the two areas affect the relative importance to the record company of local and international repertoire.
- *The perceived risk and capital cost incurred* (11) also directly affects the extent of local recording activities. A production purely for a domestic market usually involves a bigger investment and possibly more of a financial gamble than importing or manufacturing, say, 1,000 copies of a record which is already a hit on the British Top 40.
- *The policies of the transnationals* as regards sales of their products in the particular territory.(1)

It often happens that local musicians, artists and music enthusiasts reject the option of co-operating with the established companies and choose the uncertain option of running their own phonogram companies. This process has been going on ever since the phonogram was invented and has been particularly noticeable during the past then years. The factors that appear to determine the extent as well as the success/failure rate of these phenomena are as follows.
- *Control exerted over local recordings (6).*
Local producers will always wish to exert some degree of control over the artists they record. The person who puts up the money will usually want to have a say in the choice of repertoire and mode of recording. But there is a limit to how much control artists and musicians are willing to accept. After a period of frustration, the artists will back out and look for other alternatives, either another

DIAGRAM 7: MODEL 1

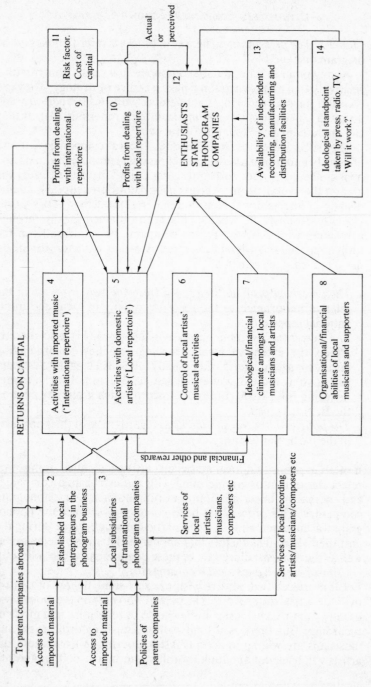

established record company, or the greater freedom of 'doing one's own thing', alone or with friends.

The exception to this rule is found in the case of very successful, established artists. The Sri Lankan *baila* singer, Nihal Nelson, has produced about 70 different cassettes over the past three or four years. Each one has sold in the region of 10,000 copies, giving the producer a profit of about 100,000 Sri Lankan rupees (app. US$ 5,000 per release). Nihal Nelson's commercial attraction is such that he does not even have to sign exclusive contracts. He can decide when, where and for which producer he records. He can sing songs of a semi-political nature about the rich and the poor, without suffering any artistic interference, rather in the same way Bob Dylan, Pete Seeger and Joan Baez could sing songs about the Vietnam War. On the other hand, another Sri Lankan recording artist, Mariazelle Goonatillake, with seven EPs and eight cassettes to her credit, has become dissatisfied with the repertoire she has been required to record. Her thoughts echo the frustration of gliding outside the accepted norms of both the public and the established record industry.

> . . . Usually, as a singer or musician, you are overruled by the producer. If he says he wants this type of song, you have to do it. Another problem about doing what you believe in is that we are all so afraid of the audience. We get popular through them. We have to cater for their needs. We are not bold enough to tell the producers and the critics: This is our music and we'll do it the way we want to do it. The result is that we get nowhere.

Mariazelle Goonatillake has taken the logical step of trying to make her own cassettes, independently of the established companies. But she has come across many other factors that have to be considered . . .

> . . . I'm keeping my fingers crossed. This will not involve any producers. The music director is a friend, so are the musicians. The only problem is the rent of the studio and the manufacture of the cassettes. But I'm prepared for it. The musicians have agreed to accept payment after the release of the cassette.

– *Ideological and financial climate (7)*
Our Sri Lankan artist continued:

> A musician-owned company could work but probably a section of the musicians would not be willing to stand by the others. They would still want to do what the producers say.

If musicians are not ideologically motivated to take the risk involved, then it is difficult to get a small record company started. Any cost breakdown of a cassette production in Sri Lanka illustrates perfectly the point Mariazelle Goonatillake is making. Fees to musicians account for 42 per cent of the fixed costs involved (there is no functioning royalty system).

TABLE 5

CASSETTE PRODUCTION ECONOMICS IN SRI LANKA

Fixed costs	Singer (1,000 to 1,500/number) ....15,000 rupees	
	Musicians (75 rp/song) .... 8,000 ,,	
	Musical director/lyric writer.............. 6,000 ,,	
	Studio, engineer, tape (2 days).......... 4,000 ,,	

TOTAL   33,000 rupees

Variable costs	Duplication in Singapore .... 20 rupees	
	Distribution................................. 5 ,,	

TOTAL   25 rupees

TOTAL COSTS (production, distribution)
  2,500 cassettes ....90,000 rupees
INCOME SALES 2,500 cassettes
  (35 rupees wholesale)..87,500 ,,
BREAK-EVEN POINT ....app. 2,500 cassettes
PROFIT ON EACH EXTRA 1,000 CASSETTES ......12,000 rupees
(NOTE: 20 rupees = app. 1 US dollar)

Of course one can not moralize and demand too much of musicians. Democracy starts with breakfast, or at least a very late supper even in the world of music. The financial state of potential artists plays a crucial role. The alternative of taking a quick payment 'up-front' from an established company is perceived as being far more secure, even if it involves considerably less income in the long term. Ideological motives for starting phonogram companies are not restricted to the issue of solidarity with other musicians. Enthusiasts can be inspired by common motives of nationalism (eg. Wales, Kenya) or by the desire to counteract unwelcome cultural tendencies (eg. anti-commercial in Sweden).

– Availability of independent recording, manufacturing and distribution facilities (13)

If all the studios are owned by and are occupied primarily by the contracted artists of established record companies, then it becomes hard to organize independent record productions. So, one of the first steps towards the growth of independent record companies is often the acquisition of recording equipment, however rudimentary. Two of the most long-lived musician-backed companies in Sweden (MNW and Silence) started in this way in the late Sixties. They grew out of a meeting between electronic know-how that loved music, and musical talent that was dissatisfied with the opportunities provided by the established companies. Bo Hansson – the man who received worldwide acclaim for his musical interpretation of *Lord of the Rings* – was one of the products of this cross-fertilization.

Manufacturing facilities are also critical. A broad range of phonograms cannot be mechanically reproduced if there is no pressing or cassette duplication plant which is willing to accept fairly short runs from a variety of customers. Thus small producers in Kenya voice much concern over Polygram achieving a manufacturing monopoly in their country. As long as Polygram still presses records for anyone who pays their bills (and as long as the prices charged are not crippling) activities can continue.

Another event illustrating the significance of manufacturing resources took place in Tunisia around 1979. Musicians and technicians returning home after a sojourn in France found that the pressing plant which was originally constructed to produce recordings of President Bourghiba's speeches was semi-idle. Engineers got the machines working again and these resources, coupled with the current liberalization in the cultural climate, enable them to produce records of a style known as *musique engagée* or *la nouvelle chanson arabe*. Some of these phonograms, notably those by artists such as Heddi Gueller, sold over 10,000 copies. Bear in mind that these songs had lyrics which only a few years earlier would have guaranteed a severe prison sentence!

– Established record companies' support for local artists

The local record industry's treatment of the local artists, including the actual or perceived financial rewards the established companies make, can also affect the drift towards new small companies and allied activities.

The Sri Lankan 'King of *baila*' referred to above – Nihal Nelson – receives a lump-sum payment of 15,000 rupees every time he records a new cassette. As we have noted, he estimates that the company producing the cassette makes a profit of around 100,000 rupees per production (an unreasonable profit in his opinion). Nihal

Nelson, however, has not attempted to form his own company, for other reasons involving his image and peace of mind. He does not want to become 'a money man', running round shops selling cassettes. This, he believes, would have a bad effect on his ability to write songs about life around him, as it really is. Maybe he is right. On the other hand, a closer study of the business would undoubtedly present him with a new wealth of topics to sing about in his calypso-style *bailas*. Nelson is trying to solve his dilemma by negotiating a royalty deal on top of his lump sum payment.

Nihal Nelson comes from a poor family, but he has not become rich enough or ideologically motivated enough to start being philanthropic towards fellow musicians. Bob Marley's Tuff Gong, as we have pointed out, is a different case. Marley felt that the established producers, both inside and outside the Island, were making too much out of Jamaican musicians – Tuff Gong was an alternative ('Before we can free South Africa we must liberate Jamaica').

Lack of support from the established companies can also spark off phonogram activity in other forms. Coupled with lack of resources, as in the case of Tanzania, the results can be very negative. Tanzania's biggest music industry problem is that the country lacks resources for mechanical reproduction. A decision to build a record pressing plant was made way back in the Sixties. Equipment was delivered in 1979. In 1982, most of it was still in packing crates piled high in the building that was to be a pressing plant. The Tanzania Film Company that has a government monopoly on anything to do with film and phonograms has not been able to get the factory together because of currency shortages. At the same time the live music scene has developed fast and there is tremendous pressure from musicians who wish to make phonograms. Some of them try to get to Kenya to record, but this is hardly a satisfactory solution, because they generally lose control of their music in the process. If Tanzania could get its own manufacturing and recording resources to function there would be a flood of activity.

Some artists claim that starting their own phonogram companies is the only solution since their music conflicts with the interests of the established companies. This would hardly seem to be a problem in every country (cf CBS in Denmark and Kenya), but does have validity where artists represent political movements that present a serious threat to authoritarian regimes.

These thoughts are echoed by Fernando Reyes Matta of the Latin American Institute for Transnational Studies in Mexico.

The development of folk song has suffered directly from the transnational expansion. And this has its cultural aims too; radio, television and the recording industry have been practically closed to the expression of commitment to structural change. Obviously, such an attitude is understandable. It is defined by the conflict of interest. And within the boundaries of that confrontation – consciously or not – radio and television stations become instruments of a kind of 'transnational culture' which encourages cultural synchronization and moves towards a model of domination of the world. Advertising, records, imported programmes, transnational news agencies, all interweave to create a communications framework which subscribes to order and coherence. Within this coherence, folk song is dysfunctional, or else it is only permitted the degree of presence which does not change the dominant model.

Fernando Matta also quotes the Mexican artist Gabino Palomares' explanation why it becomes impossible under certain circumstances to work with transnational phonogram companies.

Our music is dismissed by the transnational companies. This phenomenon is understandable, as our themes are in direct conflict with their interests. Fortunately, there are recording companies that, though small, allow us to record. Our work recalls that which the minstrels did in their time. There is a lack of truthfulness in the communications media, and we fill the gap. It is arduous work, above all because we do not have the materials necessary, but the people's acceptance of our work is what leads us to go forward.

– Organizational and financial abilities of local musicians and their supporters (8)

Once musicians and their supporters do get a record company off the ground, they find themselves thrown straight into the crass world of financial reality. Economic, technical and organizational know-how is required, if the operation is to be anything more than a one-off flash in the pan. This is why so many small companies either become dependent on or even get bought up by larger companies whose computers can organize things like accounts and distribution efficiently. Or they go bust. Two examples of the latter that come to mind are Love Records in Finland, and Demos in Denmark. Love Records, started by Finnish musicians and music lovers in the late Sixties, produced an amazing spread of musical documentation during its ten-year run. The Love records giant catalogue from little Finland covered rock, jazz, folk, political songs and even Rock-'n'roll standards with a local star band called the Hurriganes. Love discovered groups such as Wigwam and guitarists like Jukka Tolonen. At one time, Love had captured over 15 per cent of the

Finnish phonogram market. But business acumen was lacking. In spite of unlimited enthusiasm from all quarters of society, including the radio monopoly, an overdose of optimism coupled with a strangling investment in a new studio complex toppled Love. Despite a last-minute rescue attempt by selling off the distribution rights to EMI, the company folded. EMI reputedly did not lose anything in the crash, but did pick up some of Love's former artists who were scattered in the fall.

EMI's manager in Finland at the time was the Richard Lyttleton we've quoted in previous chapters (he was moved back to become International Manager EMI Records at Head Office in the middle of the Thorn take-over upheaval). Lyttleton remembered Love as

. . . an absolutely classical case. Three very talented people got together to form a record company. They had enormous success – they were up at 15 per cent of the Finnish market at one time . . . but they started losing their creative integrity. They found they had to conform to disciplines outside those they were accustomed to. For example, royalty accounting. They hit a period where even an elementary knowledge of commerce would have taught them that they were producing too many non-profitable records. I think it's a very familiar story – creative people get together, form their own company because they don't like the constraints of the larger record companies. For every successful one, there are an enormous number of failures. I would think the odds are 90 – 10 against . . .

Demos, Denmark, was another instructive case, where financial incompetence was thrust unwillingly upon the staff of a progressive operation. During the early Seventies, Demos enjoyed numerous hits with political rock groups such as Röde Mor (The Red Mothers), and Jomfru Ane (a music theatre group from Jutland). But Demos was only the music wing of a political book publishing outfit founded by the anti-Vietnam war movement. The record company was staffed by musicians and enthusiasts, some of whom were free-lancers at Danish Radio. When Sales lapsed in the mid-Seventies, the political ayatollahs on the board of Demos Books, who legally controlled the record company, called on Demos Records to adapt itself to market norms and principles of business efficiency. The result of their deliberations was that the whole staff of the record company were sacked, and new staff, including an accountant from an oil company, were brought in. A year later, Demos Records folded. This demise left a vacuum which was quickly filled by CBS Denmark, whose repertoire, as we have already mentioned, proceeded to raise a few eyebrows when it

included an LP in aid of the 'Christiania Free Town', a huge
complex of deserted army barracks that had been occupied by
squatters.

It is encouraging to note that, despite the losses of Demos and
Love, most of the people involved in their operations are back
working with new independent companies (including in Denmark a
distribution set-up based on the structure of Sweden's SAM-
distribution). It remains to be seen what they've learnt from hind-
sight.

– *ideological standpoint taken by the Press, Radio, TV (14)*
One of the reasons why the small British punk companies of the late
Seventies became so well known nationally was that they received
the ideological blessing and support of some sections of the music
press. *The New Musical Express* gave them plenty of encouragement, and their products could even be heard on the radio. Presenters like John Peel on the BBC made it their business to acquire
off-beat records from unknown labels and play them.

The same process played an important role in Scandinavia,
though certain sections of the broadcasting elite did their best to
thwart this development. In 1972, the tiny MNW company in
Sweden released an album of Russian balalaika music, recorded by
an amateur group from Stockholm. The only radio programme
where this was featured was an afternoon rock show! It really did
not fit into the format, but the host was favourably disposed to the
small, struggling independents. The other, more established
gatekeepers at Swedish Radio dismissed the repertoire of the new
independents as political propaganda which was not suitable for
'tired workers who had the right to demand a bit of musical escapism
on the radio'.

The independents' repertoire did get played, however, in specific
programmes, and this support from people within broadcasting was
crucial to their success. The introduction of Radio Cymru, the VHF
all-Welsh radio channel, provided an equally important boost for
companies producing Welsh music. And Radio Cymru needs any
amount of recorded Welsh music, to develop its all-Welsh image.
The introduction of an all-Welsh television channel will certainly
augment this effect.

The situation in Sri Lanka, Tunisia and Chile is entirely different.
In Sri Lanka and Tunisia, those in charge of broadcasting regard
local pop music as being damaging to cultural standards (Western
pop music, on the other hand is not judged so critically). All lyrics
have to be vetted by a committee before phonograms are played on
the air. This has clearly decreased the willingness and the ability of
musicians to get their own record companies going. They have to
rely on established producers with the required capital and know-

DIAGRAM 8: ENTHUSIASTS AND THEIR PHONOGRAM COMPANIES
MODEL 2. DEVELOPMENT PHASES

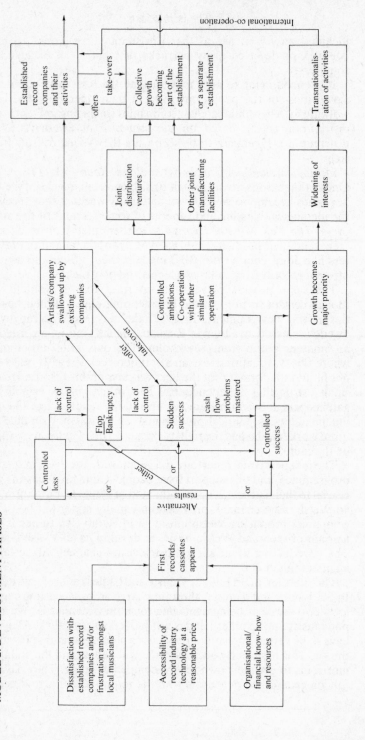

how to arrange other channels of distribution. In Chile the situation is even more critical. Radio stations simply do not play records that could be interpreted as offensive to the military government of General Pinochet (and that covers quite a wide brief).

Model 2. Development phases in the growth of small phonogram companies

Most of the observations in the preceding section concerned the prerequisites for the coming-into-being of these small organizations and the factors that decide how frequent they are. Observations of a number of these entities in different countries indicates that their development follows various phases. Model 2 is an attempt to chart this development.

If a simple production is the result of the first faltering steps, then costs might be covered with sales of as little as 1,000 – 1,500 copies. It could be a flop, leading to an abrupt termination of the process. It might just break even, leaving room for future ventures. It might 'take off', producing windfall profits. This is probably the most critical point in a small record company's development. There then follows a period of consolidation in which priorities are decided; growth, nationally and internationally, *or* controlled ambitions on a national level regarding manufacturing and distribution.

Throughout this development, phonogram companies are continuously faced with critical decisions concerning investment levels for production or marketing – the outcome of these decisions can decide in which direction they move in the model.

Consider the cost breakdown from Sain Recordiau in Wales (Table 6).

Fixed costs for a typical Welsh-language rock production requiring two weeks in a studio amount to about £4,000. With market prices being what they are, Sain would have to sell over 4,000 records to cover costs. Normally Sain reckon on sales of Welsh-language rock productions not exceeding 2,000 copies – so production decisions have to be made with care.

If Sain were content to release a very simple recording that was more or less recorded on home-taping equipment, then their fixed costs might not exceed £1,000. A break-even point would then be reached of as little as 1,200 copies. In other words, it is relatively easy to enter the record market, and just as easy to get in deep waters when investments in technical equipment are made. A heavy investment in studio equipment places high demands on sales. The equipment may not stand idle if the investment is to be recouped – so either it has to be rented out to outside customers (which is not always a satisfying occupation for enthusiasts who have built up

TABLE 6

COST ESTIMATES FOR TYPICAL SAIN LP PRODUCTION

Assumption: The artists spend two weeks in the studio, an investment of £150,000 depreciated over 5 years, with three employees.

FIXED COSTS	£
Studio 2 weeks	3,000
Cutting, plating	180
Sleeve design	200
Typesetting, separation, platemaking	450
TOTAL	3,830

VARIABLE COSTS
Assumption: 3,000 records are made and 1,500 cassettes are copied.

Record pressing, 3,000 @ 36p	1,080
Cassette copying, 1,500 @ 40p	600
Sleeves/cassette inlay (20p and 10p)	750
Labels	150
Transport from plant in England to Wales	200
TOTAL for these quantities	2,780

TOTAL FIXED + VARIABLE COSTS, of which studio
   costs amount to almost half: £6,610

INCOME FROM SALES	£
Gross in shops, incl. 65p VAT	5·00
Sain sell for a price of	2·90
LESS: artists royalty (4·5% plus	
6·25% copyright)	0·30
LESS: distribution costs and	
administrative costs, app.	0·50
RESULTS: surplus for covering investments	
and running costs	1·60

If Sain sell all the 3,000 records and 1,500
cassettes, they will generate a contribution
of 4,500 × 1·60 =   £7,200

(generating a surplus of nearly £600)
Conclusion: If Sain press 3,000 records and copy 1,500 cassettes the break-even point will be reached when 4,131 records and cassettes have been sold.

their own facilities) or the average sales of phonograms have to increase.

This is the point where the development process for many small phonogram companies comes to an abrupt halt or continues under another guise (e.g. amalgamation with other companies). This is also where the tendency to be 'sucked up' into the phonogram industry establishement becomes apparent. Only extreme determination, luck or an awful lot of money can slow down this process.

The cost picture can vary considerably from company to company and from country to country. The only pressing plant in Chile (EMI) charges US.$1.50 to manufacture an LP record (1981). The same service costs only one-third as much (about 50 cents) in Britain or Sweden. During the mid-Seventies when the pound had a low international value, some small Swedish companies ordered pressings from the United Kingdom, cutting manufacturing costs by about 40 per cent. With astronomical local prices, independents in Chile are forced to do the same, or concentrate on cassettes which are cheaper (60 US cents in 1981).

TABLE 7

LP MANUFACTURING COSTS IN A NUMBER OF COUNTRIES

Country	Cost	LP record excl. sleeve % of retail price	Cost	Cassette duplication % of retail price
WALES	36p	7%	40p	8%
SWEDEN	3·50 SEK	7%	4·50 SEK	8%
CHILE	77 pesos	30%	30 pesos	
SRI LANKA	—	—	20 rupees	40%
TUNISIA	—	—	250 milimmes	10%
KENYA	15·75 KSHS	20%	20.90 KSHS	25%
JAMAICA	2·85 J$	27%	—	—

Fixed costs for an LP phonogram production are about the same in Sweden as in Wales. But the break-even point is approximately twice as high in Sweden with a sale of around 9,000 copies required as opposed to 4,000 in Wales (comparing two similar companies with their own 16-track studios). The difference arises from distribution and studio costs.

Variable costs, as Table 8 indicates, are higher in Sweden because distribution costs more (this is partly because the separate distribu-

TABLE 8

A COMPARISON OF VARIABLE COSTS: WALES AND SWEDEN

Variable costs	WALES (£)	SWEDEN (Kronor or SEK)
Record pressing	0·36	3·50
Printed matter	0·20	3·00
Royalty	} 0·30	1·50 to 3·50 (depending on size of group)
Mechanical copyright		3·00
Distribution	0·50	9·00
TOTAL	£1·36	SEK 20·00 = app. £2·00

tion company used is also responsible for marketing operations which Sain in Wales might do itself and include in its administrative costs). Royalty payments are also higher in Sweden – a sliding scale is applied according to the number of musicians involved in a production rather than the popularity of the artist (normal in the phonogram industry).

It is also important to note that the commercial phonogram industry's habit of deducting studio costs from royalties until they have been recouped is not normally applied in small companies. Musicians recording for large companies in the United Kingdom or the USA might have to sell up to 30,000 LPs before they get a penny in royalties. A company like MNW in Sweden, on the other hand, pays an advance royalty equivalent to sales of 1,500 copies to all its artists, irrespective of popularity in the market.

One should note that in actual fact a small Swedish company such as the one we have cited would not have to sell 9,000 copies of each new release. This is because of healthy sales of older phonograms ('back catalogue') where fixed costs have already been covered or written off, producing a steady contribution to the basic running costs of the company.

At this point it is worth referring back to our discussion of the Big and the Small. Because small phonogram companies can survive in most countries with average sales well under 10,000 copies/release, they continue to play an important role, doing things the majors cannot do. Size has not produced the advantage of low production costs, except with huge series.

The enthusiasts become part of the establishment . . . .

The final state in the development model indicates that the companies that enthusiasts start, tend to become part of the establishment themselves if they survive the test of time. They might get swallowed up completely by large phonogram companies (Metronome, the Swedish company absorbed by WEA in 1969 was also started by enthusiastic musicians). They might retain a certain amount of independence by diversifying and expanding internationally (ABBA's company Polar is a typical example). They might slowly be absorbed by the phonogram establishment in their own country. Or they might form a separate establishment with its own set of norms and values.

This is what the 'non-commercial' companies in Sweden have done. They exist alongside the established giants. They control recording, manufacturing and distribution resources. Having their own separate branch association means that they enjoy the status of an identifiable negotiating partner and can avail themselves of monies that accrue from various rights, e.g. from the Rome convention. Without such a status, such monies might well 'get lost' within other organizations. (This happens in Jamaica where companies who are not members of the local IFPI branch get none of the money from radio performances.)

The Swedish 'non-commercials' have survived for over a decade with more or less the same goals (even if production decisions have become more geared to commercial realities than in the early Seventies). They have avoided being assimilated into the record industry establishment by creating their own institutionalization process (own trade organization, own norms regarding royalty payments, available studio time per production etc.).

Two events are worth mentioning here. In the late Seventies, after eight or nine years of operations, the two main phonogram companies in the Swedish music movement underwent some significant changes. One of them, Silence Records, broke away from the capital, Stockholm, and relocalized itself to a sparsely populated area some 400 kms from the city. A derelict school was converted into a modern studio, an enormous task which required many sacrifices and no small amount of voluntary contributions from friends. The other major company, MNW, did not relocate itself or change its structure. But it did change its staff. Amicably, by mutual consent, a younger generation moved in, bringing fresh air and new contacts into an operation that could otherwise have lost its raison d'être. Both MNW and Silence did continue to use and support the joint manufacturing and distribution resources they and producers like them had built up. The radical changes were at the creative end of the process, where they were most needed.

Even if this sounds like a cleverly engineered success story, both MNW and Silence could disappear tomorrow. One of Silence's founders, Anders Lindh, has said: 'We'll continue with this as long as we feel we're doing something culturally worthwhile. If we don't, we'll give it up and do something else'. If this did happen, other enthusiasts would probably move in and take over. As long as this continues, those involved will continue to provide an important cultural service; creating, documenting and spreading music, much of which would be regarded as 'not commercially viable' by the established record industry.

6
Copyright: Where does all the money go?

In my early days in music, I knew nothing about rights. I just wanted to create. Creative people are like that, especially musicians. The financial game means a lot because you have to live, but the creativity of the artist is the most important thing. That will never die. No one can steal that. They can steal the money but they can't steal the heart. Even if you've been ripped off, the satisfaction comes from knowing that you've made some people happy. So that's it. You're going to get ripped, but learn all you can so that you gradually can control your own.' (Jimmy Cliff 1983)

Few operations in the music industry have been more discussed, world wide, in the last few years than methods of remunerating creators and performers when music is distributed to the public, i.e., the various areas of copyright. The legal notion of copyright has existed for a long time (Britain got its first copyright law in 1842). But a revitalized interest in the idea is due to many factors.

- Via new international agreements such as the Rome Convention coverage has been extended in some countries to include not only composers and lyricists, but performers as well as producers of phonograms.
- Musicians and composers have also begun to become more aware of the nature of these rights; that they should get paid when works are performed on radio and television. This area was previously 'looked after' on their behalf by benevolent publishers or record company owners.
- Quite a lot of money is involved but most of it seems to go to a small number of recipients. In the case of performance fees for musical works they are mainly publishers as well as a handful of internationally famous composers. CISAC (the International Confederation of Societies of Authors and Composers) heard at its 33rd Congress in 1982 that no less than 96 per cent of authors and composers who are members of performing rights societies receive royalty income which is *below* the minimum wage level in their respective countries. On the other hand business analysts keep on reminding us that music publishing is an area where you

cannot fail to make a lot of money (publishing income comes from the same sources as composers' and authors' incomes).

- In view of the increased use of recorded music through transistorized radios, sound and video cassettes and cassette recorders, the spread of television, satellites etc, the amount of money available for copyright reimbursement should reasonably be considerably larger. But the difficulties for both legislators and collecting societies in keeping abreast of the electronic industry's ability to reproduce software are enormous. And it is even harder, once funds have been collected, to know how to divide them up fairly so that all copyright owners get a just share.

PERFORMING RIGHTS OF COMPOSERS, LYRICISTS AND PUBLISHERS

The most established form of copyright payment is that administered by collecting societies on behalf of composers, lyricists, publishers and occasionally arrangers. The first French copyright society was established in 1851. The PRS (Performing Right Society) in London was founded in 1914; STIM in Sweden in 1923. The PRS total income in 1981 amounted to almost £47 million of which 40 per cent or almost £19 million was paid in by broadcasting companies in the United Kingdom. The Swedish collecting society STIM received 25.5 million kronor (£2.5 million) from the Swedish Broadcasting Corporation for the same rights in 1981. This sum gave the writers about £5 per minute for records played on Swedish radio, £15 a minute for a popular song on television and almost £50 a minute to the copyright owners of a symphonic work when performed on television. These sums might sound quite considerable for a small country like Sweden, but as we will see later the actual sum that filters back to a composer in another country (via publishers, sub-publishers etc) could be much smaller.

The large established collecting societies exert considerable global influence in the field of performing rights. The PRS spread its activities throughout the British colonies (where British copyright law usually applied). When Britain gave independence to its colonies, the PRS was not so quick to disband its empire. The PRS still has collecting agencies in the West Indies, East Africa, Asia etc. SACEM in France has close relationships with collecting societies in former French colonies (e.g. SODACT in Tunisia). The two major American societies (ASCAP and BMI) control a large amount of the popular music repertoire which is played around the world. The 39 societies around the world with which BMI has agreements paid this American society alone about US$13 million for the use of its repertoire in 1980. Or as BMI put it in its own publication *BMI Around the World*: 'Over any given period, for every foreign title or composition used and earning royalties here, almost nine American titles are earning royalty payments from overseas., The other main collecting society in the USA, ASCAP, receives almost twice as much as BMI or around US$25 million per annum for public performances of American repertoire abroad. In other words, international copyright agreements have had considerable significance for the USA's positive 'cultural' balance of payments.

Behind closed doors . . .

To understand copyright problems around the world, one has to understand the workings not only of the relevant international conventions (Berne, UCC, Rome etc) but one also has to fathom out the policies of the leading copyright organizations. Such a task is not so easy as one might expect, as the following anecdotes illustrate.

A major collecting society with operations in a number of smaller countries annually publishes details of the funds it collects in each territory. When we requested details of how much it paid back to composers in these territories we were at first dismissed with arguments such as 'it would cost us so much to work it out.' Finally after much correspondence and verbal pressure some figures were supplied.

On another occasion we presented a written set of questions (concerning the role of publishers, activities abroad etc.) at a meeting with two of the same society's lawyers. A request to tape the conversation triggered off this response: 'Mr Wallis, I'm sure you know about "on the record" and "off the record" information. Either you don't turn your tape-recorder on and we give you some of the background information you're interested in, or you turn your tape-recorder on and . . . we don't.'

In a filmed interview with the president of another large copyright organization, the subject covered included the problems of distributing revenue to the rightful owners. The president praised at length the sampling system for radio performances which he claimed guaranteed a fair distribution of income. When one of the authors then presented material indicating that possibly up to 1,000 hours of Swedish music had been played on his country's radio stations with hardly a cent coming back to Sweden, the president had what seemed to be a minor temper tantrum. He accused the interviewer of trying to lead him into a trap and asked the film team to promise never to use that part of the filmed interview. The film team were then asked by the president's public relations officer, politely but firmly, to leave the building – she also asked them to write a letter of apology to the president.

Such experiences might tempt one to use terms such as 'cloak and dagger', 'Dickensian' or 'shady' when describing some collecting societies. There are, however, a number of logical explanations for these rather strange behavioural patterns and the occasional lack of openness.

The first is historical: most collecting societies have had to struggle hard for their very existence. Users of music rarely spring to the fold begging to pay. But collecting societies have also had problems with their own members who have not always been convinced they were getting paid properly for all performances. Some societies have tried to solve this by giving extra perks to their major income earners (e.g. extra votes at the A.G.M. as in the case of the PRS in Britain, or extra cash for performances of older songs as with ASCAP in the USA).

A lack of openness at times has led to public scandals and adventures in the courts. When PRS member Trevor Lyttleton in 1978 unravelled certain information about generous PRS loans to its top executives and publicly demanded access to the PRS voting lists at general meetings (an unidentified 4 per cent of the members effectively controlled the organization), he found himself in the courts on the receiving end of a libel suit. At the last minute the PRS withdrew the suit and paid Mr Lyttleton's costs. It is against the background of incidents like this that one must try to understand the unwillingness of certain collecting societies to be as open about their affairs as one would have hoped.

Another important historical aspect is that the established copyright societies were set up to implement copyright laws which had emerged from a creative environment that existed in Europe at the turn of the century. Composers, lyricists and artists were rarely the same persons. Publishers were independent of record companies and they made money out of sales of sheet music (see diagram 9). Conditions have changed beyond recognition but copyright laws and to a certain extent collecting societies have been slower to respond.

Historically the publisher made his money from selling sheet music. For these services, the publisher usually retained 50 per cent of all incomes generated, reasonable at the time considering the costs involved in printing music. When collecting societies were formed, they represented both composers and publishers. The PRS still has a board consisting of 12 writer-directors and 12 publishers.

Some idea of the money involved comes from comments of employees of two record companies:

If we had a hit song I would look for publishing returns in the region of £20-30,000 in our half-yearly returns[1].

If major artists constantly record a song and it becomes a standard then it could be worth about US$3 or, 400,000 a year (in copyright money)[2].

Now that sheet music publishing is virtually dead, publishing consists mainly of paperwork, registering with a collecting society, signing contracts and occasionally paying out an advance. It is normal for publishers to retain between 30 and 50 per cent of all incomes for these services.

In some of the smaller nations we have studied, integration of phonogram and publishing activities are almost total. Artists recording for the major Kenyan companies (e.g. Phonogram, AIT) are expected to assign all copyright when signing artist contracts. The phonogram industry would argue that this is a natural way to deal with a situation where works are created collectively by a group of, say, nine or ten musicians in the studio. The act of creating a work is seen as part of the performance in the studio. This system functions as long as the songs concerned are only performed publicly in the country of origin (where the artists can control what is going on reasonably well). But if East African music should

DIAGRAM 9: THE FLOW OF ROYALTIES: A COMPARISON OF THE OLD SYSTEM AND TODAY'S

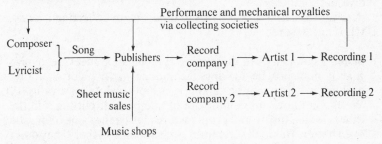

Old system, publishers act as middlemen between composers and phonogram companies

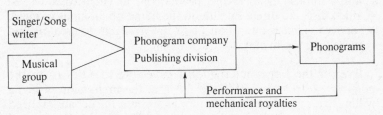

A common situation today. Artists/Song writers are the same people. Publishing is part of the phonogram company.

become very popular in, say, Europe, then the problems start. Most collecting society rules require that at least 50 per cent of performing right fees are paid to individual composers and lyricists. In other words, each song has to be identified with relation to an individual, who must be registered with an affiliated society. Is it likely that monies due to the collective composers of such works (registered under an artist's name with their phonogram company) would filter back through the international copyright system to the individual musicians involved? Probably not, unless the song in question becomes a big hit and word got around that money was being held on behalf of someone, somewhere.

The situation with mechanical rights (composers' renumeration from sales of phonograms) is even more complicated since these monies do not have to pass through official collecting societies in some countries. The flow in such cases is often based on private transactions between publishers and phonogram companies. How can individual composers check the accuracy of their mechanical returns in these cases? Consider a phonogram manufactured in factory A, sold on label B, published by company C. It could be that A, B and C are all part of the same corporation. The transnationals would tell us: we are so big and so computerized that we could not cheat, even if we wanted to. Is this a reasonable guarantee for an individual composer?

A chief executive of the USA's 'other' main collecting agency, BMI, is not so sure.

> When a company can, in looking at its balance sheet, recognize that it may not be making the money in this slot that says 'publisher', but it may be making it in another slot that says 'user'. Well, you know, it's coming out of one pocket, putting it in the other, so that the overall profit picture may be the same or may be even better. But to the creator, he or she can't do that. They don't have the same flexibility that a conglomerate does, to move and switch with the times. You have a writer, he or she can only write, whereas a conglomerate can shift emphasis from conventional music publishing to record production, to video cassettes, to video discs, to direct satellite to the home, to all kinds of music services. That is an option that's not available to creators and there's where, in part, I see a problem.[3]

Even if the larger international collecting societies (with the possible exception of BMI) do not give the impression of being willing to discuss the role of the new publishers, the debate has been hotter in some of the smaller countries. The Danish Composers' Society expressed openly its concern about the influence of publishers in a paper presented at the 1980 CIAM Congress – CIAM is an international organization of composers' and song writers' societies, as opposed to collecting societies which are organized in CISAC.

In his address to CIAM, Danish composer Sven Aaquist Johansen put forward his serious doubts about the role of publishers in copyright administration.

Publishers of music are secondary right holders or owners of *transferred rights* to works of music.

As promoters and salesmen for the composers, music publishers of course share interests with the producers of music and lyrics, and I know several publishers for whom this is the primary incentive. But obviously, as buyers of our rights, music publishers have interests opposite to ours.

Music publishers buy part of our rights, and in principle they do so after free negotiations, and we sign the contracts of our own free will. It is the task of our composers' societies, our trade unions as it were, to see to it that we get a square deal in this situation.

But it is *not at all* obvious that this private transaction, this transference of an individual composer's individual rights to an individual publisher, qualifies publishers' rights as a major concern of the performing right societies – or entitles publishers as a group to have 'democratic' representation in our national performing right societies, where they can influence decisions of vital importance to *all* composers, including an increasing majority of our colleagues who do not, or do not wish to, or are not allowed to, depend on traditional commercial publication for the promotion of their music.

What is worse is that the traditional interpretation of publishers' transferred rights and the present position of publishers within the performing rights societies are very frequently abused to the disadvantage of the composer.

In the present situation, our performing right societies are not the instruments of composers that they ought to be. They are passive paralyzed spectators to a continuous undermining of our rights and interest, which is going so far that (as I learned recently) some broadcasting corporations – when commissioning works – form *ad hoc* publishing firms in order to participate in royalties and thus reduce costs.[4]

Johansen maintained, furthermore, that the publishers' influence in Denmark had hindered the solution of one of all collecting societies' perennial problems, namely conflicts between composers of different types of music. He was referring here to what Westerners refer to rather inadequately as 'serious music', meaning Western art music, as opposed to light or popular music – which of course can be just as 'serious' in its intent.

The national performing right society has been practically paralyzed for several years due to an irrational struggle between authors of 'light' music on one side and authors of 'serious' music on the other. This struggle has developed into blind barrage shooting from trenches, from which no one seems to be able to analyze the positions any more, no one seems to remember why the whole thing started or to be able to acknowledge the fact that most of the original problems (such as outdated aesthetic criteria of apportionment of royalties) have already been solved by others. And what's worse: no one realizes that while the authors are aimlessly fighting each other, commercial interests are comfortably taking over the territories both groups believe to be defending against what ought to be an ally. Not a single composer in this country has benefited from the conflict. Not a single poet or song writer. But certainly a couple of international recording industries.

In this particular case, the general assembly based structure giving the vote to a large number of representatives of secondary or tertiary right holders has obstructed any attempt to solve the problems through quiet and reasonable negotiations between the primary right holders, the authors of music and words.[5]

The relative values Western society puts on different styles of music has not made life easier for collecting societies. Composers of 'serious' music have carefully guarded their privileges in the form of better remuneration when works are performed. Western art music performed in a small recital room might pay the composer considerably more than, say, a popular concert for a 1,000-strong audience. As the boundaries between different styles of music become more diffuse, such differentials should become less dramatic. But they still pose a problem.

With such conflicts in the air, it is, maybe, not surprising that many collecting societies, run by professional administrators on behalf of copyright holders, prefer to be as tight as a limpet when asked to express opinions about publishers, or divulge details of internal conflicts.

Dividing up the spoils . . .

It's often much easier for composers' societies to collect money than it is to get rid of it . . . and it's becoming more so today. (PRS official 1980).

One of the major problems facing copyright administration everywhere is the growing gap between the operations of collecting fees from music users and distribution to the rightful owners. In certain areas there can well be little if no relationship between the two. Collecting societies might sign an agreement with local hairdressers entitling each saloon to have the right to play music from records, tapes or the radio during business hours. This will give the society an income. But no hairdresser will ever send in lists of what is played. In other words the money goes into a general kitty and is distributed according to some other principle. Much income is generated in this fashion. Contracts are signed with hotels, jukebox owners, club owners. STIM in Sweden has blanket agreements with all the town and county councils in the country. Music users who do not pay are prosecuted under the terms of the copyright law.

Distribution is far trickier. Performing right societies usually gear their distribution to what is played on radio or television. In other words, a composer whose works are played regularly in a club, but for some reason or other are never played on the radio, could end up getting no performance fees. The situation becomes even more trickier when radio stations do not come up with proper music logs. The PRS who operate in Jamaica have had this problem. It was solved by making a so-called 'allocation', i.e. paying every registered member in Jamaica a lump sum to keep them happy. A similar case applied to a Kenyan composer with a song which was played daily on the Voice of Kenya (the VOK had been paying money to the PRS in London for some time). The composer in question was offered a lump sum compensation of £500 by the PRS.

The problems of fair distribution in the gigantic USA music market are almost insoluble. Local radio stations licensed by ASCAP broadcast a total of 54,000,000 hours a year. ASCAP samples 60,000 of these, and even if the system is 'random, stratified and disproportionate' (ASCAP's claim) the fact remains that it must be easier to win even a small prize on a Swedish national lottery than get remuneration when individual works are played occasionally on a number of small American stations.

Any sampling system must naturally favour works that turn up most frequently, in the case of the USA, across-the-nation hits. The problem here is that a small extra income for a lesser-known composer can mean far more for that person's composing activities than an extra million for Elton John, Paul McCartney or even ABBA. The small composer loses out.

Composers often exaggerate when making claims about how often their works are performed (maybe this is natural in a competitive world). But there is probably some basis to complaints made by, say, calypso singers in Trinidad, who claim that their recordings are frequently played on US local radio stations catering for West Indian communities, but that they never get any reasonable returns via the US collecting societies.

Another example concerning copyright returns from the biggest music market in the world concerns Sweden. For a number of years the Swedish Broadcasting Corporation has made available to US stations recordings of Swedish music. Full copyright details are supplied with each programme so that stations can log plays. One such series, 'Swedish soloists', featuring 13 half-hour programmes of artists playing mainly Swedish 'serious' composers (Berwald, Larsson, von Kock, Eklund etc.) was requisitioned according to Radio Sweden by 102 US radio stations during 1979. Virtually no evidence of these presumed radio performances could be found in corresponding returns from ASCAP to STIM in Sweden. Another radio series, 'Pop-rock portraits' had a similar fate. This 6 half-hour series featured popular Swedish artists performing 100 per cent Scandinavian music. It was ordered by 23 US radio stations during 1979 and 57 stations during 1980. Hardly any evidence of radio plays could be gleaned from copyright returns to Sweden.

The explanation for these apparent discrepancies is presumably that the programmes concerned were not lucky enough to get into the sample. Also the sample of non-commercial stations surveyed by ASCAP is smaller than the survey of commercial stations (since 'the fees paid are much lower than those paid by commercial broadcasters'.)

The problem of sampling an ever-increasing field of music usage is one of the reasons why performing right fees seem to go to a mere handful of composers. 12 per cent of PRS' 12,000 associated composers and publishers share 80 per cent of the Society's income. 3.5 per cent share 56 per cent and of the 3.5 per cent (500 members), about 25 per cent are music publishers[6].

Of STIM (Sweden's) almost 11,000 registered copyright owners less than 4,000 earned anything from public performance of their compositions during 1981, and of these, only 185 or less than 2 per cent earned more than £1,000.

Another trend that aggravates this phenomenon is the tendency of radio/TV stations to stick to a Top 40 format. The result is (a) that small spread of composers have their works performed publicly in the media, and (b) that, since distribution of performing right monies are closely geared to radio/TV logs, then those with Top 40 hits tend to pick up copyright monies from other sources.

Finally there is the problem of identification. STIM in Sweden has 1.2 million works of music registered in its card index. Well-known composers are easier to identify than lesser-known creators. If an ABBA song is played on a radio station in Montevideo there is a far greater chance that money will find its way back to Sweden than there is of money from radio plays in Sweden of a Zaïrean composer finding its way back to Kenshasa. Theoretically the chances should be equal, but the amount of 'undistributable income' in every collecting society is proof that this is not the case.

Uncertainty about the future . . .

Yet another explanation for the apparent lack of openness in many copyright organizations is undoubtedly a general feeling of uncertainty about things to come. We live in a music environment characterized by an ever-increasing incidence of home-taping, piracy, satellite transmissions and general usage of music where it is virtually impossible to keep track of the actual works that are performed. At times copyright societies are loath to admit the difficulties experienced in maintaining a genuine democratic profile. New sources of income are constantly sought after (e.g. a levy on sales of blank tapes) without knowing whether any such remuneration can be correctly analyzed with respect to the rightful owners.

At this point it should be made clear that any critical comments here should *not* be interpreted as a dismissal of the performing right copyright system. The difficulties are immense, particularly on the distribution side, but the needs are greater than ever before. Music is heard everywhere, but it is imperative that incomes generated go not only to established international composers, who as a rule are not badly off, but also to the lesser known who are struggling to establish themselves.

One solution which is becoming more popular in the CISAC family is the use of funds, scholarships, and grants to compensate talents that get a raw deal from the conventional distribution systems.

Collecting societies are allowed to retain 10 per cent of their national incomes for activities aimed at stimulating local composers' activities. These monies can be used for information campaigns, subsidizing phonogram productions, travel and study grants etc. The problem is that distribution of such funds is not so easy as one might think. Few composers have developed the art of filling in application forms for stipends. But funding cultural ventures of one kind or another does provide an alternative to paying more to those who already have. Funds from a levy on blank tapes which are merely distributed to the few who already receive most of performing right dues would not seem to have a very positive cultural effect – the people who are really hurt by home-taping are those who are already struggling. At least one phonogram company boss would appear to agree with this analysis (as regards artists and record companies), Ed Cramer writes:

> It hurts the fringes first. That's where it really hurts. If we take ABBA or any artist, they use musicians when they record for example. If the economics of the business change for ABBA, maybe instead of using 30 musicians, they'll use 25 and there will be 5 less who have earned a week's or a month's pay. Some of them will go off and do something else . . . Instead we lose culturally what they have to contribute. Even when it gets to record companies it will probably not affect ABBA . . . but maybe with a change in the business we will record one or two less bands. ABBA stays the same – perhaps they make a little less money, but they stay the same. But there are a couple of new artists that do not get the exposure or the chance of exposure.[7]

BMI's Ed Cramer sees things going from bad to worse unless the whole concept of copyright is subject to radical changes which can bring it up to date with current technology.

> The problem is not just, say, music on television which has been taken off a satellite. It is a universal problem that affects every area of contemporary creativity. The answer, it seems to me, is a new kind of approach to copyright, away from the conventional, with the involvement of as many countries as possible. I find it very frustrating to go to an international (copyright) meeting and find that the big item is a discussion of the Berne Convention of 1908 or the revision of 1920 or whatever it is. So far removed from the problems of the 1980s or the 1990s . . . I think basically the concept (in the copyright laws) has been wrong. We were trying to fit the problems of new technology into a preconceived scheme of copyright dealing with tangible things, with books, photo-copies . . . performing rights. But none of the new means of dissemination of information really fall within the pre-defined categories. And what we are trying to do now is squeeze this new technology and make it fit into these old forms. And frankly, it doesn't fit.[8]

MECHANICAL RIGHTS

Every time an LP is sold in Sweden, the distributor pays about 3 kronor to a joint Scandinavian mechanical copyright society in Copenhagen, NCB. NCB then distributes this money to the copy-right holders (composers, lyricists and publishers). A person in Sweden who writes all the music for an LP is adequately protected by NCB and the law not to need the services of a publisher. Such a composer would receive 100 per cent of the mechanical copyright monies less NCB's administrative costs (about 15 per cent). A sale of 100,000 copies in Sweden would generate a composer income of about £25,000. Had the composer signed away the publishing rights to a publisher then this sum would drop to anything as low as £13,000.

These mechanical right collection societies have the power to audit the books both of phonogram distributors and pressing and duplicating plants. They can also demand advance deposits from manufacturers and distributors thus ensuring that composers get their rightful dues.

The same type of principle applies within the whole of continental Europe, where mechanical copyright societies are organized in an organization known as BIEM. In Britain and the USA, however, publishers can collect mechanical royalties direct from phonogram companies, without going through an independent body, though 25 per cent of mechanical copyright collections in the UK do go through the MCPS (Mechanical Copyright Protection Society), an organization owned by the music publishers.

Mechanical copyright societies can only function if the companies involved in mechanical reproduction agree or are forced through legislation to co-operate. When the PRS and the MCPS tried to start a joint performing and mechanical copyright society in the Caribbean in the early Seventies, their endeavours were not successful. The Caribbean Copyright Organization (CCO) collapsed in 1978 after some local phonogram companies, notably in Jamaica, refused to pay dues. According to the PRS, even the transnationals supplying masters to the Caribbean did not encourage their local licensees to support the CCO. This is probably because transnationals doing lease-tape deals with the Caribbean usually add a few per cent 'for mechanical copyright'.

Attempts to start a mechanical copyright society in East Africa might well meet with the same fate as the now-defunct CCO. Phonogram companies in Kenya usually add a few per cent for mechanical copyright to artists' royalties, in effect, buying the creation outright. This practice is not appreciated by the PRS. Peter Bond says:

I think it is to the great advantage of the local composer if he can get his music recorded by the international record industry, provided there are safeguards to ensure that his interests are properly taken care of – and that's what's lacking. There aren't adequate organizations to look after the local musicians' interests vis à vis the international record industry. I have personally had some quite difficult arguments with some of the subsidiaries in Africa of the international record companies, over the terms on which local musicians' music has been recorded and sold. There's absolutely no doubt that because of lack of understanding among local musicians, and because of lack of knowledge about standard international practice, the record industry has been able to acquire rights at very small costs, and on terms it couldn't possibly have achieved in a developed country. And this is to the detriment I'm sure, of the local musicians.

Question: We were surprised to note that Polygram in Kenya still add an extra percentage to the royalty to cover copyright.

Answer: Well this has been the practice until very recently. In Africa it has been the practice to buy local material from the musician outright, to retain them virtually as recording musicians – to give them £5 and get them to sign a receipt that the whole copyright of everything recorded at that session is the property of the company. There's no doubt that an awful lot of that happens. The IFPI recognise that this is wrong, and there is a change taking place, but it's slow, unfortunately.[9]

CBS' Peter Bond makes it clear, however, that the phonogram industry would like to look after these matters itself:

In Nigeria, for instance, the deal between artists and record company always includes a clause about copyright. And there, it's fast becoming the case that there's no room for such organizations which just act as middlemen . . . if the record companies are reluctant to pay, though, I can see there is a need.[10]

On the face of it this efficiency argument might sound very reasonable, but when songs get distributed through the various branches of a complex organization to every corner of the earth, how on earth can artist/composers check up on what happens to their own intellectual property, without access to some sort of independent organization with international operations?

The smaller mechanical copyright societies in Europe have been confronted with a new problem of late. Structural rationalization within the phonogram industry has included the closure of a number of manufacturing plants. The majors have concentrated their pressing and duplicating activities to plants in Holland, Italy and Germany. If EMI move manufacturing from, say, Sweden to Holland, then NCB (which normally collects mechanical royalties in Scandinavia at the point of manufacture) would have to rely on collecting fees through the Dutch collecting society. These would be based on the inter-company EMI wholesale price, which includes certain rebates, and not on the standard wholesale price in Sweden. In other words, by moving production around Europe, the transnationals can cut their own costs for mechanical dues: the losers, of course, are the copyright holders and their organizations. Not being able to pick up advance payments from local manufacturing units that have been closed down also effects the finances of the small local mechnical copyright collecting societies, since their earnings from interest on capital suffer. Two other small countries, Switzerland and Austria, have also had similar problems. There has been a move on the part of these small countries to have new rules accepted by BIEM, but little has happened. As one Scandinavian representative put it: 'The BIEM organization is dominated by the larger European nations, particularly Germany, France and Italy. A lot of the organization's effort is devoted to conflicts arising from rivalry between the French and German representatives regarding which of them has done most for BIEM.'

It is not always easy to be small – however big the sounds are.

NEIGHBOURING RIGHTS AND OTHERS

We have already referred to the neighbouring rights that are governed by the Rome Convention. 'Rome countries' accept that remuneration should be paid to performers and phonogram companies when phonograms are played on radio/TV. In Sweden the fee in 1983 was in the region of 50 kronor or about £5 per minute (the figure being geared to an inflation index). These monies are divided equally between local phonogram companies and SAMI, a collecting society for performers organized by the Musicians Union. SAMI receives details of all commercial recordings direct from the recording studios, this information being fed into a data bank.

In some other Rome countries, musicians have been content to receive much less than 50 per cent of these dues. Indeed the first international agreement between the International Federation of Musicians Unions (FIM) and the IFPI in 1954 accepted 25 per cent as a reasonable norm! In an additional protocol signed in 1976, the performers' share was increased to 33⅓ per cent.

Neighbouring rights still suffer from the problems of reciprocity. Sweden will pay money as soon as a phonogram recorded in any Rome country is broadcast. But if there is no proper organization for distribution to performers in the country of origin, then the money will stay in Sweden and grow and grow. This problem has been circumnavigated in some cases by signing 'you keep ours, we'll keep yours' agreements such as that between the Swedish and German musicians' unions. Monies originating from Swedish performances in Germany stay there and are used for 'collective

purposes' by the German musicians' union. The converse applies to
German performers' dues in Sweden. (What the IFPI does with this
50 per cent share in such cases is less clear – normally they are
transferred to the distributor who has the distribution rights for the
phonograms in question in Sweden, *after* IFPI have deducted 20 per
cent for so-called 'administrative expenses'.)

The problems of making the Rome Convention function are
illustrated by the fact that after nigh on 15 years of operating,
Sweden's SAMI had a proper reciprocal agreement with only two
other countries, Denmark and Austria. Data are exchanged between these countries and a proper distribution of performers'
monies is attempted. The large sums of money accumulated on
account at SAMI for British performers still lie in Sweden. As early
as 1971 this unclaimed sum amounted to almost 2.5 million Swedish
kronor. A sweet tale is told of the president of the Swedish MU
visiting London in the early Seventies with a cheque for over
£100,000 and not finding anyone amongst his British counterparts
who could help him cash it. Ten years later the situation was exactly
the same, apart from the fact that the sum held on behalf of
unidentified British musicians must be well over £1 million.

These anecdotes illustrate the difficulties of making international
agreements such as the Rome Convention function, difficulties
which are further aggravated by the absence in the Rome family of
two of the larger music-producing nations, the USA and France.
This gives American and French phonograms a financial advantage
in Rome countries – they are cheaper to play – even if this is to the
ultimate financial disadvantage of individual American and French
producers and performers.

Irrespective of the Rome Convention, there are a large number of
countries where some sort of agreement exists regulating payments
from radio/TV for the right to play phonograms. An IFPI report to
Unesco lists 32 such countries[12]. The entry for Jamaica notes
contracts with radio stations dating from 1962. Remuneration is on
a 'lump-sum basis' and '50 per cent of net distributable revenue is
voluntarily paid to a fund established for performers'. We have
been unable to identify such a fund. It appears that distributions to
producers have gone solely to the larger phonogram companies that
have formed a local IFPI 'club'. This assumption is supported by the
findings of a recent Jamaican copyright committee which noted:

> The position in Jamaica now is that the makers of sound record-
> ings, by interpretation of the 1911 (British) Act, enjoy a general
> copyright for their products. The result of this is that they are
> entitled to collect public performance royalties. About four of the
> largest companies do this under auspices of the International

Federation of Phonographic Industries to the absolute exclusion of all other makers of sound recording in Jamaica. Collection from radio stations have been the source of constant income to these four companies.

In other words, none of these monies have been going to the small independent producers.

Jamaica is in the throes of getting a new copyright act and (finally, one might say) signing one or more international copyright conventions. It seems, however, that Jamaica will not give protection to performers and producers by signing the Rome Convention. This decision was apparently based on advice received from an American expert who claimed that signing Rome would make Jamaica a less attractive place for American artists to come and record phonograms. This presumably is because performers' and producers' rights are related to whether or not the country where a recording is made has signed Rome. Food for thought that a country can sacrifice the international rights of its own performers for the sake of attracting work from outside to its recording studios. The effect in Sweden, for instance, will be that Jamaican phonogram performers will not receive remuneration from radio plays for the sake of ensuring that American phonograms recorded in Jamaica will still be cheaper to play. Presumably the Jamaican government has estimated that the cash benefits of establishing the island as a centre for international film and music production outweigh the international disadvantage for its own musicians and record producers.

Where else can the money come from?

As different methods of dissemination of information develop and expand, so copyright organizations will have constantly to venture into new areas where the efforts of the creators are utilized. One area where steps are just beginning to be taken is that of copying machines which reproduce texts and music in printed form.

There are two problems here. One is the usual dilemma, that the users do not want to pay or do not even understand why they should have to pay.

People who have been very well intentioned figure that if they can get something for nothing they are better off and the public is better off . . . the part that is disturbing is that very few people except the writers seem to give a damn.[13]

Sweden is one of the countries where some photocopying agreements have been made between users and copyright holders. Education authorities have signed blanket agreements which allow them to copy material in schools and higher institutions on payment of a lump sum. But then problem two enters the scene. How does one divide up such payments? Spot checks on various samples can be made to get a rough idea, for example, how much music is photocopied, but this does not provide a basis for individual distribution in a situation where not many music or lyric sheets are sold in the open market. This problem can only be solved by making a lot of very rough assumptions.

THE INTERNATIONAL FLOW OF COPYRIGHT MONIES: SOME EXAMPLES

The international copyright system assumes that agreements are reciprocal, that organizations involved in disseminating music are honest and fair, and that some sort of international control can be exerted to maintain a high level of honesty despite any temptations to transgress.

In practice the picture is not so beautiful. Before we quote a number of cases that produce food for thought, let us first summarize the main sources of copyright income. We will consider a recording of a 3-minute popular work, produced in a country which has signed the Rome Convention, which becomes a hit in, say, Sweden. The following Table 9 gives a rough idea of the money flow, indicating that a total of 30,000 Swedish kronor could be generated from copyright and neighbouring rights alone. On top of this the recording might generate profits for local distributors and retailers, a local phonogram company, and, if they have a lease-tape deal, for a foreign phonogram company as well. Note that if the recording was a local production with local music and artists, most of the copyright money would stay in the country.

Do the books tally?

If an international exchange system is functioning properly, then one would expect the figures in the books of one collecting society to tally with those of another with which it exchanges copyright money. A spot-check shows that the figures for at least one of the societies in our sample, DAIC in Chile, do not seem to agree with corresponding figures in the books of either the PRS (UK) or STIM (Sweden).

TABLE 9

COPYRIGHT/NEIGHBOURING RIGHTS INCOMES
CASH GENERATED BY A 3 MINUTE 'HIT SONG' PRODUCED IN A ROME
CONVENTION COUNTRY

Source		Amount in Swedish kronor (SEK)	
Phonogram sales			
50,000 (Mechanical rights)	15,000	7,500 publishers and sub-publisher	
			7,500 composer and lyricist
Radio performance			
(a) Performing right (composer, lyricist, publisher, arranger) 50 plays (@ 50 kr/min)	7,500	3,750 (50%) publisher and sub-publisher	
			3,750 composer and lyricist
(b) Neighbouring rights (performer and producer) 50 plays (@ 50 kr/min)	7,500	3,750 record producer via IFPI	
			3,750 artist/ performer (accumulated with Swedish musicians' union if no recipient can be identified)
TV performances			
10 live performances (@ 165/min)	5,000	2,500 publisher	
			2,500 composer and lyricist
TOTALS	GRAND TOTAL 30,000	Publisher and sub-publisher 13,750	Composer and lyricist 13,750

The payment/receipt ratio for DAIC/STIM shows only a small 6 per cent discrepancy. In absolute terms, however, the figures seem to bear no relation to each other. A Chilean peso was worth around 0.14 Swedish kronor at this time, i.e. 33,961 pesos would be equivalent to almost double what STIM claim to have received. The figures for the PRS and DAIC are harder to compare in absolute terms because of the large fluctuations in the value of the pound during the 1970s. The disparity in the payment/receipt ratio cannot merely be explained in terms of currency fluctuations.

TABLE 10

A COMPARISON OF ROYALTY FIGURES BETWEEN DAIC (CHILE) AND STIM
(SWEDEN), AND DAIC AND PRS (UK)

DAIC's figures (pesos)		STIM's figures (kronor)	
Paid to STIM	Received from STIM	Paid to DAIC	Received from DAIC
1978/79	1978/79	1978/79	1978/79
33,961	20,273	1,432	2,552
Ratio Payments/receipts=1·67		Ratio Receipts/payments=1·78	

Not. 1 peso=app. 0·14 kronor. 33,961 pesos=4,754 kr)

DAIC's figures (pesos)		PRS figures (£)	
Paid to PRS	Received from PRS	Paid to DAIC	Received from DAIC
1974–79	1974–79	1974–79	1974–79
976,786	359,121	464	5,254
Ratio Payments/receipts=2·72		Ratio Receipts/payments=11·32	

Source: 'DAIC Chile Memoria 76–79' and figures supplied by STIM/PRS).

100 per cent becomes 12.5 or less

When Peter Seeger was touring East Africa in the 60s he 'collected' (maybe 'picked up cheaply' would be a better term) a song called 'Malaika'. Seeger arranged for a New York publishing company with which he has close associations, Fall River Inc., to acquire publishing rights outside Kenya. This was done by signing a contract with the phonogram company in Nairobi that first released a recording of 'Malaika', Equator Sound. A Fall River representative, Joy Graeme, gave us the following description of the acquisition of 'Malaika'.

It was discovered by Pete Seeger whilst on a world tour in 1963. He brought it back here, introduced it to us. We acquired the rights and he recorded it . . . . it was being played on the radio [in Kenya], he [Pete Seeger] said it was very popular. We've acquired many songs that way, which he brings back and introduces to us.[14]

The person who claimed to have written 'Malaika', a Kenyan by the name of Fadhili William, was employed at the time by Equator Sound. Fadhili William has been a member of the PRS for some time – the PRS accept that he is the composer of 'Malaika'. Fall River Inc have granted sub-publishing rights to publishers in other countries – these sub-publishers collect 100 per cent of the mechanical royalties that accrue when artists record 'Malaika'. The sub-publishers in the UK, for instance, are Harmony Music (a division of Westminster Music, formerly Essex Music).

Harmony remit 50 per cent of what they collect to Fall River. Fall River keep 50 per cent of all they collect and remit 50 per cent to Equator Sound. Equator Sound split their income 50/50 with Fadhili WEillian. Here we see how 100 per cent becomes 50 per cent becomes 25 per cent becomes 12.5 per cent etc, The money disappears into many pockets along the line.

There's another snag in the 'Malaika' case. Numerous artists have recorded the song (Harry Belafonte, Brothers Four, Pete Seeger etc, etc). It was a hit in Sweden, selling 80,000 copies in 1968 (recorded by the Hep Stars with Benny Andersson, later of ABBA). Fall River Inc. told us that over a million copies must have been sold[15]. Fall River has transferred what is left of mechanical royalties annually to Nairobi. The cheques have always been cashed. Unfortunately Equator Sound has not been more than a post-box address for years. Its owner, Charles Warrod 'hasn't been around in Nairobi for over 15 years'[16], and is believed to be living in South Africa. Fadhili William says he has never received a penny from mechanical copyright.

When presented with this information, Fall River admitted they suspected Fadhili William was not getting even 50 per cent of their remittances to Nairobi, but expressed surprise that Equator Sound was not a functioning enterprise in the Kenyan capital.

I believe he was an employee so I have no idea what the agreement would be . . . I suspect he doesn't get 50 per cent. I think that would be very rare . . . Most employees would not have that kind of contract.
Question: How do you feel about that morally?
Answer: For the average song writer having a job would be a good thing. Of all the songwriters there are, very few are a success. So therefore, if he has a permanent job and song writing is a minor part of it, at least he has employment. He may be lucky. [Regarding Equator Sound's apparent lack of operations in Nairobi] 'Really? They are still collecting royalties. They are still cashing cheques. We haven't had any correspondence with them for years. There hasn't been any need.

Question: You just send them cheques and the cheques are cashed?

Answer: That's right. I looked in the royalty file. I knew you were coming. And everything is paid up to date. But there hasn't been any need for personal correspondence. Only when there are problems.

Question: How much a year would you shift over to Kenya, to Equator Sound?

Answer: I haven't checked. I don't remember.

Question: A very rough estimate?

Answer: I honestly don't know. I don't handle the royalty part so the figures . . . I don't check.

Question: But the cheques are being cashed in Nairobi?

Answer: Oh yes. Any time there is a problem the cheque is still stapled in. You know, sometimes writers move and so we can't trace them for a while. So everything is attached in a folder until such time that we do track them down. Everything is up to date with this company.

Question: I don't know where the money goes.

Answer: That is interesting.

Question: We did make quite a conscious effort to find this company, Equator Sound, but we came to the conclusion that it was a postbox but there didn't seem to be any physical human beings there. The chap had moved to South Africa.

Answer: Oh, I see (Laugh). Then I really don't know what to say.

Question: But you don't transfer money to South Africa?

Answer: No, we have never had a different address. We have always sent to the same place. And we were under the impression that it was a functioning business.

Question: Is it possible that this guy who wrote this song, Fadhili William, in effect gave his song away for a bottle of whisky some night to this chap and that's why he doesn't get any money now?

Answer: I don't know that he doesn't get any money. I thought he was an employee. I know that, because we have a statement to that effect. But I have no idea where he is and if the company is not in existence, then I really don't know what to say. Our agreement is with the publisher. What they do with the writer, of course, is between them. One assumed, and in fact we have an authorized statement from Mr William, that they had the right to act on his behalf . . . . That's very sad, though. If there's money to be made it would be terribly sad if somebody like that were not getting paid. He could probably use the money.[17]

We shall mention that one or two doubts about Fadhili William's claim to the authorship of 'Malaika' exist. Gerhard Kubik in

The Kenyan composer Daudi Kabaka, composer of 'Helule Helule'

Volume 1 of the Cambridge University Press' *Popular Music Year-book* (page 93) claims it was written by a certain Lukas Tututu from Mombasa. This uncertainty does not affect our argument here, however. If Fadhili William is accepted as composer by both PRS and the publishers concerned, then he should be getting his fair share of copyright monies (the PRS *do* remit a percentage of performing fees to Fadhili William in Kenya).

Fall River and their German sub-publisher did have a problem regarding 'Malaika' in 1981. Boney M released 'Malaika' (Ariola 103355) and claimed it was a traditional song, arranged by Farian/Reyam. Mssrs Farian/Reyam thus claimed all copyright money (Frank Farian is Boney M's manager), including publishing (the 'arrangement' was published by Fara Music). Thus when this recording was released and distributed in the UK by WEA Records, copyright money was paid out not to Fall River's London sub-publisher (Harmony Music), but to a German collecting society. No money was flowing back to the country of origin, Kenya.

This was not the first time Boney M delved into the area of the 'public domain' (at least, so they claim) to have access to the extra rewards of copyright monies. Their big hit, 'Rivers of Babylon', was, in fact, an old Rasta chant from Jamaica. An early recording by the Melodians was on the original sound-track for the film *The Harder They Come*.

Returning to 'Malaika', Boney M's recording was not even the first to be released by Ariola without any reference to Fadhili William. In 1979 the group Saragossa recorded the Kenyan song (Ariola 200335) claiming that Rolf Dahmen and Anthony Mann had composed it. Publishing rights were claimed by a firm called Arabella. In other words, once again, nothing went back to Kenya.

As this book goes to press, the computers of the Nordic Copyright Bureau (responsible for distributing to copyright holders royalties from sales of records and cassettes in Scandinavia) read as follows:

	Song title	Copyright owner
1.	Malaika	William F Mdavida Fadhili William
2.	Malaika	Humphries Les Goldy Musikvlg. Hans Sikor
3.	Malaika	Makeba M Makeba Music Corp
4.	Malaika	Farian Frank Farian Frank
5.	Maliaka	Sarc Ronald Countdown Music
6.	Maliaka	Hjalmarsson Anders Bengt Club Mariann Music AB
7.	Maliaka	Bacardi J F Eris Musikverlag

It is interesting that one of the new claimants is Miriam Makeba's own music company, although ten years ago she with Harry Belafonte acknowledged that Fadhili William should have the credit.

Fadhili William is not the only Kenyan who claims he has suffered in this fashion. His colleague, composer Daudi Kabaka, once wrote a song entitled 'Helule, Helule'. It became a minor hit in Britain in the late Sixties when it was recorded by the group, the Tremeloes (CBS 2889). Kabaka was given credit on the record label, but he claims he never got mechanical copyright money. A British firm of publishers, Peter Walsh Music, bought the rights to 'Helule', according to a contract, for the amazing sum of 1 shilling on April 25th 1968.

What do the collecting societies do about such matters? Enquiries at PRS showed that they had both Fadhili William's *and* Boney M's 'Malaika' registered. They had not questioned this double registration, since no one had filed a complaint. Fall River Inc. said they had instructed their German sub-publisher to try to get Boney M to agree to surrender their copyright claim. No one we spoke to seemed to think it would be reasonable to get the Boney M disc blocked through litigation, unless 'it became a big hit and a lot of money is involved'.*

One of the few outspoken luminaries in the copyright world, BMI's president Ed Cramer, did have some harsh words to say about international publishing agreements that merely sap the composer.

Some of the problems that you've raised are not so difficult to solve. For example, you have a publisher in England. That publisher gives the rights to a publisher in France in return for 50 per cent. And every time it goes to another country that 50 per cent is cut in half and it's cut in half and it's cut in half. One of the things you do is you try to protect where the publishers in each country are *related* publishers, that is to say are part of the same conglomerate. You can somehow provide protections for that . . . theoretical protections in contract. I'd like to say theoretical, because I will give you what I consider to be a good example of an analogous situation. Now, this is really true. I am sorry I can't identify the individuals, because if I did anybody in the music industry would know whom I am talking about (even if I mentioned the country). But I was involved in this in my previous life as a lawyer. There was a great discussion going on as to what one of the publishers in a Latin American country would pay, what division he would get, you know (using your example, would he get 50 per cent, would he send 50 per cent back?) And the argument ensued what the percentage would be, and the publisher in that country called his lawyer aside (I was present) and he said: 'Put in whatever percentage you want and I'll pay whatever percentage I want. We'll have a deal'. Unfortunately that's true!
Question: Is that the state of honesty in the business?
Answer: Much of the international dealings are really not monitored carefully. Within each country I think that . . . I wouldn't say they are more honest dealing with their own citizens, but you have jurisdiction over them. If an American writer is being taken advantage of by his American publisher, internally there's something he can do about it. There are local laws, you can grab'em, you can take his property. The same would be true of a British or

* Some months after our first enquiry, however, the PRS decided to accept only Fadhili William (and Equator Sounds') claim to 'Maliaka'.

a French citizen in his own country. But once you depend on accountings from abroad, then you're at the mercy of the people with whom you deal. I really shouldn't say this but that is the fact of life, you know. It's very chancy as to what your returns will be. You've got a publisher who's been around a long time and has a reasonably good reputation, you take a shot at him, but that doesn't mean that you're gonna do well all the time.[18]

FOLK MUSIC: WHO SHOULD GET THE MONEY?

We mentioned that Boney M had borrowed generously from the rich folk heritage of Jamaica. Indeed the whole of the Caribbean has been a gold-mine for lovers, poachers, collectors and exploiters of music. One well-known case which even made the courts in the USA was the song 'Rum and Coca Cola' – a calypso song from Trinidad which an American comedian picked up and claimed he had written. In fact the prosecution showed that the song had already been published in a pamphlet in Port of Spain, Trinidad. Dividing up the income, which was considerable, thanks to the Andrews Sisters' recording, was another problem, since calypsonians regularly borrowed melodies from each other. It's not easy to merge the cultural norms of a society where music is regarded as a gift to the public with the legal norms of a society where individual ownership is the holiest pinnacle! The examples of Caribbean 'gifts' to the world (both voluntary and involuntary) are legion.

The song 'Guantanamera' for instance, comes from Cuba (few would contest that). The Cubans accept that the melody was written by one Joseito Fernandez, who died recently without getting any compensation via copyright. 'Guantanamera' was also a song that Peter Seeger collected. Once again the 'Malaika' publishers, Fall River feature. Neither they nor BMI have been able to send any money to Cuba because of US government restrictions. Instead the cash is held in an 'escrow' account which accumulates interest for the depositor. Fall River as the publishers, presumably retain a percentage of all copyright monies generated from radio plays and phonogram sales. They have had what their London representative described as a 'long-running case' with others who claimed Guantanamera was traditional, in the public domain.

Pete Seeger claimed to have collected it, written new lyrics for it. And a lot of people who came along and recorded it said it was traditional. But the point was that those who had heard it had done so thanks to the Peter Seeger recording. Nobody could claim to have collected it in the same way that Pete Seeger had. So the copyright was really won through that. Because Pete Seeger was the original collector.[19]

Pete Seeger's own version is somewhat different from that of the London publisher. In a letter to a Swedish television producer who was producing a documentary on 'Guantanamera' Seeger wrote:

> I did not intend to keep one penny of any royalties of that song . . . Keep in mind that when a white singer sings an Afro-American song, he/she is in effect stealing. This has happened with jazz, calypso. I used to try to ameliorate the situation by giving a rather detailed translation and story of the composition of Guantanamera, but it become so well known that I had to spare my audiences all this talk . . .
>
> Because of US policy to Cuba, Harold Leventhal (Fall River Inc.) suggested to me that unless someone copyrighted the song, it would become public domain and no money would ever reach Cuba . . . So I agreed on the understanding that all royalties would go into escrow, until they could all be sent to Cuba. My name on the copyright was simply to facilitate this. I did not want my name on it, but I was told that unless it were, the copyright could not be controlled . . . I think Joseito should get the major credit for the song.[20]

The story of 'Guantanamera' (or 'Guajira Guantanamera', 'the peasant girl from Guantanamo', to give its correct Cuban title) is both complex and dramatic. A Swedish television team who tried to clarify the facts, both in Cuba and USA, concluded the following:

Pete Seeger first heard the song from a Cuban music student, Hector Angulos, at an American children's summer camp in 1962. That Angulos knew the song well was not surprising. Every Cuban was used to hearing it daily on Havanna Radio during the 40s and 50s. It was always sung by the melody's acknowledged creator, Joseito Fernandez, 'the King of Melody'. Joseito retained the title but changed the rest of the words daily; improvising on various current events. In other words, the song had the same sort of function that many calypsos had in Trinidad from the 1930s right through to the late Sixties – they presented some of the latest news.

Hector Angulos has also added a new text, not his own, but a patriotic poem of a Cuban poet who died in 1883, José Marti. This was the version Pete Seeger sang. Seeger registered 'Guajira Guantanamera' as a song created by himself and Hector Angulos. It was published by Fall River, who thus received 50 per cent of all incomes. Joseito Fernandez, who had copyrighted the song in Cuba in 1941, received no credit on versions controlled by Fall River.

It was not until 1975 that Fall River changed the credits to include Joseito Fernandez. That was four years after Pete Seeger had visited Havanna to pay his tributes to Joseito. Fall River's chief administrator, Fred Hellerman (musician colleague of Pete Seeger in the Weavers) could give no proper explanation for this delay of nigh on 15 years in acknowledging Joseito's contribution to 'Guantanamera'.

Fall River's lead sheet now reads:

Guantanamera (Guajira Guantanamera)
Original lyrics and music: Joseito Fernandez
Music adapted by Pete Seeger
Lyrics adapted by Hector Angulos based on a poem by José Marti.

(Pete Seeger admits that his only 'musical contribution' was a mistake. He sang the first note of the refrain one tone too high!)

Back in Cuba Joseito Fernandez had this to say:

Pete Seeger thought this was an unknown song and that he could do the same as he's done with other songs . . . He owns record companies, property. What does he do? He takes his guitar and banjo, and goes out singing about the oppressed negroes and comes home with 15 or 20,000 dollars . . . First he pinches the song, then he registers it as something of him and Hector, and sings Marti's verses as though they were his own. . . .[21]

Fernandez was understandably extremely bitter. Any further research into the origins of 'Guantanamera' that rely on Joseito's co-operation would be impractical (he died in 1979). Whether in fact he did actually write the melody is a secret he took with him to his grave – maybe it was an old folk melody; Joseito certainly did popularize it on Cuba. In defence of Pete Seeger it can be said that he did try to ameliorate the situation. But it is also patently clear that Seeger was a victim of a copyright system. Unlike certain other 'collectors' of folk songs, he did at least admit his concern. The extent of Fall River's virtue is less clear. A MISC request for information on the size of the escrow blocked account was turned down. Fall River's spokeswoman said she was not sure 'if such information should be made public'. (If it was, then possibly one could estimate how much money Fall River has made out of this whole affair.)

We should reiterate here that we are not questioning the honesty of Pete Seeger. Our postulate here is that the system forces him to behave in a particular fashion. Indeed, one can observe here a pattern emerging whereby songs from small countries are often picked up and exploited internationally, with the original collector or publisher claiming the copyright on the 'first there, first claim' principle, and with the original *local* composers or 'collectors' getting left out.

This has also been the case with some of Harry Belafonte's world-wide hits. Harry Belafonte achieved worldwide acclaim after releasing an album with the song 'Day O' or 'Banana Boat Song'. The original disc credits the song to Belafonte/Burgess/Attaway. It is published by Shari Music. Shari is the name of Belafonte's daughter. Shari is administered by Fall River Inc. Fall River and Belafonte would certainly admit that 'Day O' is an old Jamaican song that the banana boat loaders sang; this took place at night, and by the end of a shift they were glad that day was 'coming and it's time to go home' (the sleeve of the original album, RCA LPM 1248, makes this patently clear). When a Dutch group, Lobo, recently recorded a disco version and claimed copyright themselves, their claim was contested via a performing rights tribunal in Holland. Fall River/Shari's claim was that they were the first publishers of the song. Earlier Fall River had even got money for themselves, Burgess and Belafonte from Stan Freeburg's parody.

> We won a case against Stan Freeburg on this years ago. He recorded it and then backed down. We claimed that and won the case . . .
>
> Question: You would describe that as an original song, not a traditional song?
>
> Answer: Oh definitely, it's an original song. We have a 100 per cent ASCAP rating on that as we do on 'Jamaica Farewell'. That's why it's so foolish for someone to come along and say it's a traditional song. And there has been nothing according to our musicologist . . . prior to our version. No one has been able to find anything. The man says it's an original song. We take his word. We said if you can find anything prior to this, go ahead. And of course they couldn't.
>
> Question: So the test is who can produce the first recording?
>
> Answer: Not necessarily recording, anything printed. It's very easy to say something's traditional, but prove it.[22]

If Fall River, Harry Belafonte or Lòrd Burgess took the trouble to visit Jamaica and went to see an elderly Scottish gentleman, Tom Murray (Musician, ex-British council representative), they could heard how he collected the 'Banana Boat Song' in the late 1940s. His notated arrangement was published in a collection of Jamaican folk songs by the Oxford University Press in 1952. In 1954, a Trinidadian singer, Edric Connor recorded a selection of these, including 'Day O', with piano accompaniment on Argo RG33 – this was a few years *before* Fall River/Belafonte released it on disc! Tom Murray receives a credit on the Argo disc.

Tom Murray's version of the 'Banana Boat Song' was published first

Why did not the original collector and publisher get the millions generated? Why did not Tom Murray and the OUP take Belafonte *et alia* to court? According to Tom Murray, OUP did consider legal action but gave up the idea because they did not think they could win over Belafonte's American lawyers. All these years, Tom Murray has been blissfully unaware of what he might have earned, with the right legal backing.

The ironic part of the Tom Murray story is that he had to subsidize the printing costs of the original OUP edition to the tune of £150 (OUP wanted a guarantee for the risk involved).

Tom Murray has a philosophic view of the whole affair:

Belafonte had too many lawyers, I got my £150 back, so that was OK with me.

Question: You might have been a millionaire?

Answer: Could I? That would have made a difference in the 50s, but not so now.[23]

Who makes all the money out of 'Day O'? Certainly no cash goes back to Jamaica where the collector lives. One of those who have profited is one Irvine Burgie ('Lord Burgess'), a US citizen from Long Island of Barbadian origin, in whose publicity material we can read the following:

```
                    FOR  RELEASE


Lord Burgess (Irving Burgie), the legendary singer-writer of the
1950's, is surfacing again with some new songs after an absence
of two decades.  Burgess is the composer of such hits as "Jamaica
Farewell," "Day O," "Island in the Sun," "Angelina," "Come Back
Liza," and 37 other songs recorded by Harry Belafonte in the
fifties.
The album Calypso, which he wrote for Belafonte, was the first
million seller album in America.
Among the songs he wrote for the Kingston Trio are such gems as
"The Seine" and "El Matador."
Burgess has been mailed some 2 million dollars in royalty checks to
date (his songs have sold over 100 million records and are still
selling well around the world).
Burgess left the music writing business in a huff in the late '60's,
claiming that the record companies were only interested in push-
ing junk.
......
```

Publicity material from Lord Burgess (Irving Burgie)

How much money did Lord Burgess make personally out of the 'Banana Boat Song'?

I'd say, to me personally, it's been close to half a million dollars. And its total value I would say to everybody is at least 2 or 3 million dollars.[24]

He went on to mention that his income was 'peanuts' compared to what Belafonte had earned from 'Day O' (Belafonte having both artist and publisher royalties).

Burgess admitted to us that 'Day O' *was* based on a banana loaders' song from Jamaica but insisted that:

. . . everything that's done in music has some origin, or some basis. There's nothing new in the world since Schubert or Beethoven, you know, nothing else to write. There's only 12 notes in all music, so how many ways can you turn it . . . .
Nothing is new under the sun. The so-called composers today are tune-smiths. They are not composers. What is there to compose? Everything has been composed before.[25]

An observation of curio can be made here regarding Lord Burgess's actual contribution to the 'Banana Boat Song'. On Belafonte's recordings the refrain reads 'Six foot, seven foot, eight foot bunch', indicating presumably that the Jamaicans must be supermen who grew and carried 'super' bunches of bananas (a plantation that produces eight-*foot* bunches would be quite a botanical sensation). In the original version the size of the banana cluster is measured in 'hands', as was the case in reality. In Tom Murray's collection the banana bunches are their normal size, measured in hands. In a bitter letter to OUP in the late Fifties, Tom Murray wrote 'the nearest Belafonte has ever been to a banana is in a shop.'

Lord Burgess was adamant that another Belafonte hit, 'Jamaica Farewell', was his original song, despite a note on the original release to the effect that it was based on a traditional Jamaican air.

> 'Island in the Sun' is a song I wrote for the film *Island in the Sun*. It's an orginal song. 'Jamaica Farewell' the same. I wrote that for the first Belafonte album and they have both enjoyed tremendous success over the years.
>
> . . . I'm brilliant. I am a great writer. I have a great sensitivity and feeling for the folk. That's why Belafonte used me for so many songs. I have the thing he wants.[26]

Lord Burgess might be interested to learn the following. Whilst rummaging around in a disused pressing plant in Port of Spain, Trinidad, we found some old labels from a Caribbean selection. This listed 'Jamaica Farewell' as a 'traditional song of Jamaica'. This is nearer to the truth than Burgess's version. 'Jamaica Farewell', in fact, is a slight travesty of an old folksong called 'Iron Bar'. It's about a guy who goes to find a girl from Kingston town. In the 'popular folk' version, however, he meets her at a bar, takes her upstairs and breaks the door down with another sort of bar. Thus 'iron bar'. The melody is exactly the same, and the lyrical concept not all that different from 'Jamaica Farewell'. The Jamaica School of Music have tapes featuring commercial recodings of this song dating from around 1950 (e.g., with Lord Fly and the Mapletoft Poulle Orchestra, or with Don Williams Orchestra). Incidentally the 'Iron bar' melody even found its way to Sweden in the early Fifties. It provided the melody for one of the late Ulf Peder Olrog's hit compositions, '*Mera bruk i baljan, boys*' (More mortar in the bucket, boys). Olrog spent some time in ths West Indies in 1948/49.

Seaga's attack and Harry Belafonte's speech of defence . . .

Not everyone in Jamaica appreciates the way their folk heritage has made money for a few in the international music business. The

Back in the Caribbean a local record manufacturer accepts that 'Island in the Sun' is a Belafonte/Burgess composition. 'Jamaica Farewell', on the other hand, is presented as a 'traditional song of Jamaica'

Prime Minister, Edward Seaga, lashed out at Belafonte in a 1983 interview:

> There's no question about it that a number of our folk songs have made a very few people very rich – one of them an internationally renowned so-to-speak calypso singer. We can't protect ourselves internationally against these violations.

(Seaga's anger was augmented no doubt by the fact that Belafonte has previously supported his political arch rival, Michael Manley.)

Belafonte reacts indignantly to charges that he has made a packet out of his own people's heritage without giving anything back. He does not deny that he has borrowed from the culture of the Caribbean. His verbal defence against accusations that he has not even paid copyright money to actual identifiable composers is impressive. This quote is reproduced verbatim from a Jamaican television interview with Belafonte.

> First of all one must understand that any people who were the victims of colonialism, and all of the peoples of the under-developed countries of the third world are the victims of cruel exploitation, a lack of knowledge in how to formulate, how to deal with legal matters; constitutional questions, international-ism and all kinds of things, plague us. When I started out singing songs that, as we say in the US, are in the public domain – this

means that they were written so long ago that two things have happened; either under law those copyrights are no longer honourable . . . or they don't know who the author is at all. So in the beginning, when I did certain songs of which adaptations were made, a lot of those songs fell into the arena of what I understood to be public domain. For instance, I don't know who was the writer of the 'Banana Boat Song' . . . There are other songs, however, where we did know the writers and in every instance it was my personal responsibility and that of my own integrity to pursue and find those writers, many of whom existed in places like Barbados and Trinidad. When I found those writers and they were notified that we were doing the tune they had written, we then found out – and it can still be checked – that other people had come to the West Indies, other publishers from North America, and had got all of these people to assign their copyrights to North American entities. So as a consequence, when the material became successful, all the cheques that were written with royalties went to the legal entity to whom those people had assigned their rights. I can specifically identify people like Lord Melody (Fitzroy Alexander) from Trinidad. When we sent money to Fitzroy, he had no legal rights over it any longer because he'd made a deal with an American firm, taking the bulk of his earnings. So if the money didn't find its way into the hands of those people, it wasn't because Belafonte didn't pay. First of all, I must tell you that I have no rights to pay. When I record for a record company it's up to the record company to pay. When I found how the mechanism works, I then set up my own legal institution that would then be able to relate to these artists directly and that problem now does not exist.

I think it is a wee bit unfair to claim that I have exploited West Indian material . . . It is true to say that I've taken a lot of material from here, that I've changed it and that it is not as identifiable with its original form as many people would like it to be – but I will always do that.

Did I at any time perform material that was abusive to black people anywhere in the world? Did I at any time perform material that violated the integrity of black people, the hopes and aspirations of black people? Did I at any time do anything that embarrassed black people? . . . .

Yes, I am guilty of having taken a lot of material, having redefined it, changed a word here or there to get an audience involved in what the West Indies was about. Because all the songs that were popular in North America at the time were not things I would wish to be associated with. All the calypsoes were very sexist, very anti-black, very anti-women; they were not to the best interests of the people of the West Indies. They put a lot of white people in North America into a wonderfully racist feeling about us; we were happy natives sitting under a coconut tree who were objects of sexuality. I found that concept terribly offensive; I didn't want to sing songs about what our sexual powers were or were not, no matter who found humour in that.

What I tried to do when I did a thing like the Banana Boat – I tried my hardest to show that work on a banana boat was hard. 'Work all night for a drink of rum' was just about the pay, 'cause we didn't get paid for the work we did for our colonial masters.

. . . I thought the people of the world should know who we are, as a people. And last but not least, I think the most important thing, because I am a person of great social consciousness, a very political person, because I am involved in the liberation movements of peoples all over the world – the most important thing . . . is that I will never be caught doing anything anti-black that would be considered racist or ever appeasing reactionary forces, I just cannot do that.[27]

The Caribbean gold mine, continued

Trinidad, as Harry Belafonte pointed out, has been another vein in the Caribbean gold mine for songs. What has made it harder for calypsonians to control their intellectual property is that from the mid-thirties onwards, they had to go to New York to record. Around 1935, a local Port of Spain businessman started taking some of the more established calypso singers once a year to New York. Artists such as the Roaring Lion, the Growling Tiger, the Lord Beginner, Attilla the Hun, Radio etc, would then record all their current repertoire straight on to wax discs (the technique used at the time). The Growling Tiger claims to have recorded no less than 35 songs on one session without making a mistake, i.e. without spoiling a single wax master!

Tiger told us that one such song, recorded in 1936 on the Decca label with Gerald Clark's Caribbean Orchestra, was entitled 'Take me down to Los Cedros'. (Los Cedros is a beach on Trinidad.) Tiger does not have the disc any longer, but he claimed that the other side of this disc was Radio's 'Maintain your child' sung by Tiger and Radio. A few years ago Neville Marcano (alias the Growling Tiger) received the lead sheet for a song called 'Take me down to Lovers' Row' published in an album. The song credits read 'Growling Tiger and Don Raye'. Neville Marcano says he has never signed a publishing contract with anyone, never received any publishing royalties and never met anyone by the name of Don Raye.

Two grand but angry old men of Calypso. Neville Marcano, alias Growling Tiger: 'It's prostitution'. Raphael de Leon, alias Roaring Lion: 'I'd like to turn Belafonte into a pin cushion'

A probable explanation for this confusion is, as Belafonte indicated, that the Tiger might have signed away all his rights forever way back in the Thirties, either to a local entrepreneur, to Decca (USA) or to an American publisher. Another complicating factor is that Tiger only recently became a member of a collecting society (the PRS) – throughout 35 years of songwriting he had enjoyed no protection for the performing right of his compositions! Both Tiger and his colleague of the same vintage, the Roaring Lion, claimed to have seen their own works exploited by others. Both accused Harry Belafonte of being one of the guilty parties. Belafonte's defence in this matter has already been cited. All we can add is that Raphael de Leon (the Roaring Lion) recorded a song on Decca in 1936 entitled 'Out de fire'. Belafonte sings a similar song with the same title on two different LPs – a 'Carter' is named as composer on each!

The confusion we have described here illustrates, once again, how international copyright systems can come into conflict with traditional thinking. Up to 1970 musicologists have estimated that about 50 melody types had been developed by the calypsonians. These 50 basic structures were used over and over again, and were traded freely between different composers. The uniqueness of a new calypso was to be found in the *combination* of choice of topic, text and melody, with the emphasis on the first two. This is quite a normal situation in folk music cultures. The identity of the actual composer becomes irrelevant in the traditional system. This 'positive' public domain attitude can of course be totally exploited by the legally wise when exposed to a system where the first registered copyright claimant is accepted as the legal owner. Many popular songs in Western music suffer from the same problems – they are variants of similar basic structures. When disputes arise in such cases, only the more spectacular examples (i.e. where there is a lot of money involved) ever hit the headlines. It is not surprising that the situation we have described backfired in the Caribbean, once calypsonians became aware of the fact that they were missing bits of the cake (however small). The same process can be noted in Jamaica. Composers have a deep mistrust not only for the international music industry but also for many of their own 'brothers', who they suspect might be its agents. When a large number of creative composers suddenly become aware of things like performing and mechanical rights, suspecting rightly that they have been ripped off for years, then the result unfortunately is a total lack of faith in those who run the business of music. This mistrust extends, sad to say, even to those who happen to be honest. Hardly a positive development.

Looking after your folklore heritage
– WIPO models and other means

It is important that any moral indignation the cases this section might have aroused is aimed at the right targets. With the system of copyright that has developed anyone is legally free to make money out of music that is genuinely in 'the public domain', i.e. truly traditional where the composer has been dead more than 50 years or cannot be identified. There are two moral aspects to this.

The first is illustrated by this quote from Belafonte's colleague Lord Burgess. When asked how he would react to someone recording 'Jamaica Farewell' or 'Day O' similar to Belafonte's version and claiming it was traditional, he answered:

> We sue them. If anybody does that, we sue them. They can't. I have an original copyright, registered with the Library of Congress. I do that with all my work. The burden of proof. They have to come up with copyright that predates mine. They can't do it, because it was original with me.[28]

This raises the first moral question. Even if Burgess was the first person to copyright the 'Banana Boat Song', albeit with a few minor alterations from the song as it is sung on Jamaica, then should this give him the right to charge anyone else who uses it?

The second moral question concerns the country of origin of a traditional song. If someone or some persons make a mint out of exploiting songs that the people of Jamaica developed through years of toil and struggle, should not something filter back to them? If the answer is YES, then a tougher question follows in its wake; if so, who on Jamaica should get the cash?

The World Intellectual Property Organization, WIPO, has considered these problems and come to the conclusion that some sort of control of folklore heritage is to be recommended. Realizing that international control is not easy, as things are at the moment, WIPO has suggested a form of national legislation. This is the essence of the Tunis Model Law for Folklore (1976). According to this suggestion, all users of folklore heritage in a country should be bound to get licences from some official authority. The income from these licences should then be used to support the activities of those who carry on the folklore traditions of that country. This would include support to researchers, archives, folk musicians etc. The WIPO law embodies a wide concept of folklore, covering everything from architecture and art to music and dance.

If enough countries accepted such legislation (however hard it is to police) then some type of international exchange and control could be organized between their countries. This would provide a theoretical way of coming to terms with the uncontrolled international exploitation of folk music that occurs at present. The future, however, would not look too bright for such a concept if it were treated in the same way as, say, the Rome Convention has been treated by the largest user nation, the USA.

Somewhat surprisingly, Jamaica, has not opted to include coverage of folklore in the new copyright legislation which was in the pipeline in 1983. The copyright committee concluded that:

> Schemes for protecting folklore do not function adequately in practice. The mechanisms necessary would include a procedure for the certification and defining of works as folklore and naturally a procedure for appeal against classification and the maintenance of a register of certified works containing the full text or description of the work. The cost in terms of skilled personnel and storage facilities would not be negotiable. Further, the mechanics of international protection do not exist so that even if provisions exist in national legislation for the protection of folklore, the material would not receive international protection.[29]

This last conclusion is somewhat surprising, since it is our understanding that an international system for folklore protection can only function when enough nations have protective legislation on a national level. Indeed the Jamaican copyright committee's ambivalent attitude to folklore is summed up in the following sentence: 'Notwithstanding the difficulties involved, the committee is committed to the principle of the protection of folklore under copyright legislation.' The committee finally recommended a sit-on-the-fence approach, until WIPO could come up with something better. In other words, Lord Burgess will continue to be able to earn money, even if Harry Belafonte's version of 'Day O' is performed publicly in Jamaica. Jamaican PM Edward Seaga explained why:

> We can't protect ourselves internationally against these violations, we can protect ourselves nationally. But even if we were to enact provisions which would protect us in the use of folk material, until it is recognized internationally, there is no protection overseas . . . Until the various conventions such as Berne, UCC etc, find a way of defining folk material, what falls in the public domain, there is no purpose in enacting legislation because you can only use that legislation effectively within your own territorial boundaries.[30]

WIPO seems to have had more success in affecting the copyright laws of our Asian sample country, Sri Lanka. The new Sri Lankan copyright law includes folklore. Folklore, according to the law, is the property of the state and should be administered by the Ministry of Culture. The law gives this ministry the power to grant permissions to users of Sri Lankan folklore and to invoke sanctions when such legislation is ignored. It will probably take some time before this law is implemented since the country's relation to the international products of the entertainment industries is somewhat unclear. Sri Lanka, like many small nations, is *not* a net exporter of mass culture. Complete enforcement of the new copyright law would inevitably mean a drain of the country's foreign currency reserves. Thus Sri Lanka does not feel the urge that one would expect to observe in the case of Jamaica, to become part of the international copyright exchange system.

The Swedish folk music fund

Swedish music in the public domain is not the property of the Swedish state. On the other hand a voluntary agreement has been made between various users of folk music. This recognizes that use of folk music does give extra profits to publishers, radio companies, phonogram companies etc. The extra monies arise either from claiming copyright in the absence of an identifiable composer, or from using such music where this is not the case, and performing and mechanical rights do not have to be observed. The agreement also recognizes that such heritage does not survive on its own without the help of those musicians, enthusiasts, archivists and researchers who devote their time to keeping folklore traditions alive.

The users who benefit financially from the fact that some music is in the public domain are:

> phonogram companies (a standard LP of non-copyright music gives in effect an extra profit of SEK 3 or about 30 pence since mechanical copyright payments will not be claimed).
> publishers and arrangers (they can copyright arrangements of public domain music and thus, in effect, claim the composer's royalties).
> concert organizations (who could claim relief from performing right fees if it can be shown that the music played has not been registered with a collecting society).
> collecting societies (who would still receive payment for performances including public domain works via the system of 'blanket licences').

These are the types of organizations that contribute voluntarily to the Swedish folk music fund. Annual payments are made by the Swedish phonogram producers, by the Swedish Broadcasting Corporation, by various concert promotion organizations, the Swedish performing right society (STIM) etc.

Those who work actively with keeping Swedish folk music alive can apply for project grants from this fund. Each year the fund receives about 70 to 80 applications and awards around 25 grants ranging in size from £100 to £2,000.

INTERNATIONAL EXCHANGE: THE OPERATIONS OF THE MCOS

In East Africa, the Caribbean and Asia we have come across the operations of the MCOS (Music Copyright Overseas Services). This is part of the overseas wing of the PRS in London. Its activities used to be described as Commonwealth Licensing by the PRS[31], an indication of the fact that its origin was to be found in the British colonial empire. The fact that so many of its collecting offices still function even in independent countries was partly the basis of our statement earlier that the PRS did not disband its empire when Britain gave independence to its colonies.

The major task of these offices is to collect performance fees, on the basis of whatever copyright law can be applied, and return them to London for distribution. In some areas the PRS has also accepted local composers as members. The extent of this has varied from country to country. Up to 1981, the PRS in Kenya had only nine members, two of which were publishing companies. The PRS representative in Trinidad has helped almost 200 local composers join the organization. This means that the PRS agrees to collect for them internationally, as well as locally. Money and data collected are transferred to London where distribution takes place. In other words, the money sent back to Trinidad should be a measure of how much Trinidadian music is played both locally and internationally. In the case of PRS operations on behalf of the 1,000 registered Jamaican composers, one would expect the returns to be considerably larger than what is merely collected in Jamaica. This, however, is not the case:

In Table 11 the low figures for money returned to East Africa would seem to indicate that no East African music is ever performed publicly in Kenya. This of course is not the case. This unsatisfactory situation stimulated a number of local composers to start their own copyright society, the MPRSK (Musicians Performing Rights Society of Kenya). The sudden small but statistically significant increase in returns to £5,000 in 1981 is probably a reflection of the PRS' desire to reach an agreement with this body. The PRS, as we will

Big sounds from small peoples

TABLE 11

A COMPARISON OF ROYALTIES COLLECTED BY PRS AND PAID BACK TO
LOCAL COMPOSERS

Country/Area	Year	For all music performances – Collected by PRS local agency (£)	Paid back by PRS for global rights of local composers (£)
East Africa	1978	24,293	1,170
(mainly	1979	43,397	600
Kenya)	1980	37,612	1,213
	1981	33,988	5,000
Jamaica	1978	56,043	35,165
	1979	58,757	51,025
	1980	69,531	78,945
	1981	75,823	80,313
Trinidad	1978	65,669	33,694
	1979	90,066	25,773
	1980	111,864	34,234
	1981	152,217	37,313
		700,000	384,345

note later, then proceded to establish a local office in cooperation with the MPRSK. However, analysis of performances and distribution was still to be carried out in London.

It might seem extraordinary that the copyright money generated by the global success of reggae should be less or only little more than the PRS collect annually in Jamaica. Indeed the returns quoted here are in the region of one-tenth of what one single group (ABBA) generate for Sweden. Can this possibly be correct? The PRS explanation is that some of the big Jamaican copyright earners (e.g. Marley) have transferred their membership to American societies (the term 'poaching' was used). Another reason according to the PRS was that some Jamaican composers register themselves in London or some other Caribbean country in order to avoid having to receive their income in taxed Jamaican dollars.

Collecting and distributing money through the MCOS would appear to be a costly business, as these figures from Jamaica indicate. The year was 1981 and the figures are quoted in the *PRS Yearbook*.

Collected in Jamaica (gross)	£75,823
Less local expenses and taxes (28%)	£21,571
Collected in Jamaica (net)	£54,252
Less PRS expenses in London (22.5%)	£12,206
For distribution to members	£42,046

Of the 75,000 collected, only little more than 40,000 was distributed to members.

Local expenses in Kenya in 1980 amounted to 27 per cent of the monies collected. A local office was established the next year by the PRS in cooperation with the MPRSK, according to the PRS principle of 'helping to establish and assist new societies' in MCOS territories. In its second year of operation, this PRS supported venture had the following budget. The VOK payment refers to the annual remuneration from the Voice of Kenya Broadcasting monopoly for the right to play music.

The income this new venture was expected to generate was admittedly somewhat higher than in 1979/80, but running costs had

TABLE 12

MPRS/PRS LICENSING OPERATIONS – 1982 BUDGET

		1982	(1981)
Estimate royalty collections	KSH	KSH	
General performances	463,000		
VOK payment	225,000	688,000	(602,716)
Estimated expenditure			
1. Personnel – Salaries, allowances, inspections and other fees, insurance	296,000		
2. Office rent	110,000		
3. Office expenses – stationery, telephone, postage, telex	32,000		
4. Office equipment maintenance	2,500		
5. Car maintenance, insurance	17,220		
6. Legal fees	4,000		
7. Sundries and contingencies	12,000	473,720	(502,555)
		214,280	

Source: MPRSK (Nairobi).

increased to nearly 70 per cent of collections. And distribution was still to be carried out in London at PRS HQ. When questioned about this, a PRS official said he would defy anyone to run an office in a cheaper way. If this is so, then some other solution would appear to be required for the composers of Kenya.

Our purpose here is not to question the administrative or business acumen of the PRS. The PRS have set themselves a very tough, if not impossible task. The aims of the MCOS are, in practice, incompatible. The agencies in the various territories are supposed to look after the interests of the PRS by generating money for PRS repertoire. In 1981 they provided an operational surplus of £340,000 and a contribution to head office expenses of £100,000. At the same time the PRS has committed itself to 'CISAC's declared policy of providing aid to developing countries in the field of copyright in co-operation with WIPO and Unesco by helping to establish and assist new societies'. If the PRS achieves this goal too efficiently, then (a) its own agencies and fund raisers would become redundant, and (b) it would lose control over those territories. This has not been a problem in places like Australia or New Zealand. But things have not been so easy in the developing countries. The PRS burnt their fingers in Ghana, where the society they helped to set up (GOPS) apparently never sent any more money back to London after the MCOS closed down. The PRS lost about £28,000 in the course of the abortive attempt to start the CCO (Caribbean Copyright Organization). This dilemma was summed up well by a MCOS representative in a small country who said about the local composers: 'There's no way we'll ever let those boys collect for our international repertoire'. With such vibrations of distrust in the air, it is not surprising that the PRS's benevolent aims regarding developing nations sometimes end up in a cul-de-sac. This was illustrated in the mid-Seventies by the case of Rhodesia. One would think that an organization that supported the cultural goals of Unesco vis-à-vis the developing nations would have avoided having deals with the regime of Ian Smith during the UDI sanctions period. The PRS maybe felt this way, but business was more or less the same as usual. MCOS collections in Rhodesia were stopped and the South Africans were asked to take over on PRS's behalf. The year after the PRS accounts showed an increase of £50,000 from the South African organization SAMRO 'in respect of arrears'. Business indeed was almost as usual.

Once again may we stress that our intention here is not to arouse pangs of moral indignation. This example merely illustrates how hard it must be for the PRS to marry the contradicting terms of the MCOS' brief, namely to increase revenue from its territories, and at the same time hand over responsibility to local interests in accordance with Unesco/WIPO principles of cultural independence. The latter becomes even harder to perform in a situation where none of the parties involved trust each other.

PAYING OUT MORE THAN THEY GET:
THE CASE OF SMALL COUNTRIES

The case of ABBA and Sweden

The small Scandinavian nations pay out far more copyright monies than they receive from performances of Scandinavian music abroad. This can be illustrated by the following two year comparison of their accounts with the PRS in London.

The fact that Norway paid the PRS £110,000 in 1980, but received only £4,000 is an indication that Norwegian music is virtually never performed publicly in Britain or any of the other PRS territories. This negative cultural balance has remained as extreme for Norway, Denmark and Finland throughout the Seventies. The figures for Sweden differ considerably. This is purely the effect of the group ABBA who copyright their own songs with the Swedish collecting society STIM. Performances of ABBA songs generated about £100,000 in PRS territories alone during 1980. ABBA account for almost 80 per cent of all the money that is returned to Sweden from public performances abroad. This does not necessarily mean that no other Swedish music is performed internationally. The spread of ABBA facilitates identification *and* access to sampling systems.

Despite the global 'successes', of ABBA, however, over 60 per cent of all the monies collected by STIM in Sweden still leave the country. This is simply because 60 per cent of the music performed on the state broadcasting corporation is of Anglo-Saxon origin. Only 30 per cent is Swedish.

TABLE 13

A COMPARISON OF TWO YEARS' ACCOUNTS FOR SCANDINAVIAN
COUNTRIES WITH PRS

Country	Year	Received by PRS	Paid out by PRS	Received by PRS	Paid out by PRS
		1974		1980	
Sweden		133,000	5,000	270,000	118,000
Norway		43,000	1,000	110,000	4,000
Denmark		106,000	13,000	134,000	28,000
Finland		69,000	17,000	100,000	34,000

These statistics prompted the Swedish Society of Composers to point out recently that: 'If only the percentage of national repertoire could be increased to 35 or 40, then there would be no real problems for our professional composers earning a living.'

This simplification might sound rather naïve, but bear in mind that with a total income for STIM of around £5 million a year, a 10 per cent increase in usage of *Swedish* music would provide an extra £500,000 for distribution amongst Sweden's active copyright holders. This is quite a considerable sum of money in a small country. Under such circumstances the Swedish Society of Composers' exhortation to the Broadcasting Corporation to play more Swedish music can hardly be dismissed as propaganda for vested interests.

The problem of supporting local composers has also been spotlighted in neighbouring Denmark. Denmark has no ABBA generating £1 million a year, even if some of their popular artists and groups have achieved international acclaim (names like Savage Rose, Gassoline, Kim Larsen come to mind). Danish composers have chosen a unique approach to the problem of an excess of foreign music on the radio draining much of the copyright monies out of the country. They have changed the weighting in the distribution system so that less account is taken of radio performances (particularly late at night) and more attention is paid to live performances in clubs where one might expect more local music to be performed. In other words, a composer will receive more for a performance at a local venue than previously, and a radio play will pay the composer less.

The aim of this Danish exercise is quite clear. Whether the means chosen will work remains to be seen. Any distribution based on returns from numerous live performances will lead to a considerable increase in administrative costs for the Danish collecting society. *If* these difficulties can be solved, then this would be one method for composers to get the support they need when broadcasters are not willing to give fair backing to local culture. This reconstruction would not appear to conflict with the rules concerning equal treatment for composers irrespective of country of origin embodied in the Berne convention and CISAC regulations. An American song performed in a club will still earn as much as a Danish song.

WILL THERE BE ANY MONEY? IF SO WHERE WILL IT GO?

A summary of music copyright problems

As our many examples have shown, the problems of remunerating creative people when their works are used in public are immense.

TABLE 14

COPYRIGHT IN THE MISC SAMPLE – SUMMARY OF CURRENT STATUS

Scandinavia –	Sweden/Denmark have observed the Rome Convention for some years. Finland signed in January 1983. Norway gives phonogram producers/performers some protection but all the monies stay in the country. All the Scandinavian nations have large 'copyright' trade deficits with the UK/USA (including Sweden, despite the ABBA incomes). Composers do not usually have to rely on a publisher to get their dues.
Kenya –	Member of the UCC. PRS via the MCOS have been collecting performing royalties for a number of years. Local composers not normally organized by the PRS have started their own society (MPRSK). Co-operation with the PRS has not been too smooth, thanks to mutual distrust. Phonograms enjoy legal protection against unauthorized duplication. No functioning mechanical copyright except when included in artist royalties by the major phonogram companies.
Tanzania –	Has not signed any international conventions. Radio Tanzania records much local music and considers that it buys the copyright outright when it pays artist fees. Pending possible international success of East African music could lead to a potential loss of income if copyright problems (including infrastructure) are not solved soon.
Tunisia –	A collection society (SODACT) was established by law in 1966. It is closely related to the ministry of culture. Has not been able to come to terms with the explosive growth of pirate copies on cassettes. Receives foreign income via SACEM in France, but considers the returns far too low.
Sri Lanka –	For many years was a territory of the PRS' MCOS. Got a new national copyright law in 1980 which was partly based on advice from WIPO. According to this, folklore is covered and is regarded as the property of the state. A collection society has been started on the initiative of the Registrar of Patents. Much pirated material from Singapore, but also much local repertoire, some of which is beginning to be pirated.
Jamaica –	One of the most productive music nations of the world which has not been attached to any international convention since it gained independence. New copyright law in the pipeline will probably lead to signing Berne or UCC (not Rome or Geneva). PRS active, mainly with collecting royalties. Distribution controlled by PRS London. Monies received from PRS only one-tenth of Sweden's receipts for ABBA.

TABLE 14 – *cont.*

COPYRIGHT IN THE MISC SAMPLE – SUMMARY OF CURRENT STATUS

Trinidad –	Active music scene for many years. PRS operations as in Jamaica, with recent increase in locally registered members (200, mainly calypsonians). No up-to-date copyright law or international conventions. Government considering moves.
Chile –	Copyright distributions organized for many years by DAIC, a department at Universidad de Chile, Santiago. DAIC has also received performers'/producers' royalties according to Rome, but none have been distributed (1981). Dissatisfaction with DAIC has stimulated some members to start a rival organization, SAIC, which has also been accepted as a member of CISAC.
Wales –	Performing rights organized totally by the PRS in London under the terms of British copyright law. Rome/Geneva also apply.

This, of course, is no reason for not tackling them. Some of our sample countries will have to give the copyright area highest priority if their composers are to retain any of their dues. This will require up-to-date legislation. Laws, however, are not enough. Any proper copyright system should have as its ultimate goal keeping the creators alive and creating. A good law, thus, is worthless if it is not backed up by a proper infrastructure for collecting and redistributing income generated. Unfortunately, all the systems currently in operation find it very hard to keep abreast of the rapid development of music industry technology. Let us sum up some of the problem areas.

Legislation

Copyright laws generally lag behind the technological state of the art. This is a natural result of any society's wish to gather data on the effects of changes before controlling them via legislation. Some of our study sample are still living with copyright legislation written at the turn of the century. Even Jamaica, which is planning up-to-date legislation that recognizes the spread of satellites etc, is still not sure how to legislate on the control of all aspects of electronic reproduction and dissemination.

> We believe that the legislation we are about to enact does take into consideration all the most advanced thinking . . . . that doesn't mean that the legislation will be up-to-date with the state

of the art, because, as you know, there is a turmoil in the industry as regards satellite transmission and a number of other areas of alleged piracy. . . . There are other developments regarding tapes and even photocopying machines that we may not be at this stage ready to incorporate in our law, and for that reason, it's true to say that there is a lag in the legislation because technology is changing so fast.[32]

Even if modern legislation is adopted, it might not be in a nation's economic interest to implement it if other countries with which it exchanges cultural material do not reciprocate. Without a proper infrastructure through which its own composers' works can be identified, a country like Sri Lanka would experience any implementation of its new copyright law or any international conventions as a loss of foreign currency. What could change this attitude would be cases arising from international exploitation of Sri Lankan music. The situation for Jamaica (and of course Tanzania) is very different. These countries are, or could develop the potential to become, net exporters of the creative works of their own people.

Technology

Music industry technology is developing by leaps and bounds. Incomes of creators and performers whose efforts provide the software have not increased at anything like the same pace. This is partly because it is not in the interests of all users to pay, and partly because of the difficulties of defining who should get what?

Collecting copyright money

Getting users to pay, as we have noted, might be easier than distributing the spoils, but it still presents plenty of head-aches. The spread of music via new technology and increasing uncertainty about the actual number of recipients has led collecting societies to sign more and more blanket agreements. But Jamaica, for example, has decided that any satellite transmissions that enter the island's airspace are the responsibility of the original transmitter and can therefore be picked up for free. Can one demand compensation from CBS or ABC for this spill-over effect? What will the situation be for small countries who cannot afford to advertise their creative artists via satellite transmissions?

Distributing copyright money

Even when the money flows in, the problem of finding a rightful owner remains. With increased usage, societies have had to rely more and more on various sampling systems which inevitably favour easily identifiable well-known composers. There are various ways of compensating for this effect. Societies make 'allocations', i.e. a lump-sum basic payment to all their active members. CISAC allows its member societies to use up to 10 per cent of their turnover for activities aimed at stimulating national music. Voluntary agreements such as the Swedish Folk Music Fund also provide alternatives.

It can be predicted that this trend towards redistribution according to ambitions of cultural policy, away from imperfect compensation will continue. This will apply to both large and small countries. In Sweden, for instance, analysis of radio performances could be carried out exactly when there was only national radio coming from one monopoly. When so-called 'Närradio' (app. neighbourhood radio) was introduced in the late Seventies, those providing localized programmes were expected to pay music licences but not to report which music they played.

The distribution of income from levies on blank tapes and similar sources provide even greater problems of distribution. Who should be compensated? The few who already have enough money but clearly lose out on home-taping? Or should the money be used to stimulate creative activity in general. Deliberations of this type result inevitably in collecting societies making decisions of a cultural policy nature. How will this affect their traditional independence from the state in many countries? Would it be a good thing to have a society of composers following one cultural policy, and their Ministry of Culture (Arts) following another?

The problems of identification leading to a small number of copyright holders receiving most of the proceeds have led to the introduction of income ceilings in another copyright area. The Swedish Confederation of Authors who administer payments to authors when their books are borrowed at libraries, have a sliding scale. Authors receive less per borrowing when, say, 100,000 people have read a book. This is regarded as a democratic way of stimulating other authors than those few at the top of the popularity poll. No music collecting society, as far as we know, has considered introducing similar principles. On the contrary, a BMI work that has been played 1 million times receives four times more per performance than a work that has been played ten thousand times on USA radio. ASCAP pay out more to the writers of older compositions than those of new ones. Such practices, even if they *can* be motivated from a musical point of view, would hardly seem to be compatible with democratic demands arising from the current problems of fair distribution.

Who created what?

The problems of *identification*, with an ever-increasing global repertoire of music, are hardly likely to decrease however much modern
information technology is applied. There will also be a growing
problem of *definition*. Does opening and shutting a gate on a pair of
rusty hinges (oh for a can of oil!) constitute a work of music?

Or consider the following. A group of Jamaican session musicians
put down a rhythm on a multi-channel recording tape. It becomes
the property of a producer. Sometime later, a pianist adds some
'fill-ins' and a basic melodic structure. Over the next year a number
of artists record songs with melodic differences on top of this tape.
This happens all the time in Jamaica. Who are the composers? How
should copyright fees be divided? Unless the concerned parties can
agree, they will almost certainly end up getting nothing.

This situation cropped up in 1982 in connection with one of that
year's biggest hit songs in the Anglo-Saxon world, 'Pass the
Dutchie' by Musical Youth from Birmingham. The record label
credits a Jamaican keyboard player and two members of the group
The Mighty Diamonds. Musical Youth and/or their advisers must
have known that it was a combination of two Jamaican records
released on the same label in Kingston, using the same backing
track but with different artists. The Mighty Diamonds had released
a song called 'Pass the Kouchie' on their album entitled *Changes*
(Music Works BS LP 11981). Gussie Clarke who owns Music Works
had also released a 'DJ' version with one Hugh Brown rapping over
the same backing track ('Gimme the Music' with matrix number
MWRT-1003-A). Musical Youth created their big hit by putting these two together. At least four Jamaican artists/composers
had a claim to this song, and Musical Youth's copyright royalties
were made subject of 'copyright control' (a sort of quarantine)
whilst the question of ownership was sorted out. Sorting this out was
not easy. Who actually owned the song? The musicians who laid the
original track, a keyboard player who came in later, the Mighty
Diamonds, Hugh Brown, Gussie Clarke's European publisher?
When we left the Caribbean in February 1983 it looked as though it
would take quite some time to sort this out.

Whose interests should dominate?

The flow of copyright monies should not only take account of
technological changes, the system should also adapt itself to organizational and financial changes in the music environment. The
significant entity here, as we have seen, is the music publisher. The
music publisher's role and organizational status have changed over

the years, and this fact must reasonably affect their activities and influence in societies whose prime interest should be the wellbeing of individual creators.

What these cases do show is that the system, including the role played by different actors, must be re-appraised if the traditional donors of raw materials (the countries where many of our popular songs have originated) are to be incorporated in a functioning system of international copyright.

Redistribution or compensation?

Probably the most vital issue we have touched upon in this chapter is the question of what principle should apply when copyright monies are to be distributed. Most collecting societies, in fact, adopt a pragmatic approach, compensating according to available data, and redistributing via allocations, scholarships etc. The two extremes, however, would still seem to be regarded as mutually incompatible opposites by different sectors of music life.

We end this chapter by citing part of a Council of Europe report on its 1982 Symposium entitled 'Creative artists and the industrialization of culture: music'. The section on copyright reported that:

> None of the discussions was more passionate than the one on compensation for private copying. In essence, there are two principles in conflict: the principle of compensation and the principle of redistribution. Those in favour of the first principle – and here the musicians' representatives were in agreement with those from the record industry – thought that the proceeds from levies on blank cassettes should all go to those whose interests suffered from private copying. In this view, the levy could not be compared to a tax but, rather, represents compensation – albeit incomplete – for injury suffered. The supporters of the second principle – which the representative of the Swedish authorities spoke forcefully in favour of – consider on the contrary that the levy must be used for general redistributive purposes. The proceeds must provide for shifts of funds made in the light of the objectives of cultural policy.

The Council of Europe report concluded finally:

> Cultural policy options seem to reflect fairly clearly the most basic choices concerning society. This is true, for example, of the choice between compensation and redistribution which dominated part of the discussions. One can see in this a resurgence of the recurring debate about the role of the state in our modern

societies. It is on this account that the reference to the constitutional, pluralist nature of our political systems was relevant. The compensation principle is based on a neo-liberal conception of the state, in which the state is responsible for proclaiming the law and remedying injustices but has no role beyond that. The redistribution principle, on the other hand, derives from a broader conception of the function of public authorities. It is associated with the idea of the welfare state in the English-speaking world and with democratic planning in the Latin world. In this way, the cultural-policy debate is linked to conflicting visions of society. To underline this is not to reduce the importance of cultural policy but rather to give it its true dimension.[33]

In view of the problems enumerated in this chapter, we can expect to see copyright administration in the years to come being geared to an ever-increasing degree of cultural policy decision-making. This does not mean that governments will have to take over or declare all music to be in the public domain. The traditional laws will have to be revised. International exchange and cooperation must improve. The existing copyright organizations will have to embrace wider responsibilities, both of a social, policy and administrative nature.

Government policies – for better, for worse

In the wake of the emergence of the new independent countries around 1960, their young governments were faced with problems concerning how they should relate to phenomena in the cultural sector. Many of these governments were made up of people with a European education. The new rulers often held an evolutionistic view of the cultural processes with European-Western culture representing the highest level attainable (cf. Chapter 1). These politicians thought that the government should support the propagation of European culture as part of their countries' development policies. A sign of this attitude is the fact that almost all national anthems in the newly independent countries are patterned on clichés taken from nineteenth-century European march music.

Opposed to such attitudes were those who had a more critical view of European culture. These were mostly young intellectuals who had studied the teachings of Mao Tse-Tung and others concerning cultural imperialism. They argued that the government should support local traditional culture.

A general debate on cultural policy developed during the Sixties out of the juxtaposition of these two views. This debate also affected the industrialized nations. In most countries direct government intervention in the field of culture had previously been of an *ad hoc* nature. Problems in this area were dealt with separately as they arose. Around 1970 governments started to formulate more comprehensive cultural policies which led to an abundance of decisions affecting cultural activities during that decade. As can be seen in the sections on government activities in our sample countries (see Profiles of change in the Appendix) practical political decisions have been many and varied during the Seventies. In some countries a more anthropological concept has been applied, with a very wide definition of the field of culture incorporating everything from song and dance to sports and traditional medicine. In other countries the limits of cultural politics have been narrower, sometimes restricted only to the arts.

From the mid-Seventies onwards, official versions of cultural policies adopted by different countries have been documented in a series of UNESCO publications. In 1979 the Council of Europe noted:

> It is now generally accepted that the cultural sphere is one in which the public authorities have specific responsibilities. All countries now have a national body responsible for cultural affairs, and sometimes even a Ministry of Culture, whose functions gradually expand as cultural matters assume greater political significance.[1]

Thus the Seventies could be termed the decade of the breakthrough of national cultural policies. But not all decisions affecting music emanate from ministries of culture. Many decisions within other governmental sectors (taxation, trade policy etc.) have an indirect effect. A borderline case between cultural and general policies is copyright legislation (see Chapter 5).

It would appear that government involvement in culture has been more intense in small countries than in larger ones. Clearly this is related to the business sector's involvement in practical cultural politics when sponsoring the arts, when designing advertisements and commercials, through choice of phonogram repertoire and so on. In a small country such activities, as we have seen in previous chapters, could quickly create trends which conflict with what politicians and others in power think are desirable. The governments would then attempt to counteract such trends either by trying to restrict the undesirable aspects or by supporting alternative, desirable activities. What, then, do governments find desirable? In the field of music it is often either some style that enjoys high status (establishment music) or something that is encompassed by the notion of 'national music traditions'. The former, in small countries, is usually related to what we call 'the Big Brother syndrome' in Chapter 3 (p. ff.), in most cases art music with roots in nineteenth-century Central Europe.

NATIONAL MUSIC

The question what a national music is and what it stands for is very intriguing and cannot be answered in full here. In the established, small national states of Europe such as the Nordic countries, two main kinds of national music have evolved during the last century. One kind is art music which uses elements from local folk music, and the other kind is a folklore music representing a synthesis of local folk music styles. Both these kinds of national music have also emerged in the small countries in the Third World, but during a much shorter time (see p. 21. and Diagram 2).

The function of these kinds of national music and national culture in general has been interpreted in different ways. Armand Mattelart writes:

> In order to define the concept of cultural imperialism, it is first necessary to try and delimit that of 'national culture'. This notion cannot be specified except by considering the relation of the national (or, in their absence, creole) bourgeoisies to the groupings of the North American Empire. National culture, in the era of the multinationals, has to guarantee the reproduction of the dependence of these bourgeoisies on the United States at the same time as that of their own hegemony as the ruling class in a particular nation; that is to say, it has to continue to sanctify their position as an 'interior bourgeoisie'.[2]

Mattelart draws his conclusions mainly from his experiences of developments in Latin America. In other parts of the world where people have a fresh experience of direct colonialism it is more fruitful to interpret the emergence of national music in terms of a reaction against the alienation from local traditions caused by the colonial rule.

President Julius Nyerere of Tanzania made the following points in a speech at the opening of the new Ministry of Culture in 1974:

> The major change I have made is to set up an entirely new Ministry: the Ministry of National Culture and Youth. I have done this because I believe that its culture is the essence and spirit of any nation. A country which lacks its own culture is no more than a collection of people without the spirit that makes them a nation. Of the crimes of colonialism there is none worse than the attempt to make us believe we had no indigenous culture of our own; or that what we did have was worthless – something of which we should be ashamed, instead of a source of pride . . .
>
> So I have set up this new Ministry to help us regain our pride in OUR culture. I want to seek out the best of the traditions and customs of all our tribes and make them a part of our national culture. I hope that everybody will do what he can to help the work of this new Ministry. But I don't want anybody to imagine that to revive our own culture means at the same time to reject that of any other country. A nation which refuses to learn from foreign cultures is nothing but a nation of idiots and lunatics.[3]

The views of President Nyerere are representative of those expressed by many radical political leaders. National culture is seen as an instrument for uniting different ethnic groups, making them feel that they all belong to the same nation. In Tanzania the activities of the Ministry of Culture with music policy led *inter alia* to the establishment of a national dance and music group within which dance and music traditions of different ethnic groups were amalgamated into the 'national ngoma style'. Throughout the mid and late Seventies this common style was adopted by young people all over Tanzania.

Whilst national styles of music based on traditional ones in the older countries have slowly developed within different popular movements as a product of geographical and social mobility, the same styles in newly independent countries are often products of government music politics during the past two decades. The first country to practise this model was Israel; its national folklore costumes, dance and music forms were more or less created in a couple of years in the early Fifties by a government committee of folklorists and musicians.

In most countries there has also emerged what can be termed 'national popular music'. These musical styles have been shaped through interaction between internationally distributed popular music and local types of music. In the small European countries this development has been going on since the end of the nineteenth century giving birth to many national popular music styles influenced by different international music trends. In the Sixties the world-wide impact of rock music and electrical instruments created a somewhat new situation. In all the MISC sample countries this triggered off developments leading to national styles of pop and rock music. We will deal more with this process in Chapter 8.

Until the Seventies, most governments left the popular music sector strictly alone or had a negative attitude to it. The cultural establishment considered it to be bad music of no value. In most of our sample countries, government attitudes towards national styles of popular music started to change during the Seventies. The governments of Sweden and Denmark started to give grants to music groups playing national pop and rock. In Tunisia popular Arabic film music was introduced into government supported festivals as was calypso music in Trinidad, reggae music in Jamaica, Welsh-language rock music in Wales and, prior to 1973, the *nueva cancin chilena* in Chile. In Tanzania the 'Swahili jazz music' is seen by many leading members of the only political party (CCM) as a symbol of development. A national pop and rock group, the Afro 70 group, with new electric and electronic instruments represented Tanzania at FESTAC 77, the big festival for black and African music and arts held in Lagos, Nigeria in that year.

Changing government attitudes also led to the funding of courses in popular music at government music schools in many countries (see below) and contributed to the emergence of academic studies of popular music. In 1981 a new society, The International Society for the Study of Popular Music, was formed as part of this process. However, at the beginning of the Eighties we still find that most governments are very ambivalent in their attitudes towards popular styles of music.

HOW GOVERNMENT POLICIES ARE PUT TO WORK

The new post-1970 emphasis on culture was marked by the setting up of government committees and bodies to formulate and carry out cultural policies. Ministries of Culture were established or reorganized. Councils for Cultural Affairs and separate government bodies dealing with music were created. Here are some examples of these developments.

In Sweden the government had given financial support to music and other cultural institutions for several decades, but had not intervened very much in the activities of these institutions. Many of the important main music institutions were controlled by the semi-private Royal Academy of Music, founded in the eighteenth century. Most government-supported music activities took place solely in the capital city, Stockholm, and a few other major urban centres. In 1968 the first step towards changing this order was taken when the government set up a new music institution, Rikskonserter (The National Institute for Concerts). It was given the giant task of making live music available to everybody in Sweden regardless of place of residence. In 1971 the government took over control of the Stockholm conservatoire and music teachers' training college from the Royal Academy of Music. Preparations got underway for a thorough reform of higher music education (this reform was completed in 1977). In 1972 the military bands were demobilized and reorganized as regional orchestras in 22 of Sweden's 24 regions. The same year a government committee laid down proposals for a government cultural policy, which was accepted unanimously by all parties in parliament in 1974. At the core of this policy was a programme summed up in eight goals.

Cultural policy shall:

* help protect freedom of expression and create genuine opportunities to utilize this freedom
* encourage people to carry on their own creative activities, and promote contacts between people
* counteract the negative effects of commercialism in the cultural sphere

* further a decentralization of activities and decision-making functions in the cultural sphere
* be designed with regard to the experiences and needs of disadvantaged groups
* facilitate artistic and cultural innovation
* guarantee that the cultural heritages of earlier periods are preserved and kept alive
* further the exchange of experience and ideas in the cultural sphere across linguistic and national boundaries.

The 1974 parliamentary resolution was formally concerned with measures to be taken by the state, but the government made it clear that it expected both county councils and municipalities to follow much the same guidelines. It was also hoped that Swedish grassroots movements and other private sector organizations would do likewise. Vital contributions to cultural life were still expected from voluntary associations with their extensive local networks.

A Council for Cultural Affairs (Kulturrådet) was set up to implement the cultural programme. This council was organized with boards dealing with different spheres of culture. Music was grouped with theatre and dance under the same board; its main task was to propose guidelines and budgets for government institutions and to distribute financial support to independent theatre, music and dance groups. In 1981 the government took over the last music institutions still administered by the Royal Academy of Music, and Music Library and the Museum of Music in Stockholm.

Throughout the Seventies, government on a regional and municipality level in Sweden has set up its own bodies for implementing local cultural politics. Most towns and county councils have formed their own cultural committees.

Not surprisingly, these developments have been accompanied by an increased spending of government money in the cultural area. Between 1970 and 1979 the expenditure of local, regional and state governments on culture in Sweden more than doubled as can be seen in Diagram 10. The fastest growth-rate is in expenditure by the state government. Of the total expenditure on culture, about 20 per cent goes to the music sector.

Similar developments to those in Sweden have taken place in most of the other Nordic countries. Denmark, however, has chosen a somewhat different approach. Instead of establishing a set of goals for cultural policies, the Danish government has introduced laws regulating the activities of public authorities in different cultural sectors. The Danish Music Law of 1976, for instance, regulates the minimum facilities to be provided by municipalities and government music institutions. This concerns municipality music schools,

DIAGRAM 10: PUBLIC SECTOR EXPENDITURE ON CULTURE IN
SWEDEN 1970–79. PRICE INDEX OF 1970.

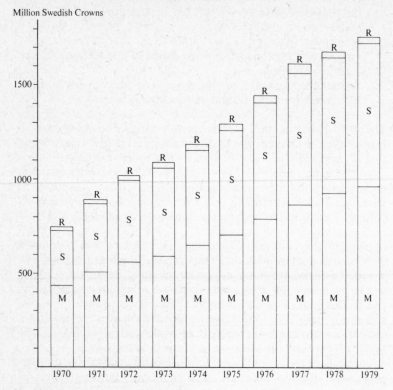

Million Swedish Crowns

M = Municipality (Local government) expenditure
S = State (Central government) expenditure.
R = Regional (Country government) expenditure.
Source: *Kulturpolitik – vad är det? (Cultural policy – what is it?)* 1981

support of orchestras and other music groups, size of phonogram
sections in public libraries etc. Being a law, this is binding for public
authorities. Regardless of changes in local, regional or even the
central political power structure, the requirements of the music law
have to be fulfilled. This provides for a certain degree of stability in
the relationship of the government to the music sector. Radical cuts
in public music budgets cannot be carried out *ad hoc* in times of
economic crises. However, the law can also be used by those in
power as an excuse for not increasing the budget for music, as long
as the minimum requirements of the law are fulfilled. Public expenditure on culture in Denmark has not risen as quickly as in
Sweden. The Swedish arrangement with a more loosely structured
government cultural policy seems to leave more leeway for pressure

and action groups to bring about changes in practical cultural politics.

In Tunisia, government engagement in culture started in a modest way with Independence (1965), mostly in the form of support to institutions inherited from the colonial period such as the music conservatoire in Tunis. In the mid and late Sixties, the Tunisian state started to build up a widespread organization for cultural administration. A network of local cultural committees covering the whole country was established. These committees consist of local cultural personalities and luminaries, chosen by the local political authorities. Each committee has its own building as well as a small staff of cultural administrators headed by a 'cultural secretary'. These buildings were termed 'People's Houses' (*Maisons du Peuple*) at first, but with a slight change in Tunisia's political orientation in the late Seventies, they were renamed *Maisons de Culture*. The most impressive of these, in the Holy City of Kairouan, has an amphitheatre, a large indoor cinema/theatre as well as areas for different sorts of hobby activities (photo, table tennis, aquarium etc.).

Local cultural committees are co-ordinated by a regional committee, and these, in their turn, are represented on a national committee. The national committee distributes state funds to regional and local cultural committees.

Another government activity which affected individual musicians was the introduction of the *carte professionnelle* law in 1969. According to this all professional or semi-professional musicians had to have their talents rated by official representatives of the music establishment – they were then granted a sort of musician's driver's licence which allowed them to perform. This also gave the police an opportunity to maintain some sort of control over the artistic sector. The *carte professionnelle* (CP) law involved big changes for the many folk musicians who used to perform at festivities such as weddings and circumcision ceremonies. They either had to perform before a committee at the music conservatoire to get their licence, or continue their musical activities illegally. But once such a permit has been granted (for one, two or five year periods) it is normally extended automatically. We were told by an official that the popular folk singer Habouba, who was jailed for drug offences in 1981, would not have his musician's licence extended, and thus would not be able to continue performing in public. However, we gather he was soon back in business after his release from jail in the summer of 1982.

Government control of performed music through the *carte professionnelle* has not been completely effective. In 1980 the chairman of the National Cultural Council, Mr Salah el Mahdi said:

Today we have approximately 5,000 professionally active musicians with a government licence, but we estimate that there are at least 10,000 more musicians making part of, or all their livelihood out of playing music who do not have a *carte professionnelle*.

DIAGRAM 11: TUNISIAN CULTURAL POLICY DURING THE SEVENTIES

Carte Professionnelle

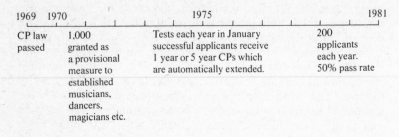

1969 1970		1975	1981
CP law passed	1,000 granted as a provisional measure to established musicians, dancers, magicians etc.	Tests each year in January successful applicants receive 1 year or 5 year CPs which are automatically extended.	200 applicants each year. 50% pass rate

Growth of Maisons de Culture

Year			
1965	1970	1975	1980
40	60	98	142

Number

The legislation concerning *cartes professionnelles* also applied to visiting foreign music groups up to 1982. The increased flow of foreign musicians to the tourist hotels during the Seventies had presented the members of the licensing board with difficulties when adjudicating what they regarded as strange kinds of music. The CP regulations initially had the effect of providing more work opportunities for Tunisian musicians at the tourist hotels. But with the spread of discothèques and the hotel managements' attempts to attract tourists by providing particularly exotic or unusual entertainment acts, the licensing authorities were presented with new problems. Often the official adjudicators who were experts on Arabic music were expected to judge the quality of music which they themselves had little experience of. One local jazz musician complained that if you played a discord in Western music for the CP committee, they thought you had made a mistake. The committee found itself in a particularly tricky situation in 1979 when it was asked to provide a work permit for a British drag show (the Tunisians referred to them as the 'group of British transvestites') –

they got a permit. From 1979, official dealings between the cultural authorities and visiting artists became more and more confused, especially when hoteliers resorted to strip-tease acts to attract the guests. The Chef du Service Musique, Fehti Zghonda, reported that an impossible situation developed after the authorities had agreed to grant temporary permits for foreign artists based on applications:

> Hotels would send a description of the act and we would approve. It often turned out that the act was something completely different. When the police complained, the artists and musicians would refer to their permit from the Ministry of Culture. I was getting very dissatisfied. Each week I had to consider about twenty artists from abroad, many of whom wanted to do strip-tease. This wasn't good for me or my job.[4]

In 1982, Fehti Zghonda and his colleagues were relieved of this duty. The responsibility of judging and issuing CPs to foreign artists who perform at hotels and night clubs has now been handed over to the police. Zghonda admits that this can lead to less work opportunities for Tunisian musicians.

> Egyptian artists are already coming in, playing for low fees. Maybe in a few years we'll have to control it again.

In Tanzania an extensive system of government bodies was set up in connection with the establishment of the new Ministry of National Culture and Youth in 1974. As in Tunisia, a government-supported national music and dance troupe had existed in Tanzania since 1964. With the exception of this and three police brass bands, government activities in the field of music were few prior to 1974, when the National Music Council (*Baraza la Muziki la Taifa* – BAMUTA) was created. BAMUTA was given the responsibility of formulating and implementing government music policy with the aid of a network of District Cultural Offices all over the country. BAMUTA also co-operates with the Tanzania Film Company (TFC) (which according to Tanzanian legislation has monopoly rights to release Tanzanian music on phonograms), with Radio Tanzania and with the Domestic Appliances and Bicycle Company, which has sole rights to import musical instruments. This network is illustrated in Diagram 12. BAMUTA also issues performance licences to music groups and to venues where music is played (dance halls, discothèques, night clubs etc.).

This infrastructure in the music sector has been created to provide a sound basis for carrying out government politics which are

DIAGRAM 12: TANZANIAN MUSIC ADMINISTRATION SYSTEM

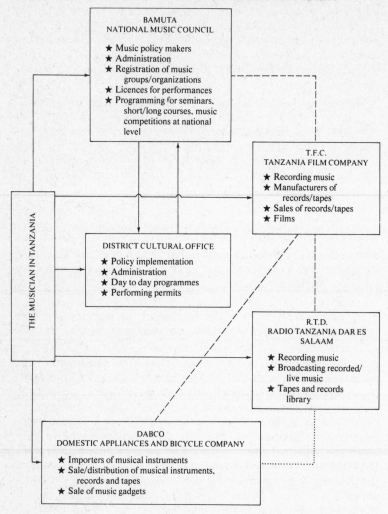

geared towards propagating the development of national and local types of music, and to screening influences from abroad. There are, however, factors that hamper the system, sometimes to an extent that it does not work at all. Currency problems, for instance, have brought the Tanzanian DABCO company's import of electrical musical instruments to a standstill. The TFC has similar problems and has been unable to get its record factory on-line. Another disturbing factor is the difficulty experienced by musicians, who often are not very good readers or writers, in coping with government music bureaucracy, knowing which body to turn to in different situations (even in Sweden musicians find this difficult and frustrating).

Economic problems in Tanzania have led to the emergence of an unofficial music sector run by private businessmen who have the right connections for importing electrical instruments illegally. Tapes with Tanzanian music are brought to Kenya and issued on records there. Quite a few musicians have left Tanzania to look for work in Kenya, but many return home after discovering that Nairobi is not the financial Eldorado for a visiting foreign musician they have been led to believe.

In spite of shortcomings in the implementation of music policies in Tanzania, the situation would probably have been much worse without the country's various official bodies. Particularly the music policy of Radio Tanzania (cf. Chapter 7) seems to have contributed to the lively music scene found today in Tanzania. An inventory in 1979 disclosed more than 6,000 traditional music and dance groups (*ngoma* groups), 120 Swahili 'jazz' bands, 60 *taarab* groups (*taarab* is a semi-traditional music with a mixture of Arabic and African style played in the coastal area and on Zanzibar), 50 choirs and 30 brass bands.

In the other sample countries trends are similar, even if developments are not so extensive as those described above. In Trinidad, in 1967, the Prime Minister's office started an annual competition between village teams in music, dance and folk literature. Similar competitions can be found in many of the sample countries. Through the standards applied by the judges, a special style of 'competition folklore' is moulded within the framework of these competitions. In 1969 the Trinidad government set up a National Folklore Archive, in 1971 a National Cultural Council and in 1973 a special Steelband Council to support the many bands in Trinidad playing on steelpans, instruments made out of empty oil drums.

In Jamaica, the Cultural Development Commission was originally set up as a statutory body in 1968. It was then known as Jamaica Festival Commission and was mainly concerned with the annual Independence celebration. As of 1980, the Festival Commission became the JCDC and its brief was expanded to include the following tasks:

* Promote cultural programmes and activities in communities throughout the Island;
* encourage and organize each year Independence anniversary

celebrations and other celebrations marking occasions of national
interest;
* stimulate the development of local talents by means of training,
  workshops, competitions, exhibitions, pageants, parades, dis-
  plays and such other activities as the Commission may from time
  to time determine;
* complement the work of other agencies engaged in the carrying
  out of community development programmes throughout the
  Island.

Activities in Kenya have been more erratic. The Kenya National
Cultural Council was established in 1972 but promptly went to
sleep. It re-emerged in a reorganized form in 1980 and was active for
a few months. Two years later the President's Commission for
African Music started to work out a policy for government support
to national Kenyan music.

In Sri Lanka an attempt was made to start a National Music
Council in 1974. The debate on music policy has been lively, but no
overall government policy has been formulated.

In Chile government music policies since 1973 have mostly been
carried out by different censorship boards. Official decisions have
mainly favoured Western Art music, have had a liberal attitude to
Anglo-American disco music and have discouraged much traditional Chilean folk music.

Only in recent decades has Wales experienced an official cultural
policy which supports the development of both Welsh-language and
English-language culture, mainly through the activities of the Welsh
Arts Council. In 1979 a spokesman for this council made the
following reflections on its role and work:

The idea of an Arts council, in its presently known form, is itself
only just over three decades old. These are young bodies, still
active and controversial. As it now stands an Arts Council is an
intervention between two powerful alternatives: on the one hand,
that of the market; on the other hand, that of the direct public
authority. It is an attempted innovation, to encourage, to support
and to extend the arts, beyond the short and indifferent terms of a
market of commodities, and at the same time beyond governmental or bureaucratic directions. As that kind of intervention and
innovation it gathers, without effort (though it has sometimes,
additionally, made efforts), both enemies and sceptical observers. Anyone who has seen it, close up, knows that it can do with
the latter. Indeed some of the best of that kind are inside it, trying
and often failing to improve it. But past all that it is a shape that
we have sketched and are trying to fill in. It is a notion of a need

and of a kind of priority. It speaks, tries to speak, to a sense of a culture which is connected with a society and yet which is never merely derivative from its more general political and economic definitions. In Britain as a whole it is having its difficulties. There is the glamorous and aching pull of a metropolis. In its precise area, of culture, there are often crippling class divisions. What is being contested, not always sensibly, is a dark area of ignorance and suspicion. What is being affirmed, through rushed meetings, is sometimes enlightenment, at other times, complacently, the mere gig-lamps of posture and fashion. But it is in process. It is where the arguments can be focused as well as the year-to-year arrangements made. It is a place where shapes are made, very practically, as the money flows or fails to flow, but at its best (a best which needs change and struggle) it is a place where shapes are also glimpsed and questioned, attempted and revised. In the larger process of shaping a culture it is a necessary agency, a necessary kind of agency.

The Welsh Arts Council has one special advantage: that it is attempting its difficult work at a time when both levels of its definitions – the Welshness and the arts – are in active movement. This makes its work harder but even more necessary. In my independent judgement, having watched comparable work in England, its spirit is quite exceptionally impressive. The very problems of Wales – the two languages of its literature, the deepening cultural crisis – have provoked, here as in other areas of Welsh life, initiatives and kinds of confidence that on their own, but especially comparatively, are remarkable.[5]

The only comment one can add to this summary of the problems of supporting both a minority and a majority culture in a country, is that most of the grants for music have been given exclusively to the so-called 'serious' sector. The Welsh National Opera gets the lion's share. Rock, beat and folk music activities have had to survive through creating their own commercial environment.

MUSIC EDUCATION

One area in which several governments in small countries have tried to introduce changes, large and small, is formal music education, both in basic compulsory schools and in institutions for more specialized training. These changes have often aimed to include traditional local music in the curriculum. Attempts have also been made within the educational system to encompass popular music and modern music technology. A common result of these changes is that musical types which have been considered to be of low value by the music establishment are given official support. Types of music that formerly were learned in an informal way or through traditional apprentice systems start to be taught in formalized and institutionalized forms. Not surprisingly, such changes have led to conflicts and tensions, of a degree that, by the early Eighties, none of our sample countries had been able to resolve.

In Sri Lanka, traditional Sinhala music and dance were first incorporated into the education system in 1964. This change triggered off a number of activities amongst supporters of high status North Indian art music. Their successful lobbying resulted in an increased emphasis on that type of music in the school syllabuses from 1974, at the expense of traditional Sinhala music. In 1981 the state of affairs was reversed, and once again an emphasis on Sinhala music was re-introduced.

In Tanzania the traditional *ngoma* (music and dance) was gradually introduced into the school syllabuses in the late Sixties. However, there was considerable uncertainty as to which types of *ngomas* were suitable for the school system. There was a tendency to concentrate on a small sample which had been standardized by the national *ngoma* group. In 1974 this concentration provoked the following remark:

> If you ask a primary school boy what utamaduni [culture] means, the answer will almost certainly be: Sindimba, a traditional dance.[6]

Tanzanian observers noted the risk that this type of policy could lead to the traditionally very broad notion of culture becoming restricted to cover only certain officially accepted *ngomas*. During the later half of the Seventies a National School of Music, Dance and Drama grew out of the National Ngoma group in Tanzania. The teaching methods developed at this school will certainly form the core of future teaching of traditional music and dance in Tanzanian schools.

In Jamaica, the island's folk and popular music was gradually introduced into the curriculum of the Jamaica School of Music during the Seventies. In Trinidad more and more primary and secondary schools have established their own school steelbands.

In spite of these gradual shifts towards local music in school curricula, much of the formal music teaching in all the former British colonies among the sample countries is still geared towards Western art music. Adjudicators from the London Royal School of Music regularly visit Jamaica, Trinidad, Kenya and Sri Lanka to listen to young music students trying to master miserable pianos and bad violins. The Dar es Salaam Music Conservatoire has introduced its own exams, which differ only marginally from those set by music institutions in London.

These experiences indicate how hard it can be to introduce local music into formal music education. There are the problems of selection out of what are almost always very prolific musical traditions, problems of acquiring teaching materials, problems of teachers not being trained in traditional music and uncertainty as to suitable teaching methods. It is often the case in developing countries, that one music teacher has the responsibility for between 50 and 70 children. What can one do in such circumstances, apart from singing the National Anthem?

Even in a developed country like Sweden much of the reform of the higher music education system decided upon by parliament in 1977 was still little more than words on paper six years later, in 1983. The reform was preceded by numerous practical experiments. Its aim was to introduce a new attitude and content into higher music education; this concerned particularly the training of music teachers. The changes envisaged have been pinpointed by Philip Tagg in Table 15.

The Swedish government experts and planners had expressed the belief that folk music and various kinds of popular music should be included in the new teacher-training programmes. Since the total time, four years, for the courses was not increased this was rather like trying to pour a gallon into a pint bottle. Many older teachers were somewhat unwilling to cut down on traditional types of training which they had got used to, so the pint bottle proved to be quite full already. However, a change is occurring, even if only very slowly. Some special courses have been started, such as a two-year course for violin teachers specializing in Swedish folk fiddling.

Meanwhile, sociological investigations continue to show that music is the highest ranking leisure time interest amongst Swedish youth. Between 80 and 90 per cent claim that music is a major interest. But when asked about school subjects only 5-8 per cent mention an interest in music. A new approach to music teaching is clearly needed to bridge this gap. But how can it come about when a planned reform of music teacher-training could not even get off the ground?

Increasing professionalism in traditional and new kinds of music together with increased diversification of music life have put added pressure on governments to adapt the formal music education system to these new conditions. At the same time the established government-sponsored institutions such as opera houses and symphony orchestras have to be supplied with highly skilled musicians playing traditional instruments. This costs more and more, and the

TABLE 15

INTENDED CHANGES IN THE MUSIC TEACHER TRAINING SCHEMES IN
SWEDEN

Former characteristics of teacher training	New intended characteristics
1 main genre (monomusicality)	No main genre (polymusicality)
Music theory *in abstracto* with quantifiable results	Arranging, instrumentation etc. with 'qualifiable' results (several genres)
Ear training *in abstracto*	Structural listening, transcription and analysis for discussion, 're-performance'
Solo achievement on instruments	Group *and* individual achievement
Individual composition	Group *and* individual composition
Music *per se*	Music as expression and communication in social and cultural contexts
Alternative to commercialism as a fixed position in art music	Alternative to commercialism as dynamic processes both inside and outside the commercial production of music
'Music history': past events as 'events' in themselves; 'great' names and works	'Music and society': events past and present as part of social and cultural processes in history
Written music only (monomodality)	Oral/aural, recorded *and* written music (polymodality)

Source: Tagg 1982: 234.

fruits of this investment are normally enjoyed by a small cultural elite.

As the Swedish example above shows, governments find themselves increasingly facing the dilemma of an ever-widening gap between the 'official' view of music as mirrored in formal music education, and the musical reality in which the majority of the citizens live.

POLICIES FOR THE MASS MEDIA

Broadcasting

Government policies regarding music in mass media clearly have considerable significance for the music life of any country. With regard to broadcasting, some governments have preferred a public service view based on the structure of organizations such as the British Broadcasting Corporation. The original concept of the BBC was that its main purpose was to educate. Financing should be through licences to guarantee its freedom from commercial interests. Music should be of high cultural value. With these goals in mind it was natural that the BBC developed a position of responsibility to the arts, retaining a number of symphony orchestras, commissioning compositions etc. Gradually the role of radio as an entertainment medium was developed, and with it the content of 'light music' expanded. The cultural goals were satisfied by devoting large resources to Western art music for a smaller section of the public. Light music for the greater mass of the listeners had its own particular transmission frequencies; the concept of generic radio emerged. Complete channels were devoted to a format of light music with little speech content other than announcements and news. To make sure the corporation did not abuse its monopoly position it was ordered to satisfy a wide range of tastes; including those of minority groups. As television expanded, the same principles applied. When the BBC got its Channel 2, this one carried the programmes with less general appeal. BBC 1 presented mass-appeal popular programmes.

This model has been preferred by many small countries – notably those in Scandinavia where public service, non-commercial broadcasting dominates. Former British colonies usually found themselves with a BBC-type corporation as part of the colonial administration. Radio Tanzania, for instance, used to play many hours of Western art music, until the government decided to concentrate on national music, a change which took all in all about eight years.

The main alternatives to the public service model are the government controlled, and the purely commercial model. Sometimes the public service, government propaganda and commercial models can be combined into various hybrid forms. Different models can also be found in the same country in the absence of a monopoly situation. In the case of the completely commercial model, a broadcasting station survives only if it attracts a large number of listeners and thus advertisers. Such stations tend naturally to adopt a popularistic rather than the educational approach. In a democratic country there is less opportunity for a government to exercise music culture policy through broadcasting. Broadcasting in Chile is very commercial in essence, having developed along the lines of the American private-enterprise system. The music output, however, does reflect the cultural norms of the ruling military junta in one respect; music styles which might offend the government are kept off the air.

Many of the nations in the MISC sample seem to have preferred a combination of some of the models described above. Thus Sri Lanka, Kenya, Tanzania and Jamaica have broadcasting companies that provide some public service, educational, output but also accept revenue from commercial entities for other programmes, usually filled with light music. The area of radio and television will be covered in greater detail in the next chapter.

Phonograms

Up to 1970 a government policy for music on phonograms was a phenomenon found only in the socialist countries. In these countries phonogram production was and still is organized by state-owned record companies. These companies are usually divided into two departments: one for art music and folk music, and one for popular music. Their popular music operations are supposed to bring in a profit which is then used to subsidize the production of phonograms with art music and folk music. Through this system, countries in Eastern Europe such as Poland, Czechoslovakia and Hungary were able to issue a great deal of their own music on gramophone records during the Sixties. During the same decade the people of the Nordic countries could note that the number of records released featuring their own music and musicians was decreasing steadily. In the mid-Sixties, for instance, more records with Swedish jazz musicians were issued in Poland than in Sweden.

The first government record company in our sample was set up in Tunisia in 1968 (Ennagham). This company had a production monopoly. It also handled all imports. Ennagham was modelled, in fact, on the phonogram companies in socialist countries. However, in 1971 Ennaghan lost its monopoly status and its operations never really expanded after that.

Another example of state involvement is the Caprice label in Sweden. In the late Sixties, Rikskonserter (the Institute for National Concerts) in Sweden started to issue subsidized records. This operation was turned into a regular government subsidized phonogram company in 1972 for a trial period of three years. The task of this company (the Caprice label) was to issue phonograms mainly with Swedish music and Swedish musicians within musical genres which were not taken care of by the other phonogram companies. The government record company was intended to be not a competitor but a complement to the already existing companies. Nevertheless there was an outcry about unfair competition from the commercial record companies.

In 1974 the goals of Swedish cultural policy had been approved by all parties in parliament. One of these official aims which dealt with counteracting the negative effects of commercialism was highly relevant to the situation in the field of phonogram production. At the end of Caprice Records' three-year test run, the Council of Cultural Affairs set up a committee to investigate the phonogram industry. Their findings were presented in March 1979[7] together with proposals for government actions. The most important proposal was that a levy should be introduced on blank cassettes and the money thus generated should be used to subsidize Swedish phonogram production, both by Caprice Records and other phonogram companies.

In 1982, after almost three years of debates and lobbying, the proposals made by the Phonogram Committee concerning a tax on tapes were accepted by parliament. The levy was set at SEK 0.02 per minute of tape (little more than 10 pence for a C60 tape). This does not constitute much of a hardship for the individual customer, but with sales of approximately 18 million blank cassettes per annum, a fair amount of money is generated. The argument for the introduction of the levy was that the blank tapes were used for the home-copying of phonograms and that the general public should pay something for this. Part of the money generated by this tax is given to the copyright owner's organizations to be divided between their members. Another part is used to subsidize live music performances and some (SEK 7 millions/year) is distributed as subsidies to phonogram productions with Swedish music and Swedish musicians. This new 'gatekeeping' function is carried out by a sub-committee of the Council for Cultural Affairs. This committee decides in effect how the 7 million Swedish Kronor should be divided up between the state company (Caprice), and private companies. Grants are based on an evaluation of applications filed by individual phonogram companies. One-third of total levy generated, however, goes straight into the government Treasury. This has evoked no small amount of protest in Sweden.

In Norway a levy or tax on tape-recorders was introduced in 1982. The main argument behind this tax reads as follows in the government bill:

When it comes to the rationale for this levy, the ministry wishes to point out the predicted infamous future role of the transnational culture industry. Current developments call for increased efforts to preserve and strengthen Norwegian culture. It will, inter alia, be of importance to attach a value to undertakings that can stimulate the production and diffusion of Norwegian phonograms and videograms in a situation where these can disappear from the market through overwhelming competition.[8]

However, nothing is stated in the Norwegian law as to how the collected tax money should be channelled back into the music life of the country. There are merely a few general statements in the commenting paragraphs to the effect that this will be done through the government's general cultural politics.

In 1982, Denmark as well was preparing to introduce a tax on blank tapes similar to the Swedish levy. According to the Danish proposals, all the money collected through the levy should be handed over to the copyright owners' organizations. How this will be done remains to be seen.

Despite generally high levels of cassette penetration, piracy and home-taping, none of the other MISC countries in 1983 were on the brink of introducing extra taxes on cassettes. Even in the UK (Wales) the government had rejected the idea of an extra tax[9] because of administrative problems envisaged and uncertainty as to how to remunerate those suffering from phenomena such as home-taping.

What happens when the phonogram industry in a small country gets into such a state of crisis that it is on the brink of disappearing? One such example is the case of Trinidad. During 1982 the operations of the local Trinidadian music industry came virtually to a standstill. This was hardly a surprise to those involved in an industry that has much of its activities concentrated to a three-month period around Christmas and the February Carnival. A local record producer summed up the difficulties:

> In all the years we couldn't get concessions out of the government. There was no way we could afford to pay the customs duty and purchase tax required. It was something like 96 per cent. Total madness . . . We find that the industry has had no encouragement whatsoever from the local media, from the local retail outlets and from the administration. We get absolutely no support. So it is extremely difficult to hold it together. Our industry is active three months of the year. It is this period, Christmas and Carnival. I am very happy that the papers now have given this some exposure. Later on after the carnival, when the industry collapses, when the people become aware of that there is no such thing as a local industry, maybe I will be able to use this as support.[10]

By the end of 1982 the difficulties referred to in this statement had led to the closing of operations at both Semp Studios and at another record pressing plant (KH Records). Since many of the calypsonians bring out their calypsos on their own record labels they now had to pay more than 60 per cent in customs duty plus shipping costs to bring in their records pressed abroad. Prices for phonograms featuring local artists jumped and sales dropped. The situation was further aggravated by organized piracy. In December 1982 the calypsonians and musicians formed a committee which presented five proposals to the government:

(a) Customs duty as well as
(b) Purchase tax on imported records with local artists should be waived.
(c) 80 per cent of airtime on radio and television should be devoted to local music and shows.
(d) Copyright laws should be updated.
(e) The government should set up a recording industry or assist to form a cooperative recording industry.

On February 3, 1983, the Trinidad and Tobago Cabinet decided that customs duties should no longer be levied on local recordings coming into the country and that a recording studio for the nation's artists should be established. Thus the Trinidad government has announced its intention to venture into phonogram politics.

INDIRECT POLICIES FOR MUSIC

Direct policies for music advocated in general cultural policy statements by governments very often are counteracted by political decisions in other areas, usually in the economic field. Ministries of Culture and Ministries of Finance do not always agree. An extreme case is that of the Tanzanian record pressing plant. The original decision to build the plant was taken in the Cabinet in the mid-Sixties. Most of the machines were delivered in the late Seventies. Completion was delayed because the necessary foreign exchange for the final assembly stage was held back by the Ministry of Finance. In 1983, the presses were still in their packing crates. A related case is the gradual closing down of the pressing plants in Trinidad which was partly due to the high costs involved in bringing in spare parts or new presses because of exorbitant customs duties.

The introduction of entertainments taxes on entrance tickets of artists' fees as a means of raising fiscal revenue is also an area that can conflict with the goals of cultural policy. Waiving such a tax in particular cases can also have a corresponding positive effect. The Sri Lankan government introduced such taxes on concert, cinema and theatre tickets in the early Seventies. The Ministry of Culture managed to get it waived for all amateur performances and, even for professional artists in the case of the first ten performances in any particular local government district (though only after an exemption permit has been granted by the ministry of Culture). This, according to a cultural official 'has made a definite difference to many artists who are poor financially, but rich in their creative work'.

Finland also had a similar tax on entrance tickets to dances – performances in theatres were exempted. This strange cultural situation led to the development of the *Iltamat* or 'Revue' tradition. An evening out at a dance hall would start off with a short 'Revue' to transform the dance into a formal theatrical performance, thus guaranteeing tax exemption. This strange fiscal manipulation actually encouraged the development of new cultural activities!

Few governments have responded to the IFPI's intensive lobbying to have phonograms classified as books for tax purposes (thus giving Value Added Tax tax relief in some territories). The introduction of VAT, on the other hand, has had some advantages for the phonogram industry. In Wales this was accompanied by the removal of a much higher purchase tax. So-called 'luxury taxes' on gramophone records have also been removed in Sweden and Denmark in connection with tax reforms.

Chile, as we have noted, has experienced a marked transition from state involvement to privatization wherever possible. The government does, however, still give some indirect support to Western art music (even if some of the symphony orchestras have been told that they are expected to pay their way). The officer responsible for promotion of cultural activities at the Ministry of Culture described a very ambitious programme of Western art music:

> We have carried out a lot of activities with serious music. Our main objective here is decentralization. We have organized concert tours all over the country. We do series with all the most important Chilean musicians. We have been doing this for four years now.

Note the notion of the word 'decentralization' as meaning the spreading of a centrally produced message all over the country. This is a common misconception among bureaucrats in many countries.

The same officer had the following to say about 'pop music':

> When it comes to drugs and pop music we haven't had any major problems yet. There are no big groups of young people who have

gone astray. Noisy music has not yet become a negative element here. It is music that does not contribute to the growth of an individual.[11]

Around the same time as that these statements were being made profound changes in music life were taking place thanks to the economic politics of the government. The 'freedom of enterprise' doctrine had led to an abundance of new radio stations, almost all of which were flooding the airwaves with different types of 'pop music'. Most government subsidies for university education had been withdrawn. Even music education was expected to pay its way. Within a year of the new directives being announced the majority of students had left the Department of Music at Universidad de Chile in Santiago. Many of the teachers had to be suspended. Some of them tried to survive by setting up small private music schools offering short, very specialized courses. One of the teachers who had decided to try to set up such a private music institute gave us this summary of this situation.

Now the government tries to get private enterprises to finance music and other arts. It is a model adopted from the USA. The Universidad de Chile used to be a great centre of music. Now it is disbanded and broken up into small units. The university still receives some financial support from the government, but now they too have to look for other sources of finance. Many people believe that this is going to be the end of the arts. Now the students have to pay for their own education and very few music students can do this. We are going to lose many talents. I don't believe we can keep our artistic standards . . .[12]

If this prophecy is correct then the indirect music policies that have been the result of the economic policies of the Chilean government will lead to a situation where the concert tours arranged by the Ministry of Culture can no longer take place because of a chronic lack of skilled musicians.

The most important indirect music policies, however, are not those carried out by government bodies but those induced by the research and development work going on in the electronic industry. The policies and actions regarding music by government in our sample countries indicate a general awareness that some sort of intervention is necessary. But the diversity of the practical decisions and actions observed indicates that no government anywhere really knows how to cope with the rapid changes in music industry technology and organization and the effects of these changes. But a number of models for supporting local and national music through government funding are currently providing the basis for experimentation. Maybe we are witnessing the start of an increased level of confrontation between the governments of small countries and the transnational music industry.

8

The power of broadcasting
in the music industry

'It's a tremendous business. You never stop. You start the day
early, turning the radio on to see if they're playing your record.
You go to bed doing the same.'
(Neville Lee, Jamaica)
'Radio is 95 per cent of promotion.'
(Byron Lee, Jamaica)

These statements by two of the men who control a major portion of
the Jamaican phonogram industry illustrate vividly the close relationship between broadcasting and the business of selling records
and cassettes. This interdependency exists, in different degrees, in
most countries, even in those with nominally non-commercial
broadcasting organizations. The phonogram industry provides
cheap programme material (or at least cheaper than the alternatives
available to radio companies) and the broadcasters provide advertising services, exposing the material to the public. A programme
director of one European broadcasting monopoly put it this way,
describing the relationship as 'a marriage of convenience . . . both
parties need each other to survive . . . we're like a department store
where the tills are closed'.[1] (Ernst Grissemann, Austrian Radio). In
actual fact the balance of interests, at least in a European context,
has always been tipped in favour of the phonogram industry. The
most important influence on the development of popular music in
Europe during the Fifties and Sixties was first Radio Luxembourg,
and then the many 'pirate' radio boats that appeared on the scene.
Radio Luxembourg's programming was largely determined by paid
advertising from commercial phonogram companies. Fifteen minutes of Decca records might be followed by thirty minutes from
EMI etc.

When the Nordic governments decided in 1963 to outlaw commercial radio stations operating off-shore from ships outside territorial limits (e.g. Radio Nord, Radio Syd and Radio Mercur), their
broadcasting monopolies were given the task of continuing to
provide the same sort of entertainment but without the advertising.
This led to a large increase of music on phonograms on the
non-commercial stations. The same thing happened again a few

years later when Britain outlawed its maritime radio pirates, and the BBC was given the task of continuing to entertain through exposing the products of the commercial phonogram industry. This new role for the public service broadcasters also gave them new and tricky responsibilities. How could they equate these new activities with the demands of impartiality and quality featured in most of their charters? Obviously the phonogram industry could not openly dictate what was played. So a new system of gatekeepers had to be introduced (with producers, disc jockeys or committees deciding which were 'the best records'). The sensitive issue of quality was often avoided by referring to high audience figures – 'giving the public what it wants' – frequently with an oblique reference to the balance provided by alternative channels with a more cultural content.

Throughout the Seventies radio continued to expand in Europe, and phonograms continued to provide a major percentage of material. In 1980, the music output from one light entertainment department at Finnish radio consisted of no less than 89 per cent commercial recordings.

While this expansion was occurring, cheap transistorized radios were becoming more available. More people became used to having a background of radio music constantly with them – the importance of radio as a promotion medium for the phonogram industry steadily increased. This relationship has been documented in a number of studies. A German study has estimated that over 40 per cent of all record purchases are initiated by radio plays[2]. A Swedish study, based on interviews with customers in record stores, showed that 60 per cent 'often' or 'sometimes' based their record purchases on radio or TV programmes[3]. Sweden, it should be reiterated, has not been exposed to commercial radio, apart from signals of varying strength from Radio Luxembourg, since 1963.

PAYOLA, LAYOLA, FLYOLA AND OTHER NAUGHTY THINGS

It is not surprising that the music gatekeepers at radio stations are people for whom the phonogram industry has a great deal of respect. The decision to expose a phonogram to the public is not a guarantee for success, but just as essential for Neville Lee in Jamaica as it is for EMI's Richard Lyttleton in London:

> Radio is incredibly important. It probably does more to influence public taste than anything else . . . . I'm sure there's a direct correlation between airplay and sales. Often airplay reports are of more interest than the sales charts since they're an indication of what's likely to happen.[4]

In view of this, it is not surprising that phonogram companies devote a lot of money and effort to getting their products played on the radio. At times this involves balancing on a narrow dividing line between what is legal and illegal. Bribery of disc jockeys as a means of getting radio plays ('payola') is a criminal offence in many countries, but there are many other dubious variations on this same theme. Philip Tagg has referred to 'layola' (arranging female company for radio presenters), 'flyola' (arranging free air trips to exotic places) or 'freebies' (donating a large number of phonograms to a disc jockey who can then sell them off cheaply)[5].

Most large phonogram companies do invest in so-called 'pluggers', that is people whose job is to make radio stations aware of their products. An IMC study entitled 'Music and Tomorrow's Public' (partly financed by the IFPI)[6] found that plugging is a widespread phenomenon, though attitudes to pluggers vary from country to country and radio station to radio station. Some broadcasting organizations do their outmost to make sure that pluggers don't get past the entrance hall. Others appreciate the presence of the industry's publicity officers. The most popular AM station in Santiago, Chile (the Spanish-pop orientated Radio Portales) welcomes the visits of record company representatives, particularly those who understand the style of the station.

> We have good contacts with the record companies. I sometimes go to them and they sometimes come to us. Their people give us tips about future hits. But if a disc doesn't suit our style, then we don't play it.
>
> Of the different companies, Quatro* is the best. We can use about 90 per cent of what they produce. EMI are pretty good. Philips are pretty bad and hardly ever bother to contact us[7].

What happens outside the broadcaster's place of work, of course is a matter of individual choice. Eyebrows were raised in Sweden when a producer of an influential pop programme on the radio took a year's leave of absence for studies and it was learned that he was working temporarily as an A & R man with EMI. He did not return to his post at the Swedish radio company.

There are very few reported cases or even allegations of bribery on record in Scandinavia. The situation is very different in many other of the MISC sample countries. Small producers in Trinidad complain that they cannot afford the payola fees demanded by some of the disc jockeys.

* Quatro is a fast-growing local phonogram company based in Santiago but closely related to Ariola (West Germany). Quatro had about 20% of the Chilean phonogram market in 1980.

You have to pay a good few hundred a week. So what happens, if you don't pay it your music is not heard. And if people in Trinidad that tune in to the radio don't hear your music, you're not going to sell any records and you'll flop. This is what has affected everybody in the industry[8].

When confronted with this statement, a representative of the state-run National Broadcasting Service in Trinidad, the director of 'Radio 610', declined to allow his comments to be taped. He indicated that the allegations were not an exaggeration but that 'I as programme director don't know anything about this officially, or I would have to put a stop to it'.

The system in Jamaica would seem to be more sophisticated. Byron Lee refers to 'gratuities'.

You take the DJs to lunch, give them a couple of samples. My promotion men have an entertainment allowance to take DJs out to lunch or to the country to see a show and find out what they think about the artist.

Neville Lee, owner of Sonic Sounds in Kingston, Jamaica, is more specific.

A person might drive a car. His tyres are worn. He's done a good job, he's broken a couple of records for you. You give him a new set of tyres. Or a nice cassette to listen to, but with your product.

The bigger the market, the bigger the amount of money at stake. A former 'inside man' has claimed that the Latin American countries, especially Mexico, are particularly corrupt. Jorge Alvarez, ex-artistic director of Capitol Records comments:

The big record companies have a budget . . . to run their public relations, their promotion campaigns. There are cases, for example, in which payola is not used, that is a cheque is not given so that a certain melody will be programmed by a station. But this is made up for by sending the broadcaster on a trip to Europe, or giving him a new car, or sending him to Acapulco . . . It has been known to happen that artistic directors ask fifty thousand pesos (US$ 2,000) per month from new, small companies, in exchange for promoting their product on a given radio station. The big companies have specialized personnel, known in the radio world, who manage these things . . . Or else, the record company sends a programmer to a concert in Los Angeles or New York, all expenses paid. In other cases, he or she is invited to Europe on a

pleasure trip, on the company's account, of course . . . Another
way to promote records is the one CBS uses: it doesn't give a cent
to the artistic directors, but from time to time it gives them a
special promotion deal of records to give the public; it may be a
thousand, two thousand, three thousand, five thousand records
by the strongest artists: Chicago, or Earth, Wind and Fire.[9]

This exposé is in sharp contrast to the official views of the EMI
management in London (the Capitol brand is part of EMI). This is
how EMI's international manager answered the question: how
about countries where bribery and corruption is common? Do you
just play the game?

There is no way EMI would condone any form of jiggery-pokery
internationally. This is one of the things we're very sensitive
about. Because when you're operating in as many countries as we
are, we not only have to be absolutely white – we have to be seen
to be white. It's a risk you can't afford to take . . . I think we have
to be more sensitive about this than many other companies, to the
extent that memoranda have been circulated internally giving
very clear instructions about the ethics we should apply. Even to
the extent that executives are discouraged from accepting over-
lavish Christmas presents. It goes the whole way through – I think
this is correct.[10]

One way of avoiding some of the 'jiggery pokery' is to make
phonogram company contributions to broadcasters official by selling time on the station.

Record companies in Kenya can buy their own weekly slots on the
Voice of Kenya – normally they do this together with a manufacturer of some other consumer product. Thus CBS Kenya have joined
up with the manufacturers of Tiger Shoes to provide the thirty
minute 'Sunday Express' on the Voice of Kenya's English–language
channel. CBS record the programme, all the records on it are from
CBS, and most of them are international repertoire since the
company relies on the VoK's own programmes for promotion of
local and other East African artists. This arrangement does not give
the VoK overall control of the music policy of the station; outside
gatekeepers with clearly defined commercial interests are allowed
to decide part of the phonogram output.

The same system is used in Jamaica – certain times of the day are
reserved for sponsored programmes. The cost is not so high that
only the largest phonogram companies can utilize the opportunity
(as is the case in Kenya) – even small producers can be heard

presenting 15 minutes of their own releases on the Jamaican Broadcasting Corporation.

One of the most long-standing examples of co-operation between the broadcasting and the phonogram industry is that of the SLBC (Sri Lankan Broacasting Corporation) and EMI/Polygram. For many years the SLBC has played the same role in Asia as Radio Luxembourg in Europe. The SLBC's Asian Beam has transmitted a stream of sponsored programmes aimed mainly at India. For some time the SLBC was the main disseminator of Indian film music on the Indian sub-continent (particularly when this music wasn't featured on many Indian stations). The SLBC also runs weekly shows for Polygram and EMI. The 'HMV Star Show' is recorded by EMI-India and sent as a reel of tape to Colombo, Sri Lanka, where the SLBC does not get paid any cash for this service – it accepts payment 'in kind'. Polygram and EMI deliver a bundle of new phonograms each month, free of charge. Thus much of the music on the SLBC's English channel, particularly on its new stereo test transmissions, consists of phonograms from these two majors. (Where the SLBC External Service does generate cash is from another source, namely from various American evangelical organizations which buy time for religious propaganda. According to one SLBC official 'they keep on paying however much we charge, even for the most unattractive slots').

CAN BROADCASTERS BE INDEPENDENT?

Whilst few broadcasting stations are so well off financially that they can say no to free samples of phonograms, many do try to retain some semblance of independence. Sometimes bureaucratic tools are applied. A senior producer or group of producers design a 'playlist' consisting of the phonograms presenters are currently allowed to play on the station. The gatekeeper function thus becomes concentrated in the hands of a few people and the individual presenters and producers, in theory at least, are not exposed to too many temptations in their dealings with the phonogram industry. The negative effect of this, of course, is that the individual presenters and producers, in theory at least, are not exposed to too many temptations in their dealings with the phonogram industry. The negative effect of this, of course, is that the individual producer's emotional involvement in the work of moulding the station's music policy becomes strictly curtailed. The BBC tried this method for a while on its Radio 1 AM channel in the UK, but returned to a situation with individual freedom of choice for producers after a few years.

Letting the listeners decide . . .

Another common method of trying to avoid getting trapped in the phonogram company snare is to pass the responsibility on to the listener, either through concluding that the music in programmes with high audience figures is solely what the station should play, or by allowing listeners' requests to dictate music policy. Each alternative can be equally treacherous from a cultural point of view.

Listeners' requests are inevitably geared to the listeners' own expectations of what the radio station is likely to play – no listener who wishes to hear his or her request played on a Top 10 request show is likely to ask for a work by Bela Bartok. Audience research figures should also be treated with care, if the notion of cultural responsibility is to play any role in broadcasting policy. It is foolhardy to assume that the public is 'getting what it wants' because a lot of people watch or listen to a certain programme on television or radio. It stands to reason that the public prefers what it has got used to. Preference refers only to the available alternatives. When the gatekeepers stick to well-proven formulae, they are in effect restricting the number of alternatives available to the public. In the case of music this means that strict Top 40 formats on radio can only have the effect of streamlining and decreasing the output of music available to the public.* This tendency is then augmented by the phonogram industry who gear their production to what they believe the radio stations will play.

This argument is supported by audience research data from the land of statistics, Sweden, where popularity ratings (in terms of actual viewers) of TV programmes rarely show any correlation with the equivalent quality ratings provided by the same viewers. This does not necessarily mean that the general public is a collection of morons; the public will choose from the available alternatives. Getting to appreciate a new form of culture requires a certain amount of mental effort – the public cannot be expected to exert themselves if mass media do not constantly make new alternatives available.

When Otto Donner, a former head of light entertainment at Finnish Radio said: 'the public will like anything if you give them time to get used to it', he was not being cynical. He was being a pragmatic visionary. Donner's analysis was based in part on his own experiences of changing programme formats at Finnish Radio. At one point Donner revolutionized the music entertainment output of his station by consciously introducing new sounds, such as Indian

---

* Even safety in numbers is no guarantee against this phenomenon. Chile's 208 different radio stations provide a small range of music. Spanish-language pop (but very little Chilean music) and Anglo-American disco style dominate (1981).

Ragas, into what had traditionally been a stream of standard light music evergreens. This led to an uproar. Listeners wrote and phoned in their complaints. The phonogram industry muttered. But Donner persevered – the new format stayed for two years. At the end of this period it was decided that Finnish Radio would return to the old, traditional light music format. How did the public at large react? There was an even bigger uproar. They had had time to get used to something and had grown to like it!

Getting phonograms from sources other than local

Radio stations in small countries are normally dependent on local phonogram companies for their supply of commercial recordings. This means that, in effect, the A & R men at the local commercial companies decide what is available for the local broadcasting stations. Thus one gets a situation where phonogram companies (particularly those who are licensees for the majors) often press up a limited number of copies merely to ensure a formal release on the market and to test the reaction of the gatekeepers at the radio. If the radio plays it, then full-scale production is started. If not, then the losses are small.

One way of avoiding this form of manipulation is to provide funds for individual producers at broadcasting stations to buy foreign phonograms independently of local phonogram companies.

This problem was the basis of one of the main complaints from European broadcasters at the 1981 European Broadcasting Union light music forum. Phonogram companies do not provide proper access to records from smaller European nations – they tend to stick to safe bets from the USA or UK Top 40 charts. The EBU was asked to organize an alternative information exchange system outside the commercial restraints of the phonogram industry. This would hopefully make it possible for radio/TV producers in, say, Austria to know about interesting phonogram productions in, say, Sweden.

The resolution of many of these problems depend ultimately, of course, on the individual ideologies and interests of broadcasters. Most tragic of all is the attitude of contempt that lies behind statements such as: 'personally I don't think much of it, but the public likes it, so we have to play it'. However simple it may seem, the fact is that an honest desire to play what the presenter/producer considers to be good music is probably the only valid defence against any tricks the phonogram industry might get up to, inadvertently or willingly. This is probably why a person like John Peel has survived so long on the BBC. Regarded by many as outrageous, he does continuously seek to provide the tasting public with new alternative musical sensations. Many other disc jockeys' only claim to fame is the ability to produce a constant stream of aural diarrhoea.

THOSE UNRELIABLE SALES CHARTS

Sales reports are frequently used as a basis for music programmes on the radio. Most countries have or have had Top 20 style programmes based on different types of sales returns which purport to reflect public demand for phonograms. The basic dual fallacy in this concept is

(a) that sales charts, even if they are accurate, do not reflect the music taste of the whole listening population, but only of the smaller percentage who actually buy phonograms, and

(b) sales charts rarely are accurate since they are always vulnerable to various types of manipulation.

Over the years, a number of broadcasting organizations have given up their chart programmes. Austria did so because they were deemed to be incompatible with the demands of impartiality in the ORF's broadcasting charter. Companies with products on the sales charts were seen as having an unfair advantage over those without. Also it was noted that this unfair bias was augmented in the case of phonograms that sell large quantities but over a longer period of time. Such products can never compete with the quick turn-over hits for a place on charts which reflect weekly and not cumulative sales.

Trinidad and Tobago's National Broadcasting Service have also discontinued chart programmes, for similar reasons. This commercial service accepts advertising from phonogram companies. It is felt that rich companies can thus 'buy their way' into the charts, giving them an unfair advantage over small producers if programmes are based on sales. Of course, if the payola accusations referred to previously are correct, then such a bias in favour of those with pecuniary resources would appear to be present with or without a Top 20 sales chart programme.

Radio Portales, the popular AM station in Santiago, Chile, has also done away with the charts.

> We used to have them, but no longer. Our audience research showed that people prefer a mixture of new and old tunes. They used to like the chart programmes, but no longer[11]

Sales charts are an obvious target for manipulation, of which there are many cases on record. Top 20 lists are usually based on information gathered from samples of shops which are asked to keep logs of sales. The chart compilers either phone or collect the logbooks once a week. There are many potential sources of inaccuracy in this system. Sometimes shops do not report actual sales, but give false returns reflecting what they *would like to sell* (phonograms of which they have many on the shelves, or for which they have committed themselves to take a large order from a wholesaler). Thus in Sweden phonograms actually appeared on the sales charts compiled by the phonogram industry that had only been distributed to a small percentage of shops. After this disclosure the Top 20 programme ('*Kvällstoppen*') was removed from the schedules of the Swedish Broadcasting Corporation (1978). Two years earlier, Danish Radio had removed their Top 20 programme. The decision was partly motivated by reports of chart corruption abroad, and partly by the fact that the charts compiled in Denmark never seemed to tally with actual sales figures reported by the phonogram companies. About the same time Finnish Radio's programme advisory council formally decided against having programmes based on charts or 'sales'; they were deemed to be incompatible with the aims of a non-commercial public service company.

THE INFLUENCE OF THE BRITISH AND AMERICAN TOP 40

Even if small countries decide not to base programming on more or less accurate measurements of public demand in the phonogram market, they can hardly avoid being affected by pronouncements of sales successes in the homelands of the phonogram industry. The British and American charts provide guidelines for phonogram licensees as regards which international repertoire is considered worth releasing in different territories. Disc jockeys the world over like to report on news from the British Top 40 or the Billboard Hot Hundred. This applies to Sri Lanka and Kenya's English-language channels, to the light music output of the Scandinavian broadcasting monopolies, to most of the fifty FM stations in Chile, as well as to the world-embracing pop music output of the influential BBC World Service.

Thus events, including manipulation, in the American and British charts have a direct cultural impact on millions of people in different countries. Not so much is said officially about the Billboard Hot Hundred, but the recent history of the British charts has been a long tale of woe. Firms have cropped up which devote their full-time efforts to 'getting records onto the charts', by identifying shops in the measurement sample, through false purchases in key shops etc, etc. The whole industry seemed to be doing its utmost to fiddle a system which its own branch organization, the BPI, together with the BBC, had designed. In 1981, RCA and WEA paid voluntary fines of £5,000 and £10,000 for irregularities. RCA reported that the wrong-doer in its organization had been identified and disciplinary

SINGLES CHART: P.13; ALBUMS CHART: P.24

AUGUST 22, 1981

MUSIC &VIDEO WEEK

Europe's leading music business paper 90p

RCA PROVIDED some buck's fizz (what else?) to celebrate the signing of its UK deal with Motown Records. From the left, RCA business affairs manager Alan Johnson, Motown International VP Peter Prince, RCA UK MD Don Ellis, and Motown business affairs manager Patrick Moncaster.

Spotlight: two launches and big promo campaign

SPOTLIGHT PUBLICATIONS, publisher of *Music & Video Week*, has announced the launch of two new consumer monthlies and a £335,000 circulation promotion budget for four of its existing titles.

The new monthlies, set for debut in mid-September, are *Kerrang* and *Video For Leisure*. The first is being produced under the aegis of *Sounds* for the heavy metal audience, and three earlier editions published two months ago sold out within days.

The second will be banded with *Hi Fi For Pleasure* for 12 issues at least, as previously reported in *MW*, with a guaranteed circulation of 66,000 for the October and November editions. Wholesale trade orders for *Kerrang* already exceed 100,000.

The promotion campaign centres on *Hi Fi For Pleasure* [with particular emphasis on *Video for Leisure*], *Sounds*, *OVER 21*, and *Record Mirror*.

CHART HYPE—RCA PAYS OUT £5,000 AFTER BPI PROBE

RCA RECORDS after "extensive internal investigation" has concurred with the findings of the BPI that "chart manipulation has occurred", and is to pay the £5,000 costs of the BPI enquiry.

This comes only four months after WEA (*MW*, April 18) volunteered to pay up £10,000 costs after BPI investigations made similar discoveries involving a freelance promotion man and false chart diary entries.

With the RCA case, investigators working for the BPI and British Market Research Bureau, compilers of the charts, had been conducting an undercover operation with the substantial assistance of a chart panel shop.

Recently they discovered that an RCA field promotion representative was attempting to influence sales entries for certain RCA product in the chart diary of the shop.

The rep, Toni Vasili, had in fact been offering the shop free LPs and singles in return for false entries in the sales diary. In addition, she had on at least one occasion put false entries into the diary herself.

Both actions contravene the BPI Code of Conduct, which was introduced at the beginning of this year, to safeguard the accuracy of the charts.

However, BMRB had been alerted to the false entries on the diaries returned by the shop, which had been excluded from the chart compilation.

With the co-operation of RCA, the wrongdoing was identified, and disciplinary action is being taken by the company which has also agreed to pay the costs of the investigation in the sum of £5,000.

Commented BPI director-general John Deacon: "I can only re-emphasise that we will not tolerate these sort of actions by individuals that bring not only their own company into disrepute, but the whole industry as well. There is only

so much that a company can do to ensure it is adhering to the Code individual reps have the same responsibility."

RCA's UK managing director Don Ellis, declined to comment on any aspect of the matter other than to state briefly: "RCA does not condone chart hyping."

Indie calls for stiffer sanctions for hyping

IN A letter to the BPI on the RCA case, Iain McNay of Cherry Red Records calls for stronger deterrents against hyping, and suggests that £50,000 would have been more appropriate in terms of the gravity of the offence.

He urges BPI director general John Deacon to put the matter on the agenda for the next BPI council meeting to gain a mandate for imposing larger penalties than the actual cost of the investigations.

Motown leaves EMI and signs with RCA

THE MOTOWN cliffhanger (*MW*, August 15) was finally resolved at the end of last week with a new long-term licensing agreement for the UK with RCA Records, which begins on October 1 this year.

The pact with RCA ends an 18 year association between Motown and EMI Records in this country. Seven people employed by EMI to work on Motown product will hear how the new arrangement affects them some time within the next week. An EMI spokesman told *MW* that the seven were the responsibility of EMI, and discussions would be taking place on their future.

The position with regard to a sell-off period on Motown product released by EMI is also the subject of discussion. A Motown spokesman said that it was "basically three months", but talks would take place on this aspect between Motown, EMI and RCA. EMI is now pressing RCA product following the latter's closure of its UK pressing plant.

Motown Records International vice president Peter Prince commented: "We are looking forward to our new partnership with RCA, and we have been impressed with the way in which they have become a real force in today's highly competitive market.

"For the past 18 years, Motown has enjoyed a highly successful relationship with EMI Records, which has helped us maintain our position as one of the leading independent record labels in the world."

RCA UK managing director Don Ellis, said: "RCA is very pleased to have this opportunity to join with the world's premier black music company. We expect great success together in the black market in the years ahead."

On EMI's behalf, UK managing director Cliff Busby stated "We have enjoyed our highly successful relationship with Motown, and we wish them all the best for the future."

● The pact with RCA is the completion of the process of re-negotiating Motown's European pressing and distribution arrangements, which have been taking place over the past year.

RCA and WEA admit irregularities, and Motown choose RCA because 'they have become a real force in today's highly competitive market'

action had been taken. The trade press informed its readers at the same time that Motown was shifting its UK distribution from EMI to RCA, because RCA had become 'a real force in today's highly competitive record market'[12]

A year later, RCA's UK managing director, Don Ellis, stated he had 'no regrets' about anything RCA had done. He dismissed the BPI's attempts to police its own members' chart fiddles as 'a terrible waste of time and effort . . . this is a competitive business and it doesn't seem an intelligent thing to set up your own police force to police yourself in a competitive business.'[13] In other words, if the opportunity is presented, take it. New electronic technology has been introduced by Gallup in the chart monitoring process in

Britain, but one can assume (human nature and economic realities being what they are) that the phonogram industry will continue to use all means at its disposal to get products on to the influential global charts.* Charts not only occasionally reflect sales – they also generate expectations, and sales. Too much concentration on charts by broadcasters (and A & R men at phonogram companies) can only have a streamlining effect, decreasing rather than expanding the musical horizon of listeners and purchasers alike.

NEEDLE-TIME RESTRICTIONS

The products of phonogram companies, as we have noted, perform the function of providing broadcasters with relatively cheap, attractive programme material. This function is balanced partly by the advertising services broadcasting provides through exposure on the airwaves. In other words, neither the broadcasting nor the phonogram industry can normally survive without each other.

This equation has gradually become modified by the introduction of other factors such as the impact of the Rome Convention (according to which producers and performers have the right to remuneration for radio plays), the financial state of the phonogram industry and labour market considerations for musicians.

With the present downward trend in the financial fortunes of the phonogram industry (augmented to some extent through home-taping from the radio) the industry has joined forces with musicians' organizations demanding higher remuneration when commercial recordings are played. The same alliance has also been active, trying to persuade more governments to sign the Rome convention. The unions traditionally regard each playing of a gramophone record on the radio as causing specific, reclaimable damages to the interests of performing musicians. IFPI lawyers had devoted considerable time to helping musicians' unions in different countries (their traditional opponents in the labour market) organize collecting societies to facilitate the introduction of the Rome Convention.

In its negotiations with broadcasting organizations, the phonogram industry can frequently be heard claiming that broadcasters exaggerate the advertising value of radio plays. The 1980 Performing Rights Tribunal, held in the UK, seemed to uphold the industry case, ruling on an increase in the neighbouring rights payment British radio stations should pay for the use of commercial recordings. On the other hand, the phonogram industry still devotes a large chunk of cash to various forms of 'plugging'. Whatever the

* In late 1982, an employee of the independent organization (British Market Research Bureau) who handled the confidential chart data was sacked after an investigation by a handwriting expert.

official standpoint, the industry still attaches a lot of importance to getting its products played on the radio.

Labour market considerations have been satisfied in some countries by negotiations on so-called 'needle-time' restrictions. According to these, broadcasters are bound to fill part of their air time, not with needles running in grooves, but with the stations' own recordings. This had provided particular problems for the BBC in Britain. To satisfy the needle-time requirements, groups of musicians have been given studio facilities where they try to reproduce their own phonograms as accurately, and as quickly as possible. With the increased use of complex multi-channel techniques in commercial studios, this has become increasingly more difficult, if not pointless. Stuart Grundy, who has been with BBC Radio 1 since its inception in 1967 has become well aware of the problems of a public service station living with needle-time restrictions in a commercial environment.

> It is important though for us to remember that we are not making records. Some bands forget that fact and, having just finished an album that has taken months to record, they get quite a shock when they realize that they have about eight hours in which to record five numbers from the same LP for transmission on the radio. Some of them seem almost incapable of doing it . . . .[14]

Needle-time restrictions might keep a few session musicians at work but they do not guarantee that radio stations will play a repertoire that extends beyond the boundaries of that of the phonogram industry.

Sweden and Denmark are signatories to the Rome Convention. There are no needle-time limits, but remuneration to performers and producers is pegged to inflation. The rate in Sweden, originally fixed by a court judgement after a 'phonogram strike' way back in the Sixties, was almost up to 3,000 kronor/hour (about £300) in 1982 for phonograms from countries which were signatories. In other words, it was fast approaching the cost of recording some forms of live music. This rise also provided Swedish radio accountants with a way of saving money. Phonograms from countries which were non-signatories involve no payments to performers or producers when played on the radio. In other words, all material from two influential phonogram producing countries, the USA and France, costs Swedish radio about £5 per minute less than, say, Swedish material. For a number of years during the Seventies, Sweden's only radio station banned *Swedish* phonograms from the air waves certain hours every night. This measure was discontinued after an outcry from the music establishment, but was re-introduced on a smaller scale (30 minutes a day) in 1982. Such an anomaly, of course, places added pressure on the domestic recording industry which is already at a disadvantage, culturally and economically, in its attempts to balance the overflow of Anglo-Saxon pop culture. One must admit, though, that the Swedish phonogram industry did pretty well out of its negotiations via the courts with Swedish radio over fifteen years ago. Remuneration in Sweden with its 8 million inhabitants is as much as 75 per cent of the fee paid by the BBC for its most popular radio channel in a kingdom of 55 million.

DOES SUCCESS DEPEND ON WHAT'S PLAYED ON RADIO?

The previous pages might have given the impression that the phonogram industry is unlikely to put any money into recording projects if the results are not likely to be played on the radio. This rule applies in most countries. But, as with all rules, there are one or two dramatic exceptions. If radio stations refuse to play a particular type of music which happens to be popular (whatever that means), then that music will find other channels of dissemination. This probably applies only to cult, pornographic and 'collector's item' phonograms in Scandinavia. It did also apply, a few years ago in Sweden, to the hundreds of phonograms released by the dance bands who used to entertain people in the provinces on Friday and Saturday nights. Their music was rarely played on Swedish radio because its quality was deemed to be too low. Some of the bands sold up to 300,000 copies of each phonogram – so they succeeded, via live performances, in using their social function to create a demand.

In two of the MISC countries we have come across phonogram industries which seem to survive almost totally independently of local broadcasting. In Sri Lanka the state-controlled SLBC broadcasts about 16 hours of music daily in the Sinhalese commercial channel. Two thirds of this is produced by the SLBC's own orchestras with guest soloists. The material has to be cleared in advance by a music committee. Recordings are stored by transferring them through a very aged cutting machine to 78 rpm acetates. These are then played over and over again. Needless to say, they sound very scratchy after one to two spins (far worse than the international phonograms played on the English-language channel). Local commercial phonogram companies can buy time and send in their own tapes, which also often sound much better than the station's own recordings, but these have to comply with the music policy of the SLBC.

The result of this system is that certain popular forms of music are rarely featured on the SLBC. But the local phonogram industry has managed to promote them all the same.

One of the pioneers of the Sri Lankan phonogram industry is Mr Gerald Wickremasooriya of the Sooriya record company. When we sought him out we found an old, almost blind man who was about to wind up his business. But he had vivid memories of his early days with the local industry.

There was a time, before the cassettes came, when we used to depend on the SLBC for publicity . . . but there were always problems. They never let you play your best songs. The SLBC had this foolish policy of banning pop songs. They started banning indiscriminately. That was because the SLBC is dominated by Indian trained classical musicians. They're not only against pop, they're even against our own traditional music . . . that crowd is in charge of Radio Ceylon [the SLBC's former name] . . . To that crowd, pop is poison.

I recorded a song called 'Dilhani' in 1969 – it was the first genuine Sinhalese pop song. When I went to the director of music on the Sinhalese service he said: 'Do you want me to play that poison?' . . . So when it became a success, I met him again and asked: 'How do you like the success of my poison?' He had nothing to say, of course.[15]

The gatekeepers at the SLBC clearly believe they have a duty to follow certain standards for the sake of the country's culture. But they are also aware, it would seem, of the need for some flexibility.

The problem we face in the commercial service is that when the businessmen ask for time to broadcast very cheap music for the teenagers, then just for the sake of selling air time we sometimes oblige. But we do have a policy. We have to maintain our standards. The problem is that there is no control over all the cassettes and discs distributed through the private record bars.[16]

One area which the SLBC only touches about 15 minutes daily, but which has become a great commercial success with the free import of cassettes, is the Baila music we have mentioned earlier. Baila, reminiscent lyrically of the calypso, rhythmically of the samba, can be bought everywhere in Sri Lanka. It has a quick turnaround, but does not rely on radio promotion. How is this possible? One plausible explanation is that a new group of gatekeepers with the means of dispersal at their disposal have entered the music arena, namely taxi drivers. They play cassettes, often very loudly, round the clock. Passengers hear them. The word gets passed around.

Taxi drivers (as well as bus and truck drivers) seem to take over this gatekeeping role in many societies where the official broadcasting services pursue a policy of ignoring popular forms which the public can get access to by other means. The early growth of pre-recorded cassettes in Finland and Norway as opposed to Sweden has been attributed to this fact. Sweden was the only Scandinavian country to introduce a fully fledged, 24-hour music channel in the Sixties. Taxi drivers in Stockholm did not feel the same need to invest in cassettes as their colleagues in Oslo or Helsinki.

Similar observations can be made in Tunisia. The popular folk songs of artists who sing at weddings, circumcision ceremonies etc, together with some Egyptian film music, form the basis of the Tunisian cassette industry. Most of this material is not featured on the Arabic service of the Radio Television Tunisienne (RTT). The RTT, just like the SLBC, has its own house bands which only record music which has been approved in advance by a music committee. The French service (international channel) – which can only be heard in Tunis – is freer in its choice of music, including even semi-political songs with an element of social criticism. But most of the promotion of the cassettes (and most of these are pirated) occurs totally independently of the RTT. Strangely enough, most of these non-radio cassettes have been recorded at the RTT studios (there are no restrictions on content when the RTT rents out its facilities to commercial companies).

The Cuban singer/composer Silvio Rodriguez has maintained his popularity in Chile throughout the period of military rule, despite his absence from the air-waves. Admittedly, one of his songs has been recorded by Chile's Gloria Simonette, and this recording has been featured on Radio Portales, but Rodriguez' music is spread by other means, via cassette recorders. The positive side of the government's free import policy has been access to music industry technology. The cassette has provided a means of circumnavigating the military junta's clamp-down on freedom of expression.

The examples quoted above show that broadcasters cannot assume that the music they do not play or do not approve of will die a quiet death without their support. Modern hardware technology has undermined the educational monopoly of the broadcaster. Disc jockeys in their clubs and taxi drivers in their cabs can also disperse music. Even if chart programmes are officially banned from the radio, the information in them however inaccurate it is, seems to find ways of distributing itself.

Although dissatisfaction about their compilation might have led to their removal, there is always a temptation to resurrect Top 20 style programmes, because they generate audiences which find the competitive element stimulating. Saying no to something which a lot of people appear to like can have a devastating effect if carried out too suddenly or too totally. This is borne out by experiences from Finland and Kenya.

Conscious attempts were made to increase the amount of Finnish music played (on the radio) . . . . today slightly over 20 per cent of all records played are Finnish by origin. A ratio of 30 per cent has been unofficially discussed within the company . . . it seems that the new policy adopted by Finnish radio in the 1970s did a great deal to encourage new talent . . . The policy was so successful that there were complaints from older, established record companies about excessive air-time given to the new companies' products.

An eclectic music policy, however, has the risk of alienating subgroups within the audience. In the late 70s there were signs of young people turning away from the radio. A new programme format, 'Rock Radio', was introduced in 1980. The programme was broadcast at different hours, several times a week with Finnish and foreign rock, interviews and commentary, and reaching a remarkably young audience[17].

The dangers of trying to implement new music policies too quickly or without adequate preparation is admirably illustrated by events at the Voice of Kenya in March 1980. The Kenyan Ministry of Information, responsible for broadcasting, suddenly decreed that 75 per cent of the music on the English-language General Service should be of Kenyan origin. The Ministry's decree was not motivated so much by cultural considerations. The order merely reflected a desire to be able to compete with neighbouring Radio Tanzania which had become very popular, even in Kenya, with a policy of 100 per cent East African music on its National Service. (Kenya and Tanzania are not the best of friends; their border has been closed since the collapse of the East African Community in 1976.)

The effect on the VoK was quite traumatic. Overnight, producers and presenters were expected to stop playing so much ABBA and Boney M and replace them with local music. The VoK did not have the necessary resources or the will-power to carry this out. The station had almost completely given up recording live music (this responsibility had been gradually handed over to commercial interests with private studios). The staff were not motivated to support the efforts of the local musicians despite the hundreds of records produced annually by Kenyan phonogram companies.

> I am underpaid. I'm overworked. Local Kenyan music sounds so awful you just can't think of anything to say in between numbers. It's completely different when you're playing ABBA or Boney M. I don't understand why they try to make us play Kenyan music which people just do not want to hear . . .
> Incidentally, I first heard ABBA's Fernando on the BBC. Then I phoned up Phonogram and suggested that they release it in Kenya. It took them 3 whole months before it appeared. But it did become a big hit. And did Phonogram show their gratitude? No – they didn't give me the slightest token of gratitude. Just the usual Christmas present . . .[18]

After no more than two weeks, the VoK directive was revoked. Local musicians and small phonogram companies claimed that VoK staff in collusion with the international phonogram companies had sabotaged the exercise. The management of Polygram thought that lobbying by local African-owned companies was the cause of the new policy.

> They probably went to the Ministry of Information, met a junior minister, convinced him, maybe with a bottle of wine . . .

The influential Kenyan press probably brought about the sudden return to normal at the VoK. Consider this editorial in *The Nation*[20] under the heading 'VoK should stop playing such boring music'.

> This decision is disappointing many thousands of wananchi [citizens] who used to enjoy music from all over the world on the General Service . . . today, that freedom is gone, and whether you like it or not, you have to listen to what the so-called cultural fighters of the VoK call indigenous music on all the services . . .
> Are we now to be subjected to the same kind of indoctrination via the radio as is happening in some neighbouring countries, where people are told that listening to Western music is the same as being imperialist stooges? Are the cultural fighters of the VoK so naive as not to understand that music is so international that it knows no political boundaries? . . . Kenyans should have the freedom to choose freely the clothes they wear, the books they read, the music they listen to and even the food they eat. Deciding for the people what they should read and listen to is encroaching on their freedom of choice, which is no business for the so-called

cultural warriors of the Voice of Kenya . . . So why don't the bosses of the VoK give the people what they want? Why?

The following week, the letters to the editor columns were opened for the subject and a debate started which was still continuing when we returned to Kenya two and a half years later. Here are two of the first contributions. They illustrate the two extremes, so common in small countries; pride or scorn for your national culture.

(1) The views of your columnist in the Nation of March 9th must not go unchallenged . . . What is wrong when wananchi are entertained by music of their own languages? . . . I don't see why Mr Kadhi [*The Nation* leader writer] was scornfully using the expression 'so-called cultural fighters of the VoK'. In fact he was arguing as though he himself was a European in African skin. There are a few like him too . . . we should promote even the meagre remnants of our shattered culture as much as possible. Let us feel proud of ourselves as a people . . .
(2) So fellow patriots at the VoK, you can't put us frustratingly at ransom because of your cultural rebirth. Have you fallen prey to Ayatollah Khomeini's sermon that Western music is like opium which was to be banished? To some of us, Western music is the only form of entertainment. You can laugh it off, but it's a fact.

In this context, it is interesting to note that the unsuccessful coup attempt against President Moi on August 1st 1982 started early on a Sunday morning at the Voice of Kenya, with a change of music policy. Instead of the soothing tones of Jim Reeves, Kenyans awoke to the rhythmical sounds of East African pop (the government described it as 'music for students' and imposed extra restrictions on the University). One VoK official who survived the events of August 1st claimed that the Kenyan Air Force personnel, who are said to have staged the coup, made a tactical error with their choice of music. 'March music should accompany any coup attempt, not East African pop'. (The Air Force did not succeed in persuading the Army to support their venture.)

Radio music policy can have far-reaching effects in small countries!

LIVE BROADCASTS – THE TANZANIAN EXPERIENCE

Since Tanzania has virtually no phonogram industry, the country's broadcasting monopoly had to decide whether to base its music output on imports of foreign records or build up its own production apparatus. Radio Tanzania opted 100 per cent for the latter on its domestic ('National') services. Its external services, which are mainly in English, beamed at South Africa, still include many Middle of the Road style international phonograms.

Radio Tanzania's national service, which is also audible and popular in neighbouring countries, is a remarkable music station. Most of its output has been recorded on tapes by the station's own engineers. Instead of relying on a record library, Radio Tanzania uses a tape library as its source of phonograms. Numbers are selected from the 1,500 or so tapes with 56 different orchestras (figures for 1980) either according to the preference of individual presenters or as a result of listeners' requests (24,500 a month in 1980). Radio Tanzania records two local electric groups (jazz bands) a week as well as choirs and traditional groups (often on location out in the provinces). Programme director, Suleiman Hegga, describes this nationalist policy as a result of

a consciousness campaign dating back to 1964. In 1973 we decided not to play foreign music on the National Service. We had to give our own chaps a chance. There were some complaints at first, but people started to understand by and by. Now they appreciate it. Even in 1974 we still had some problems with our own engineers with traditional music. They put more effort into recording jazz bands than traditional musicians. The engineers used to ignore the wishes of traditional musicians – for instance the drummers who need a fire to heat their drums (to stretch the skins). We had to arrange for an electric fire to be installed in the studio. . . . Now we can distinguish between local and foreign bands. Previously, the local bands just tried to copy the foreign groups. Now they're writing original compositions instead of just copying soul or Congolese music[21].

With music playing an important communicative role in society, these developments are understandable extensions of Tanzanian cultural policy (cf. Chapter 6).

It's easier to get a message through with music than a spoken word programme – thus music assumes an importance. Foreign groups don't care about things like this . . . our aim is to protect and develop our music culture.[22]

The positive results of the Tanzanian experience can be seen in the development of a buoyant live music scene. Radio promotes music groups through its own live recordings. The public then go to hear the groups who perform live three or four times a week. Foreign groups (mainly Zairean) who pioneered the East African jazz band style, and who have remained in Tanzania now sing in Swahili which people can understand rather than Lingala (examples are the Safari Sound. Orchestre Maquis, Macassy etc.). Tanzanian groups, such as Dar International and Mlimani Park, have developed their own melodic variant of the Zaïre/Congolese style and enjoy popularity over much of East Africa thanks partly to the resources provided by Radio Tanzania.

The negative results (if that is the correct term) of Radio Tanzania's success in developing local music, are related to the country's lack of phonogram industry resources. A shortage of foreign currency has brought record imports to a standstill. Cassettes and cassette recorders seem to be fairly plentiful despite an official ban on imports (1980). But there is a big market for stolen tapes from Radio Tanzania, particularly in neighbouring Kenya where magnetic recordings can be transferred to discs. With Tanzania enjoying virtually no international copyright protection, Tanzanian composers find themselves in a very unsatisfactory situation.

BROADCASTING'S RESPONSIBILITY TO THE COMMUNITY

Musicians all round the world frequently complain that broadcasters nearest to them give them the least support. Often their criticism is well-founded; broadcasters tend to favour established cultural trends in their own search for popularity.

Even Great Britain as a nation once experienced this situation. In 1948, British songwriters reported that only 19 per cent of music on the BBC was British. American music dominated. They advocated the same sort of quota system that had been applied to American films after the war.

> The trouble for the British composer was that American dominance, once established, became exceptionally difficult to overcome. With the interdependency of the two media (radio and publishing/phonogram industry), a sort of vicious circle came into existence. So long as American music was popular, the BBC devoted a large proportion of its programmes to American music[23]

By 1958 the percentage of British music on the BBC fell to 14.8 per cent. What rescued British music was the pop boom led by the Beatles.

This early British situation is mirrored all over the world. Welsh music suffers similar problems as a minority culture in Britain –

special Welsh channels on radio and TV, the result of political decisions, provide the only breathing space. The new all-Welsh TV channel (S4C) is a particularly interesting experiment in this context. It provides a small culture with the means of competing in the same media as the larger dominating culture. Whether this works remains to be seen. Those in charge of S4C hope it will provide a model for other small cultures, but there are still many question marks. Its inception was the result of a political decision in London aimed at cooling off an increasingly militant cultural minority in Wales. First indications after its start in November 1982, are that S4C is attracting a large percentage of those who still understand Welsh. Unfortunately it goes off the air at 9 p.m. – so anything not suitable for tender ages is out. On the positive side, S4C has given Welsh language music production a tremendous boost. Many local groups can make video recordings which will be shown on S4C. This is something small local producers in, say, Kenya, could never do. They could never produce tapes which compete with international productions presenting Boney M, ABBA etc.

The dilemma experienced by many musicians in small countries in their dealings with the broadcasters is summed up perfectly by this calypso from Trinidad. This song, 'Cultural assassination', was the Lord Superior's contribution to one of the calypso tents at the 1980 carnival.

The Right and the Honorable Doctor Eric William(s)*
Pan and kaiso is in trouble, and to get me out of this jam
eight years now I am trying to get a broadcast license from you
to help out the culture, but nothing yet
Tell me what to do!
As a born and bred Trinidadian get me out of this . . .
all I'm asking is a token, just a piece of your time
Doctor if you name the place and if you tell me when,
your humble servant Superior will be there
Hear what I want Doc:

Chorus:
I'm seeking permission to make a contribution
to the indigenous culture we got in this land
I am talking 'bout kaiso and pan
local Indian composition
and everything that evolve in this land, like parang,
Doctor we need we own radio station for
local culture promotion

* Dr Williams was Prime Minister of Trinidad at the time.

you must stop – the cultural assassination
Doctor please lend a hand, and please stop –
the cultural assassination.

I came in the calypso business some twenty-seven years ago
but then was the same damn stupidness with airplay for calypso
but those were the colonial days when the white master was still
here
his behaviour never had me amazed, I know master never cares.
But now that we are a nation, Doc, for which you have fought
why allow the radio stations to perpetuate master's thoughts.
What if we change the white slave master, so what have we done
What you should do is show cultural concern.
Hear what I want Doc:

Chorus: . . .
(last two lines:)
Tell Radio Guardian to stop
the cultural assassination

Doctor the stations broadcasting here in Trinidad
their contempt seems everlasting, they're the hardest hard,
they behave like they don't care about no cultural existence
it's only foreign stuff on the radio year after year after year.
Meanwhile Antigua, St. Lucia, Barbados, all them small islands,
if you want to hear calypso I say tune into their stations.
Doctor I don't want no finance, and I don't want no lend
just give me the chance to give culture a hand
So that's all I want Doc:

Chorus: . . .
(Last lines:)
Before the election I say
stop the cultural assassination'

It seems that many broadcasting stations and their employees
never succeed in ascending the local music threshold that Radio
Tanzania managed to clamber over in the early Seventies. One also
has a sneaking suspicion that presenters on small radio stations
prefer the emotional kick provided by playing phonograms from
international stars because of the status they believe this provides.
Far more exciting to play an untouchable rather than someone you
might meet an hour later on the street.
   When a Kenyan musician 'who requested anonymity for fear of a
total embargo on his music' called on the Voice of Kenya in a

newspaper article to change its attitude which he described as 'a conspiracy with local multinational companies to suppress local music', the Director of Broadcasting replied: 'We welcome constructive criticism through the right machinery, but we need no coaching on national patriotism. We are always open to dialogue, but not through newspapers,' the VoK DJs' answer back accused the local Kenyan musicians of 'looking for scapegoats for the chaos they have created. If we give them airtime, they will give the public trash.'[24]

Steel pan drummers in Trinidad are even more forceful in their condemnation of their radio stations' policy towards local music.

> The pseudo-yankee accents, the disco music and rockers continue to spew forth from these with sufficient intensity and regularity such that we may be tempted to believe that we are living somewhere in Alabama or Montego Bay. To say this is not to adopt a rabid anti-foreign stance but rather to affirm a belief that charity certainly begins at home.
>
> It is long overdue that we solicit from the various media some firm commitments for the promotion of local culture. This can take several forms but the bottom line must read increased airtime and television programming and greater exposure through the newspapers for local culture.[25]

WHAT IS TO BE DONE?

What can broadcasting stations do to stimulate a healthy development of local music and avoid some of the energy-consuming conflicts described in these pages?

A number of conclusions can be drawn from our qualitative data.

(1) The gatekeepers who decide which types of music are transmitted have considerable influence over public taste, and thus a great measure of cultural responsibility (even if they regard their work as a commercial operation). This responsibility is even greater in a monopoly situation where competition is absent.

(2) Even if local music is considered to be of poor quality, it will not get any better by being ignored by the local broadcasters. On the contrary, access to the media can have a stimulating effect on the quality of local music.It is significant that music from the two sample countries with the highest local content on the radio (Tanzania and Jamaica) has received international acclaim for its quality.

(3) Broadcasters' freedom of action within this area is heavily curtailed if they do not engage in their own recording activities.

This is particularly critical (a) in the case of public service monopoly organizations and (b) when financial difficulties within the phonogram industry lead to a decrease in the output of music on commercial recordings.

Activities with live music require certain minimum investments in equipment and staff training. If the recording quality at radio/TV studios is regarded as being particularly bad by local or visiting musicians, they will feel little enthusiasm for participating in live recordings. A situation where the technical quality at a broadcasting organization lags too far behind that of local commercial recording studios, is far from satisfactory. This does not mean that broadcasters need all the latest gear (digital, quadrophonic and so on); musicians should not merely try to reproduce phonograms in a live situation.

Recording of live music usually, but not always, costs more than reliance on use of commercial phonograms. In the case of state or licence-funded organizations, some form of official support via cultural policy is required. Commercial broadcasters in many countries already pay a percentage of their advertising revenue to the phonogram industry for the use of commercial recordings. A similar method of funding can also be applied to cover the costs of live music recordings. Pure needle-time restrictions are not a satisfactory solution.

(4) Within all these previous constraints, broadcasters must apply their own qualitative judgements when choosing material. Too often this responsibility is hedged by referring to other evaluations of quality or popularity. 'We're giving the public what they want', 'this is what the public have requested', 'these are the hits the sales charts are predicting' etc. are not convincing arguments.

Despite all their power, however, broadcasters cannot afford to ignore a whole genre of music which the public like and have access to through other means of dispersal (e.g. cassette machines in taxis, video tapes etc.).

Music presenters and producers tend, unfortunately, to isolate themselves in their broadcasting studios, with their thoughts revolving around the international world of art and pop music. The international successes that 'everybody's talking about in London, Paris and New York' are assumed to be the best for the cultural palate of a local listener. Local popular forms of entertainment tend to be culturally underrated and ignored, being left to develop in different directions, often without the influence of any standards of quality.

Neither cultural snobbery nor popularistic audience-hunting are satisfactory solutions. What is often lacking is a measure of education. Broadcasters in the music sector tend to shun the thought that entertainment can be combined with information – even satire is often far too sensitive an issue. Maybe the general public should be given a Top 40 programme, if they like it. But they should also be informed that it is hardly the only truth, so that they can draw their own conclusions about the music they wish to consume.

(5) Broadcasting organizations must follow closely the development of new, low-cost, music industry technology. The availability of cheap recording equipment offers new means of involving listeners in programme production. Musicians can often produce cassettes of their own work which are of a quality which is quite good enough for broadcasting, at least once, in a suitable programme format. By providing this type of opportunity, broadcasters can stimulate amateur music production.

General access to new technology combined with fluctuations in the fortunes of the phonogram industry provide new opportunities and place new demands on the broadcaster. The commercial phonogram is not necessarily always going to be the cheapest or most accessible source of programme material. Good recorded music can be found, in theory at least, in the organization's own tape library, at live concerts, on recordings made by listeners as well as on commercial material. In practice such a flexible approach is hindered by various agreements. The Musicians' Union in Britain does not allow the BBC to play cassettes sent in by listeners (individual initiative of this kind is seen as a threat to the jobs of professional musicians). In Sweden most tapes recorded by the broadcasting corporation can only be played twice before new fees have to be negotiated (for similar reasons). Such regulations restrict a broadcasting organization's ability to act freely, across the board, stimulating both amateur and professional musicianship.

Not only professional and amateur musicians but even listeners can be engaged in broadcasting. Establishing a dialogue with listeners is not the same as inviting them to send in an occasional request so that they can have their name read out, or giving them a telephone number to ring (phone-ins are popular because they are so cheap).

Sweden recently replaced a popularity poll programme where listeners voted on songs each week with a weekly opportunity for one family at a time to express their own opinions about popular tunes. Finland has also had a positive experience of this method of involving listeners.

An extension of this concept is to combine the involvement of listeners, musicians, enthusiasts and various parts of the music industry or establishment. Concerts can be arranged together with commercial or voluntary organizations. As a rule there is no lack of energy and enthusiasm available when human beings really feel involved in activities that are regarded as worth supporting. A national radio network can give a certain town or area the task of producing x hours of music during a given period, say a year ahead. Some sort of personnel resources will be required to co-ordinate the project. Technical resources will be required in the later stages of planning, during rehearsals and transmission. There is no reason why such projects should not provide a positive boost to the music life of any community. They would have the added advantage of giving the broadcasters access to interesting goings-on at a grassroots level.

(6) One way of providing more opportunities for disseminating different types of music over the airwaves is to decentralize broadcasting. Many governments are loath to do this for fear of what might happen if radio 'gets into the wrong hands' (which sometimes covers any voice critical of the government). Sweden introduced an interesting broadcasting experiment in the late Seventies, so-called *närradio* (approximately 'community radio'). A network of small transmitters was established in a number of towns and local organizations covering a variety of areas were allowed slots. Various churches, political organizations, sports, immigrant and music associations took part. Advertising was not allowed. The cost was low at first and many of the music programmes that emerged from enthusiasts gave an idea of what some people thought was lacking on the National Service. They covered everything from rudimentary recordings from jazz and folk clubs, to non-stop disco. A number of radio enthusiasts who had previously had to resort to illegal pirate transmissions could suddenly do more or less what they wanted without being chased by the authorities.

The whole nature of the experiment changed totally, however when various interested parties representing the phonogram industry, professional musicians and composers agreed on the rates they would charge these new music users. A fee of under £200 an hour was enough to remove many of the more interesting music programmes' the sponsors, usually small voluntary organizations, could not afford this. All that was left was a preponderance of religious programmes from various evangelical organizations which never seem to lack funds.

Denmark is also considering introducing the same sort of model for decentralized radio. It will be interesting to note if the same happens to Sweden's neighbour.

FINAL WORD

Radio and television are powerful but not omnipotent. Any monopoly television organization that ignores the spread of video will find the ground slipping from under its feet. Any monopoly radio station that totally ignores a particularly popular genre will find that modern technology allows other forms of distribution to take over. Satellite technology will make the world of communications even smaller.

With these developments continuing at an ever-increasing pace, it becomes more imperative that broadcasters on a local and national level do their utmost to support and develop local and national musics.

Even broadcasting needs cultural visionaries, on all levels. The culture they produce should be entertaining. And there is no reason why the entertainment broadcasters produce should not have a cultural value as well.

9
Patterns of change

My fear is that in another 10 or 15 years' time, what with all the cassettes that find their way into the remotest village, and with none of their own music available, people will get conditioned to this cheap kind of music. Then they will lose their own culture . . . I'm not being sentimental. If this disappears, then the whole world culture will lose one little aspect. However small a nation we are, we still have our own way of singing, accompanying, intonating, making movements and so on. We can make a small but distinctive contribution to world culture. But we could lose it due to lack of organization and finance. The government is all out for nationalism, but when it's a question of development, culture doesn't count for much. Filling our stomachs comes first . . . when they've paid for agriculture, roads, factories, they search in their pockets for their last coin to give it to culture. It's the same in most countries.'
(W. B. Makulloluwa, Sri Lanka 1982)
'When the disco sound orginated in Munich, a new star was born, the Producer. Regarding the future, I would predict that the predominance of the producer and the role of the 'sound, will remain. Recorded music will tend to become more international. The land of origin will become less discernible.' (Wolfgang Arming, Polygram Austria, 1979)

These two statements spotlight some of the major global effects of the growth of the music industry over the last decade, and some of the dilemma it has caused.

Music industry technology has found its way, in a very short time, into every corner of the earth. Both software and hardware can be found in even the remotest village in every country, irrespective of social or economic system. No other technology has penetrated society so quickly – what is more, the rate of penetration appears to be accelerating. At the same time governments seem to be aware that their traditional cultural heritage could be threatened, but are not sure what to do, or cannot act because of other priorities. Also, international producers of audio and visual products, partly through losses resulting from their own inventions, are forced to try to sell similar products in as many different countries as possible. A transnational form of nationless culture develops. Through a process of integration and concentration different sectors of the music, electronic and communications industries have been amalgamated into giant conglomerates, so complex in their organizational structure that even individual employees do not know who owns what. At the same time, the amount of music in our environment has increased to such a level that, even if a saturation point has not been reached, it is already getting harder to experience silence! And the problems of identifying usage of music, for the purpose of correctly remunerating creators and performers, is nigh on becoming an insoluble problem.

This scenario, however bleak it might appear at a superficial glance, is not entirely negative. The sound cassette has given thousands of people the opportunity to hear more music. To a certain extent the user can decide what music he or she wants to hear on their cassettes. The cassettes can even be used for recording the sound of the small peoples themselves. The very accessibility of music industry technology has brought about another common pattern of change, particularly noticeable in smaller cultures. It has provided the pre-requisite for a counter-reaction against the transnationalization of music – even if no local music cultures have been totally unaffected by international music products. (We will try to explain this process later in this chapter by introducing the concept of 'transculturation'.) The transformation of the business side of the music industry into a number of giant concerns has not stopped small enterprises, often run by enthusiasts, from cropping up everywhere. As regards copyright questions, musicians and composers are becoming more active than ever before in the protection of their rights and in actions aimed at compensating losses.

We will embark on our summary of changes by referring back to the developments prior to the Seventies described in Chapter 1 in connection with our mini-comparison of four sample countries (Tanzania, Tunisia, Trinidad and Sweden). Our summary noted similarities regarding changes in mode of performance, style and structure, organization, use and function of music. A continuation of the same patterns of change can be noted throughout our sample. Traditional music forms become subjected to the demands of stage shows. Quality is judged through official competitions or, in the case of commercially reproduced music, through its apparent performance in the market place. Such changes affect the music that is played and the musicians who play it. Different styles become streamlined. Virtuosity becomes a measure of individual prowess. This applies equally well to dancers and musicians in Sri Lanka, Tunisia or Kenya who perform traditional art (out of a traditional context) for tourists as it does to, say, steelpan bands who concentrate all their efforts on performing one piece of music at the annual

Trinidad panorama competitions at the expense of the rest of their repertoire. When the stage is an international competition, this process goes one step further (as in, for instance, the Eurovision Song Contest) producing a streamlining effect over national borders. This latter effect is accentuated further by the media industry's need to present a lowest common denominator in terms of cultural products that can be sold in as many countries as possible. There is an interesting interplay here between the value system applied in judging competitions and the choices made by those who enter them. ABBA from Sweden made their name initially by winning the Eurovision Song Contest – this gave them access to a world market. But they won because they prepared the right sort of stage performance for the values applied in judging the Eurovision Song Contest. Their success prompted many other ABBA-type groups to do the same in subsequent years. Selection procedures such as competitions comprise, in other words, a pattern of change.

The significance of the value system in this context is illustrated by the calypso monarch competitions in Trinidad. The 1983 winner, Tobago Crusoe, sang two songs at the finals. One was about black cricketers accepting money to play in South Africa; the other was a critical analysis of the Trinidadian economy. One can hardly imagine a European artist singing anything like that in the Eurovision Song Contest. The common denominator in Eurovision is a total absence of anything that could be interpreted as social, or even worse, political. How do the Trinidadians do it? Obviously the calypso's long tradition of social involvement plays a role. The other factor is the value system applied by the judges. Points are awarded both for subject and lyrics. (Imagine if only the same system could be tried out just once with the Eurovision Song Contest.)

Other patterns noted in Chapter 1 and observed to continue in our sample are those concerning:

- the style and structure of music (adaptation to concert hall conditions, decrease in stylistic variations of traditional forms),
- organizational changes (government involvement, integration into the economic system) and
- the use and function of music (cementing group identity, use as a time-filler, use for political or commercial information).

There is considerable overlap between these areas of change. The actual direction and speed of change is determined by a number of technological, economical and organizational factors which can affect musical activity on a local, national and international level (cf. original MISC model, Chapter 1).

The most spectacular factor, as we have already indicated, is the development and spread of music industry technology. This can be sub-divided into two areas: music instrument and amplification technology, and phonogram and mass media technology.

The effects of technology on music-making and music reception also depend on economic and organizational factors. Significant developments here are the development of what we referred to in Chapter 3 as 'the Big and the Small', government policies on a cultural and economic plane, the relationship between different types of music and different sources of finance, the cost and service requirement aspects of new technology, international agreements and money flows in the area of music, etc., to name but a few.

We will now consider the spread of music industry technology – first regarding instruments and amplification, secondly phonogram technology.

AMPLIFIED, ELECTRIFIED AND ELECTRONIC

One of the most significant developments throughout the past two decades has been the spread of amplified, electrified and electronic instruments. Instruments with microphones present the immediate advantage that, as long as electric current and amplifiers are available, performers can make their presence felt more easily in terms of decibels than with traditional instruments. It is often much easier to play a loud chord on a guitar with a microphone and an amplifier than it is to develop the technique of performing on, say, a traditional instrument that is intended to be heard over large distances. This has had a negative effect on traditional arts of producing volume acoustically rather than resorting to electricity.

Amplification has not been restricted to guitars – virtually every traditional instrument can now be heard in an amplified version. This applies both to violins, 'cellos and flutes when introduced into jazz or pop in the West, as well as to traditional instruments such as the hand piano (*mbira*) in Africa.

Adding a microphone and connecting it to an amplifier is the simplest form of adapting an instrument to electronic technology. The next stage could be termed the production of electric instruments, where notes are produced in conventional ways, but where the instrument can only be used together with an amplifier. These become totally worthless if there is no electric current. By the early Seventies, mass-produced electric guitars had spread to every country in our sample, having a profound effect on the music that was being played (both Western and adaptations of traditional tunes), but also on factors such as stage requirements – an orchestra playing on a lorry would have to have a portable generator, for instance.

Electronic instruments

Another product of music industry technology in the field of instruments is the development of electronic producers of sounds, where tones are created via electronic circuits. Electronic organs such as the Hammond did have some mechanically rotating parts for tremolo effects, but the generations of synthesizers that have emerged through the Seventies are entirely solid state (with the obvious exception of the keyboard). A common goal in the design and use of these instruments is to reproduce synthetically sounds that are as similar as possible to those produced by natural instruments. This has been developed to the stage where certain drum synthesizers even have small departures from regular tempo in their programmes to make the results sound more human. Another use of synthesizers is the production of new sounds that traditional instruments have not produced – such electronic effects have often provided the gimmicks that are added to make disco music more attractive. The development of electronic circuit techniques has also enabled these mass-produced instruments to be adapted to different cultures. Some organs imported into Tunisia have microtones so that they can be incorporated into Arabic music.

By the early Eighties, synthesizers could be found in all the MISC countries. In Tunisia we came across a synthesizer that was being programmed to produce a sound similar to that of the local bagpipes. The resulting sound was mixed with the natural sound on a cassette recording of popular folk music, thus producing different tonal qualities on the phonogram version of this music than would be heard under normal conditions, say, at a wedding reception.

Musicians everywhere are now aware of the progression through amplified and electric to electronic instruments and gadgets. There is no critical debate in the popular sector regarding positive or negative effects of always incorporating the latest 'black box' into one's music. The desire to have access to the latest means of producing new sounds encourages musicians to try to keep abreast of the 'state of the art' everywhere. Information about new 'black boxes' is gleaned from listening to phonograms, reading specialist magazines or through travelling and travellers.

We should stress that the spread of electric instruments has not led to musicians departing entirely from traditional music forms (even if some have developed completely new repertoires for the purpose of, say, entertaining tourists from other countries). It is quite usual to find musicians in any country who turn to their own traditional music for rhythmical or melodic inspiration, popularizing it through their own treatment with electronic instruments and amplification. But the electrified versions of established music forms developed in this way seem to survive at the expense of traditional versions.

The Public Address system

We return now to the first case in the spread of instrument technology, namely amplification of a very special instrument, the human voice. Common to all our sample countries is the spread of Public Address systems, involving both the use and abuse of the microphone. This has accompanied and encouraged the development of music performances from being part of traditional events and rituals, often with amateur participants, to be stage performances by professional entertainers. With the advent of the microphone, the art of projecting one's voice over large distances or to fill a large auditorium (e.g. an opera house) is fast dying out. We have found this phenomenon everywhere. Prayer callers in the Moslem mosques no longer climb up the tower to call their flock to the fold. A loudspeaker does the job – the prayer caller will be relaxing in a chair somewhere at the bottom of the turret with a microphone. Or he might even be replaced by a phonogram of some master prayer caller. An art has been made redundant by technology. The same applies to many traditional groups who prefer to bathe in a sea of microphones; the tonal impression of their performance becomes the responsibility of the engineer who mixes the sound.

Another common phenomenon we have noted, particularly in countries that have most recently assimilated PA system technology, is the tendency to push the tolerances of the system to its utmost. Sound levels are set on the verge of feedback or distortion. This is not just a phenomenon of youth; even older audiences do not seem to complain or even suffer. The result, of course, is that many of the nuances of the performances disappear in the amplification.

ECONOMIC EFFECTS ON LOCAL MUSIC MAKING

The spread of electric instruments and amplifiers has not necessarily meant that less people actually create or perform music. There are probably far more young people playing guitars in Scandinavia and Wales than used to take piano lessons two decades ago. When Sweden had its first pop boom (inspired by the Beatles) in the mid-Sixties, there were said to be over 5,000 groups singing variants on 'All you need is love' in that country of only 8 million. The motive force for many had been the status attached to pop band membership, or even wild hopes of emulating the Beatles. When most of them discovered this was not possible, many stopped playing and a lot of second-hand equipment came on the market (around 1967–68). When the Swedish music movement emerged around 1970 (cf. Chapter 4) this equipment proved to be a practical resource.

Guitars, organs, PA systems and amplifiers place considerable financial strains on the owners. The fact that so many young people got bands going in Scandinavia during the mid-Sixties was probably an indication of the buoyant state of the economy. Even if many instruments were bought on hire-purchase agreements, the purchaser would need a steady job or generous parents. In other countries with a larger spread of income it is no coincidence that rock groups are often formed by the children of upper-middle-class families. This is particularly noticeable in a country like Chile, where imported instruments can easily be acquired on hire-purchase. The same applies to the small number of groups playing Western rock music in Colombo, Sri Lanka.

The converse was true of the Punk ideology, which embodies things such as second-hand clothing and cheap ways of living. Instruments and amplifiers could well have been salvaged from a refuse tip – the music did not require sophisticated gadgets and gear. With countries like Sweden also experiencing phenomena such as high youth unemployment, it was natural that Punk ideology made its forceful entrance, affecting the music scene in the late Seventies.

The costs of acquiring and servicing the equipment of an electric group led not only to new forms of economic dependence, but also to professionalization. Groups often have to rely on some form of sponsorship or grants. In Western Europe cultural grants are normally given purely to art music. Pop and rock, though not pure electronic music, is regarded as a commercial phenomenon which should pay its way in the market place. (Sweden is an exception here and does give grants, mainly for equipment, to electric rhythmical groups.) When the commercial market does not provide enough to cover the costs incurred, some type of sponsorship has to be sought. Thus all the jazz bands in Tanzania are sponsored by organizations, official bodies (e.g. the army), companies or commercial promoters. The Mlimani Park Orchestra is run by a transport company – all the members are on its pay role. Many groups and artists in Kenya have to turn to commercial entities for sponsorship. Most of the session musicians in Trinidad find regular employment in the Police Band. Electric groups in Tunisia rely on the tourist hotels as do many of their colleagues in Sri Lanka. The Volvo car company pays the salaries of some of the members of the Gothenburg symphony orchestra.

As regards equipment costs for touring artists, the sky is the limit. This is partly why a group like ABBA perform so seldom in public. An ABBA tour is a gigantic undertaking, involving tons of equipment for sound and lighting as well as a staff of about 50 assistants. The requirements are so high because (a) ABBA must be able to reproduce exactly the sound of their records on stage and (b) the visual effect must correspond to what they regard as their global image.

Even for lesser known artists on tour, the temptation to have a few extra loudspeakers and synthesizers is too much to withstand. A large percentage of the fee for the show gets eaten up by costs for ancilliaries. A relatively fresh example from the summer of 1983 shows how little can stay in the pockets of the performers:

Every years throughout the short, hectic Swedish summer, artists tour the *folkparker* (open air entertainment centres), often putting on a 45-minute show at two or even three different parks in an evening. A new artist on the park scene was one Carola Häggkvist, a 16-year-old girl who entered the Eurovision Song Contest for Sweden. Her show cost 31,000 Swedish kronor (app. £3,000) – park managers complained it was far too expensive. A breakdown of costs shows that over a third of the 31,000 would be eaten up by equipment costs (PA and lights). Another 10,000 kronor would be divided between her backing musicians and the rest of the staff. Travelling expenses, insurance and manager's commission would consume the remainder, leaving a fee of 3,000 kronor for the artist Carola. In other words one can assume that of the 31,000 a local promoter pays out for the show, less than a third goes to the artist and her musicians.

To sum up, the spread of attractive music industry instrument technology has increased the costs of the tools for many musicians and with this their demands on regular employment. Access to service facilities becomes essential. Musicians can either rely on the commercial market or seek grants and some form of sponsorship (which increases their dependence on the sponsor). Reliance on the commercial sales of their musicianship can lead to the risk of pricing themselves out of the market, for example, by being replaced by a discothèque.

At the same time many musicians playing popular music find themselves once again in a Scylla and Charybdis situation. Irrespective of whether they live in rich Sweden or poorer Kenya, they still feel the pressure to perform with equipment as good (read: expensive or powerful) as their colleagues. This inevitably puts them in a position of being highly dependent on others, usually financiers who rent equipment.

PHONOGRAM TECHNOLOGY

By 1983, the resources for making gramophone records (from recording studios through to stamping out discs) were available in all the MISC countries with the exception of Tanzania, where a plant was still under construction. These resources have expanded rapidly throughout the Seventies. The only general setbacks concerned the supply of vinyl plastic during the first oil crisis (1973), when there was a global shortage whilst some new plants were put on line. Individual countries have also experienced raw material and spare parts problems arising from currency shortages.

During the Seventies, multitrack studio resources have become available throughout our sample (excepting Tanzania, where a multichannel studio only has a 2-track recorder). Jamaica, partly thanks to its international success with reggae, can now boast of up to seven or eight ultra modern 32-track studios.

None of our sample, on the other hand, had the resources for producing more recent phonogram/videogram industry inventions, such as the compact disc (Sony/Philips) or Selectavision discs (RCA). This is a point we will return to in our final chapter.

In the latter half of the Seventies, cassette technology had spread world wide, and with it the software of the global phonogram industry. Grease, ABBA, Boney M etc could be heard everywhere. This has also led to the infusion everywhere of the same technical norms regarding what recorded popular music should sound like. In other words, the electronic industry's norm regarding the 'sound' produced by the average recording studio, as reproduced through the average cassette recorder, provides global standards for recorded music. Anything that departs too far from this norm will be regarded as sounding weird. An illustration of the dependency on phonogram technique is that groups of musicians rehearsing will often sing and play into a cassette recorder to check that the sound is satisfactory (the significance of acoustic features becomes replaced by electronic aspects).

The accessibility of phonogram technology has provided musicians in small countries with the means of reproducing their own music. The spread of the international phonogram industry's products has also affected music-making both on a professional and amateur level, even posing a threat at times. In the disco boom of the Seventies, recordings such as those in the film *Grease* reached every continent. Disco records provided a cheap alternative to live music in the entertainment sector. These discos functioned merely as entertainment, not primarily as advertisements for the live performances of the artists concerned. A result of this was that musicians who played for tourists in hotels along the Tunisian coast found themselves out of a job. Clubs in Sweden who used to give two or three rock bands a chance to earn enough to pay for the instalments on their equipment once a week, went over to disco.

The introduction of music industry technology inevitably affects the way music is performed and the people who perform it. This applies to the prayer-caller in a mosque as much as to a vocalist in a traditional folk orchestra who has to learn where to stand without running the risk of feedback. This generalization also covers the process whereby music is fed through a recording studio with all the opportunities for adding extra sound effects.

On an international level, and sometimes even on a national level, a result of this dependency is the emergence of a professional elite who rely ultimately on the media rather than live performances to communicate with their audiences. ABBA, as we have seen, is one such example. The phonogram introduces an extra level between the performer and the audience. A general effect of this is to separate the world of the successful phonogram artist from that of the average consumer of these phonograms. This in its turn influences the subject matter of their material. Personal problems or general philosophical observations tend to dominate. Artists serving a world market would rarely choose to sing about, say, why the eight o'clock bus is always ten minutes late, or some other subject of local relevance.

Phonogram technology can affect music on several levels. Adding a synthesizer to the sound of the bagpipes on the cassette of the singer Zoubaier in Tunisia results in the bagpipe accompaniment not sounding the same as it does in a live situation. The phonogram listener will get a different impression of the bagpipe sound. The performer will have the dilemma of deciding whether or not to adapt the performance to the sound on the recording, either by playing in a different fashion or by incorporating some electronic gadget.

Sometimes this development can go so far that music becomes almost entirely a studio product. Jamaican reggae is an example. It is only in the sophisticated recording studios of Kingston that the reggae sound the world has learnt to recognize is created. Live performances of reggae are extremely rare since the demands on equipment are so great and the finances of all but the top reggae artists are so poor. Reggae can be heard live in Jamaica only at major events such as the Sunsplash Festival or the newly instigated *Rockers Magazine* awards show. On the other hand, giant discothèques dominate where the spontaneous performance would be by disc jockeys who often improvise lyrics ('toasting' or 'rapping') over reggae rhythm tracks ('dubs').

The opposite situation used to exist in Trinidad in the days when calypso singers would produce new songs daily, based on the happenings of the previous 24 hours. It was an improvised, spontaneous culture that even encompassed what the calypsonians referred to as 'calypso wars'. One calypso master would challenge another one to come on stage and engage in a verbal battle where the sword was the tongue and points were awarded for advanced rhymes, usually spiced with an element of insult directed at one's opponent. The calypsonians became walking dictionaries of rhymes and quaint grammatical constructions.

Things are different now. The same pattern can be observed as on Jamaica. Calypso is adapting to the terms of the music industry environment. With the introduction of large sound systems, calypsonians have had to structure their performances more strictly. Advanced arrangements are written for 10 – 15 piece backing bands and the repertoire is restricted. Instead of churning out new songs in a steady stream (albeit often with very similar melodies) the calypsonians will sing only two or three songs for the whole of the carnival/calypso season. Because of the time involved in getting phonograms recorded and manufactured (often abroad), the topics cannot be merely of current interest, referring to the events of the night or even the week before. At the start of the 3-month run-up period to the carnival, a calypsonian will release a phonogram and proceed to market the product. Since part of the artist's income arises from sales of discs and cassettes, an effort is made to make the live performance in the calypso tent sound as similar as possible to the phonogram version (thus decreasing the value accorded to the art of improvisation, and increasing the demands on the sound of the backing group). The disc will also, hopefully, be played on Trinidad's two radio stations; this will have both a marketing effect by boosting sales, and a publicity effect for a calypsonian entering the carnival competition for the annual 'Calypso Monarch'. The calypso has thus become adapted to the available media and music industry technology. Calypso has not gone so far as reggae yet in becoming purely a studio product – but the pattern of change is the same. Live bands used to be very much in existence on the streets of Port of Spain on carnival days. Now many of them have been replaced by disc jockeys, turntables (or cassettes) and giant loud-speaker systems. They are more reliable, functional and cheaper.

Another live music form in Trinidad has also been affected in much the same way as the calypsos. The steelbands have undergone a process of specialization whereby the National Panorama Championships become the major goal for each year's carnival activities.

A band of up to 100 members will spend weeks preparing one single piece of music for the competitions. This leaves them with no general repertoire and thus diminishes their social role as entertainers – it is not much fun going out in the streets at carnival only knowing one or two tunes. What is more, the tunes they play are often melodies sung by calypsonians, i.e. the hit songs of the year. And when a phonogram company decides to record a steelband, all their members might not even be expected to take part. The best players will take a selection of pans into a studio and create the whole effect by using multichannel techniques. What started as a social phenomenon in the ghettoes is fast becoming adapted to the music industry environment, to the demands of phonogram technology and the media.

This process whereby music becomes affected by the technology through which it is disseminated is a common facet of change everywhere. With all due respects to etymologists as well as our publisher who reacted, quite rightly, against a surplus of consecutive vowels, we have opted to refer to this process as 'MEDIAIZATION'. This refers to the adaption of music forms to the constraints of entertainment media, phonogram technology, phonogram markets etc. The example of the steelbands quoted above is particularly relevant in this context. A traditional steelband performing live a rousing, rhythmical number is a very impressive visual and aural experience. On the other hand it is extremely hard to reproduce the same type of experience through normal recording techniques (a band of 100 players, for instance covers a vast area). If this problem is solved by using multi-channel techniques (as sketched above), then a mediaized version could develop with a different sound. The bands may well then try to emulate this in a live situation, producing a different type of steelband music.

A general conclusion is that a major problem for small countries is not primarily that their own particular types of music are ignored by the local media and establishment (even if this does happen) but that this adaption process can conflict with their social function. Steelbands concentrate on a competition number – their repertoire suffers. *Baila* in Sri Lanka often functioned as music with social or satirical content that was sung at parties. Its adaptation to the demands of cassette technology has produced two mediaized versions: one with fairly smutty lyrics and another more respectable form performed by artists who would like to be accepted by the official media.

Tanzanian jazz bands still perform an important social function – they play live at clubs. Their simple mono recordings on Radio Tanzania serve merely to advertise the live function. Should they achieve world acclaim, or should Tanzania acquire the same type of technical resources as Jamaica, then an inevitable process of mediaization will take place. The result could be a fascinating 'new' sound. It could also be a devastating loss of spontaneity and live music culture.

ACTIVE PARTICIPATION OR PASSIVE LISTENING?

The spread of music industry technology has also changed the listener's role in music-making. In former times, music was very much a question of two-way communication. The performer was physically very close to his or her audience, and relied on establishing some sort of rapport. This still happens everywhere in rural areas where traditional music is still part of local rituals. But the incidence is rapidly on the decrease, simply because never before have people had such easy access to so much recorded music. In the first half of the Seventies the amount of time the Swedes devoted to listening to phonograms increased fourfold. By 1976 young Swedes in the 9 – 24 age groups spent on average one hour a day listening to their own phonograms and an extra hour listening to phonograms on the radio. Much of this is secondary listening, in other words music provides merely a background to other activities.

This is a global trend. Transistor radios and cassette-recorders are everywhere. The same goes for television – even in Tanzania where television is virtually absent and video imports are forbidden, there are plenty of VHS machines. In two of the less rich countries in our sample (Sir Lanka and Jamaica) parabolic dishes have been used to pick up television satellite signals and redistribute over local transmitters. New dishes are cropping up every day in Jamaica. Scandinavia will soon find itself in the footprints of a number of European satellites. No one knows how to solve all the legal problems of copyright that these developments entail. But what is clear is that

(a) the international distribution of music that has access to modern media is increasing at an extraordinary rate and

(b) that smaller countries are finding it harder and harder for their own music to compete with international repertoire.

Even rich Sweden finds production of a high percentage of local television programmes an impossible financial burden. Since Jamaican Television found it could pick up nigh on thirty channels on its dish, local musicians have virtually disappeared from the screen (in a country which is one of the net-exporters of music!)

One of the biggest growth rates in the music industry can be found in the area of background music. The same unobtrusive instrumental versions of standard evergreens can be heard when an Air Jamaica plane lands in Montego Bay (no reggae!), in the lobby of any international hotel, or in most supermarkets the whole world over.

Organizations such as Muzak have devoted considerable resources to investigating the positive effects (positive with relation to increased productivity or purchasing activity) of musical wallpaper. Less has been done to study its negative effects. Little is known about the possible saturation effects of living in a constant environment of recorded music. This study shows that it is not a phenomenon exclusive to large or rich countries, or even the industrialized world. Within less than three years of liberalization of import restrictions, the sound cassette had become a major disseminator of recorded music, both local and foreign, in Sri Lanka. Two years later the video cassette was firmly established in urban areas and a national television service was inaugurated.

This statement by a music researcher illustrates the feeling of despair felt by those who see their own heritage being crushed by the onslaught of relatively cheap international culture.

We are not prepared for television. Cameras and tape recorders don't make television programmes. You have to have trained people to do that. What are we getting now? The pop music of Germany, ABBA, Star Parade and so on. People see these things over and over again. But we don't have the money, experience or capacity to put on shows like that. Even if we do put on something national, it can't compete with all the glittering lights and costumes of the foreign products. People begin to believe that you have to have that sort of thing. This development could destroy everything that has come down through the ages, everything that we can proudly call national culture.[1]

The picture our research presents might seem fairly bleak; there are however some bright lights at the end of the tunnel. In every MISC country we have witnessed how people use available technology for their own cultural purposes, not merely for swallowing something that is served up on a plate.

ECONOMIC AND ORGANIZATIONAL PATTERNS OF CHANGE

The Big and the Small

No small countries have been unaffected by the structural changes in the international phonogram industry. The five largest transnational phonogram companies, as we have noted, account for a large percentage of all the music that is mass-produced and sold in the world. But their policies in the smaller nations are dissimilar. A common denominator is that they all regard small nations as potential marginal markets for international repertoire. But their attitudes to activities within the smaller nations vary. EMI has relinquished its position as the most widely spread phonogram producer – its entry into East Africa was a failure, it ceased its minor operations in Sri Lanka, lost the distribution for CBS in Chile after having a very successful run in the early Seventies, left its pressing plant in Sweden etc. Polygram (owned jointly by Philips and Siemens) have grown mainly by acquisition of other companies, notably Decca. But CBS, we noted, seem to follow an aggressive policy of getting into any country where there is a chance of breaking even, and picking up local artists where there is a chance of selling their material internationally. When presented with this analysis, CBS Records president (Dick Asher) did not disagree.

Well, as you probably have noticed we believe in having a record company any place where it is possible to have one. If it is viable to have a record company in a country, even though maybe it's a very small country, we try to have one. And as you also probably know, every place we have a record company, as soon as it gets going a little bit it begins to record local artists. We believe very strongly in local recordings and developing local artists. And then we try to spread it around to other parts of the world. Obviously with different degrees of success depending on the accessibility of the music. For example, we have recently opened a company in Inida. To my ears Indian music doesn't sound like we will ever sell a great deal of it very quickly in the US, although I hope some day we will try at least. And maybe we will. I could be wrong.[2]

Another common pattern we noted was that CBS tend to give local staff a lot of leeway regarding their policies and dealings with the national music scene. CBS appears to approve of its local personnel identifying outwardly with the cultural sentiments of local musicians – as long as the business is reasonably sound.

It's a conscious policy. It's worked very well for us. Ideas, useful ideas rarely fit into containers that are easy to live with, but the fact is that that is where the contributions usually are. Even some of our artists in the US don't necessarily say things that are particularly comfortable for the establishment or for the CBS, but we've learned to live with each other and to respect their approach and it's worked well for us and we hope we will always be able to continue that way. Obviously we are a business enterprise and if we had lost money for a long time, then some people would probably come in and say: change the way you are doing things. But fortunately what we've done has succeeded ultimately and yielded some profit as well so we hope to continue this way.

. . . I think we've done remarkably well. We are very proud of ourselves in the sense that we are sort of newcomers into international music and have achieved a very, very strong position, apparently the leading position in the world in a relatively short period of time against very heavily entrenched opposition, and opposition that had many advantages over us. And we think perhaps the reason is that we have let the local people run a little bit instead of trying to control them from New York or Hamburg, or more often, London.[3]

CBS' track-record during the Seventies indicates that this policy has paid off. The company established itself in Sweden, East Africa and Chile, tried its best to get into Jamaica, did well with unorthodox phonograms in Denmark, and so on.

Even if the phonogram division of CBS was pursuing a policy of establishing what appear to be fairly autonomous phonogram companies in a number of small countries, one should not forget that CBS records itself is only part of a larger conglomerate. Throughout the decade under scrutiny, CBS, as with the other transnational phonogram producers, has been subject to an ongoing process of diversification and integration CBS total income for 1981 was quoted at US $4,000 million of which $700 million came from operations outside the USA. The revenue from phonogram operations accounted for only one-third of the total revenue. CBS also earned quite a few dollars from selling musical instruments – CBS controls such well-known brands as Steinway (pianos), Fender (organs), Rogers (drums, Rhodes (electric pianos), Gulbransen (organs), Geimerhardt (flutes), Lyon and Healy (harps) and Rodgers (organs). CBS produce numerous full-length television films annually – both *Dallas* and *MASH* are CBS entertainment series. CBS are big in the production of text-books and medical books.[4] In other words, it is a long climb through the hierarchy from the world of a CBS record producer in Nairobi to the top of the CBS hill in New York where policy decisions are made.

The common financial experience for all the international phonogram companies during the Seventies was first an eight-year period of extraordinary growth followed by a few years of violent upheavals and decreased profits. (CBS operating profits on its Records division were $100 million in 1978, but $50 million in 1981). The phonogram industry puts the blame mainly on home-taping but does admit that high royalty agreements signed in the scramble for the superstars as well as giant investments in marketing for a few specific phonograms, could play a role. It is not surprising that under such conditions, the international phonogram industry has increased its talent-scouting efforts to find new sources of material. Many small countries have already found themselves at the focus of this telescope. Island Records, for instance, created a lot of its wealth by exploiting reggae, notably the work of Bob Marley. Island are now looking very closely to Africa. A liner note with Island's new 'Sound d'Afrique' series reads: 'African pop, in strictly commercial terms, is a massive growth industry. This is not some impoverished ghetto music'. Another British phonogram company with international operations, Virgin, is also looking at East African music.

Where such ventures have been financially successful, the changes that can be noted in the small countries concern mainly those artists who have achieved fame outside their own territories.

THE DELIGHTS OF INDIVIDUAL SUCCESS AS A STAR

Success in the Jamaican phonogram industry usually means taking a chance to get out of the ghetto. An up-and-coming producer such as Jungo Lawes might still record phonograms at Channel One Studio in Kingston's ghettoland, but he and his family have moved up the hill to an upper-middle class villa area. His house is full of the material gains from successful music-making (stereos, videos etc.). He prides himself on being able to reward his protege 'Yellowman' with a yellow BMW. Most of his business deals would appear to be done on a 'cash-in-advance' basis (or occasionally 'video machine-in-advance, basis) because he patently does not trust any of his international business partners.

Jungo Lawes was still mainly a local operator when we met him in 1983. Other Jamaican musicians such as Bob Marley, Peter Tosh and Jimmy Cliff have become household names round the world. How has this attention affected the individuals and their small country? Bob Marley is no longer with us. One thing his colleagues have all learnt is to be careful. Jimmy Cliff claims he does not get a penny out of the continuing success of the film *The Harder They Come* – which, ironically enough, was about artists getting ripped off. All of which has made him very cautious. On Jamaica he looks after his own affairs, has his own record company which he controls completely. But his international rights have been signed away to CBS.

The true story behind Jimmy Cliff's experiences with *The Harder They Come*, experiences which prompted him to write the song 'Rip Off', are hard to unravel. The film is still a money-earner. Thorne-EMI are currently releasing it on video. Island Records claim the

Jimmy Cliff: 'Intertwine and learn'

rights to the sound track. Channel 4 in Great Britain screened the film in 1983 after confused negotiations which included the UK distributor (Osiris Films) going bankrupt. The rights are now being claimed by a company registered in the Virgin Islands (International Film Management Ltd). This company, as we understand it, can only be contacted through a firm of agents or a lawyer in New

York. According to these agents the firm in the Virgn Islands is wholly owned by the original producer of *The Harder They Come*, the Jamaican Perry Hensell. The devious routes through which the proceeds drom the exploitation of Jamaican culture flow are indeed many and wondrous. Jimmy Cliff's attitude is clear.

I see the music industry as just another industry within the Babylon system. The Babylon law is a jungle law – the fittest of the fit survive. The music industry happens to be the one I'm involved in – but the whole system is a jungle of vampires, parasites, ticks . . . lice.
The only way is to study and understand how the system works, then you can start to do something about it. When you are naive, when you come with honesty in your heart, you find the world isn't so – it's really a matter of studying.
I've had a lot of hard experiences throughout my career, not only with the film but with records. These mistakes can't be made again.
The whole system is a vampire, everybody's out to dig you out or rip you off – you have to learn or you'll get burnt.
[About signing internationally to CBS record] . . . One doesn't have much of a choice in my position. Here in Jamaica I do my own distribution. But I can't do that internationally, so you need one of them. They can rip you off, but they can't take everything . . . I don't see it's wise to go to extremes and kill your life . . . I don't see it wise lock myself away either. But intertwine and learn.[5]

Jimmy Cliff has clearly opted for the alternative: action with caution ('some say go right, some say go left, I want a balance 'cause that's the best'). Bob Marley compromised with the industry at an early stage. Bunny Wailer, another colleague from Bob's former band, the Wailers, preferred to withdraw and proceded only with utmost caution. Only recently has Bunny Wailer felt that he knows enough to venture out without getting burnt.

These experiences all serve to illustrate a thesis presented at the beginning of this book, namely that small countries do have ths dual role of providing marginal markets and being sources of exploitable talent. These examples also indicate that small countries could benefit greatly from an exchange of information in these areas. If the Jamaican musicians we have mentioned could pass on their experiences to African colleagues on the brink of world exposure, the results could only be beneficial. The musicians would all become very cautious – with a risk that some might become paranoid. Phonogram companies hunting for talent would have to explain their intentions very clearly – signatures on contracts would be harder to come by. So what? It must be better to walk round a well than to fall into it and have to be rescued.

PIRACY

One of the negative aspects of the accessibility of music industry technology, as far as remuneration to the artists and composers is concerned, is the incidence of piracy for commercial gain. Copyright owners are normally remunerated via a sytem of royalties. This results in a situation where large profits can be made when royalty payments can be avoided, which is the basis of modern music piracy.

Piracy should not be confused with home-taping which, it can be argued, has certainly positive cultural advantages. The home-taper has to make active decisions as to what he or she wishes to listen to. Organized piracy with copying for commercial gain, is rife in almost every country we have visited. The only exceptions are possibly Tanzania (where there is a lack of cassettes, though pirated material from Singapore is on sale) and Jamaica (where gramophone records still dominated as opposed to cassettes in 1983).

As we have noted, many large phonogram companies have indirect interests in tape-manufacture. A pamphlet[6] produced by the British Mechanical Copyright Performing Society observes that 'Blank tape costs little to produce and the profift margins are high'. One can conclude that Philips and other manufacturers of tape are already compensating their conglomerates for the losses incurred through home-taping. Individual artists, on the other hand, have no means of doing this. This description is supported by the observed pattern of change in a high piracy country such as Tunisia. The only phonogram producers who can survive in the Tunisian recording industry are those who either manufacture and supply blank tapes to the pirates (alongside their own activities with pre-recorded tapes) or those who mainly offer facilities (recording studios etc.). The only advantage to individual artists is publicity which can give bookings for live performances. This is a completely different situation to that which existed, say in 1975, before cassettes came on the scene, when a small number of gramophone records were sold. To eradicate piracy in Tunisia would be a harder task than the one General de Gaulle set himself when he tried to squash the Algerian independence movement. Piracy could be restricted somewhat, but this would require a considerable change in the legal sanctions available.

In Sri Lanka, cassettes with Anglo–American music are all pirated (mainly imported from Singapore). They cost 25 rupees

(1982), half the price of a local artist's cassette. One local Sri Lankan dealer offers a selection of more than 2,000 titles with Anglo–American, Indian and classical repertoire. These pirated recordings range from Yehudi Menuhin to Taj Mahal, from the Chicago Symphony Orchestra to Bob Marley. They are all manufactured in the Asian region, mainly in Singapore. In 1983 there was still no evidence of large-scale piracy of local Sri Lankan repertoire on the island, even if shops did provide 'made-to-order' cassette compilation services (maybe this is because there is no manufacture of blank tapes in Sri Lanka). However, with over 100,000 Sri Lankan contract workers in the Gulf States thirsting for their own culture (and not having much to spend their money on), a market for pirated Sinhalese material has developed in the Middle East, fed mainly via Singapore.

Piracy has been able to flourish in Singapore for three reasons. (1) The copyright laws are out of date (the 1912 British Copyright Act still applies). (2) Piracy contributes handsomely to Singapore's foreign currency earnings (the 'official' figure for cassette exports is in the region of 50 million units per annum). (3) There is a very small local music scene. The effect of piracy on the few local recording artists is so marginal that the locally based anti-piracy lobby is very weak.

Of course it stands to reason that if the US government put enough pressure on its friend and ally, the government of Singapore, then Singapore piracy would disappear overnight. In a country where even front-seat passengers in taxis are meticulous about following seat-belt regulations, the eradication of large-scale pirate duplicating plants, many of which are situated in premises owned by the government, should pose few problems.

Singapore is a unique case thanks to its position as a trading centre, rather than a cultural centre with its own music scene. International pressure from those on whom Singapore's welfare depends is the only answer to organized piracy. In most countries, however, the solution to the negative effects of the cassette would seem to be some sort of combination of strict laws against piracy for commercial gain, and a levy on blank tape. The levy would have to be small enough not to create too much hardship for the average customer, and the spoils should be distributed to the real losers (e.g. by redistribution to financially non-viable recording projects, artists and composers who are struggling to survive).

The cassette, however, has not only had bad effects – in some countries its ease of usage has provided a guarantee for freedom of speech. Particularly in a country like Chile with a military dictatorship, the cassette has provided the means for spreading music culture which never gets played on official broadcasting stations.

MUSICIANS REORGANIZE

The economic changes following in the wake of technological changes also lead to new organizational developments. Professional musicians investigate new organizational forms for increasing their security and ability to meet the financial demands of new equipment. Just as symphony orchestra members in the West have formed associations or unions to attain or maintain a reasonable standard of living from their employment in an organization that costs a lot to maintain, so have musicians in the popular field moved in a similar direction. Pop/rock musicians in Scandinavia have started freelance sections in their national musicians' unions. Session musicians providing recordings for the cassette industry have also tried to organize themselves in Sri Lanka. Musicians in Trinidad who back the calypso singers have attempted to do the same.

The appearance of new groupings and associations on all levels in music life indicates a pattern of change whereby those involved in musical activities seek ways of coming to terms with their environment. The types of problems they face can be technological, financial, social, administrative. Decisions have to be made. Actions have to be taken ranging from organizing a phonogram recording, buying a PA, negotiating with the authorities regarding locales for rehearsals and performances, to seeking grants or sponsors and negotiating salaries. A need for organization emerges in a way quite unlike the situation where music is an integral part of rituals and working life. The drummers whose families have performed on their drums at fixed times daily for centuries outside the Sacred Temple of the Tooth in Kandy, Sri Lanka, in return for the right to till certain lands, have far simpler organizational problems than those of an electric dance band that tours the length and breadth of a country playing at different restaurants every weekend, or a group of folk music enthusiasts who rely on much voluntary labour and generosity from various authorities. The problems of surviving in a competitive media environment have led to an explosive development in the number of different musical organizations. Unions have been started – not always successfully, depending upon the attitude of the local authorities and the degree of solidarity shared by musicians. Where a 'union' is a dirty word, various professional associations have been started (cf. Chile). In Kenya, where conditions have been particularly hard for local musicians due to competition from Western and other East African music, a whole flora of organizations emerged during the 1970s. These included a musicians' cooperative aimed at starting a local record manufacturing plant, a performing rights society, a producers' association etc. These were augmented in the late Seventies, partly as a result of their own lobbying, by a government organization (the President's Committee on National Music) with the aim of promoting national music.

In other words, a pattern emerges whereby technological and economic developments lead to a professionalization of the corps of active musicians. This in its turn is usually accompanied by a concentration of musicians to their local media metropolis (as a rule, the capital city) or in countries with much tourism, to the tourist zones. These developments act as catalysts for the emergence of organizations. When musicians organize themselves, then those with whom they negotiate also invariably organize themselves (if they have not done so already). A ministry of culture, for instance, might form a special organization for dealing with demands and problems presented by musicians' organizations. In other words, economic and technological developments breed organizational developments, which in turn can lead to other organizations appearing. Through these developments, the music life of each country develops its interaction process.

Music organizations generally show their strength and importance when their members feel their interests are being threatened or when their leaders feel the need to demonstrate to their own members that they are doing something.

The most intense action in support of music culture can be noted in the case of large spontaneous actions involving not just the leadership of, say, one musicians union, but many different individuals or organizations. Our chapter on the enthusiasts has already described how 6,000 citizens took to the streets of Stockholm in 1975 to make their feelings felt about the commercialization of music. In 1983 another mass demonstration took place. Once again 6,000 Stockholmers took to the streets to protest about a decision by the city council to cut by half the Adolf Fredrik music school. (The school, which has produced generations of talented musicians, was situated in an old building on ground that was attractive for property speculation. The council wanted to move it to a smaller school further from the centre of the city.) Manifestations such as these are probably the best indication politicians ever can get regarding the emotional feeling of the music-making and music-loving populace. Sadly, all too often, they prefer to ignore the writing on the wall. And those who fight for their own music culture, be they local musicians in Kenya, pan men in Trinidad or Welsh language rock performers in Wales – feel growing frustration with the authorities. All too often in these situations, good healthy opportunities go to the wind. All too often, the views of the enthusiasts are ignored by those in responsible positions who think they know better.

Children from Stockholm demonstrating in support of their music school (Adolf Fredrik) which the local authorities wish to demolish (March 19th 1983)

GOVERNMENT POLICIES: GIVING THE TOURISTS WHAT THEY WANT

Tourism is a form of global commincation that has exploded during the past two decades and left its imprint on the music life of many countries.

Almost every government in any small country is keen to boost its foreign currency reserve by attracting tourists. The people of any nation feel proud to show off their culture and traditions to the tourists. A colourful bit of local culture can provide the necessary attraction that makes a tourist or tour-operator decide to come to a particular country. Thus governments organize tourist boards, instigate investment programmes in the hotel sector, and generally do their best to stimulate activities which can act as magnets to draw the tourists. Since entertainment and culture are important factors – tourist development also affects the music life of the country. The government might sponsor a major music festival in a particular area. The immediate advantage for local musicians might be work opportunities during the short festival period (though often such festivals are made 'attractive' by inviting international stars). There can also be negative effects: putting all available resources into one major festival manifestation can drain the barrel dry as far as local events for the rest of the year are concerned. The tourists get their thrill during one week in June and the local inhabitants are left with twelve months in which to hope that next year's festival will be as good, if not better.

All along the line, tourism appears to provide short-term employment advantages but leaves cultural disadvantages. The tourist hotels attract talented musicians who have to play a repertoire suitable for the majority of tourists who come to relax, not to learn the intricacies of, say, African tribal music. Thus the best local musicians end up playing tourist disco-beat music in the hotels up the coast of Mombasa, or in Tunisia in the hotels from Sousse to Hammamet. Tourism provides work (as long as the bands are not replaced by discothèques) and affects repertoire. Even when tourists are offered a small dose of traditional music and dance, the cultural experience becomes adapted to their needs. Consider these observations by a former official at the Sri Lankan Ministry of Culture:

What is offered to the tourists at many hotels is just a fake. As a practising musician and dance choreographer, I feel sorry that this sort of muck is being shown to the foreign people – many carry home the wrong impression . . .

We once called the hoteliers together, and told them that much of the stuff that was being put out was trash. Most of them get hold of one person who knows a little bit, tell him to bring along 6 or 7 who can jump around. Then there will be a lot of drum-beating and fire eating, with the least amount of art and the most amount of gymnastics and 'magic'. And the tourists go home thinking this is the culture of Sri Lanka.

We offered to put on a proper show. Of course we had demands – we had to get paid. And we refused to perform in hotels when people are munching their chicken and drinking their beer. We will perform if they come to sit down and appreciate our show. Take it between 7 and 8, and then let the people disperse. No hotelier would take it that way. That is why we have advertised that the National Dance Ensemble put on their own performances every Wednesday and Friday at a local theatre. But usually we don't get more than ten people coming a night. The reason for this? The tour guides make all the decisions – they take the tourists to the place where they get best commission. I was once asked to make a report for the municipal council of Kandy on a tourist show – they wanted me to judge whether it was a genuine traditional show or not: whether they should allow it. I went to that show. I was in a very small place. I counted 142 tourists in a place that could accommodate about 50. Most of them were standing. They had paid 50 rupees each.* Every ticket was bought by the tour guide – he gets his commission. Afterwards I wandered round the back and found a nice table laid with bottles of Arrac, all on the house for the tour guide.

The tourist authorities profess to be interested – but they never get anything going. They could – but they never do. As a result, ear-blasting electronic guitars and speakers take over. This is a very sad situation.[7]

Tourism affects not only the sounds that are heard at the hotels or those recorded on souvenir phonograms. In many country it affects the whole art of making musical instrument. Tourists often like to buy souvenir instruments to take home and hang on the wall. They do not have to function – their purpose is merely to resemble something the owner 'once saw in Africa'. This can have a devastating effect on the traditional art of building fine musical instruments. New industries develop which mass-produce mere models of the real thing.

Few government seem to be concerned about the cultural dangers of tourism. Even those individual officials who expose concern find it hard to affect the situation. The need for foreign currency gets first priority – the tourists must be given the entertainment it is assumed they want.

Job security is a rare luxury professional musicians can enjoy – tourism as an employer adds another element of insecurity. The tourists can stop coming at very short notice. A sudden outbreak of

* 50 rupees is approximately £2. 142 tickets at 50 rupees is equal to 7,100 rupees or the combined monthly salary for ten full-time musicians at the Sri Lankan Broadcasting Association.

typhoid or malaria or, as in the case of Sri Lanka, violent clashes between different ethnic groups, can bring that trade to an abrupt halt. If the tourists stop coming, or the musician gets replaced by a DJ, what will the night club repertoire and know-how be worth?

GOVERNMENT POLICIES: WARY INVOLVEMENT

Every government in the MISC sample has become involved in the music industry in one way or another. By the late Seventies, even the military government of General Pinochet had started to express concern about the demise of Chilean folk music.

The Programme Directors for Chilean television stations were ordered to give access, once again, to some local folk music – as long as the lyrical content was not too political.

In the early years of the decade one could observe a general awareness amongst governments of small nations that local culture must be actively supported if the countries were to retain any semblance of national cultural identity. The Tunisians started building more Maisons de Culture. The Swedish parliament voted in favour of its cultural goals. Strong statements of policy were announced by the Tanzanian President. Kenya got a national cultural committee. The Jamaica Festival committee extended its activities . . .

Most of the pecuniary support that was given during the Seventies, however, was for established institutions (the Welsh National Opera, the Swedish Opera, the Tower Hall Foundation in Sri Lanka etc.) In many countries, the commercial sector was relied upon to cough up the rest of the funds needed by the arts. Thus a calypso singer at a tent during the carnival season in Trinidad almost drowns in a sea of advertisements, mainly for beverages and cigarettes, almost in the same way that most sports in Britain are sponsored by the manufacturers of the most unhealthy products on the market.

The Nordic governments, and indeed musicians and artists in general in that part of the world, however, have fought hard to minimize commercial dependence. The Swedish government gives grants, not only to classical musicians but also to rock and folk music groups. The commercialization of the arts has been debated non-stop through the past ten years.

From the early Seventies' general expressions of concern, very little has happened up to the present day. Governments are still aware that some sort of involvement in the music market is needed if cultural values are to be protected. But which paths should they tread?

Some actions have been taken to support local phonogram industries. The case of Tanzania illustrates what a lack of local

A calypso singer in Trinidad (Brother Valentino) drowns in a sea of advertisements from the sponsors of a tent in the carnival season

resources can lead to – it also illustrates that even getting a record pressing plant going is more than a matter of merely erecting a building and opening a few packing crates. Sweden's decision to redistribute some of the income from a tax on blank cassettes to the phonogram industry indicates a realization of the problems of being small. The government of Trinidad has also committed itself to action now that its own industry has almost faded away.

Apart from new technology, international copyright still presents the biggest dilemma for governments, mainly because copyright law on a national level lags so far behind the technological state of the art. A general observation is that musicians and composers, i.e. those who are individually affected by such matters, seem to be far more aware of the problems than those on a government level whose job it is to provide the expertise. The result is that much of the activity concerning international copyright legislation and agreements becomes part of the international diplomatic game, far removed from the problems of the struggling creators. The only solution to many of these difficulties is a new attitude to international co-operation between governments, coupled with redistribution policies on a national level aimed at encouraging and developing local culture.

The mass communications development during the past decade has led to a completely new situation regarding the interaction between music cultures and sub-cultures. Interaction between different local types of music has been a fact since time immemorial. It became more intense throughout the nineteenth century in the industrialized countries as communications developed. This process has continued throughout this century, gradually encompassing more and more areas of the world, before exploding during the Seventies.

The kinds of interaction can roughly be classified in four categories, each one representing a new stage in the pattern of change.

The first pattern, which is the simplest form of interaction can be called *cultrual exchange*. Here two or more cultures or sub-cultures interact and exchange features under fairly loose forms and more or less on equal terms.

Culture 1 ⟵⟶ Culture 2

This very often takes place on a person to person level. For instance, travelling musicians in Europe have picked up ways of making music by playing with musicians in foreign countries ever since the Middle Ages. When groups of Turkish musicians came to Sweden as immigrants around 1970 some of them started to play individually with Swedish jazz and folk musicians. Within a very short time Turkish folk music, Swedish folk music and jazz were merged into a new kind of music played in Sweden by groups bearing names such as Sevda ('love' in Turkish), Oriental Express and Oriental Wind.

But cultural exchange is not always a matter of person to person interaction. An illuminating example is the case of the musical 'round trip' involving Africa and the Caribbean. First the Africans were brought as slaves to the Americas. There they developed Afro-American music forms following a pattern which will be further explored below. During the Forties and Fifties, records with Caribbean music found their way back to Africa, not as the crow flies, but via Europe. Black intellectuals from the Caribbean and Africa met at universities in England and France and an exchange of music took place. Colonialists (especially the Belgians) developed a taste for records with Latin-American rhythms at their parties. Through such routes, Afro–Caribbean music on disc found its way to African countries and was played in people's homes or on the radio. The music caught on and African urban areas started to copy rumbas and calypso music. During the Fifties Afro–Caribbean and African music were mixed to produce new music forms, especially in Congo/Zaïre which, as we have already described, were to provide the basis for most modern East African popular music. Musicians from Zaïre migrated to East Africa where a new cultural exchange process too place when the Tanzanians infused elements of local music into the Zaïrean sounds, producing Swahili jazz. This in its turn has been adopted by many Zaïrean musicians during the last five years. In the late Sixties records started appearing mainly in Zaïre and Kenya and Zaïrean and some Tanzanian pop music. Some of these records found their way to the Caribbean (presumably via London and Paris). They were eagerly devoured by young musicians who, in the wake of the black power movement, were seeking their African roots. This led to a new merger of music types in the early Seventies when these young West Indians developed Afro-Jazz in Martinique and Guadeloupe and Afro–Dadian music in Trinidad. In the later stages of this musical round trip, phonograms were the instrumental medium of cultural exchange.

The second pattern is *cultural dominance*. This is the case when a culture, usually that of a powerful society or group in a society, is imposed on another in a more or less formally organized fashion.

The development of Afro–American music was mentioned above. Here the culture of the white slave-master was obviously dominant. Cultural exchange on equal terms was not possible. However, the imposition of white culture on the black slaves was very loosely organized in some parts of the Americas, and more formally in others. This difference led to many variants in the pattern of change, with results varying from almost pure African music with a sprinkling of European features to the complete eradication of the African cultural heritage of the black people.

For another example of cultural dominance we can turn to Africa where missionaries working in Kenya and Tanzania supported by a colonial administration exerted pressure on local culture. Schools were established at mission stations where native pupils were taught a mixture of European-Christian values and music. The dominance even included, and still does at some missions, the banning of traditional African instruments. The form of music tuition practised by the missions has been incorporated to a large extent into the present-day school curriculum of Kenya, thereby continuing a process of change by cultural dominance. The general school system in all our sample countries teaches music according to a system of norms that reflect what is considered as 'good' by a ruling or dominant class. In Swedish schools, for instance, the singing style of Western art music is predominant. This singing style differs from that of traditional Swedish folk music, but many Swedes now perform traditional songs in a style modelled on the ideals of Western art music. Traditional songs are also performed in multi-part arrangements for choirs, a style introduced through the school system.

Radio and other mass media can also be instrumental in exerting cultural dominance. One example is the case of the domination of North Indian art music in the programming of Sri Lanka Broadcasting Corporation. However, most cases in which mass media function as part of pattern of change belong to our last two categories.

The third pattern is the *cultural imperialism*. Here the cultural dominance is augmented by the transfer of money and/or resources from dominated to dominating culture group.

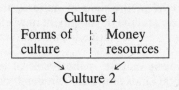

Examples of the money transferred are profits made by subsidiaries of record companies belonging to the dominating culture, or copyright money. The resources can be gifted musicians, pieces of music or unique traditional musical instruments which are removed to museums in a dominating culture area.

Activities during the past 50 years in the field of culture emanating mainly from the United States but also from some European countries are largely a process of cultural imperialism that has been described by many researchers[8]. In our study in Chapter 5 of the flow of copyright monies we touched on a few cases where pieces of music have been taken from small countries and copyrighted in the US. To enjoy the financial advantages, many gifted artists have

moved from Latin America and the Caribbean to the US. Some,
like Bob Marley, have transferred the right to collect copyright
money for their creative work to a US copyright organization.

The financial and other gains involved in cultural imperialism
contribute to placing a dominated culture under heavier pressure
than from pure cultural dominance. Cultural imperialism speeds up
the pace of change, but it also can lead to counteractions such as the
setting up of a local Musicians' Performing Right Society in Kenya
or the establishment by local musicians of small independent 'non-
commercial' record companies in the Nordic countries.

Most forms of cultural imperialism in the music sector require
that music is packaged and made into a product that can be
exchanged for money in the form of a phonogram, or a concert in a
closed hall where an entrance fee can be charged etc. This commercial aspect of cultural imperialism has contributed to the spread of
the concept of packaging and selling of music to more and more
music cultures and sub-cultures. For instance, during the Seventies
some Swedish folk fiddlers started to issue and sell phonograms with
their own music. This was a completely new development in Swedish folk music culture, and of course the technique was learnt from
the regular phonogram companies. Learning the art can contribute
to effective counteractions!

The three patterns enumerated so far: cultural exchange, cultural
dominance and cultural imperialism, have been joined by a fourth
and new pattern from around 1970: *transculturation*. This pattern of
change is the result of the worldwide establishment of the transnational corporations in the field of culture, the corresponding
spread of technology and the development of worldwide marketing
networks for what can be termed transnationalized culture or
transculture.

Transnational music culture is the result of a combination of
features from several kinds of music. This combination is the result
of a socio-economic process whereby the lowest musical common
denominator for the biggest possible market is identified by building
on the changes caused by the three previously described patterns of
change. The production of transcultural music like any other com-
modity product can involve pilot tests, industrial processing and
marketing/dissemination through mass media. Disco music, for
instance, is a transcultural music. The music of *Grease* or the group
Boney M are typical examples. It is a product that has not originated
within any special ethnic group. Disco music was marketed during
1975-78 in a massive worldwide campaign involving films, TV-
shows, phonograms and so-called merchandizing, i.e. John Tra-
volta T-shirts, Boney M buttons, ABBA posters etc. Not only
synthetically created music but also styles that have originated in a

special ethnic group can be turned into transcultural music. Usually the music in this case is stripped of its most original features. Reggae performed in Country and Western style, or Chopin melodies accompanied by a drum machine are examples. The spread of miniature organs with the *same* limited selection of synthetic rhythms to every market where they are sold is another example. Regardless of their own cultures, all performers have to relate to these pre-determined rhythms.

In the previously described patterns of change, the interaction has been bilateral, between two music cultures or in the case of cultural dominance and imperialism between a powerful, dominating culture and a number of other less powerful cultures. Through the transculturation process, music from the international music industry can interact with virtually all other music cultures and sub-cultures in the world, due to the worldwide penetration attained by music mass media during the past decade.

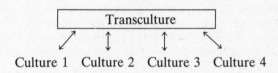

As we have noted, small countries function as marginal markets for international music as well as sources of internationally exploitable culture. What happens in practice is that individual music cultures pick up elements from transcultural music, but an increasing number of national and local music cultures also contribute features to transcultural music. The resulting process is a two-way flow which we have termed transculturation. As the music and electronic industries spread their hardware and software to different countries, this process starts.

Before we proceed to a more detailed description of the first stages in the transculturation of music in our sample countries it is important to point out that all the four categories of patterns of change described here still exist today. They overlap, strengthen or weaken each other in a complex system of relationships. For instance, there can be clear conflicts between cultural imperialism and transculturation. The process of the transculturation of music can be spread by a network of local agents for transnational companies who do not have to transfer money to any other country, or even by local entities whose official ideology is strictly opposed to that of transnational enterprises. This network is often augmented by phonogram pirates, whose activities can hardly be said to contribute positively to the riches of any 'imperialists' (apart from those who sell duplicating equipment and blank tapes).

There are clear similarities in the pattern of change in our sample countries as well as in other countries. The speed of change has increased, but not equally fast everywhere. Similar changes have taken place at different points in time and with different intervals between them. A change so profound as the emergence of popular music took place in the Nordic countries during the last decades of the nineteenth century, in Chile during the first decades of our century, in Tunisia, Sri Lanka and Trinidad during the Thirties, in Jamaica during the Forties and in Kenya and Tanzania during the Fifties and Sixties. Developments in music that have been spread out over more than 50 years in the Nordic countries have occurred within 20 years in Kenya. In the Seventies these developments reached a state where the music cultures of most countries had many features in common, maybe much more so than in other fields such as agriculture, industrial development or economic systems. This situation is a pre-requisite for the type of interaction that can lead to a general process of transculturation. In other words, translating this into practical terms, we have here the basis of an explanation for the almost simultaneous emergence of what could be termed 'national pop and rock music' in all our sample countries. Access to music industry technology, the influence of transnational music, access to local music culture and the will to create something different, all converged at the same time. The results could be referred to as the first stage of transculturation in these countries.

NATIONAL POP-ROCK OR ONE GLOBAL MUSIC?

The common development that has involved more local music-making than anything else in the MISC sample, has been the emergence of national styles of pop and rock music during the Seventies. These activities have invariably used the phonogram for distribution. One of the prerequisites, as we have noted, was access to technology by which local music could be documented and spread (first the open-reel tape recorder, then the gramophone record and cassette). The world had been flooded with Anglo–American music in the Fifties and Sixties. This influenced, but did not prevent local musicians developing their own styles, adapted to their own cultures. This seems to have happened about the same time everywhere, namely in the late Sixties and early Seventies. Throughout this period, the transnational phonogram companies might have increased or maintained their dominance in terms of sales and market percentages, but were doing less so in terms of phonograms released (and were probably quite happy to have it this way since smaller independent entities were taking the risks in the market).

We have already related how the Swedish music movement exploded around 1970. Thousands of groups suddenly started singing in their own language. The same type of process was taking place in Wales. (While Swedish groups were emerging from their cellars, singing in their own languages, young people in Wales were appearing at summer youth camps singing in Welsh.) The first pop record sung in Sinhala was released in Sri Lanka in 1969. Through the Seventies Jamaica experienced the transition from rock steady to reggae. Kenya was producing the first Lou pop records. Other local tribal variants followed throughout the decade. The Tanzanian jazz bands were developing their own Swahili version of East African popular music. After almost ten years of copying the Beatles, Elvis or Chubby Checker, musicians in the small nations started trying to develop their own national forms of popular music. Singing in one's own language or dialect was a significant change here, since it introduced a new communicative element between performer and listener.

Where recording and manufacturing and organizational resources were available, this led to the emergence of numerous small music businesses such as phonogram companies and clubs. The enthusiasts found an outlet for their energy. These changes heralded a very creative period in small country cultural history.

The creative results, however, were not always accepted by the establishment in those small countries. Radio Stations sometimes refused to play local popular music. Local politicians were slow to realize the value and importance of this development, particularly for young people. During the following ten years these local forms of pop and rock were to become accepted, first by a youth audience, and then gradually by government authorities and national mass media. Table 16 over the next few pages attempts to summarize this common pattern of change.

The charts we have just presented encompass a huge amount of cultural activity on a local and national level. They also embody the spread of the process we have termed 'transculturation'. Elements of music and music technology spread by the transnational industry are incorporated into local music. Much of the music of the Swedish and Welsh music movements was rock with local-language lyrics. Some musicians did include elements of their own culture's melodic traditions. The flow of influences was not merely one-way. Reggae began to influence global popular music, or, to use our terminology, the transculture assimilated elements of reggae. This is a relatively new process, very different from the cultural exchange of previous times. Beethoven's 5th has always been Beethoven's 5th; Western art music has stayed more or less intact throughout the process of

Table 16: DEVELOPMENT OF A NATIONAL POP/ROCK SCENE IN THE MISC SAMPLE COUNTRIES

COUNTRY	PERIOD Pre-1970	Early 70s	Mid-70s	Late 70s	Early 80s
SWEDEN	Numerous groups copying Beatles/Stones etc. Good market for English pop groups. '68/'69. Local groups emerge singing in Swedish, often at free festivals. Ignored by major record companies. Some DIY records emerge.	'Swedish trend' develops. Enthusiasts start studios, record companies and distribution companies for local pop/rock/folk productions. Political content leads to resistance from established media (radio and some sectors of press).	'Music movement' develops. Numerous associations formed to support live music. Much opposition from establishment. Though some grants given to pop/rock groups by Arts Council. Record companies expand; start a pressing plant. Mark their distance from multinationals by starting own alternative to IFPI (NIFF).	Some political rock groups collapse – others become more sophisticated, as do local recording facilities (3 24-track studios run by 'enthusiasts'). Some music associations fold up as volunteer founders grow older and/or tired. Younger Punk groups emerge; start own record companies and magazines.	Some independent record companies do well, featuring in Top 20s. Swedish pop/rock accepted as art form by press and even parts of the establishment. Punk groups find it hard to retain 'angry' identity. Records dominate over pre-recorded cassettes. Established record industry in dire straits. Puts blame on home taping.
CYMRU WALES	Mainly English language pop on disc before mid-60s. Solo artists emerge singing acoustic songs at festivals. Record companies emerge; Cambrian	Sales still good (EPs) backed up by exposure on two TV stations and BBC radio. Groups start to become electrified. Broad appeal amongst different	A 'music movement' develops. Music associations started for supporting live gigs (folk). Close relation to Welsh language society.	Sain gets development grant, goes 24-track. Groups from early 70s become more sophisticated (often more MoR).	Sain, with heavy investments finds it hard to sell pop/rock. Concentrates on MoR/Choirs etc. Cassette sales up. Rock/pop is almost accepted as Art form: is allowed to feature

Qualition (latter gets absorbed by Decca). Sain Records started by enthusiasts.	age groups *decreases*. Decca absorbs Cambrian, sticks to choirs/classical.	Sain gets 8-track studio. BBC TV try to run a folk programme (instead of rock/disco). BBC radio Cymru increase time for Welsh pop/rock.	Punk/New Wave groups emerge. New record companies (DIYs), clubs, and facilities started especially in South. BBC TV *stop* rock/pop shows.	at festivals (National Eisteddfod). Decision to start Welsh TV (Channel S4C) prompts many independent companies to work with music production. Decca, bought by Polygram, delete Welsh catalogue.
TUNISIA — Strong influence of Lebanese and Egyptian film music and French pop music.	Electric organs introduced in wedding party music in urban areas. Youth groups formed to play music patterned on film music and transnational rock. Much emphasis on solo singers.	Electric organs adapted to Arabic scales. Groups experiment with local pop and rock. Afro-American and Arabic stylistic elements mixed, but with limitations. Government counteracts influence of transnational pop and rock by extensive youth activities in network of culture houses. Many youth orchestras play Arabic film music.	Imitations of transnational pop and rock still common. Many electrified groups sing Italian-type hit songs with Arabic lyrics. (Italian TV becomes popular in northern coastal areas).	Young intellectuals (many with European education) develop *musique engagée* with political lyrics in Arabic and music combining Tunisian and French popular forms. Easing of freedom of speech restrictions combined with local manufacture of cassettes facilitate spread of national popular music. Problems with high level of piracy.

Table 16: – CONTINUED

COUNTRY/PERIOD	Pre-1970	Early 70s	Mid-70s	Late 70s	Early 80s
KENYA	English pop such as Twist/Rock 'n Roll dominate. First local record company, Mwanganza appears around '65. Congolese music becomes popular, as do groups from Zaire/Congo	More electric instruments reach Kenyan market. Singles dominate record market. Congolese groups dominate live scene. More small Kenyan record companies emerge. Two international record companies control most of market.	Congolese groups dominate live scene. Tourism provide work for musicians willing to play Anglo-Saxon hybrid music. EMI enter and leave the market. Two majors, Phonogram & AIT dominate market, one with manufacturing monopoly. More small Kenyan record companies emerge.	Local record companies explode in numbers. Form pressure group, lobbying government and radio. Start alternative organisation to the local IFPI branch. Congolese music still on top but local groups emerge, and some Tanzanian groups come in.	Local record companies try to organise a local pressing plant. Different groups organise themselves (composers, musicians, producers etc) – pressure on state radio to support more Kenyan culture, but attempts at radio fail. Singles dominate record market. Much official talk about national culture.
TANZANIA	'Jazz' bands playing popular music from Zaïre migrate to Tanzania. European string and wind instruments. African percussion. Style influenced by jazz and Caribbean music. Sung in Linguala (Zaïrean patois). Tanzanian groups formed imitating the Zaïrean 'jazz'.	First groups formed copying Western rock and soul and using electric guitars. Texts in English. Groups imitating Zaïrean music start to sing in Swahili and develop	Electric instruments gradually replace wind instruments. Almost all texts in Swahili on Tanzanian topics. Melodic and rhythmic elements from traditional	Approx. 120 'jazz' bands active in major towns. Their music has high status amongst ruling elite. Local bands supported by National Music Council. Afro 70 Band represent	Currency problems lead to virtual stop in imports of electric instruments and discs. Tanzania Film Company's pressing plant does not get foreign currency allocation needed for completion (1982).

CHILE					
	'Tanzanian' style. First recordings made and pressed in Nairobi, Kenya.	ngoma mixed with Zaïrean and Afro-American elements form 'Swahili jazz'. 'Jazz bands' sponsored by cooperatives, trade unions and students' associations. Radio Tanzania start regular live broadcasts with 'jazz'.	Tanzania at FESTAC 77 in Nairobi with full set of electric instruments incl. synthesizer. Radio Tanzania's national service broadcasts almost exclusively Tanzanian music.	Tanzanian recordings from Radio Tanzania pirated in Kenya. Many artists go to Nairobi to record. Despite problems very buoyant pop scene with local groups arousing interest all over East Africa. Musicians becoming aware of copyright problems.	
Some Beatle copies, mostly Latin American popular rhythms.	Contemporary folk music based on Andean traditions assumes importance. Music and politics closely related.	Local record companies started by musicians and political groups. Local records thrive thanks to price control and import ban. EMI's pressing plant runs at full capacity. **1973 MILITARY COUP**	Low recording activity. Many artistic groups and companies disband and/or go into exile. Virtual cultural black-out imposed by Junta.	Liberalization of import restrictions. Consumer goods flow in, including electric instruments and cassettes. Record companies find it harder to record local product and compete with foreign imports. Some musicians try to revitalize music of early 70s (*La nueva cancion* movement).	Some rock groups appear, inspired by radio output. Organize festivals. Availability of cassettes provides new means for exchange and distribution of songs (often underground). Signs that new record companies are trying to emerge (despite official opposition). New copyright society (SAIC) started which competes with established organization (DAIC).

Table 16: – *CONTINUED*

COUNTRY/PERIOD	Pre-1970	Early 70s	Mid-70s	Late 70s	Early 80s
TRINIDAD	An indigenous non-transnationalized folk/popular music firmly established: calypso played by 'brass bands' and steelbands. Indian film music and US hits imitated by some groups.	Electric instruments used in calypso bands. In spite of massive output of soul, Beatles etc. in mass media little imitation of that music. Transnational record company operations taken over by local enthusiasts.	Soul and reggae rhythms filter into the calypso music resulting in new pop style called *soca* (soul-calypso), from 1977 adopted by most bands. The heavy *soca* beat relies totally on electric instruments. Large accompanying groups and PA-systems.	*Soca* fad continues. Synthesizers adopted by most bands. Some *soca* tunes banned in mass media due to textual content. Steelbands start to play *soca*.	Live bands feel the competition from discothèques. As the economic situation worsens, political content of *soca* increases. Calypsonians and steelband musicians, through their own organizations constitute important pressure groups in society. More composers join copyright society (PRS). Local demands for new copyright law.
JAMAICA	Sound systems (discothèques) playing blues dominate popular scene, as does Western classical amongst the elite.	Growing sense of nationalism (National Festival movement). Local popular music forms	Radio stations increase Jamaican music content to high level. Even Jamaican school of music includes Jazz	World market for reggae gets established. Attracts many new entrepreneurs, not all of them merely	The Tuff-Gong label (owned by the late Bob Marley) gets off the ground, and represents an attempt by musicians to exert

			develop (reggae). Growth of local record industry. Musicians' Union uses threat of strike action to get more local music played on radio and TV.	and Folk in courses. More small local companies emerge.	enthusiastic about music. Cassettes introduced, and record company facilities (studios, pressing plants) show a marked increase.	more control over their destiny, and their music. Reggae becomes more of a media form, being played live mostly in studios. Sound systems/radio do the rest. Local demands for new copyright law.
SRI LANKA	Engish Top 40 songs popular as well as Indian film music. EMI record some local Sinhalese artists.	Sri Lankan pop emerges (this is a Western/Oriental hybrid with Sinhalese lyrics). Local record producers emerge. EMI pulls out of Sri Lanka.	Resistance to local pop strong at State Radio, which still plays much Anglo-Saxon pop. Record sales fairly good (hit singles up to 20,000 copies).	Economic restrictions on imports etc. delay introduction of the cassette. Records expensive, but can be produced in Sri Lanka's only pressing plant. Big controversy about value of Sri Lankan traditional music. Elite at state radio and elsewhere still push N. Indian music as only true form.	Liberalisation of import restrictions. Cassettes (both pirated and local) flood the market. New companies appear mainly organised and supported by businessmen, rather than music enthusiasts. Local popular form of music (*baila*) becomes a big market, but absent from radio.	Local pop productions from cassette producers receive few plays on State Radio, which prefers to record own productions, and/or play Anglo-Saxon records on popular commercial English channel. Session musicians try to form a union. Some signs that local artists want to start own production units. Copyright society formed.

Table 16: – CONTINUED

COUNTRY/PERIOD	Pre-1970	Early 70s	Mid-70s	Late 70s	Early 80s
COMMON TRENDS IN ALL NINE COUNTRIES	PA systems used. Introduction of electric instruments. Imitations of transnational pop and rock music by local groups.	Electric instruments adopted by many groups. Groups start to compose own music instead of copying. Experiments with singing pop and rock in local languages, mixing transnational music styles with national music. The emerging national pop and rock groups try to find venues (new clubs, festivals of Woodstock type etc.) and mass media outlets.	National pop and rock styles fully developed and accepted by youth audience. The cultural establishment as a rule still has an ambivalent attitude to this development.	Disco boom causes setback of live music scene and demand for a more heavy beat, i.e. more powerful amplifier systems and sophisticated multitrack studio facilities. Some kinds of national pop and rock accepted by government authorities and national mass media.	Growing awareness of areas such as copyright give added local credibility to calls for support for national pop/rock music. DJs and discothèques still posing a threat to local live music, especially where the tourist trade has financial problems. Spread of synthesizers continues into national pop/rock.

distribution around the world. Classical composers in Wales might have gone through periods during which they incorporated local Welsh folk melodies into their works – but they have not all started writing variations on Hungarian folk songs, in the way that international pop music might include elements of Jamaican pop.

We can assume that the transculturation process will continue and accelerate, encouraged by the fact that musicians in smaller cultures will continue to dream about success in the world market (thus contributing to the feed-back aspects of transculturation).

It is hard to say what is at the end of the tunnel. In its early stages (as described in our examples), transculturation has had positive effects on cultural activity. Musicians have made a lot of music, but have also looked to their own roots for extra inspiration on top of that supplied by international music. But what are the long-term perspectives? In theory at least, the result could be one single global type of popular music culture which incorporates elements of every sub-culture the international music industry has penetrated. However, such a perspective is a long way into the future and much can happen in the meantime. New expensive technology, for instance, could put the brakes on local music industry activities and stop the feed-back in the transculturation process.

10

The future

Apple Green is, or was, a Sri Lankan pop group. We found this description of their dilemma in a local newspaper.

Four years old and still no break – what a very sad situation. Apple Green, the group of musicians in question have been facing this problem throughout their career and are now quite fed up with it, they say.

The reason behind is a fact that is only too true – there is no market in Sri Lanka for musicians who don't go commercial. If they don't want to play those catchy but hacked 'Boney M' and 'Abba' numbers, they won't stand a chance. If they stick to their guns, or should we say more appropriately, their drums, guitars and other instruments, they get themselves into hot water.

This has happened only too often with groups setting out with idealistic goals, announcing – 'commercial' numbers are not our line, coming across opposition and relenting in the end.

But not so for Apple Green – they're not green at all where non-commercial music is concerned and they've been adamant that that is going to be the sort of music they always will play.

They have to face opposition and set backs of course – loads of it to be precise but they are not going to let the opinions of others upset their applecart.

'If you are not commercial they label you 'no good', says Pradeep Anthony, who manages Apple Green. 'Our group is not commercial and is good, and we've got to get that through to the people.'

'But it is difficult, we are not given the opportunity to do this. So, we sit around doing our thing (which is playing at night spots occasionally), and hope that one of these night clubs will wake up to the sound of good music. Meanwhile, if we do get a good break abroad which is one of our heart-breaking desires – we wave goodbye to Lanka, pack our bags and leave.[1]

Through development in mass communcations, music cultures interact today in a way that is totally new in human history. How will this affect the activities and ambitions of the Sri Lankan group Apple Green quoted above? Will the transnational music industry concentrate more and more on a few kinds of music with roots in

Anglo–American culture, as has been the trend so far? Will those 'catchy but hacked ABBA and Boney M numbers' be the only repertoire that will not rock the applecart? If Apple Green leave their own country, will they find a greater degree of understanding for their non-commercial ideals anywhere else? Will there be one music, long before we have one world?

OR, will local kinds of music continue to crop up, in a transcultural pattern, both giving to and taking influences from the cultural products of the international music industry, with each new transnational trend resulting in new types of music on a national and local level?

The answer to this flood of questions is that 'we do not know'. The changes have been so rapid (the penetration of technology, the collapse of traditional use and function of music etc.) that it is hard to predict what the end-result could be. All that can be done, at this stage, is to point at some of the factors which will affect the future direction of change. We start with technology.

HIGH OR LOW-COST TECHNOLOGY – ACCESSIBLE TO FEW OR TO MANY?

The Eighties have poised us on the brink of a new generation of electronic inventions that can affect music-making and the spread of music. How will new techniques with names such as laser, digital and satellite influence the music environment in different parts of the world? A critical factor will be cost. Analogue cassette technology is low-cost – thus it could be dispersed, in a very short space of time, to every corner of the globe. A digital studio, on the other hand, is and will be for some time, a high investment. Even a rich country like Sweden will find it hard to generate the investment capital for more than one or two. The new generation of software, represented by inventions such as the CD (compact disc) will mainly disseminate music that has been recorded digitally. It will only be possible to play these discs on a player that has a laser beam. Investment costs per phonogram, in other words, will be far higher than for traditional discs with analogue information recorded on a traditional tape-recorder.

If the whole world 'goes digital' and the CD becomes a global standard, then the whole world will have to buy new record-players. The old needle will not function with the new technology. If the world economy can take such an investment (and that should not be taken for granted), then such a development would accentuate the trend towards a decrease in the spread of music sold on phonograms, as well as an increase in the difficulties experienced by small countries or cultures wishing to use the latest technology on a local or national level (see diagram 13).

DIAGRAM 13: ACCESS TO HIGH OR LOW COST TECHNOLOGY IN THE FUTURE

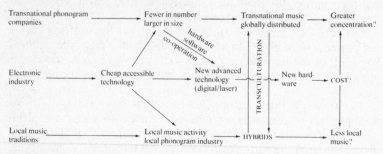

Of course, these developments do not occur overnight. The conventional LP and cassette will be with us for many years to come. However, one should not underestimate the speed at which changes can occur – this is one of the main lessons of the Seventies. If phonogram listeners do change, *en masse*, to a new generation of hardware, then this will probably occur in a similar fashion to the change-over in the Fifties/Sixties from 78 rpm players to LP stereo players; i.e. first in the industrialized countries and only later on in the developing countries. (78s were being produced in Africa as recently as the late Sixties). We might even see the electronic industry dumping obsolete analogue equipment on the poorer nations – which could even be to the advantage of their musical cultures in form of continued access to cheap, practical technology.

What complicates any attempt to analyse the future is the added factor of ever-increasing means of disseminating music through other ways than phonograms. One can envisage a system in the none-too-distant future whereby we dial a telephone number whenever we want to hear a particular piece of music. The sound will be transmitted digitally – the gatekeepers who decide on our range of cultural access, in this case, being those who programme material into the system. Gatekeepers in the ever-expanding area of radio/TV will continue to play an important cultural role, assuming (and this is an important proviso) that they still have access to plenty of music, live or recorded.

Every communcations satellite that gets into orbit can transmit up to 50 radio channels, offering, one might have thought, gigantic opportunities for pluralism in culture. But who can afford to put them into orbit? The Scandinavian nations together with Finland have ditched a plan for their own inter-Nordic TV satellite. Even plans to invest in a Nordic telecommuncations satellite (TELEX) have been hampered by lengthy and difficult negotiations about dividing up the costs. Soon the small Nordic nations will find themselves on the receiving end of British, French and German satellites, all providing an output of culture which the Nordic people have not affected either through any national democratic or commercial process. It is not surprising that those who care are both enthralled and concerned about this development. This expansion can provide a short-term financial boost to the communications industry, both internationally and nationally (parabolic dishes have to be made, erected and serviced). It also provides yet another threat to smaller cultures. Consider this warning from the head of a Canadian composers' organization:

> I'm concerned about what might happen once people get dishes and pull in programmes from satellites. More and more countries are going to lose their national identity because the originators of programmes will be those with funds to afford them like the US.[2]

This statement appears to refer to possible future developments. In fact, at the same time this statement was distributed through a trade paper, dishes were going up at a rate of one or two a day in Jamaica. This situation, and all the problems it entails, is with us already.

TECHNOLOGY AND ECONOMY

Technological and economic factors are closely related in the music industry. The invention of the sound cassette with its 'read-on/read off' function has provided the basis for profit for the pirate, access to more music for the consumer, and headaches for the phonogram producers. Questions of right and wrong become more complex in this context due to the process of concentration and integration within the international music industry (many large phonogram companies having close relationships to tape producers). As we pointed out in a previous chapter, those who lose out and suffer are primarily lesser-known artists and composers, struggling to live off their creative activity.

With increased integration of the music and electronics industries, one can assume that problems such as 'home-taping' will be harder to solve internally to the satisfaction of the phonogram producers.

With such squabbles going on within the electronics and music industry, it seems that outside forces motivated by goals of cultural policy will have to exert influence and extract from the market necessary resources for redistribution or compensation to copyright owners.

Attempts to block the pirates by producing software media which will read-off but not read-on (i.e. will play back but not record) can have a particular effect on small countries. RCA's Selectavision videodisc is such a case. RCA reckons it is pirate proof because of the millions of dollars any would-be pirate would require to set up a plant. RCA will be offering custom pressing services, but only through its own plants in the USA. In other words, a small country which might wish to produce its own Selectavision videodiscs will have to rely on the generosity of RCA. A similar situation will apply to the Philips CD, though these will be produced in a number of countries. The CD engraving procedure, however, is complex and will be available in only a very few specialized plants.

Incidentally, it is doubtful where the CD or Selectavision will put obstacles in the way of the pirates. CDs do not suffer from rumble or hiss – they provide perfect masters for copying sound cassettes and can therefore increase the quality of pirated tapes based on material that is available on the CD. What is more, the Japanese electronics industry is well on its way to developing equipment for the consumer market with a read-on/read-off type of laser disc (incorporating a mini-laser which traces pulses when recording. The signal cannot be erased, but each disc will have a capacity of about three hours!). To draw a rather unfortunate parallel, this is similar to technological 'advances' in the military. There is no ultimate super weapon – someone can always develop something more deadly. Or as one tape manufacturer told us; 'The hydrogen bomb cannot be un-invented.' One hopes the hydrogen bomb will never be used. The same cannot be said about music industry hardware. It seems to be impossible to stop it being used. Videograms, phonograms and related hardware find their way everywhere, whether the producers of software or even governments like it or not. If one reason for this is that many of the major producers of hardware are based in Japan and are *not* producers of software, then this situation is likely to continue. If the equipment is going to be there anyway, then the question to be posed is not whether it will be used, but how to make sure it is used as sensibly as possible. The cassette itself is a good, practical invention – it is what one puts on it that is of importance from a cultural aspect.

ORGANIZATIONAL CHANGES IN THE LARGE AND THE SMALL

It is likely that the growth process through concentration, diversification and integration will continue in the music, media and electronics industries. The downward trend in sales experienced by many established phonogram companies will lead to more changes of ownership and amalgamations. If the pending amalgamation of WEA and Polygram becomes a reality, this could cause turmoil in the form of losses of hundreds and even thousands of jobs. It could also spark off another amalgamation leading to a situation with only one or two major phonogram companies. Such a situation would not be in the public interest. This scenario is further complicated by the fact that other organizations with a surplus of liquid capital can also be expected to move into the music and media industries (the purchase by Coca Cola of a large film company is but one example). Small countries will find it harder to control the activities of the subsidiaries of transnationals.

The evidence presented in Chapter 3 made it clear that transnational phonogram companies might share the same ultimate goals of growth and profit but do not constitute a homogeneous group as regards policies in different operating territories.

CBS Records, we believe, intends to expand into every country where it can operate a phonogram company that breaks even. CBS policy, in 1983 at least, includes support for a high level of local recording activity.

It is not certain that every country wishes to have a subsidiary of CBS Records. If it does accept CBS' presence, then maybe in the short term, this particular transnational phonogram company presents a more attractive bed partner that one which regards a small country primarily as a marginal market which can absorb international products. Even CBS' profits, however, are sinking in the phonogram field, and economic realities could well force the Record Division to put the brakes both on its expansion, and on the degree of freedom allowed to its local employees.

The alternative policy apparently practised by Polygram of contracting and financing production companies that do the creative work and take many of the risks in the market, will also continue. ABBA's phonogram company, Polar, that developed resources by delivering products to the transnationals for distribution, is now itself financing 'younger' phonogram production units in Sweden. In return for finances, Polar demands a share of the profits, some income from distribution and (significantly) publishing rights. WEA, who bought up their Swedish distributor, Metronome, in 1979 (indicating at the time that Metronome's policy of supporting local releases would continue) sold out their studio in 1983 to an employee. The Swedish Council for Cultural Affairs was asked to provide the necessary funds to 'look after' the cultural heritage embodied in the company's unique tape library of Swedish music recordings. Such experiences are understandable and can be expected to be repeated many times in the future – obviously the global interests of any transnational must go before the national cultural interests of any one small nation. Otherwise, they would not be in business.

The integration of *music publishing companies* into the phonogram industry will continue because of the lucrative nature of these operations. There are not many business areas where an adminstrative operation can retain 50 per cent of its turnover to cover costs! The only way to change this situation is through actions by composers and their associations leading to legislation and agreements on a national and international level.

Small locally owned phonogram companies, often run by enthusiasts, will continue to wax, wane, or be swallowed up by larger operations, as long as technology is accessible. The general spread of playback equipment such as the CD, which requires a higher initial software investment than regular cassettes/records, could present a serious hindrance to the cultural activities of small, local companies. They will become more dependent on larger financial entities that can provide the latest technological services. One encouraging point here is that both conventional presses and electroplating equipment are also used in the manufacture of Selectavision discs (RCA), laservision discs (Philips) and sound recordings on CDS (Sony/Philips). Should the compact disc not turn out to be the success in the consumer market predicted by the music industry, then there are areas for improvement in conventional records (Direct Metal Mastering, or DMM, mentioned in Chapter 2 is one such development). Research, mainly by Japanese firms, into improving the mechanical qualities of the sound cassette should also improve its practical function as a disseminator of sound, especially in warmer climates where discs have disadvantages.

Small phonogram companies will not be the only groups of enthusiasts on a local or national level who will continue to contribute positively to the music life of small countries. Organization building will continue (and will hopefully find government understanding) as different groups see their musical interests and culture threatened. An exchange across borders would be invaluable for such groups. Genuine cultural exchange on a grass roots level will always be the best antidote to the negative aspects of cultural dominance.

OTHER COMMUNICATIONS MEDIA (RADIO/TV/VIDEO . . .)

Access to music and pictures via radio and TV screens is likely to follow the technological developments described above. Anything from dustbin lids to mathematically constructed steel structures will be used to pick up signals from direct transmitting satellites. Optic fibre cables, at first in the industrialized countries, will do the same underground.

The general trend towards local radio stations will continue.

The phonogram, however, may not always provide broadcasters with the same source of cheap programme material as it has done in the past. If the phonogram industry's internal financial situation should worsen, if small phonogram producers' access to technology should be curtailed, or if international agreements, such as the Rome Convention, should make phonograms harder to come by or more expensive to play, then radio stations might have to look to other ways of acquiring music. They may well have to play a more active part in recording music themselves. This would be a positive development; radio stations would provide more work for musicians. On the other hand it would cost the radio stations a fair amount – solving that problem depends on the method chosen for financing broadcasting in each country.

Producing local television programmes will continue to be expensive if small countries aim to attain the same grandeur as in the glitter shows provided by international producers. The importance of producing local programmes of high quality, featuring local artists and culture, cannot be underrated. Giving up and allowing the small screen to be filled with cheap, internationally available 'lowest common denominator' shows can only have a very discouraging effect on a nation's cultural identity.

In this context, it will be very interesting to follow the experiences gained by the minority S4C TV channel in Wales. Their model containing a small central administration with contracts to local independent producers could well be adapted successfully by other small countries if and when cheaper video recording equipment becomes available. What is needed generally is a greater level of involvement in broadcasting of local enthusiasts and groups. Let those who have sounds to make be heard.

COPYRIGHT

As things are developing now, the copyright system could collapse in a matter of years. Difficulties in keeping track of both users of music and the music they use are gigantic. Collecting societies find themselves in a situation where they have to compensate for inadequacies in the system by making their own decisions of cultural policy regarding who should get what. Compensation is gradually being replaced by redistribution. This trend can only continue.

The role of the music publishers in copyright distribution and remuneration must be reappraised.

Ideally, each small country should have its own independent collecting society representing all composers and lyricists. International distribution can only function if all nations adhere to the same conventions and if all collecting societies stick to the rules. The cloak-and-dagger atmosphere surrounding some societies would evaporate if there were better opportunities for public and (sometimes) membership access to their operations. CISAC and other international organizations with an interest in copyright should devote more effort to informing musicians about all aspects of copyright, including the difficulties of copyright remuneration.

A prerequisite for control of music use in an ever-expanding electronic media environment is the use of the latest information technology. A functioning international data bank of both copyright owners from CISAC societies and their works is a basic requirement. A more efficient exchange of computerized information between local societies and local users must be further developed with the support, where necessary, of legislation.

A Notary Public or some other impartial representative controller should be common to all. Some sort of international auditing is also necessary. The large collecting societies can continue to help small societies with purely administrative routines, but there can be no motivation for control beyond this. The developments called for here however must also include firm guarantees regarding personal integrity. The free exchange of computer tapes between collecting societies (including details of composers' country of residence *and* pseudonyms) could be misused by some governments. An unpleasant authoritarian regime might utilise the system to monitor the whereabouts of critical composers in exile.

World economic conditions will continue to affect the problems of maintaining a functioning international copyright system where funds are exchanged between countries according to the use of music. Countries that willingly or unwillingly become net importers of international music will continue to be less motivated to adhere to international agreements. Any increase in genuine exchange between the music of such countries and other nations will improve this situation. If a nation feels that its music is being played elsewhere (and copyright is being respected) then a greater amount of reciprocity is to be expected.

GOVERNMENTS AND THEIR FUTURE RESPONSIBLITY TO MUSIC

At the beginning of this book we pointed out that one reason for studying a sample of small countries rather than a sample of minority cultures is that the country is a political unit. Political decisions taken by governments often have an important effect on developments in society. How should governments of small countries tackle the future with regard to their music culture? Which are the possible options?

Of course the answers to such questions depend on the particular ideological standpoints and overall priorities that the politicians in power happen to share. Another equally important factor is the degree of awareness amongst politicians of the role of music both in society as a whole and in the life of individuals. Music plays an important role in developing the senso-motoric system of the young child, and in the development of the ability for non-verbal communcation. Music makes an important contribution to the sense of belonging to a group, in the forming of the personality and the structure of social relations. Observations of the use and function of music in different societies indicate that it is an important factor in cementing the 'common soul' of a society. This fact leads to at least two general political implications.

1. There must be a guarantee that individuals and groups in society can actively participate in different aspects of music life.
2. There must be possibilities for individuals and groups to maintain traditional activities and create new musical activities that emerge from their cultural needs and everyday conditions.

In the future, safeguarding these two features in small countries will inevitably mean more government involvement. This will be especially true in the field of new popular music. With increasing geographical and social mobility, new groupings of people will emerge, requiring changes in the structure of the music life of a country. The traditional music of a certain local rural area as a rule will not function in a suburb of a city. Essential resources such as meeting places necessary for the growth of local music activities must be provided in new living environments. It is becoming more common for ethnic groups that used to live in a limited geographical area to be dispersed over a country or even over several countries. Here mass media dissemination of music can play an important role in easing up the cultural hardships of such transitions. We also have the case of groups with similar material conditions emerging at different places within one country or within many different countries. Here a fair exchange of musical experiences between these groups through modern media can speed up the growth of a music culture appropriate to the new conditions at hand. (By 'fair' we mean a form of cultural exchange on equal terms, not one which is intended to extract a lowest common denominator type of product marketable in a larger context.)

Of particular interest in this context of learning from each other is the opportunity for cultural exchange between the industrialized and the developing world. Music seems to have a more constructive, active function in the developing world. It functions more as a catalyst, and less as a tranquillizer. No one wants to deny the stressed citizens of the 'civilized' world the right to harmless relaxation, but is it not just possible that the industrialized nations could learn much from the developing world and its use of music? Music of third-world origin, as purveyed by the music industry's products, is readily accepted, but how much is known about the function of music in other cultures? It is just possible that Europeans and North Americans could learn as much, if not more in this field, as the developing countries learn through the traditional flow of information from the 'haves' to the 'have-nots'.

Small countries shoulder not only a responsibility, but also possess some of the prerequisites for a fruitful exchange of cultural experiences in our modern 'mediaized' world. The sounds might not be so big as they sometimes deserve to be. But they are part of the world's cultural heritage. Music industry technology can be used to flood them out of a recognizable existence – it can also be used to develop and expand.

The task of governments must be to ensure that planning of new environments and mass media allows for creation and dissemination of locally and nationally grown musical activities. This will encompass a choice of technology including the availability of means for producing phonograms and music programmes for radio and TV within the country. Governments will have to decide what technology is needed and make sure that those who can use it sensibly, have it. It is important here that the yardstick used for measuring success is not purely a commercial measure. Even if phonograms with local music only sell a few copies in the commercial market, they may be very vital to the health of the 'common soul' if their content reaches many people through radio broadcasts, public libraries and home-taping.

Small countries often suffer from a lack of information when decisions regarding choice of technology are made.Small countries and their local music industries can find themselves at the mercy of middlemen, whose advice (and prices) they are forced to accept because of lack of independent counsel. Here an international organization such as Unesco could play a role through providing independent consultancy services in the area of music industry technology. Small countries also stand to gain a lot from their own exchange of information in this area.

Governments will also have to create systems for redistributing money to cover the expenses involved in keeping local music life alive and flourishing. Our research results show two emerging ways of doing this. The first involves generating funds through the taxation of hardware in the form of licences or through levies such as the levy on blank tapes in Sweden. Another way is to use copyright money, either through independent copyright societies representing creators or, failing that, through direct government involvement. As we have mentioned, the international copyright conventions already allow for 10 per cent of copyright collections to be used for the promotion of national music life. Maybe a larger percentage will have to be redistributed in this fashion in recognition of the fact that a national 'cultural capital' depends on active and widespread musical activity.

Some of the actions by governments of small countries advocated above will be far more effective if they are backed up by cooperation between several small countries. This is the case if the international copyright conventions have to be thoroughly revised or if international disseminators of culture (e.g. via regular transmissions, satellite or cable) are to be made to pay properly for the luxury of utilizing intellectual property. The music media situation is becoming more and more similar in different small countries all over the world. Lessons are learned in different countries by governments and music organizations, that could be of great interest to music activists and decision-makers in other small countries. We can predict a growing need for cooperation between small countries in the field of cultural planning in the future. It is ultimately the responsibility of the governments concerned to create the framework for such a cooperation.

Within each country governments will have to make many bold decisions, some of which will involve a certain element of risk. The role of the enthusiasts must be recognized and rewarded, even to the extent of supporting those with ideas that conflict with the more cautious, sometimes conservative thinking of the establishment. Those responsible for enacting government cultural policy (e.g. in Arts Councils etc.) must have a certain independence to support what they believe to be of value to the nation's culture. They must not merely function as the extended arm of whichever political grouping happens to be in power. (We accept that such a situation is somewhat utopian in a world of military dictatorships and authoritarian regimes – but most governments would accept that national cultural identity is something worth cementing.)

ONE GLOBAL MUSIC OR A MULTITUDE OF THRIVING CULTURES?

The continuation of the transculturation process in the future can take one of two main directions. The interaction of transculture and individual culture will either continue in a to and fro movement where more and more musical features will become common to more and more music cultures. The end of such a path would be the attainment of a global music culture available to almost everybody, long before a corresponding worldwide homogeneity in languages, living conditions etc. is reached. We would then live in a music environment that would give a little satisfaction to a lot of people, and a lot of satisfaction to very, very few. Since music is so close to the heart of man, we can predict that such a process would continually be 'disturbed' by the activities of an underground cultural guerilla.

Transculture

National and local music cultures

Global music culture

(Music guerilla)

The other main direction would involve the emergence of a multitude of types of music arising out of new living conditions and new music technologies, at the same time as traditional music is adapted to new environments where, albeit with some changes, it can be put to similar uses and functions as in a traditional society.

Whichever way it goes, technology will play an important role. But technology alone will not decide the outcome. People and governments do that.

Standardization or variety: whichever direction changes will take it is very likely that the first signs will become apparent in the smaller nations. The music cultures of small countries are very vulnerable, being easily affected by trends in the general pattern of change. It will be wise to continue keeping an eye on the music life of these entities. If big sounds from small peoples start to weaken then this could be a sign that the music of the whole world is threatened.

Epilogue

'In a world in which authoritarian power is maintained by superior technology, and the superior technology is supposed to indicate a monopoly of intellect, it is necessary to show that the real sources of technology, of all culture, are to be found in the human body and in co-operative interaction between human bodies . . . it is necessary to understand why a madrigal of Gesualdo or a Bach Passion, a sitar melody from India or a song from Africa . . . may be profoundly necessary for human survival, quite apart from any merit they may have as examples of human creativity and technical progress.'
(John Blacking in 'How musicial is man?')

References

CHAPTER 1
1. Ryan & Peterson, 1982.
2. Pearsall, 1975.
3. Kealy, 1979.
4. De Coster, 1976; Hennion & Vignolle, 1978.
5. Peterson & Berger, 1971.
6. Becker, 1976
7. Ryan & Peterson, 1982.
8. Cf. Hennion, 1981.
9. Simon Frith, 1981.
10. Gronow, 1980
11. Schiller, 1974.
12. Armand Mattelart, 1979.
13. Jeremy Tunstall, 1979.
14. Collins, 1975.
15. EMI, *World Record Markets*, 1971, p.10.
16. Hirch, 1970.
17. Denisoff, 1975.
18. Blaukopf, 1977.
19. Soramäki & Haarman, 1978.
20. Gillet, 1972.
21. Hennion & Vignolle, 1978.
22. Hennion, 1981.
23. Peacock & Weir, 1975.
24. *Fonogrammen: Kulturpolitiken* (Phonograms & cultural policy), 1979.
25. Blaukopf, 1982, p.22.
26. Laade, 1969.
27. Laade, 1971.
28. Malm, 1981.
29. A more detailed study of these four music cultures and their similarities is available in Swedish (*Fyra musikkulturer,* Malm 1981).
30. Cf. Blaukopf, 1982. p.4.
31. Ivre, 1981.
32. *Music Week*, 2.10.1982.
33. Gronow, 1980.
34. Wallis & Malm, 1980.
35. Wallis & Malm, 1983.

CHAPTER 2
1. Grundy & Tobler, 1982.
2. A. H. Sheriff, 1974.

CHAPTER 3
1. Kulatillake, 1976; Laade/Makololluwa, 1982.
2. Laade/Makololluwa, 1982.
3. *Music Week,* 29.5.1976.
4. Harm van der Wal, 1980.

CHAPTER 4
1. Beaud in Blaukopf, 1982.
2. Hirch, 1970; Denisoff, 1975.
3. Malm, 1983.
4. CIRPA, 1981.
5. Blaukopf, 1982.
6. *Dagens Nyheter*, 17.11.1982
7. Manager of the group Japan, quoted in *Music Week,* 6.11.1982.
8. Frith, 1981, p.141.
9. 'ICC Business Ratios reports', in *Record News*, 24.9.1979.
10. Mattelart, 1979.
11. Keith Richard, quoted in Gronow, 1982, taken from Ben Fong Torres (ed.), *Rolling Stone Interviews 2,* Warner, N.Y., 1972, p. 292.
12. Davies, 1980.
13. *Radio and Record News,* 14.9.1979.
14. *Music Week,* 7.4.1979.
15. MISC interview, 1981.
16. Hennion, 1982.
17. CIRPA, 1982.
18. *Music Week,* 15.11.1980.
19. Letter from CRI, CBS Records International, July 1980.
20. CBS Kenya, *Music Scene*, Vol. 1, July 1982.
21. Neville Lee, 1981.
22. Dick Asher, CBS, 1983.
23. Local radio disc jockey, 1982, Chile.
24. EMI official, 1981, Chile.
25. EMI official, 1981, Chile.
26. Frith, 1981, p.135.
27. Frith, 1981, pp. 147-8.
28. *Music Week*, 27.11.1982.
29. *Music Week,* 17.3.1979.
30. *Music Week,* 9.8.1980.
31. Richard Lyttleton, formerly head of EMI, Finland, now International Manager, EMI.
32. Mike Wells, 1980.
33. Dick Asher, Chief Operating Officer, CBS, *Music Week,* 4.12.1982.
34. Gillet, 1972; Baskerville, 1979, pp.306-9.
35. Peacock & Weir, 1975, pp.102–3.
36. Frith, 1982, p.146.
37. Gronow, 1981.

CHAPTER 5
1. Swedish rock singer on a commercial label.
2. Music researcher in Santiago, 1981.
3. Johnny Smith, concert organizer and radio presenter.
4. Ricardo Garcia, 1981.
5. Financial director, Tuff Gong, 1981.
6. Neville Lee, Sonic Sounds.
7. J. Kinzl, former managing director, Polygram Kenya.
8. Fernando Reyes Matta, 1982.

CHAPTER 6
1. Employee of Essex Music, London.
2. Employee of Fall River Inc., New York.
3. Ed Cramer, BMI, 1983.
4. Svend Aaquist Johansen, CIAM meeting in Paris, 13–14 October, 1980.
5. Ibid.
6. *PRS Yearbook,* 1982.
7. Dick Asher, CBS, 1983.
8. Ed Kramer, BMI, 1983.
9. de Freitas, PRS, 1980.
10. Peter Bond, CBS, 1980.
11. *The Rome Convention – an enquiry into its practical application*, IFPI London.
12. Ibid., Annexe IV.
13. Ed Cramer, BMI, 1983.
14. Joy Graeme, 1983.
15. Ibid.
16. Peter Bond, CBS.
17. Joy Graeme, 1983.
18. Ed Cramer, BMI, 1983.
19. Andrew King, Harmony Music, 1983.
20. Pete Seeger, 29 November, 1978.
21. Joseito Fernandez, interview with Swedish Television, 1976.
22. J. Graeme, Fall River, 1983.
23. Tom Murray, 1983.
24. Interview with Swedish Television 1983.
25. Irvine Burgie, 1983.
26. Ibid.
27. Harry Belafonte, interviewed in 1980 by Dermot Hussey of Jamaican Television.
28. Irvine Burgie, 1983.
29. Report of Jamaican copyright committee, 1982.
30. Edward Seaga, 1983.
31. *PRS Yearbook*, 1977.
32. Edward Seaga, 1982.
33. Jacques Coenen-Huther, 1982.

CHAPTER 7

1. *The Council of Europe, Aims, Operations, Activities*, 1979, p.40.
2. Mattelart, 1979, p.231.
3. Malm, p.194f.
4. Zghonda, 1982.
5. Raymond Williams in Stephens (ed.), 1979, p.2.
6. Ruhumbika, 1974, p.279.
7. See Malm, 1982.
8. *Lov om saeravgift pa utstyr for opptak eller gjengivelse av lyd eller bilder*, 1980–81.
9. Government Green Paper on Copyright Law Reform, July 1981.
10. Managing director of Semp Studios, Trinidad, 1981.
11. Sr Dominquez, head of 'extension cultural', Ministry of Culture, Chile, 1981.
12. MISC interview, April 1981.

CHAPTER 8

1. Ernst Grissemann, Austrian Radio.
2. Fischer & Melnik, 1979.
3. Grondal & Norrby, 1980.
4. Richard Lyttleton, 1980.
5. P. Tagg, 1977.
6. 'Music and tomorrow's public', IMC–IFPI, 1975.
7. 'Assecor Musical', Head of Music, Radio Portales, Chile.
8. Share Studio Center, 1981.
9. Jorge Alvarez, ex-artistic director of Capitol Records, Mexico, quoted in Matta, 1982, op.cit.
10. Richard Lyttleton, 1980.
11. Head of Music, Radio Portales, Chile.
12. *Music Week*, 22.8.1981.
13. *Music Week*, 20.11.1981.
14. Grundy in *Music Week*, 2.10.1982.
15. Gerald Wickremasooriya, February, 1982.
16. Dayaratne Ratnatunga, head of music, Sinhalese Service, SLBC.
17. Gronow, 1982.
18. Voice of Kenya disc jockey, 1980.
19. Polygram's Managing Director, 1980.
20. *The Daily Nation* (Kenya), 9.3.1980.
21. S. Hegga, 1980.
22. Ibid.
23. Peacock & Weir, 1975, p.114.
24. *The Daily Nation*, 28.11.1982.
25. *Pan Trinbago report,* 1980.

CHAPTER 9
1. W.B. Makulloluwa, Sri Lanka, 1982.
2. Dick Asher, CBS, 1983.
3. Ibid.
4. Source: CBS annual report 1981.
5. Jimmy Cliff, 1983.
6. MCPS, 1982.
7. W.B. Makulloluwa, 1982.
8. See Mattelart, 1979.

CHAPTER 10
1. Fathima Akbar in *The Sun*, Sri Lanka, 6 May, 1982.
2. John Mills, Composers, Authors and Publishers Association of Canada, CAPAC, in *Music Week*, 22.1.82.

MISC – Bibliography

Akbar, F., 'They won't let commercials upset the applecart', *The Sun*, Colombo 1982 (daily paper).

Baskerville, D., *Music business handbook*. Los Angeles 1979.

Becker, H.S., 'Art worlds and social types', in Peterson, R.A. ed., *The production of culture*, Beverly Hills 1976.

Blacking, J., *How musical is man?* Seattle and London 1973.

Blaukopf, K., *Massenmedium Schallplatte*, Vienna 1977.

Blaukopf, K., 'The strategies of the record industries', Council of Europe paper CC–GP 11 (82) 16. Strasbourg 1982

Blaukopf, K., Ed., *The phonogram in cultural communication*, Vienna 1982

CBS 1981 Annual Report, New York 1982

CBS Kenya, *Music Scene*, Vol. 1. Nairobi July 1982.

Coenen-Huther, J., 'Creative artists and the industrialisation of culture: music. Report and conclusions,, Council of Europe CC–GP 11 (82) 26. Strasbourg 1982

Collins, J., 'Etats-Unis et transnationales américaines; retour à l'envoyeur', in *Politique Aujourd'hui* Nos. 1–2, January–February 1975

Copyright law reform. British Government Green Paper publication, London 1981.

Daily Nation, Nairobi 1980. (Daily newspaper).

De Coster, M., *Le disque, art ou affaires*? Grenoble 1976.

The Council of Europe; Aims, operation, activites, Strasbourg 1979.

Dagens Nyheter, financial pages. Stockholm 17.11.982 (daily paper)

DAIC Chile Memoria 1976–79, Santiago 1980.

Davies, G., *Piracy of phonograms*, IFPI. London 1980

Denisoff, R.S., *Solid gold: The record industry, its friends and enemies*, New York 1975.

EMI World record markets, London 1971.

Fischer & Melnik, eds., 'The economics and structure of the record and tape industry: The example of West Germany', in *Entertainment – a cross cultural examination*. Frankfurt 1980.

Fonogrammen i kulturpolitiken. Rapport fran kulturradet 1979: 1. Stockholm 1979.

Frith, S., *Sound effects. Youth, leisure, and the politics of rock'n roll*. New York 1981; London 1983.

Frith, S., 'The sociology of rock – notes from Britain', in Horn, D. & Tagg, P. eds., *Popular Music Perspectives*, Gothenburg and Exeter 1982.

Gillet, C., *Sound of the city*, New York 1972.

Gronow, P., *Statistics in the field of sound recordings*. Unesco, Division of statistics on culture and communication, report C–21. Paris 1980.

Gronow, P., 'The record industry comes to the Orient', in *Ethnomusicology*, vol. 25 no. 2 pp. 251-84, 1981.

Grundy, S., in '15 years, BBC Radio 1 and 2 anniversary special supplement' in *Music (and Video) Week* 2/10 1982 (Weekly music business paper).

Grundy, S. & Tobler, J., *The record producers*, BBC. London 1982.

Gröndal & Norrby, *Music lovers – a study of people interested in music*, Gothenburg 1980.

Hennion, A., *Les professionnels du disque,* Paris 1981.

Hennion, A., & Vignolle, J. P., *L'économie du disque en France*, Paris 1978.

Hennion, A., *The place of small firms in the record industry and their role in musical creativity*, Council of Europe CC-GP 11 (82) 12, Strasbourg 1982

Hirch, P., *The structure of the popular music industry,* Ann Arbor, Mich. 1970.

Ivre, I., 'Valfriheten i multimediesamhället', in *Nya Argus* No. 3. March 1981.

Kealy, E. R., 'From craft to art: the case of sound mixers and popular music', in *Sociology of Work and Occupations* 6:3-29. 1979.

The Kenyan National Music Organizations Treaty. Nairobi 5/5 1980 (Stencil)

Kubik, G., 'Neo-traditional popular music in East Africa since 1945', in Middleton, R. & Horn, D., eds., *Popular Music* Vol. 1. Cambridge 1981.

Kulatillake, C. de S., & Abeysinghe, R., *A background to Sinhala traditional music of Sri Lanka,* Colombo 1976.

Kulturpolitik – vad är det? Statens kulturrad, Stockholm 1981.

Laade, W. & Makulloluwa, W. B., 'Music, dance, theatre and rituals of the Sinhalese of Sri Lanka'. Zürich 1982 (Manuscript in preparation).

Laade, W., *Die Situation von Musikleben and Musikforschung in den Ländern Afrikas and Asiens und die neue Aufgaben der Musikethnologie.* Heidelberg 1969.

Laade, W., *Neue Musik in Afrika, Asien and Ozeanien*. Diskographie und historisch-stilistischer Überblick. Heidelberg 1971.

Lov om saeravgift pa utstyr for opptak eller gjengivelse av lyd eller bilder. Kirke – of undervisningsdepartementet OT prp. nr. 74. Oslo 1980-81.

Malm, K., *Fyra musikkulturer,* Stockholm 1981.

Malm, K., 'Phonograms and cultural policy in Sweden', in Blaukopf, K., ed., *The phonogram in cultural communication,* Vienna 1982.

Matta, F. R., 'Popular song, the recording industry and their alternative facet.' Translation from *Canto Popular Discos v Alternativas*, prepared for Media Development 1982. Instituto Latinamericano de estudios transnacionales. Mexico City 1982.

Matterlart, A., *Multi-national corporations and the control of culture. The ideological apparatuses of imperialism*. New Jersey 1979.

MCPS, *Home taping – the case for a royalty*, London 1982.

Music and tomorrow's public, Vol. 1, Part 2, p. 141. IMC-IFPI. Paris 1975.

Music (and Video) Week; Hunter, N., 'EMI announces pragmatic policy, 17/3 1979. Hunter, N., ' Put merit before bottom line – NARM told,' 31/3 1979. 'Of international importance . . .,' 7/4 1979. Stratton Smith, T.,

'Straight talk from Strat', 15/11 1980. Mayer, I., 'RCA reveals disc, video losses,' 20/3 1982. Mayer, I., 'Lundvall strong on audio,' 15/5 1982. Hunter, N., 'Buyers queue up to bid for UK publishing firm,' 28/8 1982. Hunter, N., ed., 'Survey reveals inadequately low royalties scandal,' 23/10 1982.

Music (& Video) Week, articles. (Weekly music business paper).

Pan Trinbago 1980 Convention report. Port of Spain 1980.

Peacock, A. & Weir, R., *The composer in the market place*, London 1975.

Pearsall, R., *Edwardian popular music*, Rutherford, N. J. 1975.

Peterson, R. A. & Berger, D. G., 'Entrepreneurship and organizations, evidence form the popular music industry, in *Administrative Quarterly* Vol. 16. March 1971.

Radio and Record News, 'TV album marketing – fears of abuse come autumn,' London 14/9 1979; 'Gloom industry analysis', London 24/9 1979 (Monthly magazine, ceased 1980).

Ruhumbika, G. ed., *Towards ujamaa, twenty years of TANU leadership,* Dar es Salaam 1974.

Ryan, J. & Peterson, R. A., 'The product image. The fate of creativity in country music songwriting,' in Ettema, J. S. & Whitney, D. C., eds., *Individuals in mass media organizations: creativity and constraint*, New York 1982.

Schiller, H. I., *Mass communications and American empire*, Boston 1971.

Schiller, H.I., *The mind managers*, Boston 1974.

Sheriff, A.H., *Music and its effects,* Bilal. Muslim Mission, Dar es Salaam 1974.

Stephens, M. ed., *The arts in Wales 1950-75,* Cardiff 1979.

Tagg, P., 'Music teacher training problems and popular music research,' in Horn, D. & Tagg, P., *Popular music perspectives*, Gothenburg and Exeter 1982.

Tagg, P., 'Populärmusik och medierna'. Gothenburg 1977. (Stencil)

The tape manufacturers group (UK subsidiaries of BASF, 3M, Maxelle, Memorex, Sony and TDK), *The case against a levy on blank recording tape,* London 1983.

Tunstall, J., *The media are American*. London/New York 1979.

Wal, van der, H., *Conference on the state's role vis-a-vis the culture industries. Cost development trends in the international record industry:* Council of Europe CC-CONF-IC 19. Strasbourg 1980.

Wallis, R. & Malm, K., 'The interdependency of broadcasting and the phonogram industry. A case study covering events in Kenya during March 1980'. Mediacult documents No. 6. Vienna 1980.

Wallis, R. & Malm, K., 'The role of the Welsh phonogram industry in the development of a Welsh language pop/rock/folk scene,' in Middleton, R. & Horn, D., eds., *Popular Music* Vol. 3, *Producers and markets*. Cambridge 1983.

Appendix
Profiles of change
in the MISC sample countries

This data section summarizes the results of our study of significant incidents in the music life of our sample countries.

The countries are listed in alphabetical order. To limit data, Scandinavia is represented by Sweden.

The horizontal time axis divides the Seventies into three sections and has been extended to include events prior to the Seventies and during the most recent years (early Eighties).

The data for each country have been divided into 6 main subsections, with each subsection having a further sub-division, when relevant, as indicated by headings in a vertical column in the far left.

COUNTRY	Pre-70s	Early 70s	Mid-70s	Late 70s	Early 80s

SUBSECTION
(e.g. Phonogram
industry)

*Subdivision(1)
(e.g. Phono-
gram companies)*

Subdivision (2)

etc.

Events in the same horizontal plane do not necessarily have any direct causal relationship, apart from referring to the same area of change (this concentration of data has been chosen in order to save space).

Horizontal lines mark direct relationship between the development phases of different phenomena, or the duration of phenomena.

The subsections and subdivisions (where relevant) are presented in the same order for each country, namely:

(1) Government Policy
  - General policy
  - Phonograms
  - Radio, TV, press
  - Education
  - Copyright
  - Performances
(2) Organizations
  - Copyright
  - Phonograms
  - Musicians' unions/associations
  - Research
  - Orchestras
(3) Work opportunities for musicians
(4) Phonogram industries
  - Phonogram companies (foreign, national)
  - Studios
  - Manufacturing facilities (records, cassettes)
  - Phonogram sales
(5) Radio, TV, Film, Video
  - Radio
  - TV
  - Film, Video
(6) Trends in the music media
(subdivisions relating to different styles of music where appropriate for a particular country)

Chile

CHILE	Pre-70s	Early 70s	Mid-70s	Late 70s	Early 80s

GOVERNMENT POLICY

	Pre-70s	Early 70s	Mid-70s	Late 70s	Early 80s
General policy	Allende socialist government	1973 Military coup – Pinochet right-wing government			1981 New constitution affects media and music education
		1973–76 'Cultural black-out'			
Phonograms	Record imports banned (only license pressing allowed)			10% tax. Imports increasing	
	Record prices kept low by price control. Some subsidies to record production with folk and folk-based music		No price control		
Radio, TV, Press	1967 Law N 16.647 grants freedom of expression without censorship in all media		Freedom of expression suspended New laws regulating government control over mass media		

CHILE	Pre-70s	Early 70s	Mid-70s	Late 70s	Early 80s
	Law prescribing a quota of 25% Chilean music on radio and TV		Quota law not implemented		
Education	Government subsidies for music education at conservatories and universities				Subsidies withdrawn
		1971 Chilean folk music and dance introduced in school curriculum	Folk music instruments unofficially banned		Folk music instruments gradually allowed to reappear
Copyright		1970 New copyright act			New constitution allows for competing copyright organizations
Performances		1971 Law stating that 85% of artists in shows and concerts must be Chileans		1978 law amended – made less strict	
			1974 Law taxing shows and concerts (22% of income); exceptions are performances under 'government protection'	Concert tours with Western art music organized by Ministry of Education	
				National folklore troupe sponsored by Ministry of Education	

CHILE	Pre-70s	Early 70s	Mid-70s	Late 70s	Early 80s

ORGANIZATIONS

	Pre-70s	Early 70s	Mid-70s	Late 70s	Early 80s
Copyright	Departemento del Pequeño Derecho de Autor (DAIC) administered by Universidad de Chile			Sociedad Adminis-trativa de Autores y Compositores (SAIC) (competes with DAIC)	
Phonograms	Cámera Chilena de Productores Fonográficos (Camera del Disco)				
Musicians' unions/asso-ciations	Sindicato Orquestal Sindicato de Artistas de Variedades (SINAV) Sindicato de Folkloristas y Guitarristas de Chile				
	Consejo de Autores y Compositores (CODAYCO) Consejo Nacional de Autores y Compositores de Música Popular (CONDAUCO) Sindicato Nacional Profesional de Autores y Compositores de Musica Popular				

CHILE	Pre-70s	Early 70s	Mid-70s	Late 70s	Early 80s
	Associatión Nacional de Compositores				
			1976 Nuestro Canto (promotion of folk artists)		
Research	Institute for musicology at Universidad de Chile, Santiago				
				CENECA (group of musicologists and sociologists)	
			Taller 666 (folk music institute)		
Orchestras	Orquesta simfónica de Universidad de Chile				
	Orquesta filharmónica de Corporación Cultural de la Municipalidad de Santiago				
			Agrupación Beethoven (chamber orchestra, choir)		1981 Radio Beethoven

CHILE	Pre-70s	Early 70s	Mid-70s	Late 70s	Early 80s

WORK OPPORTUNITIES

CHILE	Pre-70s	Early 70s	Mid-70s	Late 70s	Early 80s
	Local folk fiestas				
	Concerts arranged by musicians			Nuestra Canto concerts	
					Rock groups
					organize festivals
		Festival de Vina			
		Val Paraiso			
					Some folk music re-appears on television

PHONOGRAM INDUSTRY

Phonogram companies

CHILE	Pre-70s	Early 70s	Mid-70s	Late 70s	Early 80s
Foreign	EMI-Odeon, Philips – IRT owned by RCA	IRT owned by government (takeover 1971)		IRT sold to private enterprise	IRT phonogram production discontinued
National		1970 DICAP			
		1973 Banglad			

CHILE	Pre-70s	Early 70s	Mid-70s	Late 70s	Early 80s
			1976 Alerce, Quatro, Sol de America, Brisa		
				SYM	
Studios	Radio studios. Mobile equipment	Two recording studios for phonogram production and radio commercials		Four studios	
Manufacturing facilities					
Records	EMI, IRT				IRT plant closed 1980. EMI monopoly
Cassettes				5 companies incl. IRT	
					Several small operators
Phonogram sales		Mainly local productions. Sales rapidly increasing. Culmination 1972–73 with pressing plants working at full capacity. 1973 Sales drop radically	Sales slowly increasing 2% of sales imports	More and more license pressings, less local productions	30% of sales imports

CHILE	Pre-70s	Early 70s	Mid-70s	Late 70s	Early 80s

RADIO, TV, FILM, VIDEO

Radio	Radio receivers fairly common		App. 3 million sold 1973–80		2·6 receivers/ household
		139 stations (1970) 156 (1973)		208 (1979)	230 (1981)
		All AM	FM introduced		
		6 major networks			
		Programmes fairly diversified	More and more music	Music format programming increases	70–80% music on major networks, 90% or more on local stations
			Greater dependency on records for music programming		
	Mainly Chilean music. Many music programmes sponsored by political parties		More and more Anglo–American music	Top 40 stations	
				Nuestro Canto on Radio Chilena	
TV		500,000 sets (1970) 993,000 (1973)		1,526,000 (1978)	
		Four stations (one national, three local)			

CHILE	Pre-70s	Early 70s	Mid-70s	Late 70s	Early 80s
		40% of programme material local production (1972)	28% local production (1975)	22% local production (1978)	
			Few programmes with Chilean music		A slight increase in programmes with Chilean music

TRENDS IN THE MUSIC MEDIA

	La nueva ola chilena (Chilean folk music based vocal and instrumental music)				
		La nueva canción chilena (folk-based vocal music with political texts: Violeta Parra, Victor Jara etc.)			
	Latin American popular music			Spanish language hits (international style)	
	Beatles etc.			Disco boom	
				El nuevo canto chileno (folk-based, mainly on cassette). Also some Cuban artists	
			Local hit songs, international style		

Jamaica

JAMAICA	Pre-70s	Early 70s	Mid-70s	Late 70s	Early 80s

GOVERNMENT POLICY

General   1968 Cultural Development Commission founded

Phonograms   Bureau of Standards try to create standards for record labels

Education   1973–75 Significant changes at National School of Music
1) formation of divisions: Afro–American studies, Music education and Western music
2) Jamaican studies become compulsory
3) 2 and 4 year courses introduced leading to professional qualifications

Popular music (reggae) and Jamaican folk music included in training courses for music teachers at National School of Music (1978)

JAMAICA	Pre-70s	Early 70s	Mid-70s	Late 70s	Early 80s
Copyright/ performance		Committee on copyright in Caribbean report to government. No action taken			Committee drafts copyright law based on other existing laws and a Caricom model (1983)
	1964 First significant move towards Jamaicani-zation of Jamaican National Festival (annually covering the whole island)		Jamaican National Festival becomes even more Jamaican		Jamaican Cultural Development Commission (JCDC) investigates copyright problems, starts organizing more festivals etc.

ORGANIZATIONS

Copyright	PRS opens collecting agency		Some composers join PRS London		
Phonograms		Local IFPI branch with 5 members			IFPI branch with 4 members receives money from radio stations
Musicians' unions/asso-ciations	Musicians' union				1983
					Musicians' Union tries to force recording studios to register musicians' contributions on all tracks

JAMAICA	Pre-70s	Early 70s	Mid-70s	Late 70s	Early 80s

WORK OPPORTUNITIES

JAMAICA	Pre-70s	Early 70s	Mid-70s	Late 70s	Early 80s
		Growth of record industry provides work for session musicians			
		Some overseas touring for top names			
		Few live music venues			
					1982 'World music festival' for American and some Jamaican musicians
					1982 Youth consciousness concert (Bunny Wailer) 1983.
					Rockers magazine awards festival
			Increased popularity of *mento* bands (playing instrumental dance music)		
		Work at tourist hotels on north coast			
			Reggae Sunsplash festival		

JAMAICA	Pre-70s	Early 70s	Mid-70s	Late 70s	Early 80s

PHONOGRAM INDUSTRY

Phonogram Companies

Foreign

			CBS try to enter the market but are not allowed to start a local company		CBS try to join up with Dynamic Sounds who distribute CBS, WEA and Polygram

National

Some small record companies in 50s (e.g. Coxone and Federal)	5 main manufacturers in local IFPI branch	Many small time producers. Tapes often distributed via London as reggae gets more internationally accepted		

'Dynamic Sounds' emerges by absorbing 'West Indies records'	Tuff Gong registered as phonogram company		Tuff Gong buys pressing plant	Tuff Gong expands solely with local music. Rita Marley continues after Bob Marley's death

	Phonogram industry expands as reggae gains international fame and local companies gain distribution rights in the Caribbean	Financial constraints lead some local companies to move operations to Miami or other Caribbean islands, or to run down local operations	Tuff Gong goes international

JAMAICA	Pre-70s	Early 70s	Mid-70s	Late 70s	Early 80s
Studios	3 studios		Expansion of studio facilities (multitrack)		Several studios with highly sophisticated equipment
Manufacturing facilities					
Records	A few pressing plants			App. 10 pressing plants	Tuff Gong buys automatic presses
Cassettes					Cassette duplication facilities available but records dominate
Phonogram sales			Sales of Jamaican music dominate local market	Increase in local sales of international repertoire	Increased exports to Caribbean region of both local and international repertoire

RADIO, TV, FILM, VIDEO

JAMAICA	Pre-70s	Early 70s	Mid-70s	Late 70s	Early 80s
Radio/TV Licenses/ sets			550,000 (radio) 100,000 (TV) (Source: IFPI report)		
	Redifussion start RJR (wholly commercial)		Rediffusion pulls out of RJR	RJR's popularity as a commercial station increases	
	JBC (partly commercial) radio+TV	2 VHF channels started			JBC TV goes colour from 625 Pal to 525 line US system

JAMAICA	Pre-70s	Early 70s	Mid-70s	Late 70s	Early 80s
		1971 Musicians' Union strike leads to increase in local music content on radio/TV	Local music increases	Music output 50/50 local/foreign on radio stations	Less local music on radio/TV
					Satellite disc picks up and transmits more American TV programmes
Other	Mobile 'sound s systems' (big PAs) established from early 50s onwards				

TRENDS IN THE MUSIC MEDIA

	Rhythm and blues develops into rock steady. Reggae emerges		Growth of reggae locally and internationally		
		Disc jockey personalities emerge – become infused into record production			
					American disco takes over part of reggae market

Kenya

KENYA	Pre-70s	Early 70s	Mid-70s	Late 70s	Early 80s

GOVERNMENT POLICY

		Early 70s	Mid-70s	Late 70s	Early 80s
General		National Cultural Council formed	Low activity		Many African members brought in as attempts are made to rejuvenate council in early 1980. Discontinued after 3 months
		'Culture' enters government activities as a section in the Ministry of Cooperatives	'Culture' is a division in the Ministry of Housing		'Culture' becomes a division in the Ministry of Culture and Social Services
					President makes many speeches in support of national culture. Instigates 'Presidential Committee on African Music' (1983)
Phonograms			Government considers revoking Phonogram's distribution licence (the pressing plant, EAT, owned 100% by Phonogram). No action taken	31% sales tax on records removed after lobbying of government by local producers	Anti-piracy law passed; gives phonogram producers extra protection

KENYA	Pre-70s	Early 70s	Mid-70s	Late 70s	Early 80s
Education				Ministry of Culture encourages ethnomusicologists to catalogue and classify field recordings of tribal songs	Government announces intention to start a national school for music and dance (1982)

ORGANIZATIONS

Copyright	PRS (London) opens office in Kenya mainly for collecting of royalties			Composers/ performers start their own Performing Right Society (MPRSK) PRS have only 12 members organized in Kenya	Conflict and negotiations between PRS and MPRSK
Phonograms	Local IFPI group formed in Kenya by large phonogram companies	1971 Local producers form own record producers' association		Local producers start a co-operative aimed at getting a pressing factory going	Lobbying of authorities for support
Musicians' unions/associations	1965 Musicians' union formed (KUEMIE)				
Orchestras	Nairobi Symphony Orchestra				
			Bomas of Kenya (national folklore troupe)		Bomas develop as important tourist attraction in Nairobi

KENYA	Pre-70s	Early 70s	Mid-70s	Late 70s	Early 80s

WORK OPPORTUNITIES

| | | | Session work for local studio musicians develops as local record companies and studios expand in numbers | | |

| | | Night clubs provide work opportunities for
 (a) tourist music (big internatio- nal hotels)
 (b) East African jazz music at local night clubs | | Growth of discothèques remove some opportunities for live bands | |

| | | Very few festivals or tours because of lack of organizers. Some opportunities for dance bands at annual 'Agricultural shows' | | | |

KENYA	Pre-70s	Early 70s	Mid-70s	Late 70s	Early 80s

PHONOGRAM INDUSTRY

Phonogram companies

	Pre-70s	Early 70s	Mid-70s	Late 70s	Early 80s
– foreign	Associated Sound, a locally based company, represented Decca. Bought up by Philips. Did well with Congolese (Zaïre) music on 78's in early 60s (up to 80% of total production)	AIT (formerly Teal, close links Lonrho) pioneer Luo sound. AIT exports 5 times as much as sales in Kenya	EMI enter and leave the market after bankruptcy	AIT tries to buy out Lonrho interest so that AIT is formally Kenyan	Phonogram consider selling some of its shares to local luminaries Plan never carried out European/ American record companies put a spotlight on East Africa. Activity centred on Nairobi
– national	MWAN-GAZA started shortly after independence (around '65). 50 singles during 60s. First in English, then in local languages	Local producers emerge		Explosion of local producers (some estimate there are 150)	
					CBS open in Nairobi together with a local partner
Studios			Commercial studios open as record market for local artists expands and VOK decreases live music recordings		CBS builds 16 track studio. Phonogram, goes 8-track

KENYA	Pre-70s	Early 70s	Mid-70s	Late 70s	Early 80s
Manufacturing facilities	Plant for 78's started by AIT owners together with Gallotone of South Africa				
Records	Philips buy out AIT from pressing plant 1966	SAPRA's pressing plant constructed (72–73)	SAPRA pressing plant closes (77) giving Phonogram manufacturing monopoly		
Cassettes				Local manufacturing plant opens for blank cassettes Diverse cassette duplicators open up, including small pirate operators	
Phonogram sales	Limited sales of 78 rpm discs		Increased sales, mainly of 45 rpm singles		1982 Singles: 1·8 million LPs: 150,000 Prerecorded cassettes: 115,000

RADIO, TV, FILM, VIDEO

Radio		Former British colonial administration's broadcasting corporation becomes the Voice of Kenya after Independence	Commercial companies (often phonogram company + sponsor) buy time for packaged programmes on VOK radio		

KENYA	Pre-70s	Early 70s	Mid-70s	Late 70s	Early 80s
			Steady decrease in recording of live music at the VOK, increased reliance on records		
	VOK monopoly goes semi-commercial in 1962				March 80. Directive to play 3 Kenyan records for every foreign record on English language service. Order reversed after 2 weeks after a 'traumatic experience'
TV		Order to show more programmes of Kenyan origin led to some programmes being repeated over and over again			Debate rages amongst musicians, in the press, about the VOK's role and responsibility regarding local Kenyan music
Film/Video	Big markets for Indian films				Video market develops for Indian films

TRENDS IN THE MUSIC MEDIA

International			Sweet pop and disco (ABBA, Boney M) popular on radio		
Congolese (Zaïre)	78's from Kinshasa popular	Congolese groups dominate market (80%)		Less Congolese music on disc/live	

KENYA	Pre-70s	Early 70s	Mid-70s	Late 70s	Early 80s
Tanzanian			Tanzanian groups compete with Zaïrean groups	Tanzanian Swahili groups become very popular	Tanzanian musicians do well on Nairobi night club scene
Kenya hybrids	Kenyan twist (Chubby Checker hybrid)				Tourist records (some Swahili + European disco beat)
	Tribal songs, embryonic local pop songs on local labels	Nairobi based Congolese style bands gain popularity	Benga beat (Luo) develops, spreads to other countries in Africa	Kikuyu country style music sells to tribe members	Local groups make many singles – find it hard to compete with Tanzanian music and Congolese sounds
					International phonogram cos look for bands to export (Virgin, CBS, Island plan releases in Europe)

Sri Lanka

SRI LANKA	Pre-70s	Early 70s	Mid-70s	Late 70s	Early 80s
			GOVERNMENT POLICY		
General			1974 Abortive attempt to start National Music Council		1982 New attempt to start National Music Council and affiliation to IMC/Paris
			Liberalization of import restrictions opens door for cassette and electronic hardware imports		
			Government sponsors Tower Hall Foundation (Arts Centre in Colombo)		
Education	1964 Traditional music from Sinhala folklore incorporated into education system		1974 Emphasis on N Indian music in school syllabuses increased at the expenses of traditional Sinhala music		Increased emphasis on traditional music for 2nd time
		1972 First teachers' training college for Art, Music and Dancing inaugurated in Kandy	1974 Influential supporter of traditional music moved from Ministry of Education	1977 Government Institute for Fine Arts upgraded into faculty at Colombo University	No exams granted. 1981 Strike at music faculty which is closed temporarily

SRI LANKA	Pre-70s	Early 70s	Mid-70s	Late 70s	Early 80s
			1976 Ministry of Culture starts section for research		
Performances	Late 60s. Army band incorporate dancers and traditional music			1977 State Dance and Music ensemble made permanent	
		Entertainments tax introduced	Exemptions granted for certain amateur performances		
Copyright				1979 Intellectual copyright law passed	Registrar of Patents ordered by Ministry of Trade to start a PRS

ORGANIZATIONS

Copyright					1981 Sri Lankan PRS founded by government official (Registrar of Patents)
Phonograms			1976 Record producers start a loose Association, based on advice from IFPI representative in Hong Kong	Cassette producers join to discuss piracy	Association's president allowed to join committee of new PRS
Musicians' union/associations				1979 Recording session musicians form a union	Rates negotiated for recordings/ title

SRI LANKA	Pre-70s	Early 70s	Mid-70s	Late 70s	Early 80s
	Sinhala Sangeetha Sangamaya (Sinhala music society) founded		1975 Sinhala Sangeetha fades out due to lack of funds	Musicology Society founded	(12 members, headed by a dentist)
			1975 Sangita Padanama (Society for North Indian music) founded		
Orchestras	Colombo Symphony Orchestra (amateurs interested in Western Art Music)				

WORK OPPORTUNITIES

	Pre-70s	Early 70s	Mid-70s	Late 70s	Early 80s
	Weddings, New Year Festivals, Kandy Perahera parade (annually in August), provide work opportunities for musicians				Colombo Perahera parade; 112 elephants + hundreds of drummers/dancers (annually in February)
					Cassette industry provides work for session musicians
		Night club/restaurant music	Pianists playing MOR selection	Demand for beat groups playing Western music	
	Tourist influx starts	Traditional music performances		Dance/music groups of varying abilities putting on shows for tourists	

SRI LANKA	Pre-70s	Early 70s	Mid-70s	Late 70s	Early 80s
	Film music (session musicians + playback singers)				
	'Observer Talent Search' finds new pop singers			Old revue venue 'The Tower Hall' revived as Arts Centre. Government Sponsorship	

PHONOGRAM INDUSTRY

Record companies					
Foreign	EMI (via India)				
				Pirate productions on cassette via Singapore/ Hong Kong/ Jakarta	
National	2 or 3 local recording companies. Sinhala pop/baila/folk music			New cassette companies emerge	8 major cassette companies + 15 others
	SLBC (Radio Ceylon) release occasional discs of Sinhala music				
Studios	SLBC – live music recorded for radio				
	EMI mobile equipment		Local studios appear	Expansions of local facilities	11 studios – 4 multitrack

SRI LANKA	Pre-70s	Early 70s	Mid-70s	Late 70s	Early 80s
Manufacturing facilities					
Records	SLBC. 78 rpm acetates				1983 Radio production still stored on 78 rpm acetates
			Sangita pressing plant. 1 press. LP or single		Low record pressing activity at Sangita
Cassettes					Sangita cassette duplicating ca 300/day
					Gypsy studios cassette duplication capacity 1,000/day
					Singlanka small production of cassettes

RADIO, TV, FILM, VIDEO

Licences Radio	300,000 (68)	500,000 (71)	550,000 (75)	1,500,000 (78)	2,000,000 (80)
TV	—	—	—	—	50,000 (81) 170,000 (83)
Radio			Investment in transmitting stations. Low investments in studio equipment		

SRI LANKA	Pre-70s	Early 70s	Mid-70s	Late 70s	Early 80s
	1950 Commercial service started by Australian consultants	Local record companies start buying own programme time			
	1967 Government dept corporation self financing via licences + advertising revenue 1952 Tamil/Sinhala studio orchestra founded	Music Research Unit established at SLBC Sinhala drummers auditioned for first time (71) 5 recruited to SLBC	SLBC research unit issues first commercial LP of traditional Sinhala music (74) Increased amount of live music with own orchestras + contracted vocalists	Conflict grows within SLBC regarding relative merits of traditional Sinhala music and N Indian Music. Increased emphasis on N. Indian music	Experimental stereo transmissions with Western disco/jazz-rock music cover 100 mile radius from Colombo Own recordings produce 10 hrs Sinhala light music/day
	British Top 40 influences music on English channel		74 English Service transmits series presenting Sinhalese traditional music	British and USA charts exert strong influence on English channel	
	1969 Tamil service starts recording 15 mins of Tamil light music/day (= *Indian film music*)	1972 Tamil Service starts recording 'Tamil pop' artists			45 mins of Tamil light music from own studios daily
	Via external services, SLBC becomes *the* major disseminator of Indian film music on Indian sub-continent	Policy of not favouring various forms of popular culture (Baila, Sinhala pop)		Music Board created to vet records/ cassettes for suitability	Perceived norms of quality led SLBC to follow a very different path than local recording industry

SRI LANKA	Pre-70s	Early 70s	Mid-70s	Late 70s	Early 80s
	HMV/Polydor (India) buy programme time on Asian beam	SLBC receives HMV/Polydor payment in form of records for record library			
					English service music on disc mainly HMV/Polydor
TV	Government turns down an offer of a black and white TV station from West Germany			Japanese government donates transmitting station (colour)	National TV (commercial) starts Feb 1982
				Private TV (ITN) starts. State takes it over within months	ITN continues mainly with imported material
Film		Sinhala films develop similar to Indian films		Fewer love songs, more theme music	
Video					Video cassettes appear in cities. Distribution through video clubs. Market explodes, reaching all urban areas

TRENDS IN THE MUSIC MEDIA

Western	Records. Pop/rock/ sentimental MOR			Pirated cassettes type ABBA, Boney M	Disco

SRI LANKA	Pre-70s	Early 70s	Mid-70s	Late 70s	Early 80s
Baila	Some EPs/LPs				
				Cassette boom with	
				baila artists	
Sinhala pop	Pop sung in Sinhala emerges	Pop boom Sinhala song		New recordings of old standards	'Disco' cassettes
	'Caribbean groups' e.g. La Ceylonians, Los Cabelleros, Mainly for tourists			Hindi songs translated into Sinhala	
Indian	Records; film music/classical			Pirated cassettes; film music/classical	
Media					
Discs/ cassettes	Records dominate			Cassettes dominate	
				Records luxury items or for radio purposes	

Sweden

SWEDEN	Pre-70s	Early 70s	Mid-70s	Late 70s	Early 80s

GOVERNMENT POLICY

General	Government sponsors Western art music				
		Government committee on cultural policy	Bill on national cultural policy passed by all parties in parliament	Government increases resources for the propagation of Swedish music abroad	Government takes over Royal Academy of Music Library and Museum
		Local governments set up cultural boards	Council for Cultural Affairs is set up, i.e. giving grants to freelance music groups (jazz, rock, folk)		
	1968 Rikskonserter (Institute for National Concerts)	Rikskonserter introduces pluralistic programme policy and sets up department for sociology of music			
		1972 Military brass bands turned into regional orchestras			

SWEDEN	Pre-70s	Early 70s	Mid-70s	Late 70s	Early 80s
Phonograms		Government subsidies to phonogram production at Rikskonserter		Council of Cultural Affairs sets up Committee on phonograms	Bill passed introducing levy on blank cassettes and subsidies to phonogram producers
					Bill passed introducing compulsory deposit of 2 copies of all phonograms and videograms in government archives
Radio, TV, press			Government committee reports on organization of radio/TV in Sweden		
Education		New institutes for musicology at Universities of Gothenburg and Lund			
		Many municipality music schools started			
		1971 Government takes over the Royal Academy School of Music in Stockholm			
		Bill passed introducing folk, jazz, pop into higher music education			

SWEDEN	Pre-70s	Early 70s	Mid-70s	Late 70s	Early 80s
Performances					Ban on street music lifted

ORGANIZATIONS

SWEDEN	Pre-70s	Early 70s	Mid-70s	Late 70s	Early 80s
Copyright	1923 STIM (copyright organization)			Folk Music Fund formed to collect copyright money for Swedish folk music	STIM receives part of money collected from blank cassette levy
Phonograms	Swedish branch of IFPI		New trade association (NIFF) formed for non-commercial phonogram companies	IFPI 12 members NIFF 20 members	
Musicians' unions/associations	1970 Musicians' union	Musicians' union forms SAMI, an organization for collecting copyright for performers on phonograms		Musicians' union sets up section for freelance musicians	
	Labour movement organizes People's Parks and People's Houses for cultural activities	Established labour movement hostile towards new music movement		Labour movement adopts more positive attitude towards music movement	
		Several new organizations and co-operatives formed by freelance musicians and music groups outside Musicians' union			Many local associations formed by amateur rock groups

SWEDEN	Pre-70s	Early 70s	Mid-70s	Late 70s	Early 80s
		Start of new music movement. Local associations open music pubs all over Sweden for Swedish rock, folk and other music labelled as 'non-commercial'	Kontaktnätet – national organization for non-commercial culture formed	Several local music movement associations disbanded. New local associations formed by punk rock groups and fans	
			Jazz clubs and musicians form the Swedish Jazz Federation		
			Immigrant musicians form association		

WORK OPPORTUNITIES

			More and more musicians perform music illegally in streets and other public places		Street music activities made legal
	People's Parks, People's Houses, restaurants provide work for musicians playing popular music		More work opportunities for rock groups at local youth centres Boom for dance bands performing mainly at restaurants for 20–40 age group	Many discothèques open. Youth centres turned into discos. Fewer work opportunities	
	Folk musicians play at local feasts and fiddlers' meets	Fiddlers' meets get new youth attendance			

SWEDEN	Pre-70s	Early 70s	Mid-70s	Late 70s	Early 80s
	Five professional symphony orchestras				
	Several societies for chamber music				
	A few jazz clubs				
		Many new local music pubs and cafés opened			
		Youth music festivals arranged by music movement activists	1975 'The Alternative Festival' organized with the support of the majority of Swedish music organizations as a protest against the Eurovision Song Contest		
		Local governments and Rikskonserter start and sponsor local music festivals			
		Rikskonserter arranges app. 15,000 concerts a year mostly in schools			

PHONOGRAM INDUSTRY

Phonogram companies

| *Foreign* | EMI, CBS, Polydor, Phonogram (Philips) | | | EMI cuts down Swedish production and concentrates on distribution. Polydor and Phonogram merge into Polygram | |

SWEDEN	Pre-70s	Early 70s	Mid-70s	Late 70s	Early 80s
National	Metronome, Electra, Sonet and five smaller companies		Sonet opens subsidiary in UK	Metronome taken over by WEA	WEA sells Metronome studio and cuts down on local production
		Several small companies start operations 15 companies	40 companies	Many small companies in financial difficulties 50 companies	45 companies
		Phonogram company with government subsidies starts (Caprice label)			
			ABBA company Polar booms	ABBA diversifies business. Buys publishers, starts art leasing, buys swimming hall, bicycle factory etc	
Studios	Swedish Broadcasting Corporation and large phonogram companies operate studios	New small companies set up own studios App. 10 studios 4–8 tracks	15 studios 16–24 tracks	30 studios 16–32 tracks	40 studios 16–32 tracks
					1 studio with digital equipment

SWEDEN	Pre-70s	Early 70s	Mid-70s	Late 70s	Early 80s
Manufacturing facilities					
Records	Four pressing plants – two with disc cutting and electro-plating	Five pressing plants	EMI gets government subsidy to build pressing plant with capacity to cater for the whole of Scandinavia Small independent 'non-commercial' companies lobby government and get a small subsidy to build a pressing plant	One of the old plants closes	EMI sells plant and moves operations to the Netherlands. Another local plant closes
Cassettes			Three large and several small cassette copying facilities	Seven large cassette copying facilities	12 large cassette copying facilities. Hundreds of smaller Factory for making blank cassettes opens
Phonogram sales	1965 4 million records sold	1970 9 million sold	1975 17 million sold	1977 21 million sold	1980 20 million sold
			Sales of blank cassettes increase rapidly 1975 8·5 million sold		1982 20 million sold

SWEDEN	Pre-70s	Early 70s	Mid-70s	Late 70s	Early 80s
			Slower increase in sales of pre-recorded cassettes 1975 2·8 million sold		1982 4·5 million sold
					1983 Marketing of compact discs starts
		Distribution and sales dominated by cartel formed by 8 largest companies			
		1972 93% of sales through distribution cartel		1978 80% of sales through cartel	
		Cooperative distribution company formed by new small companies			
			1976 Rack jobbers cause close down of regular record shops. 30% of sales through rack firms		

RADIO, TV, FILM, VIDEO

	Radio receivers and TV sets available in almost every Swedish home				

SWEDEN	Pre-70s	Early 70s	Mid-70s	Late 70s	Early 80s
Radio	Swedish Broadcasting Corporation (Sveriges Radio) has monopoly on broadcasting. No commercials in broadcasting			Swedish Broadcasting Corporation split into a national, a local and an educational broadcasting company and a TV company	
	Closure of maritime pirate broadcasters leads to an increase of light music on Swedish radio		Stereo transmission starts Regional transmissions start	Local radio stations formed Neighbour-hood radio run by associations starts (no commercials), transmitted on low-power local transmitters	
	Three radio channels (speech, art music, light music)	Increased listening to light music programmes, less to all other programmes			
		Much debate as to relevance of music programmes which were based on sales statistics	Frequent changes in chart programmes	Some Top 20 format programmes dropped	
			More diversified music programming with special programmes for folk music, music of immigrant groups etc.		

SWEDEN	Pre-70s	Early 70s	Mid-70s	Late 70s	Early 80s
TV	Two TV channels. No commercials				
	American music shows dominate music programming	Increased amount of special programmes with Swedish music	1975 TV1 shows Eurovision Song Contest while TV2 shows Alternative Festival	Music departments of both channels reduced	More transmission time devoted to pop music shows based partly on promotion videos
Film	Government film institute and foundation sponsor Swedish film production				
		No emphasis on music film productions			
Video				Video explosion	No apparent decrease despite new taxes on tapes and recorders

TRENDS IN THE MUSIC MEDIA

	Foreign repertoire dominates	British pop (Beatles etc.)	Hard rock	Disco, reggae, punk rock	
	Some phonograms released with Swedish popular music and a few with art music and jazz	More Swedish music released on phonograms: songs in Swedish, rock in Swedish, phonograms for children, music for dancing	Swedish folk music released on phonogram	More phonograms with art music released by small specialized companies	
	Anglo–American pop music dominate				

SWEDEN	Pre-70s	Early 70s	Mid-70s	Late 70s	Early 80s
			App. 800 new releases every year by phonogram companies in Sweden		
			App. 3,500 phonogram titles imported every year		
		Steady increase in phonogram sales		Stagnation in sales figures	
		Number of hours spent listening to phonograms fivefold during the 70s			
					Video boom

Tanzania

TANZANIA	Pre-70s	Early 70s	Mid-70s	Late 70s	Early 80s

GOVERNMENT POLICY

	Pre-70s	Early 70s	Mid-70s	Late 70s	Early 80s
General	1962 Principles for national cultural policy laid down in speech by president Nyerere	US soul music banned	Ministry of National Culture and Youth		
			Baraza la Muziki la Taifa (BAMUTA) National Music Council		
Phonograms					Import of records and blank tapes banned due to lack of currency, but occur all the same. Same applies later to video cassettes
Education				National college for music, dance and drama founded	
Performances	National *ngoma* group (music and dance) founded		An attempt to oust Zaïrean jazz bands failed	BAMUTA vets visiting bands and music groups	
				BAMUTA jazz band	

TANZANIA	Pre-70s	Early 70s	Mid-70s	Late 70s	Early 80s

ORGANIZATIONS

	Pre-70s	Early 70s	Mid-70s	Late 70s	Early 80s
	Local ngoma societies all over the country				
	Dar es Salaam Music Society (Western classical music)				
			Ruhija music centre (missionaries)		
	Culture and entertainment sections in trade unions, sports clubs etc				

WORK OPPORTUNITIES

	Pre-70s	Early 70s	Mid-70s	Late 70s	Early 80s
	Traditional festivals and rituals				
	National festivals, campaigns etc				
	Dance clubs				
		Regular recording sessions at Radio Tanzania		Work opportunities increase in Kenya due to popularity of Tanzanian music	

TANZANIA	Pre-70s	Early 70s	Mid-70s	Late 70s	Early 80s

PHONOGRAM INDUSTRY

*Phonogram
companies*

	Pre-70s	Early 70s	Mid-70s	Late 70s	Early 80s
Foreign	NONE				
Local	Tanzania Film Company (TFC) imports records from Kenya and Europe				
		TFC monopoly on Tanzanian music on records. A few discs issued, mostly EPs			
			1973 LP with traditional Tanzanian music co-production Tanzania – Sweden Some EPs produced by churches with aid from parent organizations in Europe		
				Cassette piracy	
		EPs and a few LPs with Tanzanian music issued by record companies in Kenya			Kenyan piracy of Tanzanian recordings

TANZANIA	Pre-70s	Early 70s	Mid-70s	Late 70s	Early 80s
Studios	Radio Tanzania				
			TFC studio		
Manufac-turing					
Records		Records cut and pressed in Kenya		TFC tries co-operation with CBS, London	Discontinued
				Plant for cutting and pressing under construction	1983. Plant still not operational
Record sales	Sales slowly increasing			1978 App. 40,000 records	Sales drop, no records available due to import restrictions

RADIO, TV, FILM, VIDEO

Radio	Few receivers				Radio receivers (and cassette recorders) quite common, but shortage of batteries limits use
	Radio Tanzania (government) AM transmitters				

TANZANIA	Pre-70s	Early 70s	Mid-70s	Late 70s	Early 80s
	Mixed European and African pop music		Only Tanzanian music on National Service (popular and folk) Mainly RT's own tape recordings		
			Committee formed for music policy in radio		
TV/Video		Small TV station on Zanzibar (gift from DDR)		No mainland TV. Video finds its way in despite official ban	

TRENDS IN THE MUSIC MEDIA

	Western rock and pop				
	Kwaya (religious)				
	Zairean groups popular	Tanzanian 'Swahili jazz' electric bands			
		develop			
				Taarab music on cassettes	

Trinidad

TRINIDAD	Pre-70s	Early 70s	Mid-70s	Late 70s	Early 80s

GOVERNMENT POLICY

	Pre-70s	Early 70s	Mid-70s	Late 70s	Early 80s
General		1971 Attempted military coup fails. Clamp down on black power movement			
		1969 Start of National Folklore Archive			
		1971 National Cultural Council formed			
	Government supports and tries to control carnival celebrations				
Phonograms		High duty on imports and no concessions to phonogram companies hampers development of industry		Government promises to wave import duties for phonograms with local artists	
			15% purchase tax on records		
		1975 Survey of phonogram industry. No action taken		1979 New survey. No action taken	

TRINIDAD	Pre-70s	Early 70s	Mid-70s	Late 70s	Early 80s
Perform-ances	From 1967 Annual folklore competition between villages organized by government				
		1973 Steelband Council established to support development of steelband movement (few accomplish-ments)			

ORGANIZATIONS

Copyright	Copyright law = British 1912 law				
	Local branch of PRS London established		Most copyright owners not registered		Change of management. Local PRS collects more money. More local members join
Phonograms		No local association, larger companies members of IFPI			
Musicians' unions/asso-ciations		1971 Calypsonians form associations (few accomplish-ments)			Session musicians try to start a union but fail

TRINIDAD	Pre-70s	Early 70s	Mid-70s	Late 70s	Early 80s
		Steelband association reorganized and renamed 'Pan Trinbago' (PT)		1979 PT organizes steelband boycott of government carnival shows, organizes own shows Presents a policy document covering a wide range of activities	
Orchestras	Police brass band, numerous calypso brass bands, several hundred steelbands				

WORK OPPORTUNITIES

	Traditional Festivals (carnival, Christmas, Hosse, Eid, Phagwa)				
	Calypsonians group together and perform in 'calypso tents' during carnival seasons				
					Musicians start to organize concerts outside festival seasons

TRINIDAD	Pre-70s	Early 70s	Mid-70s	Late 70s	Early 80s
		Local parang music competitions. Parang introduced into Christmas commercials			
	Bands sponsored by companies and used for promotion				
	Tourist entertainment at hotels (mainly Tobago)				

PHONOGRAM INDUSTRY

Phonogram companies					
Foreign	1965 International Recording Company owned by RCA		RCA leaves Trinidad	KH Records takes over from RCA	
National	1963 TELCO – Caribbean Sound Studios				Sporadic studio activities
		SEMP			Low activity
		Windsor Records (East Indian music)			
			Romeo Abraham Records		

TRINIDAD	Pre-70s	Early 70s	Mid-70s	Late 70s	Early 80s
			Sharc		Studio closed for long periods
			Numerous labels owned by calypsonians		
Studios	Two recording studios (IRC, Caribbean Sound)			Caribbean Sound closed	
		SEMP 4-track	16-track	Sharc Studio Centre 24-track	3 multi-track studios (KH, SEMP, SHARC)
Manufacturing facilities					
Records	TELCO and IRC		IRC becomes KH Records	TELCO closed	KH pressing plant runs into trouble and closes
				SEMP pressing plant	Low activity
Cassettes					Large street sales of pirate copies
				Record shops make custom ordered pirate copies	
Phonogram sales		No reliable figures available			1–2 million/year 20% local repertory local labels

TRINIDAD	Pre-70s	Early 70s	Mid-70s	Late 70s	Early 80s

RADIO, TV, FILM, VIDEO

	Pre-70s	Early 70s	Mid-70s	Late 70s	Early 80s
Radio		Receivers in every home	1975 IFPI estimate 500,000 sets		
	National Broadcasting Corp. (government) and Radio Trinidad (owned by Rediffusion) both with commercials				
	AM only		FM starts		
	DJ programmes with mainly Top 40 format 20–30% local music increasing during 70s	Share of local music 50% during carnival season			45% Caribbean music on NBC. 25% on Radio Trinidad
TV	Not common		1975 IFPI estimate 90,000 sets		Fairly common
	Trinidad and Tobago Television (TTT) (government owned – commercial)				
	95% US and British programmes – more and more steelband and folklore shows				Local music shows app. 1 hr/week
Video					Rapid growth of video

TRINIDAD	Pre-70s	Early 70s	Mid-70s	Late 70s	Early 80s

TRENDS IN THE MUSIC MEDIA

	International hits				
	Soul			Reggae	
	Calypso		App. 15 LPs and several singles every year (incl. soca)		
		Steelband and local folk (mostly parang) 5–10 albums every year			
				Disco	
	Indian film music, imports from India – local covers				Indian film music app. 40 LPs released per year

Tunisia

TUNISIA	Pre-70s	Early 70s	Mid-70s	Late 70s	Early 80s

GOVERNMENT POLICY

General	Cultural committees and 'Cultural Houses' established around the country. Numbers of 'Maisons de Culture': 40	1970: 70	1975: 98		1980: 142
	1969 law. Control of musicians via 'Cartes pro-fessionelles' applying to all performing artists			Slight relaxation of censorship by government	1980. Centrally produced cassette recordings distributed as instruction material to cultural houses
		1970 1,000 artists are granted permits as a transitional measure	2,000 apply each year. 50% pass	CP used more and more as control function by local police when checking on musicians at tourist hotels. Still applies in theory to foreign musicians as well	1982 CP requirement for foreign musicians rescinded due to control difficulties. 4,550 artists have CP, a good %-age of performing artists have been registered according to the authorities

TUNISIA	Pre-70s	Early 70s	Mid-70s	Late 70s	Early 80s
Phonograms	Mid 60s Government committee recommends building a record factory to provide recordings of all the president's speeches	Ennagham plant created			
		1972 law regarding free trade zones paves the way for creation of video/film production centre in Sousse			
	Imports of hardware taxed highly (350% on stereo)	Import restrictions on records relaxed (Ennagham loses monopoly)	High taxes on imports (imports of records restricted to small quantities). 150% tax on records/ cassettes when imported	1979 Import of cassettes and records virtually blocked by legislation. Local manufacturing facilities supported by this legislation	
Radio, TV, press		Amalga-mation of ministries of Culture and Information	Radio/tele-vision/film cultural activities under same ministry		Ministry of Information and Culture separated for 'political' reasons. Radio/TV no longer controlled by Ministry of Culture
Education		Music Conservatoire more of a school than conservatory. Drift from Western to Arabic music			1980 Tuition at Music Conservatoire in Arabic, not French

TUNISIA	Pre-70s	Early 70s	Mid-70s	Late 70s	Early 80s
		1972 School for religious chanting (Koran reading) opened. 100 pupils			
	Support for lute workshops via L'office National de l'Artisan	Lute workshops expand operations and even exports instruments to Algeria/Libya			

Copyright	1966 Tunisian copyright law passed which paved way for SACEM France to be replaced by SODACT in 1968				
Performances	Major festivals (Carthage, Monastir, Gafsa etc.)				

ORGANIZATIONS

Copyright	1968 SODACT copyright organization formed (somewhat under the wings of the government)	SODACT takes over collecting role of SACEM in Tunisia			

TUNISIA	Pre-70s	Early 70s	Mid-70s	Late 70s	Early 80s
Musicians' unions/asso-ciations	Professional association or 'union' for members of the two radio orchestras			1979 New loose association for professional and amateur musicians formed	
Orchestras		Symphony orchestra (Western) created in Tunis. Amateur members; with some state support		French conductor replaced by Tunisian	
	1934 Rachidia (Malouf association) formed as an antidote to Egyptian oriented music		Rachidia receives government support – annual festival is organized with state support		

WORK OPPORTUNITIES

	Pre-70s	Early 70s	Mid-70s	Late 70s	Early 80s
	Growth of cultural houses	Some opportunities for concerts		Increased opportunities as a result of a slight liberalization in cultural policy	
	Many foreign groups (mainly Italian, French, Spanish) perform as dance combos at tourist hotels	Control introduced regarding musicians qualifications	Drift towards more work for Tunisian artists		Fewer work opportunities. Discos replace live bands. Control relaxed – easier for foreign bands to replace Tunisian

TUNISIA	Pre-70s	Early 70s	Mid-70s	Late 70s	Early 80s
		Local cultural committees active in providing folk music 'spectacles' for tourist hotels		Professional impresarios take over this role from cultural committees	'Folk culture' becomes 'show business' in tourist sector
	State increases its support for annual or biannual festivals around Tunisia (many organized as competitions open to amateurs/professionals)				1982 Festivals temporarily cancelled as act of solidarity with Palestinians
		1970 Tunis symphony orchestra (45 musicians) formed. Mainly amateurs			
				1979 Conservatory orchestra (Arabic music) formed	

PHONOGRAM INDUSTRY

Phonogram companies

Foreign

	Pre-70s	Early 70s	Mid-70s	Late 70s	Early 80s
	NONE				
	Some imports via local shops mainly from Beirut	Beirut business transferred gradually to Athens/Cairo	Various deals between EMI/Athens and phonogram companies in Cairo with Mellouliphone (see below)	Conflict between Ennagham and Mellouliphone regarding Sonodisc (Cairo) rights	Presence only through exchanges deals

TUNISIA	Pre-70s	Early 70s	Mid-70s	Late 70s	Early 80s
National	1968 Ennagham (state record company) given import monopoly after its inauguration by the president	1971 Ennagham loses import monopoly			
			1976 Mellouliphone starts with cassettes	Mellouliphone expands cassette production 1980: 300,000	1981 Mellouliphone buys El Fen (competitor). Mellouli-phone's major artist (60% of business) jailed for drug offences
				Growth of pirate producers up to 60%	Piracy up to 80 or 90%
Studios	RTT (Tunisian Broadcasting) studios rented out for commercial recordings		Most recordings made at RTT. Mono only		Stereo introduced at RTT
					Independent studio established with 8-track equipment, first at Sousse, then moves to Tunis

TUNISIA	Pre-70s	Early 70s	Mid-70s	Late 70s	Early 80s
Manufacturing facilities					
Records	1968 Ennagham, state controlled pressing plant, established (3 presses, bought secondhand from Phonogram Kongo)	1974 Ennagham gets cutting and plating facilities	1976–78 Fairly low activity for Ennagham	Rejuvenation	Ennagham releases 2 titles/year
Cassettes				Cassette duplication added. Individuals encouraged to make own records with Ennagham supplying custom pressing	Many more releases on cassette. Activity at Ennagham decreases after technical manager moves to 'Oasis' (see below)
				1979 Oasis cassette plant started. Import of blank tapes	1982 Oasis 2 million cassettes per annum. 20% increase annually 33% exported

RADIO, TV, FILM, VIDEO

Radio		Radio music committee vet quality of text and music before accepting for use on Radio's Arabic channel			

TUNISIA	Pre-70s	Early 70s	Mid-70s	Late 70s	Early 80s
				Tunis 2 (international channel) plays some modern Tunisian/Arabic music (*Musique engagée*)	
TV	One channel with much French material			Competition from legal and pirate Italian TV	
Film, Video	Egyptian film music starts making inroads in the 30s, 40s	Egyptian films popular		Number of songs decrease from 7–8 per film to one or two	
			Tunisia becomes favourite location for many international film productions (*Life of Brian*, *Star Wars* etc)		March 1982, Sousse free trade zone. 'Zinifilm' video complex inaugurated producing TV films mainly for Egypt/Saudi Arabia
					Video cassette recorders on sale generally

TRENDS IN THE MUSIC MEDIA

	Pre-70s	Early 70s	Mid-70s	Late 70s	Early 80s
	Egyptian influences on modern music				
		1970 First 'protest songs' emerge 1973 Lebanese modern Tunisian composers	Contemporary Moroccan influence on the politicized music scene (Instruments/ songs)	*Musique engagée*, folk music + thoughtful political lyrics	Popular among the young, rejected by establishment as a passing fashion

TUNISIA	Pre-70s	Early 70s	Mid-70s	Late 70s	Early 80s
				Wedding artists become 'mediaized' – cassette distribution	
				Italian radio popularity for music from other side of Mediterranean	
	Cultural committees provide folk music for evening entertainment at tourist hotels		Responsibility taken over by 'professional' impresarios	More show business	
	Italian, French, Spanish groups provide music for tourists	Tunisian 'electric' groups emerge mainly for the tourist trade replacing many foreign groups			Some Tunisian electric groups produce disco versions of Arabic songs
					Discos replace live bands
			Chanters/ prayer callers rely more and more on microphones/ amplifiers But absence of the Iranian discussion of the relationship between music and religion		

TUNISIA	Pre-70s	Early 70s	Mid-70s	Late 70s	Early 80s
			Arabiani-zation/Wester-nization, two movements which introduce dynamics and conflict into the music media environment		
	Limited sales of records			Cassettes replace most records	

Wales/Cymru

WALES/CYMRU	Pre-70s	Early 70s	Mid-70s	Late 70s	Early 80s

GOVERNMENT POLICY

	Pre-70s	Early 70s	Mid-70s	Late 70s	Early 80s
General	Decentral-ization of British Arts Council. Wales treated as separate region with own budget, administration etc.	Welsh Arts Council joins with BBC to upgrade symphony orchestra to full size	Support given to phonogram projects and festivals (only for 'art' music)		£1·5 million distributed to opera, symphony orchestra, festivals and stipends ('Art' music only)
Education			Welsh College of Music increases emphasis on training performers	Welsh College of Music moves to impressive new building in Cardiff	
		Music taught to degree level in three university colleges			
	Music advisers appointed in some counties (duties: arranging instrumental courses on county and regional basis). First appointed 1942				

WALES/CYMRU	Pre-70s	Early 70s	Mid-70s	Late 70s	Early 80s
Phonograms	55% purchase tax on records	40%	Purchase tax replaced by 10% VAT	8% VAT 15% VAT	
Performances			10% VAT on concert tickets	8% VAT 15% VAT	

ORGANIZATIONS

	Pre-70s	Early 70s	Mid-70s	Late 70s	Early 80s
Copyright	PRS London supervise Wales				
Musicians' unions/associations	1968 Welsh amateur music associations		Amateur association engages professional musicians and orchestras		
		Welsh youth leagues organize festivals	Folk clubs appear around Wales		
				MACYM (N Wales), MAC (S Wales) start arranging Welsh rock/pop evenings	
Education	1955 Guild for promotion of Welsh music		1976 Welsh music archive founded	Various anthologies published	
Orchestras	Various attempts to start Welsh symphony orchestra	BBC Welsh Orchestra (40 members)	Upgrading to symphony size (Arts Council funds)		

WALES/CYMRU	Pre-70s	Early 70s	Mid-70s	Late 70s	Early 80s
	1943 Welsh National Opera (WNO) formed	WNO gets permanent orchestra (Welsh Philharmonia)			
	1944 National Youth Orchestra				

WORK OPPORTUNITIES

WALES/CYMRU	Pre-70s	Early 70s	Mid-70s	Late 70s	Early 80s
	National Eisteddfod alternates N and S Wales annually		1974 First rock opera commissioned by Eisteddfod		Rock music allowed on Eisteddfod site
				Alternative Eisteddfod stage for rock/pop/folk	
	Welsh Youth League festivals. Emerging acoustic artists enjoy great popularity across the board in Wales				
				Dolgellau festival Pan-Celtic folk/Welsh rock	
				Aberystwyth rock festival	Fades out 1982
				Rural Development Board festival in Aberystwyth (many imported artists)	

WALES/CYMRU	Pre-70s	Early 70s	Mid-70s	Late 70s	Early 80s
		1970 Fishguard Festival			
		1970 N Wales Cathedral festival (ASAPH)			
	1958 Llandaff festival, Cardiff				
	1947 Llangollen Musical Eisteddfod (mainly choirs, with international participation)				
	1948 Swansea festival				
			BBC Radio Cymru regular sessions of rock/folk		
		TV on BBC/HTV	BBC TV show ceases		Welsh S4C TV
				Folk clubs and rock/disco clubs (e.g. MACYM in North, MAC in South)	
	BBC Welsh Orchestra		Upgrading to symphony size		
		Welsh opera company gets permanent orchestra		Welsh National Opera extends tours	

WALES/CYMRU	Pre-70s	Early 70s	Mid-70s	Late 70s	Early 80s

PHONOGRAM INDUSTRY

Phonogram companies

Non-Welsh	EMI records some choirs		EMI continues to record some choirs (some on contract) plus occasional tourist albums		
			Non-Welsh companies dabble in occasional tourist albums. Some classical recordings via Arts Council money		
	Decca with certain pre-war presence decided to build Welsh catalogue. Absorb Qualiton	Decca absorbs much of Cambrian catalogue. Some recordings of choirs/folk/soloists	Deccas steers clear of Welsh pop/rock scene	Decca absorbed by Polygram	Decca deletes Welsh catalogue
Welsh	Welsh Teldisc, Cambrian/Qualiton and Wren enjoy big sales of Welsh EPs from mid 60s on	Teldisc catalogue goes to Sain	Wren folds up		
	1969 Sain records started by artists. Sells 15,000 EPs	Sain grows as others disappear	Sain has virtual monopoly on pop/rock/folk scene. Sells 25,000 LPs	Sain expands	1980 Sain sells 100,000 LPs and cassettes

WALES/CYMRU	Pre-70s	Early 70s	Mid-70s	Late 70s	Early 80s
Studios			Sain gets 8-track	Sain builds 24-track complex in N Wales	New studio in Cardiff
		Some studios appear in Wales, mainly functioning for English artists (weekend parties)			BBC gets 16-track
Manufacturing facilities					
Records	Qualiton pressing plant bought by Decca – closed and moved to London	No make-up facilities for record sleeves in Wales			
		Plastic Sound (2 presses) in mid-Waes			Closed 1980
		Caerffili Pant (12 presses) changes ownership many times			
Cassettes			Various small operators		
		EMI cassette tape plant in Rhondda valley, S Wales (regional development area)			

WALES/CYMRU	Pre-70s	Early 70s	Mid-70s	Late 70s	Early 80s
		3M cassette tape plant near Swansea, S Wales (regional development area)			

RADIO, TV, FILM, VIDEO

Radio/TV sets			1·6 million radio receivers. 0·7 million TV sets		Almost every household has radio and TV sets
Radio (UK)	Pop pirates of the 60s replaced by BBC Radio 1 and 2	BBC Radio One continues to exert large influence on youth of Wales			
Radio (Welsh)	1968 BBC Wales Cymru starts covering pop/rock 40 minutes/week		Radio Cymru's Welsh pop/rock/folk coverage increases to 1 hour/week	. . . and then to 2 hours/week	
			Radio Cymru records art, pop, MoR music as well as many choirs at festivals		
			BBC symphony orchestra upgraded to 66 members		
					BBC Cardiff gets 16-track recording facilities

WALES/CYMRU	Pre-70s	Early 70s	Mid-70s	Late 70s	Early 80s
Local radio (commercial)			Swansea Sound on air. 3% of advertising revenue must go to live music		2 hours Welsh pop/rock per week
TV	1964 BBC starts pop show with broad appeal	1973 Pop show changes from acoustic to electric format	BBC turns disco show into folk show	BBC attempt bilingual music show (failure)	
					Decision to combine all Welsh TV in new channel S4C
HTV (commercial) and predecessor (TWW)	1966–69 TWW pop show	1973–74 HTV music show	Some Welsh language pop in afternoon shows		
					Many producers leave HTV and BBC to start independent film/video production units for S4C. Many music shows commissioned

TRENDS IN THE MUSIC MEDIA

	Pre-70s	Early 70s	Mid-70s	Late 70s	Early 80s
Traditional religious	Hymn singing male voice choirs (tend to become more secular)			Male voice choirs 'popularize' repertoire	
		Star soloists emerge		Max Boyce on EMI, Trebor Edwards on Sain	

WALES/CYMRU	Pre-70s	Early 70s	Mid-70s	Late 70s	Early 80s
			Folk music revival – groups make records and sing at festivals, on radio/TV		
Popular MoR Secular	MoR Country and Western style sung in Welsh gains popularity				
			Increased interest in brass bands		
Youth culture, protest, electric	Late 60s. Protest or message songs sung acoustically	Groups get electrified		Some former protest artists stick to acoustic style. Others develop as instrumentalists	
	Lyrics most important in popular songs		Lyrics assume less importance	2 trends. (a) Musical quality assumes more importance (b) Reaction against technical extremes in music	
Punk/new wave				Punk/new wave groups emerge, often in South Wales. Make own records	

WALES/CYMRU	Pre-70s	Early 70s	Mid-70s	Late 70s	Early 80s
Art music	Established composers become Europeanized		Through subsidies from Arts Council, BBC Welsh symphony orchestra makes discs with Welsh works		
			Some young composers stay tonal, seeking Welsh roots. Others go very avant-garde		

Index

Note: numbers in *italics* refer to illustrations, tables, diagrams